SARTOR CALLED RESARTUS

Song

BY THOMAS CARLYLE

Poor Thomas Cairel,
Foolishest of men,
Bought him new apparel;
And what followed then?

Bought him new apparel,
Lectured unto men,
Gaped and gasped, poor Cairel,
Foolishest of men.

He wrote a Revolution,
Book without its like;
Then he took a resolution
That he was a wretched tike.

Sartor called *Resartus*
This my published theme;
"May no chance e'er part us!"
Nonsense said to teme.

But then came no money,
Not a coin of money in,
Then was gall instead of honey,
'Stead of peace was din.

Hapless Thomas Cairel
Foolishest of men
Bought him new apparel
And what followed then?

—*From a manuscript in the
Yale University Library
(quoted by permission)*

SARTOR CALLED *RESARTUS*

THE GENESIS, STRUCTURE, AND STYLE OF THOMAS CARLYLE'S FIRST MAJOR WORK

BY G. B. TENNYSON

PRINCETON UNIVERSITY PRESS

PRINCETON • NEW JERSEY

1965

1384255

For Emily
and A. Betty

Preface

In a sense that I think Carlyle would have endorsed, this is a book about Thomas Carlyle—the sense Carlyle meant when he said, "the Man is the spirit he worked in; not what he did, but what he became." If today Carlyle the eminent Victorian appears much more Victorian than eminent, it may be because we have concerned ourselves more with what he did than with the spirit he worked in. But that spirit is at its freshest and most vital in the early Carlyle; and it culminates in what has proved to be his most durable work, *Sartor Resartus*.

During the more than three generations since Carlyle's death critical studies of *Sartor* and other Carlyle works have not been wanting. In fact, Carlyle holds the record as the most popular subject for dissertations in the field of Victorian literature. But such data are misleading. The years after Carlyle's death in 1881 have in general been lean years in Carlyle scholarship. (Not only German dissertations are marred by the sound of grinding axes.) In recent years, however, more and more studies of Carlyle as a literary artist have appeared. The new edition of the letters of the two Carlyles should reopen the biographical question to more dispassionate investigation than was possible immediately after Carlyle's death. A new Carlyle may be palingenetically stirring in the ashes of the old.

The present study was conceived of a contribution to the general revaluation of Victorian literature and the specific revaluation of Carlyle as a literary artist. From its first inception to its final form I have had the benefit of advice from Professor E. D. H. Johnson of Princeton, for which I am deeply grateful. I also owe a debt of gratitude to Professor Hans Aarsleff of Princeton and to Professor Hill Shine of the University of Kentucky, each of whom read different stages of the manuscript and offered sound counsel. I thank Hans Schreiber of Frankfurt, Germany, for calling my attention to several valuable works and Professor W. Heiske of the Deutsches Volksliedarchiv,

Freiburg, for researches on my behalf. I am very grateful to Princeton University for support during the early stages of this study and to the Universities of North Carolina and California, Los Angeles, where it was completed. Special thanks are due to Miss Ellen Cole and her staff of the University of California, Los Angeles, for the typing of the manuscript, and to my wife for help with the index. At Princeton University Press I have benefitted from the aid of Miriam Brokaw and Jean Lilly.

I acknowledge with thanks permission from the Yale University Library for the Carlyle poem which appears opposite the title page and which provided the title for this work. I also want to thank the National Library of Scotland, Edinburgh, for permission to quote from an unpublished Carlyle letter and Professor Charles Richard Sanders of Duke University for making a copy of that letter available to me.

G. B. T.

Los Angeles, California
January 1965

Contents

SARTOR CALLED RESARTUS

LIST OF ABBREVIATIONS

The following abbreviations have been used for works to which frequent reference is made.

Early Letters   *Early Letters of Thomas Carlyle, 1814–1826,* ed. Charles Eliot Norton (2 vols.; London, 1886)

Froude   James Anthony Froude, *Thomas Carlyle: A History of the First Forty Years of His Life, 1795–1835* (2 vols.; London, 1882)

Letters   *Letters of Thomas Carlyle, 1826–1836,* ed. Charles Eliot Norton (2 vols.; London, 1888)

Love Letters   *The Love Letters of Thomas Carlyle and Jane Welsh,* ed. Alexander Carlyle (2 vols.; London, 1909)

Last Words   *The Last Words of Thomas Carlyle* (New York, 1892)

Reminiscences   Thomas Carlyle, *Reminiscences,* ed. Charles Eliot Norton (2 vols.; London, 1887)

Sartor   Thomas Carlyle, *Sartor Resartus,* ed. Charles Frederick Harrold (New York, 1937)

Two Note Books   *Two Note Books of Thomas Carlyle, from 23 March 1822 to 16 May 1832,* ed. Charles Eliot Norton (New York, 1898)

Works   *The Works of Thomas Carlyle,* ed. H. D. Traill, "Centenary Edition" (30 vols.; London, 1896–1899)

Introduction

Those who seem to be the chief writers of our time have found their subjects in attempting to dramatize at once both the culture and the turbulences it was meant to control, and in doing so they have had practically to create—as it happens, to re-create—the terms, the very symbolic substance, of the culture as they went along. . . .

Performance, the condition we are after, cannot mean the same thing to the audience and the artist. The audience needs instruction in the lost skill of symbolic thinking. The arts need rather to be shown how their old roles can be played in new conditions. To do either, both need to be allied to the intellectual habits of the time. Besides analysis, elucidation, and comparison . . . criticism in our time must also come to judgment.

—R. P. BLACKMUR

· I ·

After reading her husband's just-completed manuscript of *Sartor Resartus* in 1831, Jane Welsh Carlyle declared, "It is a work of genius." Following an initial period of perplexity the world has largely come to agree with her. For many a Victorian the book became a bible showing, above all, the way from doubt to faith. Even today when Carlyle enjoys far from universal acclaim, there is general agreement that *Sartor Resartus* is a work of genius. But the acknowledgment is grudging; and from the start the area of dispute has been the same—the artistic merit of *Sartor Resartus*. Has the book a coherent plan? Is the style truly felicitous? For that matter, does it show the way from doubt to faith? The questions were raised early but remain unresolved.

John Sterling in 1835 privately wrote to Carlyle the most balanced early criticism of *Sartor*. Nevertheless, he objected to the language and to the "Rhapsodico-Reflective" form of composition. Public critics were of a similar mind. In the first English edition (1838) Carlyle impudently tweaked his critics by including "Testimonies of Authors," a selection from editorial and journalistic commentary that *Sartor* had evoked on its first appearance as a serial in *Fraser's Magazine* in 1833–1834 and as a book in America in 1836. The critic of the *Sun* called it "a heap of clotted nonsense," acknowledging however "here and there . . . passages marked by thought and a striking poetic vigour." He lamented chiefly that the author did not write "so as to make himself generally intelligible." The publisher's reader who had rejected the book in 1831 complained that its heavy wit "reminds one of the German Baron who took to leaping on tables, and answered that he was learning to be lively." The *North-American Review* referred to the language as a "sort of Babylonish dialect."[1]

The observations of Carlyle's contemporaries have found echoes in many quarters for more than a century. *Sartor* has, to be sure, found its advocates, but like most of the Victorian readers they have been more concerned with the ideas in the book than with the arrangement of parts or with the style. Where stylistic matters are treated, one finds only a few defenders willing not only to assert that the work is the product of conscious literary artistry but also to engage in examination and analysis of it. All this need not surprise us. It is obvious that *Sartor Resartus* is an uncommon work and one likely to repel many on first encounter. Those who persevere try to penetrate to the thought. Carlyle himself intended the work to carry a message to its readers. He always affected to be disinterested in the manner by which a work of art was

---

[1] For Sterling's letter and Carlyle's response and the testimonies of authors see *Sartor Resartus,* ed. Charles Frederick Harrold (New York, 1937), pp. 305–325. Hereafter all references to *Sartor* are to this edition, but I have adopted a method of referring to *Sartor* also by book and chapter to make for ease of reference to any edition. Thus *Sartor,* i, iii, 40 refers to *Sartor,* Book One, chapter three, in any edition, and page 40 in the Harrold edition.

created (although his letters make clear that he was himself quite painstaking in his writing).

Since Carlyle's emphasis fell on the matter rather than the manner, and since Victorian readers accepted *Sartor* primarily as a moral document, it is small wonder that scholarly emphasis has fallen on Carlyle's ideas and their sources. The result has been a substantial literature on Carlyle's philosophy and his relations with previous philosophic systems, especially German, but only scant treatment of Carlyle's literary artistry. Yet every treatment of Carlyle as a philosopher has served to make more necessary a real understanding of Carlyle's literary methods. For Carlyle adumbrated no consistent philosophy; he was neither a metaphysician nor a logician. He had, to be sure, a definite philosophic stance, and his works are patently more than entertainments. Indeed, it may be wondered whether any serious writer on topics akin to Carlyle's has ever enjoyed greater esteem and popularity in his own lifetime than Carlyle did in his. But Carlyle's ideas commend themselves to the reader not because of their philosophic rigor and clarity, but because of their compelling literary manner. That manner is of the essence. If Carlyle continues to be read because he was a literary artist, it is only because that is why he was read in the first place.

Recognition of Carlyle's literary artistry has been growing. With it there has been a corresponding increase in studies of his literary achievement. There are likely to be still more in the future. As yet, there are few full-length treatments of Carlyle as an artist, and thus one only occasionally encounters studies of the artistic merits of Carlyle's most enduring work, *Sartor Resartus.* These studies are generally confined to specific literary devices or isolated passages. The old judgments that *Sartor* is chaotic in form and merely grotesque in style have never been effectively countered. Carlyle's merit as a literary artist, however, must stand or fall on *Sartor.* It is his first mature full-length work and, curiously, his only entirely imaginative full-length work. If Carlyle has not created a work of literature in *Sartor,* the case must be all the more dubious for the rest of his output. But countless readers know that *Sartor* is a work of high literary artistry, even if that artistry has never received full explication. The time is certainly ripe for just such explication.

Paradoxically, the uniqueness of the structure and style of *Sartor Resartus* has operated to obscure just what its structure and style are. Otherwise sympathetic critics have been content to assert that there is a coherent plan and an effective style, without clarifying for the reader how they arrived at their evaluations. If we can sense that the form has a coherence, it ought to be possible to explain in greater detail what it consists of. And so with the style. Further, if *Sartor* is a work of the imagination, we may legitimately expect structure and style to contribute to the meaning. To detach matter from manner (apart from an artificial detachment for critical purposes) is justified only when the two are not significantly related. The accuracy of a scientific treatise is (to judge from many of them) not destroyed by an infelicitous style, although our enjoyment of the work may be. In a work of art, however, accuracy is far from the goal. The aesthetic (and even the moral) meaning of a work is fundamentally conditioned by the way the artist has arranged and expressed his materials. Literary artistry in *Sartor,* shut out at the front door, comes in at the back. For the work is not a scientific treatise, nor a philosophic one; it is a work of the imagination, an unorthodox novel by an inventive and original mind. As such, it deserves the same attention to its literary and artistic dimensions that we direct to any other work of art.

The questions that persist in plaguing the literary critic of *Sartor* are those posed so early in the career of that remarkable work. What kind of plan holds the whole work together, and what is the key to the idiosyncratic style? Laying aside the answers that there is no discernible plan and that the style was adopted merely for shock effect, let us consider two means of coming to genuinely illuminating answers to these questions. Since *Sartor* is indisputably original, one cannot expect to find a key to its form in pre-existing literary works, or in an established theory of literary kinds. If *Sartor* fails to fall in the great tradition of English realistic fiction, it may be necessary to look beyond that tradition for a rationale that Carlyle would have endorsed. The intent of the author is still worth considering, despite the assaults that have been made on that critical bulwark in recent years. Thus the first step is to examine Carlyle's pre-*Sartor* writings to ascertain whether any light is cast on the structure and style of *Sartor* by the author's own literary habits and aesthetic convictions. Such an examination must be based on a chronology by composition and not by publication, as has generally been the case, for the two are by no means identical. Once we make such an examination, we can proceed to the second step, a critical analysis of the work itself, a sympathetic reading of the book from the vantage point of Carlyle's previous practice and ideas with an eye toward discerning a pattern to the organization and a logic to the style.

The approach in the following pages has been of this two-fold kind: a study of the background, followed by a critical analysis of *Sartor*. The method is not new; it is, after all, the method of historical criticism. If there is any relevance in Carlyle's output before *Sartor*, it will become apparent as that material helps to clarify *Sartor* itself. And if there is any merit in the analysis of the literary dimension of *Sartor*, it will become apparent as that analysis helps to clarify the whole meaning of *Sartor*.

Like other original and independent works, *Sartor* retains its own individuality no matter how much we murder to dissect. But from Carlyle's pre-*Sartor* writings emerges a pattern of continual refinement of literary methods that subsequently determines the nature of *Sartor;* and from

8 Introduction

the wealth of critical pronouncements that Carlyle made in the pre-*Sartor* period emerges an aesthetic that goes far toward explaining why *Sartor* took the form it did. A systematic study of Carlyle's methods and ideas serves as a pointer to a close critical examination of *Sartor* itself. It is, in fact, as a preliminary to the task of examining *Sartor* that all of the material in the first three chapters must be judged, for there the reader will find considerable attention directed alike at works of slight intrinsic merit and works of undisputed eminence. The criterion is always how important the pre-*Sartor* work is for an understanding of *Sartor*. Readers more concerned with *Sartor* as a finished product than with how it developed may want to begin with Chapter iii or iv, but for those who want a complete picture of Carlyle's maturing literary methods, the early chapters will prove essential. In the dozen years before Carlyle wrote *Sartor* he produced everything from highly transient hackwork to some of the seminal essays of the nineteenth century. Hackwork and major essays are both examined for what they tell us about Carlyle's literary skill or for what they tell us about his aesthetic, as these operate in or determine the shape of *Sartor Resartus*. Post-*Sartor* writings naturally occupy no prominent place in the present study, although the student of Carlyle will recognize many of the features discussed here as part of Carlyle's permanent literary arsenal, called into service from *The French Revolution* to *The Early Kings of Norway*. In that sense this book is a propaedeutic to the study of Carlyle as a literary craftsman.

After the initial chapters of pre-*Sartor* investigation comes a critical study of *Sartor* itself. The study naturally focuses on structure and style. It also covers what lies between, here called texture. In the final chapter I attempt to bring the lessons of literary criticism to bear on the question of the whole substance and direction of *Sartor Resartus*. The one should not be undertaken without the other. Let me confess at the outset that I do not at all doubt that *Sartor* is a work of conscious artistic integrity and a work of abiding aesthetic and intellectual interest. The following pages are therefore not impartial. Yet they are directed to the doubter as well as to the believer. The former I hope will be persuaded, the latter strengthened in his belief.

· II ·

Although Carlyle's biography is only incidental to the present study, some biographical details are of consequence to the shape and nature of *Sartor Resartus*. For example, it is of some consequence that Carlyle's very early writings were composed on the order and under the supervision of others, whose chief interests were not literary but scientific or journalistic. Likewise, the sequence of composition, essentially a biographical matter, must play a part in our assessment of Carlyle's literary development because that sequence varies from the order of publication. Thus biography has undoubted relevance even in a study like the present one that is concerned with technique. Throughout these pages I have cited biographical incidents when they appear consequential, but no attempt has been made to write the biography of Carlyle's early life as such.

Despite the fact that Carlyle's life has been one of the most intensely researched and widely discussed lives in Victorian literature, it seems to be always in danger of falling into formula: humble origins, lost religion, dyspepsia, conversion experience, marriage to Jane Welsh, elevation to Sageship from Chelsea, fame and honor, and death. One cannot precisely deny any of the components, but one can wish for a little more flesh and blood to adhere to the skeleton. But that is a task for another work. Here we are concerned with the general outline of Carlyle's early life, even at the risk of repeating parts of the formula.

Nowhere does Carlyle seem to be so human as in the early years before the ermine of the Sage had been placed about him, when he was still wearing the clouts of the unsung prophet. These early years to 1834 are the years of Carlyle's literary apprenticeship, the years that form the background to the writing of *Sartor Resartus*. The specialist will know the story well; but many nonspecialists with an interest in *Sartor* may find it helpful to review the main events of the pre-*Sartor* years. Accordingly, a brief survey of the important events in Carlyle's early life is in order at the outset.[2]

The unlikely story that Carlyle's first words (spoken at age three) were "What ails wee Jack?" has a certain appropriateness, apart from the Scottishness of it; for Carlyle's great labor was to be ascertaining what ailed the world and then broadcasting his findings. But otherwise no more unprepossessing a beginning could be imagined for the future Sage of Chelsea than the facts of Carlyle's birth and childhood. The eldest son of James Carlyle, stonemason, and Margaret Aitken Carlyle in the Scottish village of Ecclefechan in Dumfriesshire, Thomas Carlyle was born on December 4, 1795, the same year in which Keats was born and only three years after the birth of Shelley. Yet both Keats and Shelley had been dead almost a decade before Carlyle wrote *Sartor Resartus*. Carlyle's late flowering and long life, rather than the date of his birth, made him a Victorian. But that he became a great figure at all must be credited to the combination of remarkable literary gifts wedded to indomitable perseverance.

The Carlyles were poor, proud, thrifty, and sternly Calvinist, of a variety indeed that found the Kirk of Scot-

[2] The most readable life of Carlyle is still J. A. Froude's *Thomas Carlyle: A History of the First Forty Years of His Life, 1795-1835* (2 vols; London, 1882) and the sequel *Thomas Carlyle: A History of His Life in London, 1834-1881* (2 vols; London, 1884). The most accurate biography, however, is David Alec Wilson's six-volume work. For matters of fact in the following account I have relied chiefly on Wilson's first two volumes, *Carlyle till Marriage* (London, 1923) and *Carlyle to "The French Revolution"* (London, 1924).

For a chronology of Carlyle's writing to 1834 by date of composition see below, Appendix, pp. 329-342.

land wanting in earnestness. Thomas attended local
schools, where discipline stood second only to godliness.
The last and chief of these was Annan Academy, which
was also the alma mater of Annan's most famous son,
Edward Irving, three years Carlyle's senior, a young man
already gaining distinction as a brilliant divinity student
in Edinburgh when Carlyle was still in Annan.[3] After the
Academy Carlyle quite literally made his way to Edinburgh
University for the fall term of 1809 by walking the entire
distance from Annan to Edinburgh, about one hundred
miles. He spent the years from 1809 to 1814 at Edinburgh,
studying as a prospective candidate for the ministry; but
he abandoned Edinburgh in 1814 (and later the ministry)
when he returned to Annan Academy as mathematics
master. He never took his degree from the University, even
though in 1865, as the Sage, he became its rector.

In 1816, after two years teaching at Annan, he was lured
to the seaport town of Kirkcaldy in Fifeshire (across the
Firth of Forth from Edinburgh). In Kirkcaldy Carlyle was
set up in the burgh school as a kind of rival to Edward
Irving, who was teaching there at a private school. Some
parents resented Irving's severe discipline and engaged
Carlyle to teach their children. But the rivalry did not
prevent Irving and Carlyle from striking a deep friendship,
the most profound friendship Carlyle had with another
man for the rest of his life. He said of it later: "But
for Irving, I had never known what the communion of
man with man means." Certainly the friendship with Irving
makes the two years in Kirkcaldy of great importance in
Carlyle's early life.

The Kirkcaldy experience has earned a permanent and
perhaps exaggerated place in Carlyle's biography for other
reasons as well. It was here, in Irving's library, that Carlyle
read Gibbon and allegedly lost his faith, although it must
be stressed that serious misgivings about religion had

[3] A statue to Irving stands today in Annan. See John MacGavin
Sloan, *The Carlyle Country* (London, 1904), p. 183.

earlier caused him to abandon the ministry as a vocation (he had not delivered the requisite yearly sermon at the University since 1815). It was in Kirkcaldy too that Carlyle fell in love with the unattainable highborn lady Margaret Gordon, afterwards Lady Bannerman, one of the supposed originals for Blumine in *Sartor*. Carlyle himself was poignantly eloquent on the subject as late as 1867, when he wrote in recollection of seeing Margaret Gordon again years after Kirkcaldy: "I saw her, recognisably to me, here in her London time (1840 or so), *twice*, once with her maid in Piccadilly, promenading, little altered; a second time, that same year or next, on horseback both of us, and *meeting* in the gate of Hyde Park, when her *eyes* (but that was all) said to me almost touchingly, 'Yes, yes; that is you!' "[4]

But teaching in Annan or Kirkcaldy proved to be an abrasive to Carlyle's soul, and in late 1818 he took himself back to Edinburgh, where he determined first to study for the law, then to make a living by writing. His legal studies he quickly gave up, leaving himself both free and without prospects for writing. He listened to some of Jameson's lectures on geology at the University. At the same time he began the (for him) momentous study of German, quickly gaining a remarkable proficiency. Finally, he succeeded in finding some writing jobs through David Brewster, a Scottish physicist and editor then editing a scientific journal and the *Edinburgh Encyclopaedia*. Between 1819 and 1823 Carlyle did a few translations and abstracts of articles for Brewster's *Edinburgh Philosophical Journal*, before being graduated to articles on biography, geography, and history for the *Encyclopaedia*. Through Brewster he also translated a French manual on geometry, and on his own he contributed a few reviews to an Edinburgh magazine. These journalistic, rather than literary, labors and some private tutoring supported Carlyle for

[4] *Reminiscences*, ed. Charles Eliot Norton (London, 1887), II, 58–59.

about four years. They were years of both physical and spiritual torment. His lifelong suffering from dyspepsia seems to have assailed him with special force during this period, but more painful than that was the spiritual torment he suffered. These were the years in which Carlyle felt that life had no meaning. These are the years often, and sometimes too glibly, equated with Teufelsdröckh's sorrows. But they are also the years that mark the turning point in Carlyle's struggle with doubt and unbelief. During this period he met Jane Welsh, and during this period he experienced his much discussed "newbirth" in Leith Walk.

Edward Irving was Carlyle's point of contact with Jane Welsh of Haddington. Irving had first tutored, and later courted, Jane before Carlyle met her in 1821. Called the "Flower of Haddington," Jane Welsh enjoyed not only a comfortable fortune from her late father but the high regard of all who knew her. Later, it would seem she provoked some to feelings of pity on account of her subordination to the demanding Carlyle. It is now a commonplace of Victorian studies to claim that Carlyle ruined Jane Welsh's life, and, further, that he nipped in the bud an immense literary talent. In a more malicious vein Samuel Butler remarked: "It was very good of God to let Carlyle and Mrs. Carlyle marry one another and so make only two people miserable instead of four, besides being very amusing."[5] But all indications are that Thomas and Jane had a sincere and moving love for each other that transcended mere psychological dependency. Certainly their early letters, as Alexander Carlyle has been at pains to show in his edition, bespeak a deep and growing love that quite understandably led to marriage, despite the sometimes open opposition of Jane's mother. The courtship lasted five years.

Possibly in the summer of 1821, after meeting Jane

[5] Quoted by Holbrook Jackson, *Dreamers of Dreams* (London, 1948), p. 67.

Welsh, possibly not until the following summer, Carlyle, still a prey to despair, experienced what he later called a "Conversion," and what in *Sartor* is called a "Spiritual Newbirth." It was an experience of intense, mystical awareness and understanding that occurred to him in Leith Walk in Edinburgh on the way to the strand between Leith and Portobello. The sensation, surely the most powerful Carlyle experienced in his entire life, ushered in, albeit slowly, a transformation of personality and outlook that is central to the whole nature of the mature Carlyle. He did not cease to be the Carlyle he had been up to 1822; in a sense he became that same person in a more powerful and compelling guise. Nor did he overnight burst onto the literary or any other scene as a new man. The working out of the experience on what Teufelsdröckh would call "the living subject" actually required the following decade; and *Sartor Resartus* is in a real sense the outcome of the period introduced by the incident in Leith Walk. But, as a result of the experience, Carlyle did see a meaning and purpose in life, and his interest in life and our interest in Carlyle quicken with the occurrence that took place in 1821 or 1822.

Before the Leith Walk experience Carlyle had undertaken to tutor the children of Mr. and Mrs. Charles Buller, first in Edinburgh, then in 1823 at their country home, Kinnaird House in Perthshire. He had met the Bullers through Edward Irving, who was now a minister in the Kirk of Scotland, enjoying an almost notorious, but soon to prove ephemeral, success in Hatton Garden, London. Again through Irving, Carlyle received a commission to write on the German playwright Friedrich Schiller for the *London Magazine*. The articles were written in Edinburgh and during his stay with the Bullers in Perthshire in 1823–1824. In 1824, as his tutoring assignment expired, he wrote a translation of Goethe's *Wilhelm Meisters Lehrjahre*. By now he was launched on the work that dominated the remainder of the decade, translating and writing as the Voice of Germany in England. In 1824 the Schiller articles were slightly revised and expanded for publication the next year in London as a book. The occasion provided Carlyle with an opportunity to travel to London and, briefly, to Paris. Despite the fact that *Schiller* and *Meister* were establishing him as one of the few specialists on contemporary German literature, this was Carlyle's first trip outside of Scotland, and even then it did not include Germany.

Throughout these years Carlyle continued to court Jane Welsh, seeing her in Haddington or Edinburgh whenever possible, writing letters to her at an immense rate. At the same time he grew farther apart from Irving, whose success in London soon turned to scandal and who died prematurely in 1834.[6] Upon returning to Scotland from his London trip in the spring of 1825, Carlyle settled at Hoddam Hill, a farm in Dumfriesshire, where he set to work on further translations, subsequently published in four volumes as *German Romance*. Hoddam Hill for the year 1825–1826 marks another point of consolidation and reflection that grew out of the conversion experience. At the end of the Hoddam Hill period, in the fall of 1826, he married Jane Welsh at Templand, a Welsh family estate in the Nithsdale section of Dumfriesshire. The couple settled at Comley Bank, Edinburgh, where Carlyle gained entrée into the intellectual and social life of the Scottish capital and friendship with such figures as Francis Jeffrey, editor of the *Edinburgh Review,* and John Wilson, editor of *Blackwood's.* Carlyle now began writing major essays for the *Edinburgh,* at that time by all odds the most prestigious and influential periodical in the British Isles.

A lesser man might have settled then for what Carlyle already had: growing celebrity, a charming wife, association with his country's leading writers and politicians. But Carlyle was not content, partly because he was ambitious, but more because he was deeply disturbed by aesthetic,

[6] See below, p. 41n.

social, moral, and ethical questions that others seemed
not to be grappling with. Earlier, with some short stories
and poems, he had tried his hand at more imaginative
writing than that represented by *Schiller* or his translations.
He did so again in Edinburgh in 1827 with an abortive
novel, "Wotton Reinfred." Then at Whitsuntide 1828 he
and Jane removed to an isolated farm at Craigenputtock
in the moorland hills of Dumfriesshire near Templand.
The name means "Craig of the Hawks" and, even more
than Hoddam Hill with its old Border watchtower called
"Repentance Tower," Craigenputtock was a lonely and almost desolate spot. But just as at Hoddam Hill, so at
Craigenputtock, Carlyle needed the isolation to continue
to work out with himself the full terms of the understanding of life that had first burst upon him in Leith
Walk in 1821–1822. From 1828 to 1834 the Carlyles lived
in semi-seclusion in Craigenputtock. To be sure, there were
occasional trips to Edinburgh or to Jeffrey's estate Craig-
crook, but for the most part the couple saw only relatives
and a few friends. Carlyle, later joined by Jane, made
one substantial trip to London during the period.

Carlyle's intellectual development and literary output increased as his social life became more restricted. In
Craigenputtock he wrote the great bulk of the essays that
established him as the primary British authority on contemporary German literature, essays for the *Edinburgh Review* and other leading journals. In Craigenputtock he
entered into correspondence with Goethe, whom he considered to have been one of the few, perhaps the only,
spiritual guide during his years of doubt and denial. There
he also received an American caller, Emerson, the first
outsider to recognize Carlyle's genius. Finally, in Craigenputtock in 1830 he wrote a long article called "Thoughts
on Clothes," submitted it to, then recalled it from, *Fraser's
Magazine;* and, still in his Scottish retreat in 1831, he expanded it into *Sartor Resartus.* He took the manuscript
of the completed book to London in 1831 in an unsuccess-

ful effort to find a publisher for it. But all England, he reported, was "dancing a Tarantula Dance of Political Reform" and had no time for a puzzling work like *Sartor*.[7] He returned to Craigenputtock with his manuscript and kept it for two years before submitting it again for serial publication in *Fraser's*.

When *Sartor Resartus* at last began appearing in *Fraser's* in 1833, the Craigenputtock period, and with it Carlyle's literary and spiritual apprenticeship, was drawing to a close. To the end of his life he never ceased considering the Craigenputtock years the happiest years he had ever spent. He would fondly contrast the blessed silences of the Scottish mountains with the unceasing clangor of London, or the cool summer breezes that waved round the moorland cottage with what he considered the infernal heat of summertime London. But when the Carlyles moved from Craigenputtock to London in 1834 the change proved to be permanent. The move coincided with the final installments of *Sartor* in *Fraser's*, and it fell between the passage of the First Reform Bill and the accession of Victoria. The publication of *Sartor* and the move of the Carlyles from Scotland to London are signs that the Victorian age had begun.

[7] *Correspondence between Goethe and Carlyle,* ed. Charles Eliot Norton (London, 1887), p. 290.

I

Apprenticeship
1819–1827

Im Ganzen, Guten, Wahren resolut zu leben!
—GOETHE

Cecily. We might have a good influence over him, Miss Prism. I am sure you would. You know German, and geology, and things of that kind influence a man very much.
—*The Importance of Being Earnest*

The earliest recorded compositions by Thomas Carlyle are two sermons, one titled "Before I was afflicted I went astray," the other "Num detur religio naturalis." These were composed and delivered to the faculty at Edinburgh University in 1814 and 1815 as part of the required program for ministerial students. Carlyle abandoned the ministry shortly after his second sermon, and both of these early works are lost. Yet there is something significant and appropriate in the fact that Carlyle began by writing sermons. It suggests that much of the earnestness and much of the hortatory tone characteristic of Carlyle stem from the earliest period of his literary awareness. Partly because of his manner, Carlyle became an apostle of faith for countless Victorians, even though more than one of them must have shared the puzzlement of the philosopher E. E. Caird when he said, "What is Carlyle's religion anyway? Or does he have one?"[1]

---

[1] The sermon titles are recorded by Carlyle himself in his *Reminiscences,* ed. Charles Eliot Norton (London, 1887), II, 20–21. "Before I was afflicted I went astray" comes from Psalms 99: 67. Despite Caird's skepticism, he wrote glowingly of Carlyle in *Essays on Literature and Philosophy,* (Glasgow, 1892), I, 230–267.

The question still requires an answer, but so does the less comprehensive question, why should a student of the ministry turn to what we today would call science? For that is what Carlyle did. In 1817, two years after his second sermon, his name appeared in print for the first time, as the "ingenious young mathematician" who provided the great professor Leslie with the solution to the problem of how "to divide a straight line, whether internally or externally, so that the rectangle under its segment shall be equivalent to a given rectangle."[2] Two years later still, in 1819, Carlyle gained his first money from writing with a translation of an article on mineralogy. The fact is that at the time scientific studies seemed to offer answers to many of the questions that perplexed the former divinity student. Biographers have told us that Carlyle experienced a profound loss of faith during his university years, and that he was unable to sustain the total commitment to Calvinism that had characterized his upbringing. Clearly, he had to abandon the ministry. Less a cause than a consequence of his loss of faith was his preoccupation with natural philosophy.

In the early nineteenth century natural philosophy was conceived of as the handmaiden of religion. Since the eighteenth century, only the illustrations had changed. Of course, the day was not far distant when natural philosophy could no longer be called upon to prove divine providence. Already the venerable notion of the Great Chain of Being had been retired as an illustration of the concept of Providence. Still the concept survived when the Chain had lost its illustrative force. Nor were there in England any overt attacks on providence in nature until well into the nineteenth century. Early in the century, when Carlyle was

---

[2] John Leslie, *Elements of Geometry, and Plane Trigonometry,* 3rd ed. (Edinburgh, 1817) p. 340. In David Masson's *Edinburgh Sketches and Memories* (Edinburgh, 1892), p. 261, Masson claims that the solution of this problem was not original with Carlyle, but could be found in an old Scottish book of geometry; but it is not clear whether Carlyle knew this.

abandoning his ministerial studies, there was still a great
deal of hope that from science would come a synthesis
that would unite in meaningful harmony the multiplicities
of modern life, that would somehow strike down the blank
wall of atheism toward which eighteenth-century thought
seemed to lead.[3] The Romantic movement is permeated
with such hopes, doomed to fail again and again. There
was a considerable preoccupation with mysticism and with
science at one and the same time. Natural philosophy still
appeared in the early years of the nineteenth century as
a potential means of setting the time right. For most people
natural philosophy appeared as a way to bridge the gap,
not as the cause of it. And so with Carlyle.

As a teacher, first at his own Annan Academy, later
at a similar school in Kirkcaldy, in proximity to the rising
young preacher Edward Irving, Carlyle studied literature
and history, science and language, even, for a time, law.
His post-University pursuits culminated in the commencement in 1819 of the study of German, and for the next
ten years his activities were largely literary. Carlyle undertook to study German, according to Emerson, on the advice
of one who told him he would find in that language what
he wanted. As we know, he assuredly did. But what he
wanted at first appears to have been a knowledge of
geology.[4]

[3] Charles Coulston Gillispie, *Genesis and Geology: A Study in
the Relations of Scientific Thought, Natural Theology and Social
Opinion in Great Britain, 1790–1850* (Cambridge, Mass., 1951),
pp. 3–40. See also Gillispie's penetrating study of the romantic
response to science in his *The Edge of Objectivity: An Essay in
the History of Scientific Ideas* (Princeton, 1960), pp. 151–201.

[4] Carlyle himself confirms this explanation in *Correspondence between Goethe and Carlyle,* ed. Charles Eliot Norton (London, 1887),
p. 157. Another suggested cause is his reading of Mme de Staël's
De l'Allemagne; see Richard Garnett, *Life of Carlyle* (London,
1887), p. 27. However, Carlyle refers as early as 1817 to de Staël's
works; yet he does not begin the study of German for two more
years. Moreover, the first German word to appear in Carlyle's writing
comes from geology—*Thonschiefer* ("clay slate")—used in a letter
of 15 February 1819 to Robert Mitchell, a fellow student, who
became secretary to Henry Duncan, finder of the Ruthwell Cross.

Carlyle's selection of geology is as significant for his early career as his initial inclination toward the ministry. Geology was the keystone science of the first half of the nineteenth century, much as chemistry had been for the late eighteenth century, and as biology was to be after Darwin. In geology, as in so much else in the early nineteenth century, the Germans were the masters. Carlyle learned German to uncover the secrets of geology (or geognosy) and mineralogy. But almost immediately he found a dead end, for in 1819 he complained to a friend that in Werner there was no real light cast upon the nature of things.[5] It seemed to him that knowledge through geology must remain superficial because the Wernerian school adhered rigorously to "external characters" of minerals. Yet he was attracted to geology by the very fact that, of the contemporary studies in natural philosophy, geology seemed the one that undertook to explain the most. Carlyle knew Werner at first hand and doubtless through Professor Jameson of Edinburgh, Werner's chief British disciple; he read Saussure, Cuvier, and Playfair, and he knew Newton.[6]

Early Letters of Thomas Carlyle, ed. Charles Eliot Norton (London, 1886), I, 214. In the same letter Carlyle dismisses the German lessons he was acquiring from a certain Robert Jardine, who had studied at Göttingen, as a "slight tincture of the German language." Carlyle paid for his German lessons by giving Jardine French lessons in exchange. Latin Carlyle had acquired along with French at school, and he continued his study of it at Edinburgh under the celebrated Professor Christison, of whom Carlyle later said that he "never noticed him, nor could distinguish him from another Mr. Irving Carlyle, an older, bigger boy, with red hair, wild buck teeth, and scorched complexion, and the worst Latinist of his acquaintance" (Froude, I, 25).

[5] *Early Letters,* I, 214 (letters to Robert Mitchell, 15 February 1819).

[6] For a detailed chronological account of Carlyle's reading see Hill Shine, *Carlyle's Early Reading, to 1834, with an Introductory Essay on His Intellectual Development* (Lexington, Ky., 1953). Carlyle's scientific inclinations have never been very thoroughly explored, but a suggestive study of his response to Newton has been made by Samuel Gill Barnes, "Formula for Faith: the Newtonian Pattern in the Transcendentalism of Thomas Carlyle," unpublished Ph.D. dissertation, University of North Carolina, 1953.

He also read Paley, whose works on natural theology continued the eighteenth-century British tradition of accommodating the latest findings in the natural sciences to the question of the truth of Christianity. It matters not so much that Carlyle later claimed to have found Paley unconvincing as that early in his career his reading was flavored with the kind of works Paley wrote, and that in his own writing Carlyle made free use of analogies drawn from natural sciences like geology to advance arguments sometimes strikingly similar to those made by the physico-theologists.

Religion, natural philosophy, history, literature—these were Carlyle's early interests; and he held them with no concern that they were necessarily incompatible. In pursuing so many diverse interests, Carlyle was not at all out of character in his time. One thinks first of Goethe, with his simultaneous scientific, governmental, administrative, and literary activities, and then of the mystic Novalis, a serious student of the mining operations at Freyberg, home of Werner and the Neptunist school. After Carlyle, Ruskin read in geology, erratically but with great conviction. Carlyle's studies in natural philosophy co-exist with his studies in literature and history, but the former do begin to diminish as natural philosophy breaks up into more technical specialities, as the term "science" displaces the more inclusive natural philosophy. Thus there is no record in Carlyle's reading of Lyell, Buckland, Sedgwick, and the various disputants in the catastrophist and uniformitarian controversies of the late twenties and thirties.[7] Carlyle's scientific interests do not disappear altogether, of

[7] For an account of these early theories of the origin of the earth see Gillispie, *Genesis and Geology*. In *Sartor*, i, i, 4, Carlyle mentions Werner and Hutton by name, but not later geologists. Nevertheless, Teufelsdröckh's frequent insistence on the immense age of the earth suggests that Carlyle may have been familiar with the theories circulating in the eighteen-twenties, almost all of which served to push farther back the putative age of the earth. See *Sartor*, i, v, 39; ii, iii, 102; and iii, viii, 258.

course. There is, until about the mid-thirties, a great catholicity of interests on his part. It is not surprising to find him suggesting as early as 1814 to a friend that they exchange essays on subjects of interest and reporting that he had done one on the rainbow. Nor should it surprise us to learn that among other lost early writings there was a travel piece on Annandale and a review of Pictet's *Gravitation,* or that he enjoyed submitting answers to mathematical puzzles to the *Dumfries Courier.*[8] Yet side by side with these interests Carlyle wrote poetry and fiction. What is probably his earliest preserved work, apart from letters, is his 1818 poem "Tragedy of the Night-Moth." And at the same time that he was engaged in writing for the *Edinburgh Philosophical Journal* he turned out a translation of a portion of the *Thirty Years' War.* During his years of hackwork for the *Edinburgh Encyclopaedia* he also wrote critical essays, poetry, and a short story. Part of the variety of Carlyle's early writings can be accounted for on the grounds that the young Carlyle was casting about for an area in which he could make a living by his pen. At first it appeared that he might be able to do so with scientific and philosophic writings for scholarly journals, but later it became evident that he could not make an adequate living there, and he turned to translation and finally to the great reviews. Both economically and intellectually Carlyle was finding his own way. Thus as late as 1834, when social and political readings had largely supplanted readings in natural philosophy (literary readings remaining abundant and relatively constant), Carlyle could urge a disciple to study geometry. And in the same year, when Carlyle could claim to be pre-eminently the Voice of Germany in Britain, he was seriously considered for the Chair of Astronomy at Edinburgh.[9]

[8] *Early Letters,* I, 3–21; *Reminiscences,* II, 233–235.
[9] David Alec Wilson, *Carlyle to "The French Revolution,"* (London, 1924), pp. 354–355. The appointment went instead to a Thomas Henderson. In 1828 Carlyle had more vigorously pursued the appointment to the Chair of Moral Philosophy at St. Andrews,

Carlyle's apprentice writings and his reading up to 1834 in many ways run parallel. His reading shows certainty that he read voraciously (as many literary men have done), and, further, that much of what he read was directed toward finding answers to philosophic questions. He sought his answers, not alone in the specific discipline of philosophy as we know it, but, in keeping with his age, in Philosophy broadly conceived. This included natural philosophy as well as humane letters, mathematics as well as poetry, contemporary journals as well as the classics. His writings too are extremely varied. He begins in the area of natural philosophy and moves through literary criticism and fiction to social tracts and history. Throughout the early years there is also a liberal seasoning of poetry.

Carlyle's early writings have a good deal of relevance to a study of his mature literary methods and style; for Carlyle did not throw off the lessons he learned writing for the *Edinburgh Philosophical Journal,* just as he did not abandon all interest in German once geology failed to yield all he sought. He applied both to other areas. Thus the fundamental relationship of Carlyle to his materials in the *Edinburgh Philosophical Journal* recurs in *Sartor Resartus,* and the first German words Carlyle knew, geological terms like *Thonschiefer,* give way to philosophic and literary terms that enliven the pages of *Sartor Resartus,* terms like *Selbsttötung and Entsagen.* A large number of the methods and concerns of Carlyle's early writings ultimately became part of what we know today as Carlylese.

The apprenticeship clearly begins in 1819 with Carlyle's first article for the *Edinburgh Philosophical Journal.* When

---

even obtaining testimonials from Goethe and from John Wilson ("Christopher North"), then Professor of Moral Philosophy at Edinburgh. But the appointment went to the "safe" Rev. Dr. Cook. In 1827 Carlyle had hoped for a similar chair at the new London University, yet he was considered, in Jeffrey's words, too much of a "sectary." See Wilson, *Carlyle to "The French Revolution,"* pp. 29–33.

it can be said to end is less clear. It is a case of several apprenticeships. As journalist Carlyle ends his apprenticeship only with the publication of his Schiller biography in 1825. As a translator he ends his apprenticeship with the translation of *Wilhelm Meister* in 1824–1825. As a literary critic he finishes his apprenticeship with the writing of *German Romance* in 1826. As an essayist Carlyle has surely arrived with the 1827 *Edinburgh Review* essay on Jean Paul. As a novelist Carlyle had to write "Illudo Chartis" and "Wotton Reinfred" before his apprenticeship ends with *Sartor Resartus* in 1830–1831. As a poet, however, Carlyle took the better part of valor.

What we have, then, for *Sartor* is the cumulative acquisition by Carlyle of various kinds of writing skills and techniques and their eventual assimilation. The first apprenticeship Carlyle served was as journalist, the second as novelist. The period of the first ranges from his efforts as a science hackwriter in 1819 to his abandoned 1827 novel, "Wotton Reinfred," first published posthumously. A subsequent chapter will treat the partly overlapping apprenticeships in translation and the essay. The whole period of the eighteen twenties was the seed-field for *Sartor*. Carlyle, we must suppose, little realized how much of his early work would find its way into *Sartor*. In drawing attention to it here, I am giving my study incidentally a psychological dimension which, along with the literary, can only be justified by how well it fits the facts of *Sartor Resartus* itself.

JOURNALISM

Three central features in terms of the later *Sartor Resartus* emerge from a study of Carlyle's journalistic apprenticeship. We may call these "situation," "structure," and "subject matter." There are also some stylistic elements worth at least passing attention. "Situation" refers to Carlyle's relation to his material, "structure" to the dominant patterns in his early essays, and "subject matter" to the topics that appear in and around Carlyle's early writing. The most revealing, situation, appears from the very first, in the essays for the *Edinburgh Philosophical Journal*.

The *Journal* was largely a personal project directed by David Brewster (later Sir David), an influential Edinburgh physicist and savant, and Carlyle's first point of contact with professional writing. The *Journal* ran only seven years (1819–1826), never attaining supremacy in its field; but as the organ of the Edinburgh Philosophical Society it had thoroughly respectable credentials. Under new auspices it continued as the *Edinburgh New Philosophical Journal* from 1826 to 1854. Carlyle's contributions to the *Journal* consist of three articles written between February 1819 and June 1820. Two are translations (one from French, one from German); the third is an outline of the substance of a German work.[10]

The articles have only limited interest in their own right, but one aspect of them stands out for the student of *Sartor*—Carlyle's relationship to his material. He is the editor-translator of the material he presents to the readers of the *Journal*. We may legitimately call this Carlyle's fundamental literary role of the eighteen-twenties, for he is cast in it again and again up to, and including, the composition of *Sartor*. In the *Journal* articles Carlyle's role is only barely discernible by virtue of a few editorial intrusions and a few explanatory footnotes signed "Transl." The situation, however, leads to a device of clarification that was

[10] The three are Jacob Berzelius, "Examination of some Compounds which depend upon very weak Affinities," *Edinburgh Philosophical Journal*, I (1819), 63–75, 243–253; "Remarks on Professor Hansteen's 'Inquiries Concerning the Magnetism of the Earth,'" *EPJ*, III (1820), 124–138; IV (1821), 114–124; "Outline of Professor Mohs's New System of Crystallography and Mineralogy," *EPJ*, III (1820), 154–176, 317–342; IV (1821), 56–67. Part three of the Mohs article is followed by a line reading "To be concluded." This is evidently in error, for no fourth part ever appeared and it was described as a three-part article on its first appearance. There is no convincing argument for doubting Carlyle's authorship of these articles, as does James C. Malin, "Carlyle's Philosophy of Clothes and Swedenborg's," *Scandinavian Studies*, XXXIII (1961), 164–166. See Appendix II for evidences of composition and dating.

later to become a feature of Carlyle's own style. It is the citation of a foreign language expression in parenthetical apposition to the translation. In his outline of Professor Mohs's system of mineralogy Carlyle writes: "The foundation of a natural system of mineralogy, depends on what may be called natural historical similarity (*naturhistorische aehnlichkeit*)." The stylistic device has arisen from the editorial situation, and it serves to remind us of what the situation was. We can hardly overestimate its importance.

Since the *Journal* articles were commissioned and subject to Brewster's supervision, it is not surprising that, overall, the style is not much like the style we associate with Carlyle. A few suggestive passages occur in which rhetorical questions and a certain intensity and emphasis of expression seem to betray Carlyle behind the impassive façade of scholarship. "Who [he writes] has yet been able to explain the cold of Siberia, Greenland, or Terra [*sic*] del Fuego? Who the strange variations of the polar climate, or Cook's observations upon the different distances to which the solid ice extends from the south pole, in the Pacific and Atlantic Oceans?"[11] But for the most part the style is merely workaday. More pertinent is the very subject matter of Carlyle's articles and of others in the *Journal*. He wrote on chemical compounds, magnetism, and mineralogy. Elsewhere in the *Journal* appeared notices of researches by Humboldt and Cuvier, accounts of Lagrange's theories and Laplace's, reports of the transactions of the Wernerian Society, even a history of pendulum clocks. To

[11] *Edinburgh Philosophical Journal,* IV (1821), 63. Of some interest is Carlyle's treatment of magnetism in the Hansteen article, where expressions like "state of indifference" argue for an even earlier source for the imagery in the "Centre of Indifference" chapter of *Sartor* than C. F. Harrold suggests (*Sartor*, pp. 169n., 182n.). In the Mohs article Carlyle intrudes his presence occasionally with such devices as underlining, as in the following example: " . . . *hitherto few mineralogists have been enabled to gain a knowledge of the productions of inorganic nature, in any other way, than by methods, which, though enveloped in much erudition, are strictly empirical.*" Apparently Carlyle was using "empirical" in a pejorative sense, a sense it retained until the mid-nineteenth century.

pinpoint the source of every allusion in *Sartor* would be
a hopeless and probably thankless task, but there is some
point in calling attention to the number and variety of
topics in the *Journal* that have their Sartorian counterparts.
In the first two paragraphs alone of *Sartor Resartus,* there
is mention of Lagrange, Laplace, Werner, Hutton, nautical
logbooks, geology, geognosy, and the Royal Society!
Carlyle's almost diabolic gift for allusion to the topical
and factual had an immense store to draw on in the
Edinburgh Philosophical Journal.

Before he had completed his last work for the *Journal,*
Carlyle began writing articles for Brewster's *Edinburgh
Encyclopaedia.* In progress since 1809, the *Encyclopaedia*
was not to be completed until 1830. Carlyle's association
with it extended from 1820 to 1823. Although encyclopaedia writing was apparently a promotion on Brewster's
ladder, it was still hackwork, and years later Carlyle called
his labors "wretched little translations, compilations, which
were very welcome too, though never other than dreary."[12]
By the time Carlyle began writing for the *Encyclopaedia,*
it had reached the letter M. He replaced the poet Thomas
Campbell in turning out articles to Brewster's specifications
and deadlines. At first his articles were biographical; later
geographical and historical articles were added. In all there
are thirteen biographical essays by Carlyle, from Montaigne
to the two Pitts, and seven historical and geographical
essays, from the Netherlands through the Quakers.[13]

[12] *Reminiscences,* II, 93.
[13] Carlyle's twenty articles are: "Montaigne," "Montagu,"
"Montesquieu," "Dr. John Moore," "Sir John Moore," "Montfaucon,"
"Montucla," "Necker," "Nelson," "Netherlands," "Newfoundland,"
"Norfolk," "Northamptonshire," "Northumberland," "Park," "Pascal,"
"Persia," "Pitt," "Pitt the Younger," "Quakers." See appendix for
composition dates. Seventeen of the essays were reprinted in *Mon-
taigne and Other Essays, Chiefly Biographical,* ed. S. R. Crockett
(London, 1897). The three missing essays, all later attributions,
are "Pascal," "Persia," and "Quakers." For the arguments for the
attribution of "Persia" and "Quakers" see G. B. Tennyson, "Unnoted
Encyclopaedia Articles by Carlyle," *English Language Notes,*
I (1963), 108–112.

The encyclopaedia experience was essentially a continuation of the relationship established in the *Philosophical Journal.* Carlyle is still the anonymous author of factual material. The difference lies in the material itself, broader in appeal, less concerned with translation. But the factual is still paramount. Carlyle retained a lifelong bias for it.

Since Carlyle had thirteen existing encyclopaedia volumes as guides, not to mention Brewster's editorial hand, he hardly exhibited much originality in the encyclopaedia articles. The obvious procedure was to follow chronology. To a large extent Carlyle's essays do. But one can discern in these essays two other structural tendencies: the two-part and the three-part division. The biographical essays are patterned either in two divisions—life and works—or three—introduction, biography, evaluation. Geographical-historical essays are similarly organized into statistics and history, or statistics, history, and culture. What makes these two structural patterns significant is that they anticipate Carlyle's later methods of organization—in the Schiller biography, in the critical essays, and in *Sartor Resartus.*

A glance at the way Carlyle's structural patterns work in two typical essays may stand for the encyclopaedia articles in general. The early Montaigne essay falls into three main divisions. The essay runs about 1,200 words. The first 200 are devoted to Montaigne's youth, with one central event that seems to capture the quality of the period (in this case Montaigne's peculiar mode of acquiring Latin); the following 800 words deal with Montaigne's chief works and the events of his mature life, culminating in his death; finally, about 200 words are devoted to an evaluation of Montaigne's total achievement. The pattern is rudimentary, to be sure, but then "Montaigne" is Carlyle's first encyclopaedia essay.

With Carlyle's longest essay, the recently discovered article on Persia, we have a good example of the two-part pattern of organization. The essay is formally divided into two separately tilted parts: "Statistics of Persia" and "History of Persia." Altogether "Persia" occupies thirty-seven of the oversize, double-columned pages of the *Edinburgh Encyclopaedia*.[14] Fifteen pages treat the statistics of Persia, chiefly geographical and economic data; and nineteen pages cover Persian history. There appears to be an internal tendency for the article to separate into three parts, but the formal divisions operate against it. Like the biographical essays, "Persia" proceeds from the superficial to the more complex and demanding aspects of the subject.

"Persia" is an especially rich example of that other constant of Carlyle's early writing, allusions to topics that appear in Carlyle's later writing. There is a discussion of modes of dress, for example, and in the historical portion a treatment of the aprons revolt led by Kahweh (or Gao as it appears in *Sartor*); there is mention of the poet Firdausi, known to Carlyle and Jane in the early twenties, discussion of Pilpay (or Bidpai), a name Carlyle later jocularly assumed as a pseudonym. More arresting is Carlyle's adoption of the tripartite division of Persian history postulated by Sir William Jones, for it corresponds strikingly to Carlyle's own division of European history in his 1830 "History of German Literature."[15] Throughout the encyclopaedia essays appear subjects that find their way later, often much altered, into *Sartor*. Pascal, for example, was the subject of one essay, as well as a constant Carlyle interest. The Quakers, whose George Fox figures in *Sartor*, were the subject of one essay, as were Montaigne and Montesquieu, who also surface again in *Sartor*. The Gueux of the Netherlands article come forth in the discussion of symbols in *Sartor*. The Pitt diamond makes its appearance in Carlyle's article on Pitt and again in *Sartor*. Obviously a considerable list could be compiled, but the point is to emphasize the heterogeneity of materials that Carlyle himself dealt with. Of course, everyone knows and

[14] *Edinburgh Encyclopaedia*, xvi, 369–406.
[15] *Carlyle's Unfinished History of German Literature*, ed. Hill Shine (Lexington, Ky., 1951).

has been exposed to countless numbers of unrelated facts. Carlyle may not have known or been exposed to more of these than many other men before or since. What matters is that he made an imaginative use of them in his writing, and, since this is a qualitative observation, it is not much illuminated by compiling a list of possible sources for this or that fact.

The abundance and variety of *Sartor* appear the less surprising when we remind ourselves that the work followed years of Carlyle's dealing with factual material for publications like the *Journal* and the *Encyclopaedia* and the great reviews. Therefore, we can see, not so much that he knew about Montesquieu's *Esprit des Lois* from his essay for the *Encyclopaedia,* but that, having written of Montesquieu for the *Encyclopaedia,* he was perhaps more readily disposed than another man to introduce Montesquieu into a work like *Sartor,* and that he knew from personal experience how a subject like the *Esprit des Lois* was normally treated in informative prose. Consequently, Carlyle knew what use *he* wanted to make of it in *Sartor.* The astonishing result is Teufelsdröckh's ridicule of Montesquieu's work as superficial, followed by the witty paraphrase of the *Esprit des Lois* as an *Esprit de Coutumes* to parallel Teufelsdröckh's own *Esprit de Costumes.* Clearly, it took more than an essay for the *Edinburgh Encyclopaedia* for Carlyle to transform the *Esprit des Lois* as he does, but the *Encyclopaedia* experience gave him a common denominator of received opinion and received style that he had to know before he could parody and modify.

In the *Encyclopaedia* itself we find little to suggest the verbal pyrotechnics of which Carlyle was capable. Those who have examined the articles have sought to find foreshadowings of his later manner. Thus, Crockett, who collected Carlyle's encyclopaedia contributions into one volume, makes much of Carlyle's comment on Montaigne's style: "With him, more than with any other, words may be called the garment of thought; the expression is frequently moulded to fit the idea, never the idea to fit the expression." The clothes image notwithstanding, it is an act of imaginative faith to see anything seminal in Carlyle's observation. There are early indications enough of the direction Carlyle's style took without exalting what is, after all, a conventional observation into a guidepost. There are in the *Encyclopaedia* essays here and there, as in the *Journal* articles, touches that may betray the Carlyle we know under the anonymity of the encyclopaedia hack: an occasional emphasis in style (he calls Nelson "a HERO"), a leaning toward parallelism (although often of the Johnsonian sort), a wryness, and even irony, of tone. For the most part, however, the *Encyclopaedia* style, along with that of *Schiller*, has furnished more support to the sometimes exaggerated allegations about Carlyle's "two styles" than to demonstrations of the consistency of Carlyle's manner.

Stylistic generalizations from the *Journal* and *Encyclopaedia* articles are simply more unreliable than those based on Carlyle's independent work. He evidently carried out his tasks with due diligence and sincerity, but biographical indications actually point to disinterest on his part with any serious merit in this early work. Nor can we overlook the extent to which the manner was dictated by Brewster's editorial demands. By contrast, however, it is hard to escape the fundamental aspects of situation, structure, and subject matter in the *Journal* and *Encyclopaedia* essays, whether these are independent of or in conformity with Brewster's dictates. Whatever Carlyle may have thought at the time of his role as editor and editor-translator of factual materials, or of the convenient two-part and three-part essay divisions, the fact is that these recur in his writing experience with such frequency that they cannot be overlooked. Whereas the style of his early writings shades increasingly into a style that was all his own, situation, structure, and subject matter remain in many respects the same for ten years. When Carlyle came to write an original work, like most writers he used what he knew.

While it is apparent that Carlyle wanted to dispense with writing encyclopaedia articles, he was obliged to continue them until 1823, when he obtained a commission to write a biography of Schiller. Still, he endeavored to find other channels for his talents during the three years that he sustained himself largely by writing for Brewster. In 1819–1820 he wrote a review of Pictet's *Gravitation*, which was never published.[16] In 1820 he tried a translation of the *Thirty Years' War*, which was apparently rejected but preserved by him for later use.[17] In 1821 he translated a portion of Malte Brun's *Geography* from a French edition, but it too was never published.[18] Two early essays for an obscure Edinburgh literary review brought little money. Therefore, in 1821–1822, to supplement his encyclopaedia work, he accepted a commission from Brewster to translate Legendre's *Geometry*.[19] It turned out to be his last substantial work in "science." Years later he felt only the most distant sympathy for geometry, while recalling that he had once been highly proficient at it. In the early twenties Carlyle's was a much more versatile intellect than it was in the sixties.

As a straightforward treatise on geometry Legendre's text seems far removed from the concerns of *Sartor Resartus,* but in fact it holds the same kind of relevance to the situation of *Sartor* that we have been investigating up to now. Carlyle was again an editor-translator, even

[16] Carlyle was probably trying to exploit topical interest, since Pictet was well known in Edinburgh. See Maxwell H. Goldberg, "Carlyle, Pictet, and Jeffrey," *Modern Language Quarterly,* VII (1946), 291–296.

[17] See below, pp. 68–69.

[18] *Early Letters,* I, 326 (letter to his parents of 25 February 1821).

[19] *Elements of Geometry and Trigonometry* (Edinburgh, 1824). The original *Éléments de Géometrie* was first published in 1794. Carlyle's is a translation of the 11th ed.

though Brewster took full credit for the work when it was published, cagily subtitling it: "Translated from the French of A. M. Legendre: Edited by Sir David Brewster." But Carlyle did the work. Apart from translating, it consisted in some rearrangement and in the composition of an introductory essay on proportion that Carlyle in his *Reminiscences* confessed himself proud of, calling it "complete really and lucid, and yet one of the briefest ever known." Of the whole work, Carlyle said he felt "as if it were right enough and felicitous in its kind!"[20] Once we grasp the importance of the constantly recurring situation of Carlyle as editor, we need not detain ourselves with details of the geometry text itself. The essay on proportion does indeed set forth with clarity the essentials of measure and balance, which may surprise Carlyle detractors; and the translation overall (a portion of it completed by Carlyle's brother John) appears thoroughly competent.[21]

But Carlyle was ambitious, and by 1822 he had published two critical essays in which we can see the inclination of his interests.

CRITICISM

Both of Carlyle's early critical essays appeared in the shortlived *New Edinburgh Review*. The first essay, published in October 1821, bore the title of the work under review, "The Metrical Legends of Exalted Characters," a series of historical portraits in verse by Joanna Baillie. The second essay, published in April 1822 was originally titled "Goethe's Faust," but it is now more generally known by its anthology title "Faustus." "Crude," D. A. Wilson's

---

[20] *Reminiscences*, II, 105–106.

[21] Of proportion he wrote: "Its Object being to point out the relations which subsist among magnitudes in general, when viewed as *measured* or represented by *members*, the connexion it has with Geometry is not more immediate than with many other branches of knowledge, except indeed as Geometry affords the largest class of magnitudes capable of being so measured or represented, and thus offers the widest field for reducing it to practice" (p. ix).

word for the essays, is too harsh, although we may not
dispute Carlyle's disinclination to reprint them in his lifetime. Still, students of Carlyle have been justified in ex-
huming them, even if not in trying to reinvest them with
full-bodied life. The *New Edinburgh* essays are of greater
interest for their ideas than for their structure or style,
and it is on this basis that "Faustus" has received periodic
re-examination.[22] The Baillie essay, however, also com-
mands our attention as an illustration of Carlyle's early
critical views, especially since it has been neglected in favor
of "Faustus." **1384255**

In the Baillie essay Carlyle confronts the problem of
the rival claims of truth and fiction and decides on behalf
of fiction. His concession to the historian is to urge the
poet to concentrate on the lesser-known figures of history,
for whom he sees the poet as a "kind of new creator."
It is in just such observations and in the following discussion of credibility in fiction that we find material of
interest for Carlyle's later career, rather than in his treatment of the *Metrical Legends* themselves (although who
would dispute his judgment that Miss Baillie is out of
her depth?). When he examines the question of credibility
in fiction, he comes down firmly on the side of imagination
rather than fact, so that even in 1821 the serious student
of the facts shows himself even more committed to the
truth. He argues that if a literary means were found whereby verisimilitude could be dispensed with without
"violating, not the transient, but the permanent belief we
have of [the] reality" of an event, we would have a "more
intense, and therefore more poetical" work of art. Since

[22] The *Faust* essay has been reprinted no fewer than four times
by students of Carlyle, never by Carlyle himself. See Isaac Watson
Dyer, *A Bibliography of Thomas Carlyle's Writings and Ana* (Port-
land, Me., 1928), p. 78. I have not had access to the original
periodical and I have referred to the work by its anthology title
"Faustus," as it appears in *Collectanea Thomas Carlyle, 1821–1855*,
ed. S. A. Jones (Canton, Pa., 1903), pp. 59–92. The Baillie essay
is printed in *Collectanea*, pp. 19–56.

one's actions are never "more than a feeble and imperfect emblem of what is passing within," considerable latitude must be allowed the writer in creating true proportion:

> Hence, to give a *true* picture of any character, particularly of a great character, true, we mean, both in its *proportions* and *vividness* it must often be requisite to forsake the straightforward track of narrative, to accumulate, either secretly, as historians do in forming their judgment, or avowedly, as poets do in presenting theirs, and combine the several impressions which the story has produced upon us,—uniting them in their proper situations and relative strength to establish the true *proportion*, and accompanying them with all the influence of poetry to impart the true degree of *vividness*. (*Collectanea*, pp. 34–35)

In short, Carlyle shows himself no slavish student of the facts, but an advocate of imagination and "true proportion," whether in science or literature (his geometry essay on proportion was written close to this same time).

Stylistically Carlyle seems to write with a little more verve in his Baillie essay: he employs italics with greater freedom and a syntax looser than that of the *Journal* and *Encyclopaedia* articles. He also finds occasion to introduce a device of emphasis first explored in his *Journal* articles, for we find him writing of Schiller's Tell in contrast to Miss Baillie's Wallace:

> Tell died beside his own hearth, amid affectionate grandchildren; a people blessed him, (*des Vaterlandes Schütz und Erretter*); and a poet, fitted to appreciate and fathom his manly soul, has embalmed the memory of its worth forever. (*Collectanea*, p. 37)

Here the citation of a foreign-language expression works more toward expansion than toward the clarification sought after by the same device in the *Journal*, since here Carlyle has not given the literal equivalent of his English phrase, but has introduced an entirely new phrase into his description. It may be doubted that many readers recognized the phrase, which after all requires familiarity with Schiller's *Wilhelm Tell* in the original, but it adds another dimension to the thought, distending the sentence, slowing the reading, and convoluting what is already somewhat cumbersome syntax. Here, rather than in the Montaigne essay, we are perhaps justified in saying that it is Carlyle speaking. These incipient flashes of Carlyle's later manner appear in generally unremarkable contexts, but they suggest that the famous Carlyle style is a development of long present inclinations rather than an overnight concoction.

So much has been made of Carlyle's 1822 *Faust* essay that one hesitates to traverse again those main-travelled roads. Recently it was even argued that the whole scheme of *Sartor Resartus* lies embedded in it.[23] Something by way of seminal insight is certainly there, but *Sartor* is more than an expansion of the often quoted lines of the *Erdgeist*.[24] Neither Goethe's impact on Carlyle nor Carlyle's early essay on Goethe's masterpiece can be brushed aside in an examination of *Sartor. Faust,* as a work, profoundly touched Carlyle's affections, although probably less so than *Wilhelm Meister.* Yet Carlyle wrote *Sartor* before the second, redemptive part of *Faust* appeared, so the work was not the means by which Carlyle gained a positive outlook

[23] Lore Metzger, "*Sartor Resartus:* A Victorian *Faust*," *Comparative Literature,* XIII (1961), 316–331.
[24] In Lebensfluten, im Tatensturm
wall' ich auf und ab,
webe hin und her!
Geburt und Grab,
ein ewiges Meer,
ein wechselnd Weben,
ein glühend Leben:
so schaff' ich am sausenden Webstuhl der Zeit
und wirke der Gottheit lebendiges Kleid. (*Faust,* I, 501–509)

Carlyle's translation appears in *Sartor,* I, viii, 55.

on life. Indeed, in the *New Edinburgh* essay and throughout the twenties Carlyle lamented the apparent damnation
of *Faust*. Carlyle's new grasp on life had commenced in
the very year in which his *Faust* essay appeared. Since
we can no longer lay Carlyle's conversion at Jane Welsh's
door, as Froude tried to do, there seems no justification
for laying it at Goethe's.

What the *Faust* essay does show is Carlyle's respect
for Goethe and his dawning awareness that in literature
the new dispensation was coming from Germany. Even
more important, the essay reveals Carlyle's understanding
of the artistic integrity of *Faust*. Repeatedly Carlyle calls
attention to the very defects in *Faust* that critics were
later to charge *Sartor Resartus* with: lack of coherence,
flamboyant style, and improbable characters. His justification of Goethe's method shows a marked capacity for sympathetic criticism. *Faust*, he argues, aims "to show the
great vortex of human life, an end to which much of the
rich mixture of discordants actually contributes." For that
reason *Faust* excels Marlowe's *Faustus*, for the former is
in fact about modern man. Mephistopheles is "emphatically
'The Denyer,'" i.e., Carlyle's *bête noire*, an eighteenth-
century French *philosophe*. The difficulty of placing *Faust*
in perspective, he argues, is that it transcends genre: "We
scarcely know under what class to arrange it, or how to
work out its rank in the scale of literary dignity." The
chief merit, then, of Carlyle's *Faust* essay is its revelation
of Carlyle as a critic sympathetic to experiment and originality when the result is, however unorthodox, an artistic
whole.[25]

---

[25] An incidental feature of the article is the inclusion of Carlyle's
early translation of "Faust's Curse," which he subsequently revised
and printed in Ottilie von Goethe's Weimar coterie journal *Chaos*
(1830). I have not seen a copy of this later printing, but it was
evidently the same version as the one printed, much to Carlyle's
dismay, in the *Athenaeum*, 7 January 1832, p. 5. See *Two Note
Books of Thomas Carlyle*, ed. Charles Eliot Norton (New York,
1898), p. 232. The two versions show substantial differences both

Both "Faustus" and the Baillie essay are structurally akin to the encyclopaedia articles. The Baillie essay divides into two major portions: the first is a theoretical discussion of the claims of fact in fiction; the second is a detailed examination of Miss Baillie's way of dealing with the problem. In short, the essay divides into two approximately equal portions, theory and practice. "Faustus," however, is organized on a three-part plan. The first introduces the English reader to the general tenor and impact of *Faust,* the second treats the story itself and the verse, and the third assesses the deeper meaning and ultimate significance of the whole work. It appears that these two methods of organization represent organizing principles fundamental to Carlyle's imagination. In *Sartor* the three-part principle determines structure, whereas elsewhere in Carlyle—in *Past and Present,* for example—the two-part principle dominates.

The later exclusion of these early essays from Carlyle's canon reflects no doubt a sincere recognition of their imperfections. In addition, Carlyle may have excluded "Faustus" because it appeared to be too harsh a judgment of the revered Goethe, but even at the time, in his characteristically self-deprecatory manner, Carlyle told Jane that

---

in Carlyle's comprehension and in his versifying skill:

> Accursed be the grape's enticing juice—
> Cursed be love, and hope, and faith—and cursed
> Above all cursed, be the tame dull spirit
> Which bears life's evils patiently.
> —From "Faustus" (*Collectanea,* p. 75)

> A curse on juice of Grapes deceiving,
> On Love's wild thrill of raptures first,
> A curse on Hoping, on Believing,
> And Patience more than all be cursed!
> —From "Faust's Curse" (*Athenaeum,* 1832)

Note the liberal use of capitalization of abstracts in the later version. Alexander Carlyle dates the later version 1822, but this appears to be an extremely early date.

the *Faust* essay was "a paltry rag," that it was "so ambitious, so bombastic, so jejune."[26] His next literary endeavor pleased him a little more. It was the *Life of Schiller*.
Before the writing of *Schiller,* in July or August 1821 or
1822, Carlyle experienced that mystic illumination in Leith
Walk, Edinburgh, that has since become one of the best-
known personal experiences in all English literary history.
The Leith Walk experience is central to *Sartor Resartus,*
where it is also symbolically recorded, and there will be
subsequent mention of it in these pages; but it will not
be treated now in all its fulness, partly because it is so
celebrated, and partly because its most important
aspect—its genuineness—has been thoroughly authenticated
and can be taken as established.[27] The profundity of the

[26] *Love Letters of Thomas Carlyle and Jane Welsh,* ed. Alexander
Carlyle (London, 1909), I, 17.
[27] Carlyle later reported that the mystic illumination described
in "The Everlasting No" chapter of *Sartor* "occurred quite literally to
myself in Leith Walk, during three weeks of total sleeplessness in
which almost my one solace was that of a daily bathe on the sands
between Leith and Portobello. Incident was as I went down; coming
up I generally felt refreshed for the hour. I remember it well, and
could go straight about the place" (Froude, I, 101). Masson,
Edinburgh Sketches, p. 299, has identified the very spot, "just below
Pilrig Street, which was Carlyle's starting point from his lodgings
in Moray Street (now Spey Street) on his way to Leith."
Froude is responsible for the earlier dating of June 1821 which
may have been influenced by Froude's desire to link the regeneration
to Carlyle's first meeting with Jane Welsh, which occurred in May
of that year. Alexander Carlyle in *Love Letters,* II, 380–382, and
D. A. Wilson in *Carlyle Till Marriage* (London, 1923), pp. 250–252,
argue for July or early August 1822.
The genuineness and long-term impact of the experience are fully
set forth in Charles Frederick Harrold's "Carlyle and the Mystical
Tradition," *Catholic World,* CXLII (1935), 45–49, and "The Mystical
Element in Carlyle (1827–34)." *Modern Philology,* XXIX (1932),
459–475. That the deepening of Carlyle's understanding as a result
of the Leith Walk experience required the whole decade of the
twenties is convincingly shown by Carlisle Moore, "*Sartor Resartus*
and the Problem of Carlyle's 'Conversion,'" *PMLA,* LXX (1955),
662–681," and his "The Persistence of Carlyle's 'Everlasting Yea.'"
Modern Philology, LIV (1957), 187–196. See also W. Witte,
"Carlyle's Conversion," in *The Era of Goethe: Essays Presented*

conversion and its implications for all that Carlyle subsequently did becomes increasingly apparent as we examine his literary output in the years up to *Sartor*. A new man is gradually emerging, even if only the most indistinct outlines appear in the first substantial post-conversion work, the *Life of Schiller*.

Originally a series of three articles in the *London Magazine* in 1823–1824, the *Life of Schiller*, published in 1825, was an expansion of the original series that had been commissioned through the good offices of Carlyle's Annandale countryman, the preacher Edward Irving.[28] The book re-

---

to *James Boyd*, (Oxford, 1959), pp. 179–193. Carlyle himself speaks of "Conversion" in respect to his life at Hoddam Hill, 1825–26: "I understood well what the old Christian people meant by 'Conversion,' by God's infinite mercy to them. I had, in effect, gained an immense victory, and for a number of years had, in spite of nerves and chagrins, a constant inward happiness that was quite royal and supreme, in which all temporal evil was transient and insignificant, and which essentially remains with me still, though far oftener *eclipsed* and lying deeper *down* than then." *Reminiscences*, II, 180.

[28] "Life of Friedrich Schiller," *London Magazine*, VIII (1823), 381–400; IX (1824), 37–59; X (1824), 16–25, 149–163, 259–269.

Life of Friedrich Schiller (London, 1825) appears as vol. XXV of *The Works of Thomas Carlyle*, ed. H. D. Traill ("Centenary Edition," London, 1896–1899). Hereafter all references to Carlyle's works, unless otherwise noted, are to this edition, cited as *Works*.

Edward Irving (1792–1834) exerted a profound influence on Carlyle which has been generally neglected, although by Carlyle's own admission (*Reminiscences*, II, 41) some of Irving's flamboyant style stands behind Carlyle's own: ". . . of attitude, gesture, elocution, there was no neglect:—his voice was very fine; melodious depth, strength, clearness its chief characteristics; I have heard more pathetic voices, going more direct to the heart, both in the way of indignation and of pity, but recollect none that better filled the ear. He affected the Miltonic or Old-English Puritan style, and strove visibly to imitate it more and more, till almost the end of his career, when indeed it had become his own, and was the language he used in utmost heat of business, for expressing his meaning. At this time, and for years afterwards, there was something of preconceived intention visible in it, in fact of real 'affectation,' as there could not well help being—to his example also, I suppose, I owe something of my own poor affectations in that matter, which are now more or less visible to me, much repented

ceived generally favorable notices, and it marks the completion of Carlyle's journalistic apprenticeship, for it is the
culmination of the kind of writing undertaken for the
Edinburgh Encyclopaedia; it is Carlyle's crowning achievement in conventional biography. It merits neither Carlyle's
own censure after the writing of it, nor the extravagant
praise heaped upon it by those who cite it as evidence
of Carlyle's capacity for sane, clear prose, perversely
thwarted after 1825. *Schiller,* like the *Journal* and *Encyclopaedia* articles, was commissioned work by a literary unknown striving to please a distant editor. A certain degree
of caution must therefore accompany any generalizations
about the style.

Schiller firmly establishes Carlyle's understanding of a
major German literary figure. His sympathy for Schiller
was perhaps as great as that for any German writer, including Goethe (although he accorded a higher place to
Goethe's achievements), for Schiller touched Carlyle's response at many points: he was the child of poor parents;
he was the victim of tyrannical pedagogy, against which
his spirit rebelled; and yet he succeeded in excelling in
a diversity of fields—drama, poetry, history, philosophy,
and fiction. By contrast, Goethe's struggles appeared minor.
In endeavoring to communicate the magnitude and scope
of Schiller's achievements, Carlyle chose to present him
from a magisterial, encyclopaedic viewpoint. He had to
assume that his readers would be, if anything, hostile to
many aspects of German literature and thought. The basic
situation found Carlyle again in the role of an Englishman
introducing and commenting on the work of a foreigner,
the role he had filled for the *Journal* and *Encyclopaedia*
and, in his *Faust* review, for the *New Edinburgh.* Nat-

---

or not." Irving died a broken man, deposed from the Kirk of
Scotland, after being convicted of maintaining the heresy of the
sinfulness of Christ's human nature. See Mrs. [Margaret] Oliphant,
The Life of Edward Irving (New York, 1862) and Andrew Landale
Drummond, *Edward Irving and His Circle* (London, [1937]).

urally, he adopted the same format and essentially the same style that had proved acceptable to Brewster and like-minded editors in Scotland.

Conveniently, there were three magazine articles. The book expands the articles but retains the original divisions. Part one, shortest of the three, introduces Schiller and offers some reasons for his distinction; part two, slightly longer, discusses his life and some important achievements; and part three, double the length of part two, dwells on the major works and the philosophic implications of Schiller's writings. The similarities between the structure of *Schiller* and the encyclopaedia articles is striking enough. Here again, it is hard to know how much of the pattern was owed directly to the encyclopaedia experience, although we should remember that Carlyle was writing encyclopaedia articles probably as late as January 1823. It is obvious that the degree of supervision Brewster may have exercised was impossible for the editors of the *London Magazine* while Carlyle was writing in distant Perthshire.[29] To some extent, therefore, the structure of *Schiller* was more freely chosen by Carlyle than any of the Brewster work of the past.

The much-discussed eighteenth-century style of *Schiller* is in the encyclopaedia vein. Carlyle adopts a somewhat distant tone, and his sentences are much more likely to reverberate than to rend. Still, the style of *Schiller* is considerably more emphatic than that of the *Journal* or *Encyclopaedia* articles. An exclamatory tone begins to emerge, as Carlyle treats subjects that go directly to his heart. He waxes rhapsodic, for example, on the fate of Karl Moor in Schiller's *Die Räuber*: ". . . We follow him with anxiety through the forest and desert places, where he wanders,

[29] At the time, he was tutoring the sons of Mr. and Mrs. Charles Buller, a wealthy Anglo-Indian couple, at their home, Kinnaird House in Perthshire. The Buller family is frequently "identified" as the prototype of the Towgoods in *Sartor*. The elder son, Charles, later became an M.P. and counted for a time as a disciple of Carlyle's.

encompassed with peril, inspired with lofty daring, and torn by unceasing remorse." He mixes scorn with pity as he contemplates the fate of literary men: "Look at the biography of authors! Except for the Newgate Calendar, it is the most sickening chapter in the history of man. The calamities of these people are a fertile topic; and too often their faults and vices have kept pace with their calamities." (*Works*, xxv, 19, 41–42). Examples of this sort could be multiplied. They mark a departure from the more sober tone of the encyclopaedia essays or even the *New Edinburgh Review* essays. Carlylean overtones are evident too in the emerging assumption of his role as the Voice of Germany: "Influences still more mysterious are hinted at, if not directly announced. An idea seems to lurk obscurely at the bottom of [the German dramatists'] abstruse and elaborate speculations." And his treatment of Kant is couched in the same language:

> The air of mysticism connected with these doctrines was attractive to the German mind, with which the vague and vast are always pleasing qualities; the dreadful array of first principles, the forest huge of terminology and definitions, where the panting intellect of weaker men wanders as in pathless thickets, and at length sinks powerless to the earth, oppressed with fatigue, and suffocated with scholastic miasma, seemed sublime rather than appalling to the Germans; men who shrink not at toil, and to whom a certain degree of darkness appears a native element, essential for giving play to that deep meditative enthusiasm which forms so important a feature in their character (*Works*, xxv, 108)

Something close to the Editor of Teufelsdröckh's papers is in those lines. And that is the significance of *Schiller* for *Sartor*. Carlyle well knew the tone suitable to the serious and clear-eyed British reviewer. He had used it himself.

In the history of Anglo-German literary relations Carlyle's biography marks the first major assessment of

Schiller's work, and even among German works Carlyle's takes precedence as the first substantial appraisal of Schiller's whole achievement. Goethe, who supervised a translation of the work into German, justly called it "merkwürdig";[30] but it must be evident too that *Schiller* is no work of art. It is at best a work of scholarship. As such it was destined to be superseded. Although it has abundant historical interest, it reflects the ignorance of its author and its times. There is not much point in lamenting that the style of *Schiller* was not maintained in Carlyle's later work.[31] To cast a work like *Sartor* in the language of *Schiller* would have been to condemn it to oblivion. Those who cavil at the loss of the "lucid" style of *Schiller* for the turgidity of *Sartor Resartus* are objecting to more than they may realize—they are objecting to the very point and essence of Carlyle's purpose in *Sartor*. They are asking that Carlyle remain a popularizer and biographer rather than become the individual, idiosyncratic, sometimes exasperating Carlyle we know, and on whose account only we read the *Schiller* biography at all. *Schiller* marks the end of apprenticeship for Carlyle; there is no virtue in lamenting that it was not a beginning.

FICTION AND VERSE

While Carlyle was doing piecework for Brewster, studying German and geology, tutoring the Buller children in Perthshire, and projecting a history of the English

[30] *Correspondence between Goethe and Carlyle*, p. 14. The German work appeared as *Leben Schillers, aus dem Englischen, eingeleitet durch Goethe* (Frankfurt/Main, 1830).

[31] See Francis X. Roellinger, Jr., "The Early Development of Carlyle's Style," *PMLA*, LXXII (1957), 936–951. The article is a good corrective to exaggerated attempts to establish an unwavering consistency in Carlyle's style, but it lends more support than necessary to the late Victorian assertion that Carlyle put on Carlylese for fancy occasions and dropped it for everyday ones. The notion has perpetuated in subtler form the weary charge of insincerity in Carlyle's writing. The charge of insincerity continues to bedevil Carlyle's reputation. See Henri Peyre, *Literature and Sincerity* (New Haven, 1963), p. 318.

Commonwealth, he was also courting Jane Welsh of Haddington and proposing to her numerous plans for their future as writers. In November 1822 he conceived of a novel about a "fiery but benignant spirit" who comes to grief against the obstacles of life and society. In December he modified the plan, to provide for his and Jane's composing the novel together in epistolary form. He was to write the man's letters, she the woman's. He even wrote the first two letters before abandoning the scheme because he "wrote with no *verve*."[32]

Verve *Sartor Resartus* has. And it is verve that most of Carlyle's early stories and poetry lack. At the same time that he proposed the joint novel to Jane he enclosed for her consideration a short story he had written and which he contemptuously called a "sooterkin," justified only on the grounds that "a man must write a cart-load of trash before he can produce a handful of excellence."[33] The story was "Cruthers and Jonson." It was written by November 1822, but it was not published until 1831, when Carlyle was in need of money and sufficiently established to publish his old story in *Fraser's*.[34] Ironically, it enjoyed a favorable reception, while *Sartor* two years later was almost driven from the magazine by irate readers.

[32] *Love Letters*, I, 123–124. The novel he described has more affinities with "Wotton Reinfred" than with *Sartor*: "At length [the hero] must grow tired of science, and Nature, and simplicity, just as he had of towns; sickening by degrees till his heart was full of bitterness and ennui, he speaks forth his sufferings—not in the puling Lake-style—but with a tongue of fire—sharp, sarcastic, apparently unfeeling, yet all the while betokening to the quick-sighted a mind of lofty thoughts and generous affections smarting under the torment of its own overnobleness, and ready to break in pieces by the force of its own energies. Already all seems over with him, he has hinted about suicide, and rejected it scornfully—but it is evident he cannot long exist in this to him most blasted, waste and lonely world,—when *you*—that is the heroine—come stepping in before him with your *espiègleries* and fervency, your 'becks and wreathed smiles,' and all your native loveliness. . . ."

[33] *Love Letters*, I, 125.

[34] *Fraser's Magazine*, II (1831), 691–705. It is reprinted in *Works*, xxx, 168–198.

Carlisle Moore has examined "Cruthers and Jonson" with care as an early instance of Carlyle's narrative methods prior to his writing history.[35] It is also an early instance, probably the earliest, of Carlyle's writing fiction. "Cruthers and Jonson," subtitled "The Outskirts of Life. A True Story," was actually a true story, one which Carlyle had heard in his youth on the Scottish border. At the same time, it is not history; it is a short story. Thus Moore's division of Carlyle's narrative methods into "detailed narrative" and "running narrative" is only of limited utility in examining "Cruthers and Jonson" as a work of the imagination. Detailed narrative is the term Moore uses to describe passages depicting events as they happen; running narrative is that which is summary, in which the story passes swiftly over long periods of time in order to reach a point at which detailed narrative resumes. But we must still inquire whether "Cruthers and Jonson" is an artistic success, whether it has unity, pace, interest, and style. And we must ask whether there are any discernible traces of Carlyle's methods of writing fiction that apply to his general practice. In truth, the story lacks unity, its pace is uneven, and interest and style vary excessively. But there are structural and stylistic elements that anticipate Carlyle's later practice. Moore's running narrative (the summary passages) does little but serve the function of moving the story forward in time. Some passages of detailed narrative, however, have a life and vitality, a verve, if you will, lacking in the story as a whole. The battle scenes in particular enjoy this distinction.

The story tells of two Annandale boys from contrasting backgrounds—one a son of the gentry, the other of peasant stock—who become fast friends in youth and resolve to remain so until death. Cruthers grows up to become a

[35] Carlisle Moore, "Thomas Carlyle and Fiction: 1822–1834," *Nineteenth-Century Studies,* ed. H. Davis et al. (Ithaca, 1940), pp. 131–177. See also Moore's "Carlyle as a Narrative Writer: 1822–1833," unpublished Ph.D. dissertation, Princeton University, 1940.

self-sufficient, honest farmer, whereas Jonson improvidently
loses his ancestral lands and, almost by chance, joins the
Jacobite rebellion of 1745. He is captured when the uprising
fails and is condemned to death, but at the last minute
he gains a reprieve and is exiled to Jamaica. There he wins
the hand of the daughter of a rich planter: he prospers
and eventually returns to Scotland to repurchase his ancestral lands. He dies in old age, with Cruthers, true to
his promise, there to see that he is properly buried.
It is not an especially entertaining or edifying story, but
much of that is due to Carlyle's execution. His conception,
like Joanna Baillie's, may have been good. Three features
of the story arrest the attention of the student of Carlyle's
methods in *Sartor*: the use of a frame, passages of conscious
eloquence, and passages of ludicrous humor.

The frame of "Cruthers and Jonson" is the merest
shadow of a frame, used to no advantage, but fundamental
in Carlyle's approach to fiction. A narrator appears at the
beginning of the story, later drops out of sight in favor
of an omniscient author, and then re-emerges at the end
with a commentary on the story. The use of this frame
is sufficiently crude to make it appear that the story was
done in two separate stages. In the first the narrator has
a certain prominence. By the second the very presence
of the narrator seems to have been forgotten, to be recalled
only at the end. Nevertheless, the use of a frame serves
two purposes. It gives the story an immediacy it might
otherwise lack, and it helps direct the reader's responses
to the material. The narrator's claim to have been a witness
to most of the events related helps lend credence to the
story and maintain in the reader's mind the fact that he
is reading a true story. In the early part of the story the
narrator comments on the action in such a way as to suggest
that his is a normative voice which can help the reader over
the rough spots.

Some of the rough spots the narrator guides the reader
over are the very passages of conscious eloquence which
distinguish this story from Carlyle's other early writing.

First, Carlyle gives full vent to his feelings for the majesty of nature:

It was a lovely evening, as I have been told, and the place itself is not without some charms. Around them lay an undulating tract of green country, sprinkled with trees and white cottages, hanging on the sunny sides of the declivities. Cattle lowing afar off in the closes; ploughmen driving home their wearied teams; and columns of blue peat-smoke, rising from every chimney within sight, gave notice that the goodwives were cooking their husbands' frugal supper. . . . On the left rose Woodcockair, to which the rook was making wing, and Repentance Hill, with its old Border watch-tower, now inhabited by ghosts and pigeons; while to the right, and far away, the great red disc of the sun, among its curtains of flaming cloud, was hanging over the shoulder of Criffel, and casting a yellow, golden light athwart the whole frith of Solway; on the other side of which, St. Bees' Head, with all the merry ports and granges of Cumberland, swelled gradually up into the hills, where Skiddaw, and Helvellyn, and a thousand nameless peaks, towered away into the azure vault, and shone as if they had been something far better than they were (*Works*, xxx, 174)

Immediately the narrator intrudes to undercut the passage with another exploiting the ludicrousness of the situation:

These boys were no poets. Indeed, except the author of Lagg's elegy and Macnay, whose ode, beginning with
"A joiner lad has ta'en a trip
Across the Atlantic in a ship,"
—(not a cart, or washing-tub, the usual method of conveyance)—has been much admired by the literary world, Annandale has had few poets of note, and no philosopher but "Henderson *On the Breeding of Swine*"; yet the beauty of such a scene, the calm, rich, reposing loveliness of nature, will penetrate into the dullest heart. (*Works*, xxx, 175)

The effect in "Cruthers and Jonson" is rather disquieting, for the reader has not been adequately conditioned by the narrator for the sudden shift in mood. Thus, to carry off his game, Carlyle needed more narrator, not less. It is likely that Carlyle's purpose here is to deprecate the popular eighteenth-century concept of philosophy as useful knowledge by the introduction of Henderson on Swine at so inappropriate a juncture. There is thus a relevance, not immediately evident to the dullest heart, in the sudden juxtaposition of the two passages. But there is no way of conveying the point to the reader, although Carlyle's later means—the narrator—lies close at hand, inadequately exploited. Indeed, the inadequacy of "Cruthers and Jonson" lies largely in the reader's uncertainty as to tone. It is not clear where the author stands, so it is not clear where the reader may stand. The result is a fictional crossbreed.

There is little to associate the story proper with the later Carlyle. The presentation of first love, in the form of Jonson's love for Margaret in Jamaica, has litttle in common with Teufelsdröckh's Blumine, a creature of entirely different nature and function. Margaret in "Cruthers and Jonson" may recall Carlyle's own first love, Margaret Gordon, but little else.[36] As a story "Cruthers and Jonson" hovers between two worlds. It is at best an incipient comedy, but there is no integration of the comic and serious aspects, so that they alternate rather than mingle. In general, the humorous portions are found chiefly in part one, the serious ones in part two. The narrator, returning at the end of the story, takes the occasion, not to summarize or capture for the reader the essence of the story, but

[36] Margaret Gordon is also widely regarded as one of the originals of Blumine in *Sartor*, although such identifications do more to obscure than to clarify the meaning of *Sartor*. Carlyle knew Margaret Gordon when he was teaching with Irving in Kirkcaldy. For accounts of her life and importance to Carlyle see Raymond Clare Archibald, *Carlyle's First Love, Margaret Gordon, Lady Bannerman* (London, 1910); *Love Letters*, II, 387–400, 426–430; and *Reminiscences*, II, 57–59.

merely to comment that all of the events described are now vanished, and to muse "upon the vast and dreary vortex of this world's mutability."

That Carlyle had an early inclination toward the comic is dimly discernible in "Cruthers and Jonson," but in his next story it is very much more apparent. In late 1826 he began a novel, then abandoned it after one chapter. The manuscript lay unnoticed until 1954, when Marjorie King discovered it and made it the basis for a study of Carlyle's early mode of composition. The fragment of a novel is called "Illudo Chartis."[37] It preceded the more widely known novel fragment "Wotton Reinfred." Miss King has rightly stigmatized "Illudo Chartis" as a work having too much "insignificant detail" and "Wotton Reinfred" as a work having too many "large generalizations." She suggests that *Sartor Resartus* achieves the balance. So it does. But the distinctions between "Wotton" and "Illudo" go even beyond those Miss King identifies. "Wotton Reinfred," with it windy generalizations, is an earnest work deriving from *Werther* and Byron. "Illudo Chartis," on the other hand, is a comic work deriving from Sterne and Jean Paul. Of the two fragments, "Illudo Chartis" is closer to Carlyle's proper direction than "Wotton." The very title is in the Carlyle manner, and Carlyle had a genius for

[37] Marjorie P. King, "'Illudo Chartis': An Initial Study in Carlyle's Mode of Composition," *Modern Language Review*, XLIX (1954), 164–175. The article contains the only printing of "Illudo Chartis" itself. Although the dating of 1825–1826 is conjectural, Miss King's arguments are very persuasive. The first sentence of "Illudo Chartis" ("My whole life has been a nightmare, and my awakening will be in Hell") is a line borrowed from Tieck's "Trusty Eckhart," which Carlyle translated for *German Romance*. The same sentence forms the first entry in Carlyle's journal for 7 December 1826 (*Two Note Books*, p. 81), and in a letter to Mrs. Montagu at Christmas 1826 Carlyle paraphrases the expression that provided him with the title of the story. Miss King also points out that the manuscript paper is watermarked 1825. She does not note that, in the letter to Mrs. Montagu, Carlyle also quotes from Tieck. The letter is quoted in Masson, *Edinburgh Sketches*, p. 329, and reprinted in *Letters Addressed to Mrs. Basil Montagu and B. W. Procter by Mr. Thomas Carlyle* (London, 1881), pp. 8–15.

choosing titles. It manifests itself earliest in this appropriation from Horace:

> ubi quid datur oti
> illudo chartis. Hoc est mediocribus illis
> ex vitiis unum. (*Satires*, ɪ, iv, 138–40)

Or, as Carlyle wrote at the time, "I, like the Roman poet,
and many British ones, 'disport on paper!'" *Sartor Resartus*
as title bespeaks the same amusement and affection of the
author for his creation, concealed in a cryptic Latin term.

In "Illudo Chartis" Carlyle has chosen again to employ
a narrator, not an editor of a manuscript but nevertheless
a narrator with his own identity. The author knew Stephen
Corry, the protagonist of the novel, and he justifies writing
about him on grounds we recognize as Carlylean: "His
[Corry's] biography in truth is of no great moment; but
it has the merit of being true, and it is in the case of
remarkable facts of private life that ink and paper ought
least of all to be spared." If we recall Carlyle's concern with
the facts of natural philosophy and mathematics, and his
wrestling with the claims of truth versus fiction in the
Baillie essay, it appears that truth is the single most important factor, Carlyle requires in any literary work. And yet,
in a sense, truth is precisely what no literary work can
lay claim to, in any common-sense understanding of the
term. Carlyle knows this. His decision in favor of the higher
claims of imagination in the Baillie essay makes it clear.
Why, then, does he habitually insist that the stories he tells
be "true?" There is ony one explanation: he wants to win
the reader's assent, and he recognizes that the claims of
truth can do it for him. At the same time Carlyle rarely tells
what we can call a conventionally true story. Even his
most straightforward stories—"Cruthers and Jonson" and
"Wotton Reinfred"—have such strong elements of authorial
intrusion or of purely improbable situation that, by standards of realistic fiction, they fail to convince. The fact
is that, until the periodical essays and *Sartor*, Carlyle was

using a misleading vocabulary. He speaks of truth as its own justification without making clear that he is talking about a higher truth than mere verisimilitude. He puts forth biography as justification for itself without explaining that even the lowest biography is justified because it opens a way into the interior life. But his instincts are right when his vocabulary errs. The story that he tells in "Illudo Chartis" is far removed in tone from a "true story"; it is rather a highly selective creation of an atmosphere of the ridiculous, touched here and there by the sublime.

Carlyle's picture of Stephen's Uncle Isaac has been called a self-satire by Miss King. It may be. It is also a Carlyle exercise in the comic manner of a Sterne or a Jean Paul:

> But the flower of that eloq race was Isaac the uncle of Elshender, a man who had been at the College of Edinburgh, and become a licentiate (alas! never a pastor) of the Church: he taught for many years the parish school of Croudieburn; could decipher all manner of Latin inscriptions; wrote a *Glossary of Corderius,* for which he could find no publisher, and in his old days, a Prophetic Poem on Napoleon Bonaparte, the manuscript of which, for this also is still unprinted, I have seen, tho' at this distance of time, I can only recollect from it that the first stanza was:

> "I will not sing of that mighty Beast
> Whon the river Siene that stays,
> Who proudly raiseth up his crest,
> And many men he often slays."[38]

[38] King, p. 165. The errors in Uncle Issac's poem—such as "whon" for "who on" and the misspelling of Seine—are evidently intentional. The "eloq" of the first line quoted is not a word, so far as I have been able to determine. It may be an abbreviation for eloquent. Parallels between "Illudo Chartis" and the manner of Sterne and Jean Paul are striking. As Uncle Isaac writes a curious and useless book on Corderius, a sixteenth-century Belgian Jesuit and exegete, so Dr. Slop in *Tristram Shandy* writes a history of midwifery, and so in Jean Paul's *Katzenbergers Badereise* Katzenberger writes a book on miscarriages. In Jean Paul's *Flegeljahre* twin brothers

Still, even though it caught some of the humor, "Illudo Chartis" failed to catch in matter or manner the desperate earnestness that Carlyle wanted to convey: it was altogether too frivolous, or so it appears, since he wrote only one chapter and a few pages of a second. To render his more serious convictions, he began to write "Wotton Reinfred" in January 1827.

It is to "Wotton Reinfred" rather than *Sartor* that most of Carlyle's avowals before 1827 about writing a "*Kunstwerk* of my own" clearly point. There is a youthful naïveté about the phrasing of these early resolves that disappears after the failure of "Wotton." Thenceforward, Carlyle expresses his intentions more subtly and cryptically: "I have some thought of prophesying next year," he writes in 1829. But at the time he began "Wotton" it appeared to him to be the work he had long yearned to write, and he swore to finish it. Yet he abandoned it six months later for the first of his review essays, and when he came to recall "Wotton" in 1866 he claimed that it "proved to be a dreary *zero*, and went wholly into the fire."[39] In fact, it was preserved among his papers and published posthumously.

"Wotton Reinfred" is Carlyle's most ambitious fictional work before *Sartor Resartus*. It is, by and large, a less

---

compose a joint novel, "Hoppelpoppel oder das Herz" (loosely: "Syllabub or the Heart"). "Illudo Chartis" in fact is far closer to the cheery *Kleinstädterei* of Jean Paul than is the much more sardonic *Sartor Resartus*.

[39] He expressed his inclinations toward prophecy in a letter of December 1829 to John Wilson. See Mrs. [Mary] Gordon, "*Christopher North*": *A Memoir of John Wilson* (Edinburgh, 1862), II, 151. Similar sentiments appear in letters of 1828 and 1829 to many other recipients. Cf. *Letters of Thomas Carlyle, 1826–1836*, ed. Charles Eliot Norton (London, 1888), I, 174; William A. Speck, "New Letters of Carlyle to Eckermann," *Yale Review*, xv (1926), 740; *Correspondence between Goethe and Carlyle*, p. 158. The disclaimer of "Wotton" is quoted by Norton from unpublished Carlyliana. See *Letters*, I, 62n. The only printing of "Wotton Reinfred" appears in *Last Words of Thomas Carlyle* (New York, 1892), pp. 1–206.

satisfactory performance than "Illudo Chartis" or even than
"Cruthers and Jonson," which, rough as it is, has at least
the merit of avoiding lugubriousness. "Wotton," however,
is Carlyle's *Werther,* and by 1827, when he wrote it, it
lacked even novelty. The execution, moreover, is so unvary-
ing and so ponderously sentimental that the reader struggles in vain to remember who is speaking and to discrimi-
nate one character from another. It is no accident that
Carlyle subtitled it "A Romance," a subtitle that should
alert us to its fundamental difference from *Sartor.*

A good deal of attention has been paid to the plot situation of "Wotton Reinfred" because of its alleged "incorporation" into Book Two of *Sartor Resartus.*[40] This "incorporation" has been accepted too uncritically. The plot situation
that occurs in both "Wotton" and *Sartor* is, after all, the
eternal love triangle. Moreover, indications are in "Wotton"
that the triangle was to be resolved ultimately in favor
of the hero, whereas the whole point of the Blumine-Tow-
good-Teufelsdröckh triangle is that the lady herself (with
some slight regret) chooses the other man.

The story tells of a sensitive young man, Wotton Reinfred, who has been disappointed in love because of the
difference between his worldly estate and that of his be-
loved, Jane Montagu. Jane is expected to marry a superficial, insincere army officer, Edmund Walter, but the
marriage does not take place. Wotton departs on a long
trip through the hills and valleys of southern Scotland and
northern England, accompanied by his faithful friend, Bernard Swane. They come upon the House in the Wold,
a forest retreat where a certain Maurice Herbert and his
wife Dorothy reside and receive all manner of callers. In
the House in the Wold, Wotton and the other guests, including a certain Dalbrook, engage in long discussions of

[40] For a list of parallels see Harrold's ed. of *Sartor,* p. 318, and
the notes to *Last Words of Thomas Carlyle.* For the relation of
"Wotton" to *Wilhelm Meister* see Heinrich Kraeger, "Carlyles
deutsche Studien und der 'Wotton Reinfred,'" *Anglia Beiblatt,* IX
(1898), 193–219.

metaphysics and aesthetics. Dalbrook supports a Kantian view. To Wotton's dismay his rival Edmund Walter appears at the house. The next day in the wood Wotton encounters Jane Montagu and two of her cousins. They are evidently fleeing some terror which Jane is reluctant to disclose. But she agrees to explain her presence and conduct to Wotton the next day. She begins by telling him, at great length, the story of her life. She has reached the point where she refused Walter's hand when the story breaks off.

It is clear that parallels with *Sartor* are few. A point of similarity between the two works, less frequently cited than the plot, serves to cast some light on the lessons "Wotton" taught Carlyle—the treatment of the character Dalbrook. At the House in the Wold, Dalbrook indulges in an interminable philosophic disquisition, revealing here and there some Goethe and Coleridge amid the Kant. He attacks eighteenth-century philosophy in general and David Hume in particular.[41] The story thus offers some typical Carlylean polarities: Wotton the romantic, Dalbrook the skeptic, Wotton the man of feeling, Dalbrook the man of reason. In "Wotton" these two distinct personalities sunder the book. They represent two central tendencies of the novel—romantic and didactic—and they remain irreconcilable. The question was, how could Carlyle incorporate two tendencies without setting them in opposition. The answer lay in creating a character that could contain these opposites within himself. The ultimate result was that, not only Wotton Reinfred, but the philosopher Dalbrook was metamorphosed into Diogenes Teufelsdröckh.

The technical difficulties brought about by Carlyle's split conception of his novel further illustrate how doomed the work was from the start. In "Wotton" Carlyle was obliged

[41] Olle Holmberg, "David Hume in Carlyle's *Sartor Resartus*," *Arsberättelse 1933–34* (Kungl. Humanistika Vetenskapssamfundet i Lund), pp. 91–109. "Wotton" as a biographical document is treated by Alexander Carlyle in *Love Letters*, I, 124, and II, 361–430.

to cast most of his ideas into dialogue, since the ideas were attached to characters who lived and spoke in the real world. Neither Carlyle's ideas nor his literary gifts show themselves to best advantage in dialogue unless some convention be established whereby his idiosyncratic language can be accepted by the reader. Thus, the following passage, which clearly foreshadows the *Sartor* manner, is in "Wotton" unwieldy:

> There hast thou sat poring over thy Geometries and Stereometries, thy Fluxions direct and inverse, by the Newtonian and the Leibnitzian method, thy Universal History, thy Scotch Philosophy and French Poetics, till thy eyes are dazed with so many lamps, and so very little light thou canst not see a glimpse, and so in thy head the world is whirling like a sick man's dream, and for thee it has neither top nor bottom, beginning, middle, nor end! (*Last Words*, p. 4)

The passage is unwieldy in "Wotton" because Carlyle has chosen to put it in the mouth of Bernard Swane, up to that point depicted as a stalwart and unimaginative companion to Wotton, a kind of Cruthers to Wotton's more tempestuous Jonson. To encounter Swane, then, speaking in the language of a Teufelsdröckh strikes the reader as absurd. Indeed, there is not a single character in "Wotton Reinfred" who could deliver those lines without causing disquiet. Carlyle did not establish any device whereby he might utter such observations. Even Wotton, a complex enough personality, has not been developed in a way that makes the following utterance seem normal from his lips, although from Teufelsdröckh it would be—in fact it is—perfectly acceptable:

> The pebble I strike from my path was severed from distant mountains in the primaeval convulsions of Nature, and has rolled for ages in the depth of waters. This

streamlet was meted out by the hand of the Omnipotent as well as the great ocean; it is ancient as the Flood, and was murmuring through its solitude when the ships of Aeneas ascended the Tiber, or Siloa's Brook was flowing past by the Oracle of God. (*Last Words*, pp. 71–72)

The reader may recognize that the passage quoted is paralleled closely in *Sartor Resartus*. It shows clearly that by 1827 a large part of Carlylese had been developed. More arresting is the knowledge that the passage is similar to an earlier one from "Illudo Chartis," and paralleled more closely by one in a letter to Jane Welsh in June 1825:[42]

Earth, sea, and air are open to us here, as well as anywhere: the Water of Milk was flowing through its simple valley as early as the Brook Siloa, and poor Repentance Hill is as old as Caucasus itself. There is a majesty and mystery in Nature, take her as you will; the essence of all poetry comes breathing to a mind that feels, from every province of her empire. Is she not immoveable, eternal, and immense, in Annandale as she is in Chamouni? (*Love Letters*, II, 131–132)

Yet nowhere does the passage seem more at home than in *Sartor Resartus* itself:

[42] The passage from "Illudo Chartis" reads ". . . the place was softly situated, in a little circular valley, while in primeval times the brook that now flowed thro it hemmed in by trim borders, might have hollowed out from the neighbouring uplands. . . . At the bottom was a hill, where 'strong ale and twopenny' tempted the thirsty wayfarer; below this the brook foamed furiously thro' the 'Linn,' a wild rocky chasm, in the wooded clefts of which dwelt or were fabled to dwell many minor beasts of prey . . ." (King, p. 166). Note that in *Sartor* Carlyle has expanded and emphasized his point while ceasing to state it baldly. He develops balances with alliterative doublets: Joshua . . . Jordan . . . Caesar . . . Commentaries, lasted . . . lasts. The *Sartor* version is a single sustained sentence that builds as though it were designed for oral delivery, a frequently overlooked strength of Carlyle's mature style.

"It struck me much, as I sat by the Kuhbach, one silent noontide, and watched it flowing, gurgling, to think how this same streamlet had flowed and gurgled, through all changes of weather and of fortune, from beyond the earliest date of History. Yes, probably on the morning when Joshua forded Jordan; even as at the mid-day when Caesar, doubtless with difficulty, swam the Nile, yet kept his *Commentaries* dry,—this little Kuhbach, assiduous as Tiber, Eurotas or Siloa, was murmuring on across the widerness, as yet unnamed, unseen: here, too, as in the Euphrates and the Ganges, is a vein or veinlet of the grand World-circulation of Waters, which, with its atmospheric arteries, has lasted and lasts simply with the World."(*Sartor*, II, iii, 102)

Why does the passage sit so much better in *Sartor?* Because it corresponds to the tone and texture of the entire work. In "Illudo Chartis" it is not entirely out of place, but in "Wotton Reinfred" it is simply a purple passage lacking harmony with the whole. Likewise, in its post-*Sartor* appearance, in the 1832 poem "Drumwhirn Bridge," the passage is limp in comparison to its Sartorian counterpart. In the poem Carlyle apostrophizes the river itself:

> From Being's Source it bounded,
> The morn when time began;
> Since thro' this moor has sounded,
> Unheard or heard of man.
>
> That day they crossed the Jordan
> When Hebrew trumpets rang,
> *Thy* wave no foot was fording,
> Yet here in moor it sang.[43]

[43] The poem dates from November 1832 and was first printed in *Leigh Hunt's London Journal*, I (1834), 238, and later in W. H. Wylie, *Thomas Carlyle* (London, 1881), pp. 230–231. In both places the title is given incorrectly as "Drumwhinn Bridge." Alexander Carlyle gives the title correctly in *Love Letters*, II, 348.

The successful integration of the passage into *Sartor* is a measure of the rightness of Carlyle's style in *Sartor*. That the sentiments and much of the language go back to 1825, the date Carlisle Moore gives as that of the intensification of the Leith Walk Conversion experience, is a measure of how fundamental and thoroughly assimilated Carlylese was.

Carlyle was still an apprentice in the writing of fiction after both "Illudo Chartis" and "Wotton Reinfred," so that the leap to *Sartor Resartus* is still unexplained. Some light is cast by a look at the poetry Carlyle composed in the decade of the eighteen-twenties.[44] If many are willing to concede Carlyle the titles essayist, journalist, biographer, historian, and even novelist, few would be disposed to add the title poet. For sufficient reason his poetry remains unsung. He himself had no illusions about it: "I am no poet, 'have no genius,' I know it well," he wrote to Jane as early as 1822; but, just as he proposed a joint novel, he urged that they should try to write poetry to exchange with each other, for "I *can* learn to make words jingle." It is a fair estimate of what he did in his poetry. For a man whose prose can so justly be called poetic, it is surprising to find his poetry so prosaic. Meter and compression seemed to defeat him, and his poetry possesses at best only a monotonous regularity. Still, there are several revealing aspects of Carlyle's poetry. First, he uses again and again a few central images. Second, he attempts to make his not a pure but a didactic poetry. Third, his very failures in verse clarify by contrast some of his successes in prose.

Carlyle's earliest surviving poem dates from 1818 during

[44] For a treatment of all Carlyle's early poetry see G. B. Tennyson, "Carlyle's Poetry to 1840: A Checklist and Discussion, a New Attribution, and Six Unpublished Poems," *Victorian Poetry*, I (1963), 161–181. The poems cited in the present discussion are, except for "Peter Nimmo," available in *Love Letters*, II, 341–360. Some of them also are printed among Carlyle's "Fractions," in *Works*, XXVI, 469–476.

his year as a teacher in the Fifeshire town of Kirkcaldy. The poem is "Tragedy of the Night-Moth." It may have undergone some revision between composition in 1818 and first publication in Ottilie von Goethe's *Chaos* in 1830, such as the addition of a reference to Goethe, whose works Carlyle could hardly have known in the original in 1818; but the central situation is what interests us. The poet tells in fourteen four-line stanzas of a night-moth attracted by a candle flame. The moth darts in and about the flame and is finally consumed by the fire. The poet then makes an explicit comparison between himself and the moth: as the moth to the flame, so the poet to philosophy. This early analogical exercise calls to mind Carlyle's inveterate inclination toward analogy. When expressed in this and other poems—such as the analogy between the swallow building under the eaves and the house-dwellers, or the comparison of a homeward-bound beetle to man the Pilgrim—Carlyle's insights are unremarkable; but when analogy is drawn to the sometimes fantastic points of comparison explored in *Sartor,* the insights are quite remarkable enough. Carlyle, like many romantics, saw analogies where others see only contraries; but Carlyle, the Victorian, saw these not so much with mysterious emanations, exotic flowers, or cabalistic rites, as with the commonplace, everyday, multifaceted life of his time, so that his analogies reveal how a world spinning down the ringing grooves of change was nevertheless a world of wonder and coherence.

For its imagery the "Night-Moth" turns on a contrast between light and dark, heat and cold, attraction and repulsion. Some early Carlylisms also appear: "speck of boundless Space," "nature's majesty," and the like. Similar images mark his other poems. The 1822 poem "The Wish," a reply to Jane Welsh's poem on the same subject, contrasts light (goodness and happiness) with dark (evil and sorrow). Other early poems are similar. After 1825 a calmer tone pervades Carlyle's verse, and images of organic growth appear. He becomes increasingly addicted to the refrain poem in preference to the short narrative, and rightly so, for his refrain poems are generally superior to the narrative ones. The one or two Carlyle poems ever to attain popularity are refrain poems—"Today" and "Adieu." Sometimes he sought to combine refrain and narrative. One such poem has a special relevance to *Sartor Resartus*. It is "Peter Nimmo."

"Peter Nimmo" was apparently written in the early twenties, although Carlyle's failure to refer to it in his published correspondence until well after its composition, makes certainty impossible. When he needed funds, he published his old poem, anonymously, of course, in *Fraser's*, and at that time he wrote a preface for it (signed "O. Y.") in the manner of *Sartor Resartus*, which he was then writing.[45] The preface to "Nimmo" and the publication date of the poem have misled the few commentators on it to assign the poem to the time of *Sartor* and to write commentaries oddly at variance with the poem itself. If we distinguish between poem and preface, the difficulties in "Peter Nimmo" begin to disappear, and its true significance for *Sartor* begins to emerge.

The poem is divided into three parts, "Rhapsody," "To Peter Nimmo," and "L'Envoy." The introductory "Rhapsody" sets forth the poet's intention to write about a subject he knows well. The long central section, "To Peter Nimmo," constitutes the poem proper. It tells how for twenty-five years Nimmo has attended classes at the University of Edinburgh. Nimmo's brain, being "of substance adipose,"

---

[45] *Fraser's Magazine*, III (1831), 12–16. It has never been reprinted. O. Y. were the initials of Oliver Yorke (also called "Nol" Yorke), the fictional editor of *Fraser's*. William Maginn was the most frequent user of this *persona*, but other *Fraser's* contributors also made use of it. See Miriam M. H. Thrall, *Rebellious Fraser's: Nol Yorke's Magazine in the days of Maginn, Thackery, and Carlyle* (New York, 1934). For the impact of *Fraser's* on *Sartor*, see Chapter III. Carlyle submitted the poem to *Fraser's* in November 1830 at the same time that he sent the first draft of *Sartor*. Masson, *Edinburgh Sketches*, p. 291, argues for composition "before 1821," and he provides the only information about the real-life Peter Nimmo. See *Letters*, I, 239.

has never absorbed any knowledge, and so he wanders through the world, mounted on an ass, and at length comes upon a church, the door of which flies open; whereupon he decides to become a priest. Nimmo, however, is attracted not by the substance of religion or learning, but merely by the exterior. Those who wonder about Nimmo's nature speculate that he neither eats nor sleeps, that he is perhaps the Wandering Jew. But the poet dispels all such fancies when he reports, after a visit from Nimmo himself, that Peter's great appetite is reserved for rum. Nimmo drinks himself into a stupor and is carted home in a wheelbarrow. The poet has penetrated the mystery:

> Thus, solv'd in sheephead juice and rum,
> That soul's whole secret you might see:
> *His* essence (in strange menstruum)
> Like yours and mine, was—VANITY.

Then the envoy takes up an earlier refrain to close the story:

> *Sure, 'tis Peter, sure 'tis Peter,*
> *Life's a variorum.*

The poem is comic. Meter and language are awkward but crudely effective nevertheless. Carlyle's only poetic gifts actually lay in comic verse, although he rarely indulged himself in it. The poem is also cynical: it discloses that the whole secret of this man, thought by many to be strangely gifted, is nothing other than vanity. Thus, critical interpretations of Nimmo as a tragic figure who makes the way clear for Teufelsdröckh are a little wide of the mark. To write of a Nimmo who is "a child of God, an old thinker, the *one* whom the many others do not properly understand,"[46] is to write of a Nimmo not to be found

---

[46] Heinrich Kraeger, "Carlyles Stellung zur deutschen Sprache und Literatur," *Anglia*, xxii (1899), 170. Kraeger writes that Nimmo "steht . . . vor unsern augen wie eine wunderbare hieroglyphe im

in the poem. How, then, could Nimmo's readers be so wrong? I believe the answer lies in what has happened to Carlyle and his creative methods between the writing of "Nimmo" in the early twenties and his writing of the preface to "Nimmo" in 1830. The two pieces are as distinct—and in the same way—as "Cruthers and Jonson" and *Sartor Resartus*.

The Carlyle of 1830 did see in "Nimmo" a depth not conveyed by the poem itself. Perhaps he always had, but the problem was how to transmit it to the reader while still maintaining the humor, the ludicrousness, the cynicism of the poem. The method Carlyle chose is essentially the method of *Sartor Resartus* and much of his subsequent writing: he framed "Nimmo" with a preface that tells the reader what to look for. That every reader of the poem has found what Carlyle told him to find is a tribute to the persuasiveness and brilliance of the preface, for it is the preface that commentators have been, all unconsciously, echoing, not the poem itself. Through the device of a preface and an editor Carlyle gains a double vision. The poem becomes an object imbedded within a prose work, and Carlyle, in the *persona* of O. Y. of *Fraser's Magazine*, directs the reader's response. O. Y. writes, for example, that Nimmo is a hieroglyph, and that we are to look through him as through a mystic window into the soul. So eloquent is the preface that the critical observations quoted above turn out to be merely a paraphrase of the preface by way of interpreting the poem. Carlyle has cleverly imposed his own interpretation on the poem, and no one has ever called

buche des lebens da," and argues: "Wichtig ist uns aber die persönlichkeit des heldengedichtes, die lächerlich vor der welt, aber ernsthaft vor Carlyles augen dasteht, ein kind gottes, ein alter denker, der *eine*, den die vielen andern nicht recht verstehen." Arthur Mämpel, *Thomas Carlyle als Künstler* (Bochum-Langendreer, 1935), p. 59, claims that "Nimmo" made the way clear for the writing of *Sartor*, an assertion that also rests on the mistaken assumption as to the date of the poem.

him to account for describing things that simply are not there.

My purpose is not to accuse Carlyle of fraud—he was merely disingenuous. But I do want to call attention to the kind of exposure Carlyle's method made possible and to the vast advance it enabled him to make in expressing contrary points of view simultaneously. The problem that remained unsolved in "Wotton Reinfred" is solved by the preface to "Peter Nimmo." The poem itself is apprentice work, but the preface is the work of the author of *Sartor Resartus*. The writing of "Illudo Chartis" and "Wotton Reinfred" is not enough to explain the mastery of the preface to "Nimmo." What explains the preface to "Nimmo" is the intervention of three years of serious and successful writing for the leading literary reviews of Great Britain. In the periodical reviews Carlyle attains mastery of methods of style and structure that enabled *Sartor* (and derivatively "Peter Nimmo") to take the form it did.

By June 1827 Carlyle had served well and capably as a writer of instructive material in natural science and mathematics, as an author of informative encyclopaedia essays, as a promising literary critic, as a conventional biographer, and as an aspiring novelist. He needed yet to gain mastery in two areas crucial to *Sartor Resartus:* translation and the essay. To these we must turn to see how Carlyle's literary experience made possible the structure and style of *Sartor Resartus*.

II

The Voice of Germany
1824–1832

Die Gattung und Gestaltung, die allgemeinen
Verhältnisse und Schranken eines Kunstwerks zu
bestimmen, das gehört nur zu den Vorbereitungen
des eigentlichen Kunsturtheils; wiewohl manche
über alles entscheiden, die nicht einmal vom Fach-
werk der Kunst gründliche Kentniss haben. Das
Wesentliche ist, einen Widerschein des Werks selbst
zu geben, seinen eigenthümlichen Geist mitzuteilen,
den reinen Eindruck so darzustellen, dass die Gestalt der Darstellung schon das künstlerische Bür-
gerrecht ihres Urhebers beglaubigt; nicht bloss ein
Gedicht über ein Gedicht, um eine Weile zu glän-
zen; nicht bloss den Eindruck, welchen das Werk
gestern oder Heute auf diesen oder jenen macht
oder gemacht hat, sondern den es immer auf alle
Gebildete machen soll.

—FRIEDRICH SCHLEGEL

Between 1824 and 1831 Carlyle produced a body of
work that alone would have sufficed to secure him an
important place in Anglo-German literary history. His
translations and essays infused new vigor into the waning
cult of Germanism and gave it a different and much more
intellectual direction. In England the Romantics had discovered Germany; so the stress fell on the *Sturm und
Drang*, the gothic, the ballad, folk songs, and legends.
The dominant English figures were men like Coleridge and
the early Walter Scott. Later, interest was kept somewhat
alive by DeQuincey, Crabb Robinson, and, especially in
Edinburgh, by the *Blackwood's* circle of Lockhart, Wilson,
and Gillies. Chief of the popularizers was William Taylor
of Norwich, whom Carlyle was to demolish in a periodical
essay. But all of these figures were men of the first quarter

of the nineteenth century and their German enthusiams were confined to the old favorites. Coleridge, of course, had seen rather more than the others; he had translated Schiller's *Wallenstein,* for example, and he knew the idealist philosophers. But his influence remained limited to the literati. Carlyle made a point of visiting him on his 1824 London trip, although he managed to withstand the fascination of the Sage of Highgate. While Coleridge had not translated his lofty concerns into popular enthusiasm, the *Blackwood's* circle had rarely risen above the transiently amusing. Carlyle, however, with the publication of *Wilhelm Meister,* began to invade the popular arena with serious German works, and he became the undisputed master of things German with his review essays. Although his essays and translations are Carlyle's most outspoken work on behalf of German culture, *Sartor Resartus* stands as the capstone of his career as a professional German zealot, and it cannot be understood apart from that career.

Unlike his *juvenilia,* the translations and periodical essays that made Carlyle the Voice of Germany deserve and repay study for their own sake. His *Meister,* for example, became *the* English translation of that work in the nineteenth century; some of his translations in *German Romance* remain today the only, as well as the best, available English versions; and essays like those on Goethe, Jean Paul, Novalis, and the "State of German Literature" are central works by one of the great Victorian essayists. Much of the interest in this material, however, must here be subordinated to the study of Carlyle's German gospelizing as the seedfield for the growth of *Sartor Resartus.* For it is in the translation and essays that the characteristic literary methods of the mature Carlyle are perfected.

TRANSLATION

Carlyle began the study of German in 1819, and almost immediately he applied his new knowledge to the scientific

abstracts and translations that came his way from David
Brewster. The first fruits appear in the articles on
Hansteen's magnetism and Mohs's mineralogy. These translations, interesting as they are, afford little hint of the power
that was to come only five years later in his translation
of *Wilhelm Meister*. But his skill was not developed overnight. In addition to having a profound and intuitive feeling
for the German language, he applied himself to the mastery
of it with surpassing diligence. As early as December 1820,
not yet two years after he had commenced the study of
German, Carlyle was advanced enough to undertake a
translation of a portion of Schiller's *Thirty Years' War*.
The translation was designed to demonstrate his ability
to the London publishing house of Longmans, which, it
was hoped, would then engage him to translate the entire
work. The project was never realized, and the translation
has been believed lost. But it appears that Carlyle saved
his rejected translation and used part of it in the 1825
Schiller as an illustration of Schiller's historical style.[1] This
fortuitous preservation is also fortunate, for it provides
an instance of Carlyle's early translating skill as a spring-
board to his major works as the Voice of Germany in
England.

The brief passage Carlyle included in *Schiller* was taken
from the end of Book III of the *Thirty Years' War*. A
comparison of Carlyle's translation with the standard
English translation by A. J. W. Morrison reveals several
interesting points of difference. One example must stand
for many. Schiller wrote in the original: "Endlich erscheint
der gefürchtete Morgen; aber ein undurchdringlicher
Nebel, der über das ganze Schlachtfeld verbreitet light,
verzögert den Angriff noch bis zur Mittagsstunde."[2]

---

[1] Carlyle tells of submitting the translation to Longmans in *Early
Letters*, I, 311 (letter to Alexander Carlyle, 2 January 1821). The
translation appears in *Schiller, Works*, xxv, 317–320. For a fuller
treatment see G. B. Tennyson, "Carlyle's Earliest German Translation," *American Notes & Queries*, III (1964), 51–54.

[2] *Schillers Sämtliche Werke*, ed. Eduard von der Hellen et al.,
"Säkular-Ausgabe" (Stuttgart and Berlin, 1904), xv, 304–305.

Morrison's translation reads: "At last the fatal morning dawned; but an impenetrable fog, which spread over the plain, delayed the attack till noon."[3]

Carlyle's version is at once more faithful to the original and more moving: "At last the dreaded morning dawned; but a thick fog, which lay brooding over all the field, delayed the attack till noon" (*Works*, xxv, 317).

The difference here lies chiefly in Carlyle's choice of "dreaded" and "brooding," but these make a considerable difference in the whole. Morrison's "fatal" is hackneyed, his "spread" workaday; Carlyle's "dreaded" conveys the feeling of the troops, his "brooding" suggests active force. In Carlyle's version, too, there is the alliteration of "dreaded . . . dawned," and "fog . . . field," which is missing in Morrison's. Comparison of other passages by Carlyle with those by Morrison show similar small but significant differences.

Other stylistic features evident in the Carlyle translation (not illustrated here) are his use of the intimate personal pronoun *thou* to render the German *Du*, and his frequent retention of the German tense, the historical present (parusia). Morrison ignores *Du* and tends to homogenize all into the past. Carlyle's method gives a sense of earnest concern that was to distinguish his later style. Carlyle also usually abides with the German sentence unit rather than to break up the longer German unit of thought into separate English sentences.

Whatever the verdict of Longmans (and one is inclined to think the publisher erred), Carlyle must have been aware of his own uncommon skill in translating, for it was to translating that he turned after the publication of

[3] *The Works of Friedrich Schiller*, ed. Nathan Haskell Dole, trans. C. B. Eastwick and A. J. W. Morrison (New York, 1901), v, pt. 2, p. 296. The Morrison translation has virtually pre-empted the field. It was used from the mid-nineteenth century on in such popular editions as the Bohn Library Edition in England and the Household edition in America and many others. In a later edition (London, 1916) there are some insignificant variations in the wording. Only one occurs in the passage here cited: in the later text "fateful" is used instead of "fatal."

the Schiller articles. In 1824, at the very time that the final installment of the Schiller articles was appearing in the *London Magazine,* and a year before the book publication of *Schiller,* Carlyle published his first major translation—*Wilhelm Meister's Apprenticeship* (*Wilhelm Meisters Lehrjahre*). It was a success. In the summer of 1824, when he went to London to supervise the publication of *Schiller,* his *Meister* was, in his words, "growing a kind of small very small *lion*" among the London literati. The *Blackwood's* German circle also knew the authorship of the translation of *Meister* (although the book was published anonymously), and commented favorably on it. The London publishers were impressed with Carlyle's work and said that he was "a clever fellow and must translate them much more."[4]

Meister proved to be one of the most influential foreign books of the nineteenth century in England. Yet critics have sometimes taken a superior attitude toward Carlyle's translation. They point to infelicitous translations of poems, Germanisms and Scotticisms in Carlyle's style, and indications of an overzealousness on Carlyle's part to protect the delicacy of English feelings on the matter of sex.[5] But these niggling criticisms cannot obscure the fact that Carlyle's is one of the great translations of a German work into English and that its recent republication is justified on historical and aesthetic grounds.[6]

[4] *Love Letters,* I, 387–388; the *Blackwood's* comments appeared in the "Noctes Ambrosianae" for August 1824. See *Noctes Ambrosianae,* ed. R. Shelton Mackenzie (New York, 1854), I, 473–474.

[5] The complaints began with DeQuincey's review in the *London Magazine,* IX (1824), 189–197, 291–308. The review ironically ran concurrently with the final installments of Carlyle's Schiller articles. Modern estimates of Carlyle's translation appear in J. M. Carré, *Goethe en Angleterre* (Paris, 1920); Olga Marx, *Carlyle's Translation of Wilhelm Meister* (Baltimore, 1925); and C. T. Carr, "Carlyle's Translations from German," *Modern Language Review,* XLII (1947), 223–232.

[6] *Wilhelm Meister's Apprenticeship,* trans. Thomas Carlyle, ed. with introd. by Victor Lange (New York, 1962).

More important for a study of *Sartor* than the language
of the translation is the widespread conviction that *Sartor*,
borrowing from *Meister*, is an English *Bildungsroman*. The
notion forms a comfortable corollary to the contention that
Sartor incorporates "Wotton Reinfred." The genealogy is
best expressed as *Meister* > "Wotton" > *Sartor*. *Meister*
is thought to stand behind both, and "Wotton" is seen as
Carlyle's equivalent to the "Theatralische Sendung" that
was Goethe's germ for *Meister*. Both ideas must be so
seriously modified as to render them almost useless. They
both rest on a reading of *Sartor* as Carlyle's literal autobiography, which in turn is a *Bildungsroman*. There are
some obvious affinities between *Sartor* and the two earlier
works. Carlyle has appropriated passages from "Wotton"
in *Sartor;* Teufelsdröckh's is in a broad sense a biography
of the development of a sensitive young man; and ideas
from *Meister* can be found in *Sartor*. But we need more
swallows than this to make a summer. As the previously
cited passage from "Wotton" indicates, Carlyle's borrowings from that work have nothing to do with plot, but
rather they have to do with lyrical passages that he tried
unsuccessfully to integrate into "Wotton." Teufelsdröckh's
biography can be broadly denominated a *Bildungsroman*
or *Entwicklungsroman,* or—and here critics have been
laggard indeed—even a *Künstlerroman*. But when all is
said and done, the borrowings from "Wotton" and the
convenience of the literary category cast very little light
on *Sartor Resartus* as a work of art. As Susanne Howe
makes clear in her valuable study of *Meister* in English,
"nothing at all in common . . . has the tone of *Sartor* with
the German book to which it owes the most in ideas—*Wilhelm Meister*."[7] One must say the same of "Wotton
Reinfred." *Sartor's* paternity is not to be found in *Meister*,
or "Wotton," or *Faust* but in Carlyle's own writing.

Carlyle's debt to Goethe's ideas in *Meister* is more veri-

[7] *Wilhelm Meister and His English Kinsmen* (New York, 1930),
p. 117.

72 The Voice of Germany

fiable than his debt in style and structure. It too has been sometimes overstressed, but C. F. Harrold rightly places the burden of influence on the concept of *Entsagen*.[8] Even that has undergone a sea change, for to Goethe *Entsagen* meant the subordination of discordant strivings to attain total harmony of personality, and it had much to do with his concept of culture in a broader sense. Carlyle, however, employs *Entsagen* in a meaning closer akin to Novalis' and Fichte's *Selbsttötung*, the word he actually uses in the "Everlasting Yea" chapter of *Sartor*. For him, as Harrold says, "*Entsagen* came more and more to mean . . . a puritan denial of self, a chastising of natural impulses in order to attain spiritual good" (p. 219). It is also the case that Carlyle's mystic strain responded more warmly to Novalis than to Goethe's pantheistic humanism. Apart from *Enstagen*, Goethe's discussion in *Meister* of the three reverences and his dispatching Wilhelm on his travels as a means of self-education may have had some impact on *Sartor*. Otherwise the case for *Sartor* as Carlyle's English rewriting of *Wilhelm Meister* is grossly exaggerated.

Meister meant for Carlyle something other than a work he could readily render in his own version. What it seems to have made clear to him is similar to what *Faust* suggested as early as 1822. It is essentially a critical insight. Carlyle said it in a later essay: "For the great law of culture is: Let each become all that he was created capable of being; expand, if possible, to his full growth; resisting all impediments, casting off all foreign, especially all noxious adhesions; and show himself at length in his own shape and stature, be these what they may. There is no uniform of excellence, either in physical or spiritual Nature: all *genuine* things are what they ought to be."[9] *Meister* demonstrated to Carlyle the imperative of critical tolerance. Yes tolerance, although the subject here is Carlyle; for the

[8] Charles Frederick Harrold, *Carlyle and German Thought* (New Haven, 1934), pp. 214–230.
[9] *Works*, xxvi, 19 ("Jean Paul Friedrich Richter").

Carlyle of the eighteen-twenties was probably the most tolerant English critic then writing. Certainly, when it came to German letters, Carlyle's tolerance was unsurpassed.

What does this mean for *Meister?* We must remember that *Meister* is, while clearly a novel, a very loose novel. Jean Paul, of all people, is said to have charged that *Wilhelm Meister* defied all the canons of the novel.[10] Carlyle, in translating it, exploded from time to time in exasperation: "Goethe is the greatest genius that has lived for a century, and the greatest ass that has lived for three." "There is not properly speaking the smallest particle of *historical* [i.e., novelistic] interest in it, except what is concerned with Mignon." "Bushels of dust and straws and feathers, with here and there a diamond of the purest water."[11] But when it came to the point of public utterance, Carlyle wrote an extremely appreciative preface for the *Apprenticeship,* and for the *Travels,* two years later, he exceeded his earlier laudations, calling it "a light and living poem" and comparing it to the *Faerie Queene.*[12] In other words, Carlyle came to see the integrity of *Meister* as a work of art subject to its own laws.

If there are intimations of Carlyle's own methods in *Meister,* they are only to be found in the liberality of the form, especially in the *Travels.* There Goethe intrudes with editorial notes and *Zwischenreden* (one of which Carlyle liberally translates as "Exculpatory Word"), and he permits frequent digressions, letters reproduced,

[10] Cited by Howe, p. 61. Although not documented in Howe, Jean Paul's observation was probably made to Friedrich Schlegel. See Eduard Berend, *Jean Paul's Persönlichkeit in Berichten der Zeitgenossen* (Berlin, 1956), pp. 31–32.

[11] *Early Letters,* II, 224; *Love Letters,* I, 339–340.

[12] *Works,* XXIII, 23, 32. The *Apprenticeship* was published as a separate work in 1824; the *Travels* first appeared as vol. IV of *German Romance* (1827). Later editions joined the two as a single work, and *German Romance* was subsequently printed without the *Travels.* When he translated these works in 1823–1824 and 1826, Carlyle naturally used the 1821 edition of *Meister,* which differs in many particulars from the final version Goethe published in "Ausgabe letzter Hand" (Stuttgart, 1828–1834).

disquisitions on geology, and discussions of papers left to
be edited.[13] By contrast, *Sartor's* organization is much
tighter; but Goethe's use of a fictional form for the inclusion
of varied materials and as a platform for all manner of
discussion must have been suggestive to Carlyle. If Goethe's
license did nothing more than condition Carlyle for the
reading of the much more experimental and unorthodox
Jean Paul, it would be an important precondition for *Sartor*.
The matter of license, however, has little to do with tone,
and we must except stylistic elements in drawing even
the most general comparisons. Goethe's style is ever con-
trolled and at the same time flowing; it cannot be mistaken
for Carlyle's hortatory one. For similarities of style we
must turn to Carlyle's essays and translations in *German
Romance*.

Considering how unremittingly Carlyle complained in his
letters about each writing task he undertook, it is surprising
to find him so amiable during the writing and translating
for *German Romance*.[14] From the relative absence of ex-
postulations one is inclined to believe that the task of

[13] One such editorial observation from the *Wanderjahre* will indicate
the kind of ironic distance and freedom in the form that may
have been instructive to Carlyle: "Again it is to be observed, that
in the Novel, as in Universal History, we have to struggle with
uncertain computations of time; and cannot always decisively fix
what has happened sooner, and what later. We shall hold, therefore,
by the surest points" (*Works*, xxiv, 318).

There are also a number of purely Carlylean footnotes, usually
of linguistic explanation. Most suggestive are Carlyle's notes on
Anempfinderin, which he translated as a "*spiritual chameleon or
taker-on*" (*Works*, xxiii, 139), and his note on the precise meaning
of *Lehrjahre* and *Wanderjahre* (*Works*, xxiii, 32).

[14] The writing occupied Carlyle for a little more than a year,
1825–1826, while he lived at Hoddam Hill, Dumfriesshire. He had
completed his work by August 1826 and awaited publication in
the fall, but it was delayed until January 1827 by the publisher.
See *Love Letters*, ii, 308; *Letters*, i, 5, 13, 18. These difficulties
with the publishers probably strengthened Carlyle's resolve to write
without regard for publishers and public, an important factor in
Sartor. Cf. Camille Pitollet, "Lettres inédites de Thomas Carlyle,"
Révue Germanique, iv (1908), 304.

translating the stories in *German Romance* was Carlyle's most congenial labor as a translator. It is also one of the most instructive for the student of *Sartor Resartus*. If *Wilhelm Meister* has some broad similarities in thought and attitude with *Sartor,* much of the material in *German Romance* has the more revealing feature of similarity in method and style. This aspect of *German Romance* will be examined later in connection with the periodical essays. But first let us consider the clear relevance, hitherto ignored, in the type of story Carlyle chose to include in *German Romance,* and in the critical precepts enunciated in the prefaces to the stories. Carlyle's role, of course, became even more consciously that of the voice of Germany and his subject matter became, far more patently than in *Meister,* the biography and works of authors.

In the preface to *Wilhelm Meister,* Carlyle felt called upon to urge the reading of Goethe upon an indifferent public. Carlyle was the English editor-translator presenting one of the works of the master to a public ever skeptical of things German. If his earlier role of editor-translator of scientific materials was a purely fortuitous one, dictated more by Brewster and the needs of Carlyle's pocketbook than anything else, his role as editor-translator of Goethe's novel was a matter of conscious choice. In *German Romance* the same role assumes even greater importance. Goethe, if not *Wilhelm Meister,* was known in England by 1824 (he was then seventy-two); his *Werther* four decades before had been an international sensation. If he did not then, or later, command the adoration his name evokes in Germany, he was still not altogether a cipher to the English reader. The case with the authors in *German Romance* was totally different. Since Goethe's *Märchen,* which Carlyle wanted to include, had already been translated, the authors left for inclusion were largely unknown in England. Moreover, *Meister* was recognizably a novel, not, as Carlyle remarked, merely a novel of the sort useful for driving away the "tedium of mental vacancy," but a novel nonetheless; whereas the stories in *German Romance* were chiefly *Märchen,* a species of writing never domesticated in English. Whatever may have been Carlyle's consciousness of his previous roles as editor-translator, he was in *German Romance* fully alive to the nature and size of the task before him and to the need to present his material as an advocate rather than as a silent and distant editor. In the general preface to the collection he sounded the note of earnestness and defiance appropriate to his task: "They are German Novelists, not English ones; and their Germanhood I have all along regarded as a quality, not as a fault" (*Works,* xxi, 4). From here on, Carlyle's consciousness of his editorial and translating role is indisputable.

The material presented in *German Romance* needed the advocacy of a Carlyle. The collection contains no fewer than thirteen stories and novels by representative German authors from the late eighteenth and early nineteenth centuries.[15] That Carlyle's selection is exceptionally judicious accrues chiefly to his credit as a student of German letters. More to the point in considering *Sartor* is the fact that the stories Carlyle chose have in common that most German of forms, the *Märchen.*

To the English reader the *Märchen* is simply the fairy tale, suitable enough for children but hardly a serious literary form. To the German Romantic the *Märchen* was the one characteristic form their own times had produced Literary historians now distinguish between two types of *Märchen:* the *Volksmärchen* (the anonymous folk and fairy tale) and the *Kunstmärchen* (the conscious literary product

---

[15] The contents of the original edition were: Vol. i: Johann August Musäus, "Dumb Love," "Libussa," "Melechsala"; Friedrich de la Motte Fouqué, "Aslauga's Knight"; Vol. ii: Ludwig Tieck, "The Fair-Haired Eckbert," "The Trusty Eckhart," "The Runenberg," "The Elves," "The Goblet"; E. T. A. Hoffman, "The Golden Pot"; Vol. iii: Jean Paul Friedrich Richter, "Army-Chaplain Schmelzle's Journey to Flaetz," "The Life of Quintus Fixlein"; Vol. iv: Johann Wolfgang von Goethe, "Wilhelm Meister's Travels." The first three volumes are printed in two in *Works,* xxi-xxii.

of an author using legendary and folk materials).[16] Carlyle
does not use this terminology—not then current in any
case—but he senses some of the differences. In *German
Romance* he is concerned with *Kunstmärchen* only.

The *Volksmärchen* proper first appears in the collection
of the brothers Grimm, *Kinder-und Hausmärchen* of 1812–
1815, although the type was well known from oral sources
long before the Grimms recorded it. Musäus was in his
own time considered to be a collector of such *Märchen,*

[16] The distinction is especially German, but it is paralleled by
our own insistence upon separating genuine anonymous folk songs
from composed ones—the difference between "Barbara Allen" and
"Way Down Upon the Swanee River." For the *Märchen* the following definitions set forth the German view:

Märchen. "Kürzere volksläufig-unterhaltende Prosaerzählung von
phantastisch-wunderbaren Begenbenheiten und Zuständen aus freier
Erfindung ohne zeitlich-räumliche Festlegung: Eingreifen über-
natürlicher Gewalten ins Alltagsleben, redende Menschengestalt,
annehmende Tiere und Tier-oder Pflanzengestalt, annehmende
verwunschene Menschen, Riesen, Zwerge, Drachen, Feen, Hexen,
Zauberer u.a. den Naturgesetzen widersprechende und an sich
unglaubwürdige Erscheinungen, die jedoch aus dem Geist des
Menschen heraus glaubwürdig werden, indem eine gedanklich
mitvollzogene Unwahrscheinlichkeit die andere schon wahrschein-
lich macht. Der ethische Grund ist eine denkbar einfache
Weltordnung: Belohnung des Guten, Bestrafung des Bösen, je
nach dem Grad an Sympathie oder Antipathie für die Haupt-
gestalt, Wendung zum Guten oder Schlechten entsprechend den
Wünschen des naïve moralisierenden kindlichen Aufnahmekreises.
. . . .
[Das Volksmärchen steht], geprägt von seiner Erzählweise, mit
Variationen und Umdichtungen, im Gegensatz zum Kunstmärchen,
das als Schöpfung einer Dichterindividualität Erzählweise und
Motive des Volksmärchen übernimmt und mit bewusstem Kunstver-
stand gestaltet, dabei jedoch teils das unbewusste Phantasiespiel
durch allegorische Verkleidung von Gedanken, Tendenzen und
Meinungen zerbricht. (Gero von Wilpert, *Sachwörterbuch der
Literatur* [2nd. ed., Stuttgart, 1959], p. 355.)

An indispensable study of the German *Kunstmärchen* containing
abundant insight into the ontological implications of the form will
be found in Marianne Thalmann, *Das Märchen und die Moderne:
Zum Begriff der Surrealität im Märchen der Romantik* (Stuttgart,
1961). Thalmann quotes Novalis as saying, "Der Roman soll
allmählich in Märchen übergehen" (p. 20).

and so Carlyle takes him in *German Romance*, with no
quibble over the fact that Musäus reshaped the stories
he collected to emphasize his gentle, satirical points and
thus by contemporary standards was writing *Kunstmärchen*.
The other authors in the text made no pretense of reporting
genuine folk stories but simply wrote tales in the vein of
the *Märchen*.

Carlyle customarily translated the term *Märchen* by
"Fabulous Tale" and sometimes by "Traditionary Tale" or
"Antique Tale." It profits us nothing to tax Carlyle with
less than our understanding of what the *Märchen* really
is.[17] Rather it is necessary to understand what he meant by
the term. His most complete statement occurs in the essay
on Ludwig Tieck, the most accomplished creator of
Kunstmärchen of all the writers included in *German Romance*. Tieck excelled in adapting the fairy tale and its
subspecies, the beast fable, to modern ends. Of Tieck's use
of the beast fable in *Puss-in-Boots* (*Der gestiefelte Kater*),
Carlyle revealingly writes that under the "grotesque mask"
of this form Tieck

> had laughed with his whole heart, in a true Aristophanic
> vein, at the actual aspect of literature; and without
> mingling his satire with personalities, or any other false
> ingredient, had rained it like a quiet shower of volcanic
> ashes on the cant of Illumination, the cant of Sensibility,
> the cant of Criticism and the many other cants of that
> shallow time [i.e. the eighteenth century], till the gum-
> flower products of the poetic garden hung draggled and
> black under their unkindly coating. (*Works*, XXI, 259)

[17] Olga Marx, p. 25, inclines toward this error in expressing dissatisfaction with Carlyle's term "Antique Tale" for *Märchen* in *Meister's
Travels*. Later Carlyle uses "Traditionary Tale" and finally "Fabulous
Tale." There is every reason to believe that by these terms Carlyle
meant much the same as the modern "folk tale." Sir Walter Scott
uses "Traditionary Tale" in this way, indicating that perhaps it
is a Scotticism. See Ian Jack, *English Literature, 1815–1832* (Oxford,
1963), p. 200.

On Tieck's use of the *Märchen* proper Carlyle is led to a statement of the purposes of the writers of *Märchen:*

> It was to penetrate into the inmost shrines of Imagination, where human passion and action are reflected in dim and fitful but deeply significant resemblances, and to copy these with the guileless humble graces which alone can become them. Such tales ought to be poetical, because they spring from the very fountains of natural feeling; they ought to be moral, not as exemplifying some current apophthegm, but as imaging forth in shadowy emblems the universal tendencies and destinies of man. (*Works*, xxi, 266)

Carlyle's concern with the *Märchen* in *German Romance* is of more than academic interest. It has to do with his own methods in writing *Sartor Resartus,* especially in Book Two, Teufelsdröckh's biography. As we shall see, Carlyle himself in Book Two made a contribution to the *Märchen* that can only be appreciated when we know what the *Märchen* is.

In his preface to each author's work Carlyle provides a substantial measure of biography. Even in 1825 he considered biography essential to literary criticism. There is a distinct correlation between the quality of the author's life and Carlyle's respect and affection for his work. For Carlyle did not seek merely to explain away but to discern a moral pattern, a lesson that could be extracted and made useful for others. Thus his admiration for Schiller as an author is conditioned by his vast respect for Schiller's personal triumph over enormous difficulties, and his distaste for E. T. A. Hoffmann as a writer is colored by his disapprobation of Hoffmann's profligacy. It is almost with relief that Carlyle pronounces Jean Paul's biography to be worthy of his writing.

Let it not be misunderstood that Carlyle sought in biography a staid and empty conformity. Far from it. Jean Paul's biography would disprove such a contention—as would Carlyle's own—and Carlyle painted a colorful and sympathetic account of the rebellious Jean Paul in a later essay for the *Edinburgh Review*. To Carlyle biography gives us the measure of the man—his courage, his honesty, his determination, his seriousness of purpose, his refusal to compromise. Outward actions symbolize the inner man, and Carlyle's concern is to understand what these outward actions truly symbolize. He did not make biography the excuse for unearthing any fact, however insignificant, that relates to the subject. When he seizes upon an apparent triviality, it is unfailingly for the purpose of displaying it as a highly symbolic act, and when he passes over a public event of some celebrity, it is largely because he feels its significance is either clear or is not in fact so great as has been claimed. His constant endeavor is to penetrate to the essence of things. He is nowhere so grippingly convincing as when he has a biography with which he is in fundamental sympathy but which must be explained to the skeptical reader for its true meaning to be laid bare. Again we are reminded of *Sartor*.

There are, finally, specific points of similarity in allusion and reference between *German Romance* and *Sartor*, as there are between *Sartor* and the *Journal* and *Encyclopaedia* work. To catalogue them would serve little purpose. But to observe that these details are there—from E. T. A. Hoffmann's Johannes Kreisler as a Teufelsdröckh prototype to Jean Paul's manner of naming characters—suggests again that the endless variety of materials Carlyle was exposed to were brought into play when he wrote *Sartor*, and it puts us on notice to seek a rationale for Carlyle's heterogeneity of reference.[18]

---

[18] Some specific echoes are noted in annotated editions of *Sartor*. Other points of similarity lie in more general areas: Hoffman's Johannes Kreisler, for example, is an eccentric musician in whom some Teufelsdröckhian qualities can be discerned; Jean Paul's naming of characters was surely instructive for Carlyle. To cite but a few, Jean Paul's Fixlein is confused in the novel with the near homophone *Füchslein* (lit., "little fox"), in *Flegeljahre* Jean

The style of *German Romance* will be treated subsequently. For the present we can consider the most significant features of *German Romance* to be four: the intensification of Carlyle's role as editor-translator; Carlyle's intimate association with the *Märchen;* the increasing emphasis on biography in criticism; and his continued exposure to a multiple of facts that he stored up for later use.

THE ESSAY

German Romance performed the necessary service of consolidating Carlyle's position as a translator and introducing him as a serious essayist. On the strength of *German Romance* Carlyle, then living in Edinburgh, gained an entrée to the literary circles associated with *Blackwood's* and the *Edinburgh Review.* He attended one of Christopher North's "Noctes Ambrosianae" and, more important, he met Francis Jeffrey, editor of the great *Edinburgh Review. German Romance* also helped confirm in Carlyle's mind the direction his writing would take. His venture into periodical writing was posited on the assumption that his would be the task of speaking as the Voice of Germany. When he was approached in 1827 by Jeffrey to write essays for the *Edinburgh,* Carlyle warned him to read *German Romance* first. If Jeffrey could stomach the Gemanism and mysticism in *German Romance* and still want articles,

---

Paul contrasts Gottwalt ("God's love or dispensation") with his more willful brother Vult (cf. Lat. *volo*), Fibel in *Leben Fibels* is a character and the word for a primer or hornbook, and the town of Flätz in *Schmelzles Reise* has the same sound as the word *Flätz* which means "lout." Note that the name Carlyle used for the uncle in "Illudo Chartis," Isaac, means "laughter" in Hebrew.

But the distinguished Jean Paul scholar Eduard Berend takes a dim view of such glosses on Jean Paul's characters and argues that Jean Paul did not intend secondary meanings to accrue to the names. See his "Die Namengebung bei Jean Paul," *PMLA,* LVII (1942), 820–850, as well as a shorter version of this article, "Die Personen- und Ortsnamen in Jean Pauls Werken," *Hesperus,* No. 14 (1957), 21–31.

Carlyle felt he would be free to write as he chose. He took a certain pleasure in his reputation in Edinburgh as both a mystic and a Germanophile. Accordingly, when Jeffrey persevered and asked for an essay, Carlyle obliged him with "Jean Paul Friedrich Richter."[19]

The *Edinburgh* Jean Paul essay is actually Carlyle's second major essay on Jean Paul, the first being the preface in *German Romance;* but it is Carlyle's first essay for a major review journal, and it ushers in the period of review essays and the retreat to Craigenputtock. The periodical essays written between 1827 and the completion of *Sartor* in 1831 have the most profound critical, structural, and stylistic significance for *Sartor Resartus*. First, their scope: It is merely hinted at by statistics, but in the four years in question Carlyle wrote sixteen major essays for journals like the *Edinburgh*, the *Foreign Review*, and *Fraser's* and the incomplete "History of German Literature."[20] He wrote eleven more essays and two translations between the completion of *Sartor* in 1831 and its publication in 1833–1834.[21]

---

[19] For Carlyle's reputation as a mystic and as the Voice of Germany see Wilson, *Carlyle to "The French Revolution,"* pp. 14–15; *Letters,* I, 77, 104, 107, 182, 131, 201–202.

[20] Twelve of the sixteen were written initially for the literary reviews: "Jean Paul Friedrich Richter," "State of German Literature," "The Life and Writings of Werner," "Goethe's *Helena,*" "Goethe," "Heyne," "Burns," "German Playwrights," "Novalis," "Voltaire," "Signs of the Times," and "Jean Paul Friedrich Richter Again." The remaining four came out of the unfinished "History of German Literature": "On History," "Taylor's Historic Survey of German Poetry," "The Nibelungen Lied," and "Early German Literature" (also known as "Reinecke Fuchs," and "German Literature of the Fourteenth and Fifteenth Centuries"). Three other pre-*Sartor* items are translations: "Richter and Mme. de Staël," "Luther's Hymn," and "Schiller." In addition during this period Carlyle continued writing verses. Of the total of nineteen, eight appeared in the *Foreign Review*, five in the *Edinburgh,* four in *Fraser's,* and one each in the *Westminister Review* and the *Foreign Quarterly Review.*

[21] "Characteristics," "Biography," "Johnson," "Goethe's Portrait," "Schiller, Goethe, and Mme. de Staël," "Death of Goethe," "Corn-Law Rhymes," "Goethe's Works," "Diderot," "Cagliostro," "On History Again." The translations were a revision of "Das Mährchen,"

This is almost thirty essays in all, plus translations, stories, and poems, written during the six years the Carlyles lived in seclusion in Craigenputtock.[22]   When he broke that seclusion to move to London in 1834, he was no longer an apprentice in translation or the essay. Above all, he had completed and published *Sartor Resartus*. If Carlyle was justified in attaching the importance he did to biography, we are justified in emphasizing that the period of his essays and his vast labor on behalf of German letters is the Craigenputtock period and that *Sartor Resartus* is both part and culmination of it. The 1822 conversion experience in Leith Walk required for its fulfillment the six years of seclusion in Craigenputtock, and for its expression *Sartor Resartus*.

There is a direct relation between *Sartor* and Carlyle's role as the Voice of Germany. Twelve of the sixteen pre-*Sartor* essays treat German literary topics. Only seven of the fourteen post-*Sartor* essays deal with German literature, and four of these seven are adaptations from the pre-*Sartor* "History of German Literature." This leaves but three truly post-*Sartor* German essays. All three are on Goethe and were occasioned by his death in 1832. Carlyle's active interests in the post-*Sartor* period are reflected by the seven essays on history and society written between 1831 and 1834. It has long been recognized that Carlyle's interests shifted in the eighteen-thirties from German literary topics to his-

and a translation of "Novelle." Of these thirteen, eight appeared in *Fraser's*, two in the *Edinburgh*, two in the *Foreign Quarterly Review*, and one in the *New Monthly Magazine*.

[22] The Carlyles married in the fall of 1826 and settled in Edinburgh, where he wrote his first four review articles. They moved to Craigenputtock at Whitsuntide 1828 and remained there until 1834, during which time he wrote all of the other articles cited above and *Sartor Resartus*. His output escaped even Carlyle, who in 1833 assembled and had bound as a gift for Jane his periodical writings between 1827 and 1833. The unique volume, now in the Yale Library, contains twenty-seven items, yet it still lacks a half-dozen others printed in the period and, of course, the unpublished materials.

torical and cultural ones. The record of his books documents the shift: *The French Revolution* (1837), *Heroes and Hero-Worship* (1841), *Past and Present* (1843). But the record of his essays makes it possible to date the shift more precisely as occurring immediately after the completion of *Sartor Resartus*—in fact, with the writing of "Characteristics" in November–December 1831. I suggest two causes for this shift. First, with *Sartor* Carlyle expressed his most profound convictions on things German; it is the capstone of his whole Germanizing endeavor of the eighteen-twenties. Second, with the essays and *Sartor* he developed a method and a style that he found adaptable to other topics, especially to the writing of social criticism and history, which interests were in any case evident also in *Sartor*. Thus post-*Sartor* essays like "Cagliostro" and "The Diamond Necklace" are artistically inconceivable without the lessons of *Sartor,* but their subjects mark a turning away from German matters. Since it is always first the literary quality that makes Carlyle's works live, the mastery Carlyle acquired in the essays has far-reaching significance for the rest of his output.

The writing of essays for the popular reviews differs from Carlyle's previous literary activity in degree rather than in kind; it is an intensification of what he had been doing for ten years. Thus the situation of editor-translator for the *Philosophical Journal* material is substantially the same as the one he faced in writing the essays. Of course, a great deal had been added, not least of all Carlyle's own awareness and choice of role and his elaboration of an aesthetic theory to match his literary ardors. In the essays Carlyle is closer to being his own man than ever before.

We are apt to forget today, when his essays are often reprinted for their own sake without identifying information, that every essay Carlyle wrote was a *review.* His procedure in the essays makes it easy to overlook the point of departure, but that point was always a review of some published work. His first essay, the 1827 "Jean Paul

Friedrich Richter," is a review of Heinrich Döring's *Life of Richter;* the important "State of German Literature" is a review of two literary reference works by Franz Horn; "Heyne," "Novalis," "Goethe," are reviews of collected editions of the works of those authors; and even the far-ranging "Signs of the Times" was provoked by three works (one by Edward Irving!), despite the fact that virtually no reprint in collected editions or anthologies ever includes this information.[23] That he took the occasion for much more than mere reviewing is what has insured Carlyle's essays a permanent place in literary and cultural history, and that his practice is the rule rather than the exception in the journals of the time is what makes Victorian literary reviews so influential in the period. But in a study of *Sartor* the review situation needs to be emphasized, for *Sartor* is also a review of a foreign work. And it too transcends its topic.

Carlyle officiated as editor-translator, advocate, and interpreter of the mysteries of German letters in twelve of his major review essays before *Sartor*. In the other four he did not stray further afield than Burns or Voltaire. And in each of the essays he grappled again with the problems of biography. "History," he tells us in an often quoted line in a pre-*Sartor* essay, "is the essence of innumerable Biographies."[24] What Carlyle means by biography is beginning to come clear in the essays. He says it exceptionally well in the 1830 Jean Paul review essay:

> It has been said that no Poet is equal to his Poem, which saying is partially true; but, in a deeper sense, it may also be asserted, and with still greater truth, that no Poem is equal to its Poet. Now, it is Biography

[23] The three works are: *Anticipation; or, an Hundred Years Hence* (London, 1829), *The Rise, Progress, and Present State of Public Opinion in Great Britain* (London, 1829), and *The Last Days; or Discourses on These Our Times,* by Rev. Edward Irving (London, 1829).

[24] *Works,* xxvii, 86 ("On History").

that first gives us both Poet and Poem, by the significance of the one elucidating and completing that of the other. That initial outline of himself, which a man unconsciously shadows forth in his writings, and which, rightly deciphered, will be truer than any other representation of him, it is the task of the Biographer to fill-up into an actual coherent figure, and bring home to our experience, or at least our clear undoubting admiration, thereby to instruct and edify us in many ways. Conducted on such principles, the Biography of great men, especially of great Poets, that is, of men in the highest degree noble-minded and wise, might become one of the most dignified and valuable species of composition. (*Works*, xxvii, 100–101)

Note that the essence of this definition is the extent to which biography and literary works mutually elucidate each other and thus edify the reader. Carlyle's lofty concept of biography exposes him often enough to disappointment with biographies by other hands. He denounces them repeatedly in his essays. Döring's Jean Paul biography is compared to faulty building construction, and the result is called "a perfect architectural enigma." Heeren's biography of Heyne is likened to the productions of Gulliver's turning loom. The demon of mechanism always lurks in Carlyle's description of inadequate biographies in contrast to the creative indwelling in the spirit and nature of the subject that distinguishes good biographies. Even autobiography, which Carlyle calls "a favourite sort of reading with us," can fail of Carlyle's high standards, as is the case with Heyne's autobiographical notes: "We could have wished to get some view into the interior of that poor Chemnitz hovel, with its unresting loom and cheerless hearth, its squalor and devotion, its affection and repining; and the fire of natural genius struggling into flame amid such incumbrances, in an atmosphere so damp and close! But of all this we catch few farther glimpses."[25] When Carlyle

[25] *Works*, xxvi, 3, 322, 325.

writes "Jean Paul Friedrich Richter Again" in 1830 (his third Jean Paul essay) he uses an ostensible review of Jean Paul's autobiography, *Wahrheit aus Jean Pauls Leben*, to supply what Jean Paul's biographer had missed. By such touches as three pages devoted to Jean Paul's "clothes martyrdom," in which a trivial incident is made to illuminate the subject's whole character, Carlyle justifies the stress he places on biography.[26]

Editor-translator, critic, reviewer, essayist, all these Carlyle was in the Craigenputtock period. To these we must add biographer. Further, as Carlyle presents the biographies of literary men, a pattern of incidents begins to emerge that will be recognizable to readers of *Sartor*. Usually of undistinguished antecedents (Schiller, Heyne, Werner— Novalis is a notable exception), the typical man of letters whom Carlyle describes experiences in childhood a sense of wonder at the world. By early manhood this typical figure undergoes a period of storm and stress (Schiller, Goethe, Klingemann, Werner). Disappointment and defeat mar his efforts to gain social or literary advancement, and not infrequently severe material deprivation burdens his existence (Jean Paul, Heyne). He must eke out a precarious living at translation, hackwriting, teaching, and other employments on the lowest slopes of Parnassus. The period

---

[26] The incident recurs again and again in the essay, becoming a kind of leitmotif in a manner we associate with Carlyle's mature style. The term "clothes martyrdom" itself is a characteristic Carlyle coinage in which sympathy, scorn, and humor mix in inseparable union. The incident involves Jean Paul's having adopted in his student days what was called the English fashion of dress, including a "docked cue" and "shirts *à la Hamlet*" (i.e., open-breasted). In Leipzig Jean Paul outraged sober citizens with his affectation, and he was asked not to take walks in the garden of his boarding house because of the offense his appearance gave to a more distinguished resident. Upon his return to provincial Hof the outcry was greater, but he persisted in his dress for seven years. When he decided to dress conventionally, he announced the fact to his friends by distributing a circular letter.

Other instances in which Carlyle seizes upon a seeming triviality and expands its significance appear in his treatment of Werner, E. T. A. Hoffmann, Heyne, and Voltaire.

88   *The Voice of Germany*

of poverty frequently coincides with a period of religious doubt. Those who survive the joint afflictions of poverty and doubt emerge either with a positive grasp on life, as reflected in their works (Jean Paul, Schiller, Goethe), or they never succeed in throwing off their spiritual problems, and their work is hollow, confused, strained, or even insincere (Hoffmann, Werner, Klingemann). The parallels with Carlyle's own life, not to mention Teufelsdröckh's, are striking; but Carlyle's autobiography therefore becomes typical, not unique.[27] In writing the review essays, Carlyle acquired a more graphic education in the lives of artists than anything in the *Calamities of Authors*. With his own experience clearly before him, he had the substance of the life of Diogenes Teufelsdröckh. Add to that the concept of an English editor-translator presenting foreign-language works, especially German, to the public, and the dimensions of *Sartor Resartus* begin to take shape. Still unexplored are the aesthetic principles Carlyle advances in the essays, and the specifics of style and structure toward which I have directed so much anticipatory attention.

The older Carlyle got, the less he liked to speculate about aesthetics. He was always inclined to attribute artistic creation to the unconscious. In its earlier less doctrinaire form, however, the theory of the unconscious is a very real aesthetic principle, so that the pre-*Sartor* Carlyle is far from being a man without an aesthetic. In the *Edin-*

---

[27] Knut Hagberg, *Thomas Carlyle: Romantik och Puritanism i Sartor Resartus* (Stockholm, 1925), pp. 156–163, has seen some of the peculiarities of Heyne in Teufelsdröckh. He is certainly right in doing so, but Heyne is only one of many figures from the essays that find echo in Teufelsdröckh, for Teufelsdröckh is by no means Heyne as such. Some of the similarities between Heyne and Teufelsdröckh are that both are scholars who write extremely learned works and live in university towns. Also—and hitherto unnoted—Heyne edited the *Göttingen Gelehrte Anzeigen,* for which he wrote 7,500 book reviews, of which achievement Carlyle writes: "Shame on us degenerate Editors! Here of itself was work for a lifetime!" (*Works,* xxvi, 344).

burgh Jean Paul essay, indeed, he introduces the word *aesthetic* into English. Throughout the essays he speculates on some fundamental aesthetic questions—the nature of poetry and the poet, the form of literary works, the task of the critic. He also treats some particular aesthetic questions that deserve the attention of the student of *Sartor*—allegory and symbolism, the *Märchen,* and the nature of humor.

Not until *German Romance* does Carlyle begin using a terminology that is adequate to his meaning. Two especially helpful expressions actually go back to the early twenties, but it is not until the period of the essays that Carlyle uses them with sufficient consistency and clarity to make them serviceable aesthetic terms. These are "shadow forth" and "body forth," and taken together they suggest almost a whole aesthetic. That which shadows forth is that which reflects, usually fitfully, some deep inner truth; it is Carlyle's closest approach to mimetic theory, although it is not terribly close at that. Shadowing forth conjures up pictures of the cave with its fleeting and often distorted reflections of reality, but it is still ultimately an inner light that makes the picture possible. More laudatory is his use of the term *body forth.* It falls in the category of creative aesthetics, the lamp of Abrams' discussion of Romantic theories of art.[28] When an author has bodied forth his conception in Carlyle's sense, he has placed his inner vision in a form that does justice to it, so that it may stand forth in its own form with its own dignity; the poet has found his objective correlative. In both cases, shadowing forth or bodying forth, the poet is projecting something that comes from within rather than mirroring that which is outside. It is enlightening to see that Carlyle in 1823 adopted as his own pictorial device a kind of unofficial coat of arms, a burning candle underneath which was written: *Terar dum prosim*—"I burn that I may be

[28] Meyer Abrams, *The Mirror and the Lamp: Romantic Theory and the Critical Tradition* (New York, 1958).

of use."[29] It constitutes a statement of Carlyle's aesthetic creed that unites the glow of art with the earnestness of morality. Carlyle the artist is a seeker after truth, and truth, like the inspiration for a work of art, comes from the invisible not the visible world. Thus mimesis is quite out of the question. The poet's fundamental problem is to find some means of projecting that which is within. When the projection falters or is mere lantern slides, it has been shadowed forth; but when it has found a local habitation and a name, it has been bodied forth. The poet has created a symbol to lead others to his same perception.

It is in the means of presentation that the poet differs from the philosopher, not in what is presented: the philosopher, of course, uses systematic discourse, but the poet uses an imaginative creation. Carlyle lets a spokesman in "Wotton Reinfred" declare that the philosophy of Kant is merely the systematization in more rigorous philosophic terms of truths known intuitively and from practice to all genuine poets.[30] The equation of poetry and philosophy puts an indelibly didactic stamp on everything Carlyle did.

If Carlyle's artist, or, as he always called him, the poet, must like the philosopher see through appearances and employ what Carlyle would call Kantian Reason as opposed to mere Understanding,[31] then the poet is in the literal sense a *seer* who penetrates through the visible universe to the invisible but truly real universe, of which the visible is indeed but the garment or symbol. What the poet sees is, in the phrase Carlyle borrowed from Fichte, the Divine

[29] *Two Note Books,* p. 44. Immediately adjacent to the drawing Carlyle commented: "But what if I do not *prodesse?* Why then terar still,—dum I cannot help it!"

[30] *Last Words,* p. 138.

[31] C. F. Harrold, *Carlyle and German Thought,* pp. 120–147, makes clear that Carlyle's virtual equation of Reason with intuition is not Kantian, but akin to the thought of Jacobi and Coleridge. Much as he did with Goethe's *Entsagen,* however, Carlyle seized upon Kant's *Vernunft* and made it into his own *Reason.* Cf. Carlyle's definitions in *Last Words,* pp. 60–63, and "Novalis," *Works,* xxvii, 26–27.

Idea of the World. The Divine Idea in Carlyle is synonymous with the Open Secret, his appropriation from Goethe.
The Divine Idea–Open Secret is hidden from the eyes
of the vulgar, "but clear to the poet's; because the 'open
secret' is no longer a secret to him, and he knows that
the Universe is *full* of goodness; that whatever has being
has beauty."[32] Carlyle is not telling the poet specifically
what he must see in his penetration of the *visibilia* of
the world, he is merely trying to channel the poet's efforts
in the proper direction. He is positing an ultimate purpose
for art: the presentation of truth. As to the manner in
which the poet's insight is to be conveyed, Carlyle shows
himself less restrictive than proponents of mimetic theory,
for he sees form as a highly individual matter, something
to be determined in each specific case. What is universally
true is only that the poet must see what others miss: "He
is a *vates*, a seer; a gift of vision has been given him.
Has life no meanings for him, which another cannot equally
decipher; then he is no poet, and Delphi itself will not
make him one" (*Works*, xxvi, 272).

The only circumscription in Carlyle's theory is his insistence on the prophetic nature of art. Since a poet is a
seer and a *vates*, what he writes must be visionary and
vatic. Nor does the effort alone necessarily bring success.
Witness Werner who fails as a *vates* in Carlyle's eyes and
gets something like an E for effort. Only poets who capture
the Divine Idea merit the name "poet" and their work
"poetry" (Carlyle uses the terms as the Germans do *Dichter*
and *Dichtung*).[33] The poet who successfully addresses him-

[32] *Works*, xxvi, 225 ("Goethe"). Harrold, *Carlyle and German
Thought*, pp. 116–119, notes the philosophic objections to Carlyle's
identification of the Open Secret with the Divine Idea. A good
history of the development of the term Open Secret is found in
Joseph Slater, "Goethe, Carlyle, and the Open Secret," *Anglia*, lxxvi
(1958), 422–426.
[33] Of Werner, Carlyle wrote: ". . . taking up the character of *Vates*
in its widest sense, Werner earnestly desires not only to be a
poet, but a prophet; and, indeed, looks upon his merits in the
former province as altogether subservient to his higher purposes
in the latter" (*Works*, xxvi, 115–116).

self to the Divine Idea need not worry overmuch with
the form in which the Divine Idea is expressed, not because
form is unimportant, but because the visible manifestations
of the Divine Idea change with different ages and different
authors. They are more difficult to predict. It is hard to
feel superior to Carlyle's awareness of shifts in taste, for
that is what his subordination of form to meaning really
reflects. He recognized that the form of poetry not only
may, but must, change. What he insisted on was that the
subject matter and form for expressing the Divine Idea
come from the present.[34] He saw this as the great strength
of German literature, because in it modern life was presented not mimetically, or for its own sake, but in conjunction with the perceptions of ultimate reality that each
author had painfully won for his own. Among his German
favorites he rarely complained of the escapism that dis-
tressed him in the English Romantics, almost all of whom
he persistently underrated.[35] Only the Germans, he felt,
had wedded the unchanging essence of poetry to modern
subject matter; only the Germans had found a means of

Carlyle's use of the word *poetry* in the eighteen-twenties as approximately equivalent to "creative writing" is too frequent to call
for citation. I have found only one instance in which he appears
to use poetry in a more restricted sense: in "German Playwrights"
he writes that the "essence of a Playwright [is] that he works
not in Poetry, but in Prose which more or less cunningly resembles
it" (*Works*, xxvi, 359). But even here the distinction is not so
much formal as qualitative.

[34] See *Works*, xxvi, 66 ("State of German Literature"), 128
("Werner"), 155, 195 ("Goethe's *Helena*"), 213, 217, 225
("Goethe"), 271–272 ("Burns"), and xxvii, 159 ("Jean Paul
Friedrich Richter Again").

[35] Byron alone of the Romantics won Carlyle's qualified approval,
but he felt that Byron never passed beyond the *Sturm und Drang*
stage. He called the Lake poets "puling" (*Love Letters*, i, 123),
and he said that all of Keats consists "in a weak-eyed maudlin
sensibility, and a certain vague random tunefulness of nature"
(*Works*, xxvi, 277—"Burns"). See also Charles Richard Sanders,
"The Byron Closed in *Sartor Resartus*," *Studies in Romanticism*,
iii (1964), 77–108.

bodying forth their insights into the Divine Idea of the World.

According to Carlyle's theory, any work of art must be an organic whole, with the execution growing from the conception. Carlyle insists on organicism as strongly as Coleridge or the German theorists, although without giving much attention to practical problems of composition.[36] The questions he asks, for example, of Jean Paul are: "How nearly does this manner of writing represent his real manner of thinking and existing? With what degree of freedom does it allow this particular form of being to manifest itself; or what fetters and perversions does it lay on such manifestation?" Shortly after these questions he makes the previously cited assertion, "All *genuine* things are what they ought to be." The rule for the critic is that "the outward style is to be judged by the inward qualities of the spirit which it is employed to body forth" (*Works,* xxvi, 19). Similarly he asks, in "State of German Literature," of Shakespeare's plays: "Are these dramas of his not verisimilar only, but true; nay, truer than reality itself, since the essence of unmixed reality is bodied forth in them under more expressive symbols? What is this unity of theirs; and can our deeper inspection discern it to be indivisible, and existing by necessity, because each work springs, as it were, from the general elements of all Thought, and grows up therefrom, into form and expansion by its own growth?" (*Works,* xxvi, 51–52)

The frequency with which Carlyle calls for organic form in literary works is matched only by the frequency with

[36] These are not entirely neglected in the early writings, however, and he occasionally mentions the need for conscious intellectual exertion to perfect the form of a work. See, e.g., his citation from Jean Paul on Werner (*Works,* xxvi, 145) and his comment on Goethe's works (*Works,* xxvi, 244). For an instance of Carlyle's concern about changes in a text of his own see Maxwell H. Goldberg, "Jeffrey: Mutilator of Carlyle's 'Burns,'" *PMLA,* lvi (1941), 466–471, and Macvey Napier (ed.), *A Selection from the Correspondence of Macvey Napier* (London, 1879) p. 96. See also W. C. Brownell, *Victorian Prose Masters* (New York, 1902), p. 77.

which he employs organic metaphors throughout his writing.[37] Thus, by direct statement and by insinuation and comparison, he always returns to art as organism. Nowhere is his insistence on organism so vividly set forth as in the epigraph he adopted from Goethe to precede *Sartor Resartus:*

> *Mein Vermächtniss, wie herrlich weit und breit!*
> *Die Zeit ist mein Vermächtniss, Mein Acker ist die Zeit.*

In those two lines he combines two favorite ideas, growth and time. Time becomes the field in which growth takes place, thus to some extent freeing organicism from the curse of inertness. The sum of Carlyle's aesthetic speculations is well expressed in his evaluation of the *Nibelungenlied:* "[The] poem, unlike so many old and new pretenders to that name, has a basis and organic structure, a beginning, middle and end; there is one great principle and idea set forth in it, round which all its multifarious parts combine in living union . . . and the living soul of Poetry being there, its body of incidents, its garment of language, come of their own accord" (*Works,* xxvii, 234).

Given Carlyle's axioms, some corollaries are inevitable. If the real world presented by the poet-philosopher is an invisible one, what is the visible world? It is, of course, a symbol. It represents the invisible world. For this reason Carlyle equated the Divine Idea with the Open Secret. The Divine Idea is invisible and not physically verifiable. But the Open Secret is visible to anyone who will look; it is the manifestation of meaning in the real world. Mean-

[37] Typical is the following from "On History": "When the oak-tree is felled, the whole forest echoes with it; but a hundred acorns are planted silently by some unnoticed breeze" (*Works,* xxvii, 86). In another instance we find Carlyle distorting a German proverb to suit his organicist bias. He renders "Zeit brigt Rosen, nicht der Stock" as "Time brings Roses; the stem helps" (Shine, *Carlyle's Unfinished History of German Literature,* p. 35). Carlyle's version argues the indissolubility of the plant from the whole; the German is rather an exhortation to patience: "Time brings roses, not the stem."

ing is what Carlyle is ever seeking; so he readily seizes upon that which makes the Open Secret open—physical phenomena—as a means of reaching the Divine Idea. Everyday reality is a symbol of the greater reality. By realistic signposts the poet can lead the reader to the perception of truth. Without them there is no means of engaging the reader. Carlyle's symbolism, then, is a function of his concept of the Divine Idea and the Open Secret. Once he has committed himself to these concepts, his theory of symbolism must follow.

Now, symbols suggest the possibility of allegory, although symbolism in itself is not allegory. But Carlyle *is* led to embrace a kind of allegory as a desirable contemporary form. He frequently finds allegories in *German Romance* and in the essays. Of the "Helena" episode in *Faust*, for example, he says: "This doctrine [Faust's salvation through art] is to be stated emblematically and parabolically." He appears to have skirted close to the idea of allegory but never to have been fully satisfied with the term itself, perhaps because he was aware of the more rigorous definition of allegory that requires the existence of symbols prior to, and independent of, the work in question. The traditional symbols (Christ the fish, the rose of passion, the pearl of innocence) no longer carried much force in the nineteenth century. Meaningful symbols were those that grew out of the work itself, and any concomitant allegory might be fitful. Perhaps that is why, after calling "Helena" emblematic and parabolic, Carlyle said: *"Helena* is not an Allegory, but a Phantasmagory" (*Works*, XXVI, 196). For an allegory to work, the symbols, from whatever they derive, must cohere in a consistent and sustained pattern. But what of a work in which an allegorical pattern emerges and then subsides again? It is not a conventional allegory, and yet the symbolism is at least intermittently allegorical. Carlyle found a number of German works that display this sort of allegory, an allegorical symbolism, and he was much attracted to them. But to what genre do such works belong? As he wrote of *Faust* in 1822: "We scarcely know under what class to arrange it." By the "Helena" essay of 1828, however, he has come to a clearer understanding of the category of these allusive, semi-allegorical works. After calling the "Helena" interlude emblematic, parabolic, not an allegory but a phantasmagory, he reveals that "properly speaking, *Helena* is what the Germans call a *Mährchen* (Fabulous Tale), a species of fiction they have particularly excelled in" (*Works*, XXVI, 196). The *Märchen*, is the proper vehicle for contemporary allegorical symbolism. Nor is Carlyle deterred by the fact that "Helena" is a part of the larger work *Faust*. He notes with approval Novalis' habit of inserting *Märchen* into his stories, chiefly *Heinrich von Ofterdingen*.[38] It is noteworthy that both Goethe's and Novalis' *Märchen* are subplots of larger works and that characters and themes from the major story appear in the *Märchen* as well.

In addition to providing the poet with an opportunity for allegory, the *Märchen* touches the deepest fibers of the folk psyche. Carlyle credits the fable (for him a variety of the *Volksmärchen*) with introducing the Age of Apologue, or the Didactic Age, in European literary history, for "fable, indeed, may be regarded as the earliest and simplest product of Didactic Poetry, the first attempt of Instruction clothing itself in Fancy."[39] The *Märchen*, he felt, had a role to play again in literature. The Age of Apologue was the second of three stages he discerned in

---

[38] *Works*, XXVII, 11 ("Novalis"). Carlyle speaks of only one *Märchen*, but actually there are at least three *Märchen* in *Heinrich von Ofterdingen*. Carlyle probably had reference to Klingsohr's *Märchen* at the end of part one in which "die blaue Blume" of the story proper also plays a part. In quoting Carlyle, I use the *h* in *Thonschiefer*, *Mährchen*, etc., as he did.

[39] *Works*, XXVII, 301. Carlyle discusses the *Volksmärchen* frequently and with great intelligence in his "History of German Literature" (esp. p. 38) and in the essays that grew out of it (*Works*, XXVII, 324—"Early German Literature"; and XXVII, 343—"Historic Survey of German Poetry"). He calls the *Volksmärchen* "Popular Fable" and translates two of them in the "History of German Literature."

European history in his 1830 "History of German Literature." The first was the Chivalric Age (the world's youth);
the second was the Age of Apologue (the world's manhood). The second age had lasted even into the eighteenth
century, which was but the degeneration of the didactic
spirit. The next stage was dawning: the union of Understanding (the didactic spirit) with Poetry (modern imagination) to produce a true age of Reason (that which, in the
Kantian sense, passeth Understanding). Carlyle anticipated
Arnold in seeing literature replace religion in the new age.
However, it would have to be a literature which, like the
German, was eminently philosophical and poetic, one that
had found a means of uniting truth and beauty, instruction
and fancy.[40] Into this vision Carlyle's conception of the
Märchen fits exceedingly well. Seen both as an historical
phenomenon in Carlyle's three-fold historical division and
as a fertile contemporary form, the *Märchen* has a limitless
potential for good. In Carlyle's lofty conception of the
historical and future role of the *Märchen* is to be found,
I believe, what Carlyle really meant when she said that
the *Reineke Fuchs* fable gave him the whole idea of *Sartor
Resartus*.[41]

As the *Märchen* can unify separate elements (instruction and fancy), so, to Carlyle, can humor. His concept
of humor is the last important corollary of his aesthetic
principles. The full implications of his concept of humor
for *Sartor Resartus* will be examined later. However, in the

---

[40] *Works*, xxvi, 30. A part of Carlyle's interest in international
literary cooperation was doubtless stimulated by Goethe's concept
of *Weltliteratur* and other German theories on the amalgamation
of all knowledge (cf. Novalis' *Totalwissenschaft*). There is a good
deal of discussion of *Weltliteratur* in *Correspondence between Goethe
and Carlyle*. For Carlyle's views on the ominous *Zeitgeist* which
could only be placated by literature replacing religion see *Works*,
xxvi, 88 ("Werner") and 211–217 ("Goethe"); xxvii, 55
("Novalis"); and throughout "Signs of the Times," xxvii, 56–82.

[41] Froude, ii, 372 (extract from Carlyle's Journal, 1833). No doubt
the importance he attached to fable led him to retitle "Early German
Literature" as "Reinecke Fuchs" in later publications of that essay.

review essays it is clear that humor has become for Carlyle a ruling principle. His concept of humor presupposes a vast range, not only of intellect, but of sympathy. Humor is the joining together of the ridiculous and the sublime; it is the means of uniting the visible and the invisible worlds, an occasion for embodying eternal truths in the very multitudinousness of nineteenth-century life.[42]

Such, then, are the aesthetic axioms and corollaries Carlyle expounds throughout the essays: poetry as the expression of the Divine Idea–Open Secret; the poet as a seer and *vates* who penetrates the visible world to grasp the invisible; the artistic form of literature as an organic growth around an essential and unchanging meaning; symbolism as the means of embodying permanent truths; allegory as a logical extension of cohesive symbolism; the *Märchen* as a form uniquely suited to allegorical symbolism; and humor as a means of unifying contraries. Indeed, Carlyle's whole aesthetic appears to be posited on the assumption that art is a means of unifying contrary or disparate things: visible and invisible, truth and beauty, instruction and fancy, finite and infinite. We turn now to the manifestations of Carlyle's theory in the practice of his essays.

STRUCTURE AND STYLE

Since Carlyle's aesthetic continually returns to the principle of polarities and their unification, it is not surprising

---

[42] Significantly, Carlyle set forth his theory of humor in his first *Edinburgh* Jean Paul essay: "True humour springs not more from the head than from the heart; it is not contempt, its essence is love; it issues not in laughter but in still smiles, which lie far deeper" (*Works*, xxvi, 17). In Burns, too, Carlyle discerned a spirit animated by love which "under a lighter disguise . . . occasionally manifests itself in the shape of Humour" (*Works*, xxvi, 283). By contrast, Voltaire exhibits pleasantries but not humor: "We look in vain, through his whole writings, for one lineament of a *Quixote*, or a *Shandy*; even of a *Hudibras*, or *Battle of the Books*" (*Works*, xxvi, 451). Coleridge also echoes Jean Paul on humor. Cf. Thomas Middleton Raysor (ed.), *Coleridge's Miscellaneous Criticism* (London, 1936), pp. 111–121.

that the structure of his essays reflects these principles, for they are as much emotional dispositions as intellectual principles. They are the way Carlyle thinks. His earliest works divide either in two parts or three. So do the essays; but the process has become more sophisticated, more elaborate. A great deal more must be kept in balance, and the flow of the language must be maintained. Still, the essential pattern is there. The two-part division in the essays conforms to the visible and invisible worlds of which Carlyle's aesthetic theory makes so much. Thus factual data and biography normally fall in the first part, and evaluation and meaning in the second. The three-part essay follows in broad outline the pattern observed in the earlier three-part encyclopaedia essays. In terms of Carlyle's aesthetic theories, the tripartite essay pattern illustrates his effort to unite visible and invisible, finite and infinite. But usually in the essays the three-part division is less completely realized than it is in *Sartor*. Often, the first part is merely preliminary, as in the Montaigne encyclopaedia essay, and the essay proper is reserved for the following two parts.

The arrangement of Carlyle's essays is also substantially conditioned by Carlyle's role of editor-translator. The structural impact of this role becomes progressively greater as the essays approach *Sartor Resartus* in date. Likewise, biography is always sure to loom large in the plan of the essays because of Carlyle's intense concern with the light that biography casts on literature. We shall examine some of the essays for characteristic structural elements. Meantime, what of style? Francis X. Roellinger argues that on the appearance of *Sartor* no one was heard to remark, "I know who wrote the article in the last month's *Fraser's*—Mr. Carlyle. You couldn't mistake his style." After reading the periodical articles, however, one can only wonder why. That they were all published anonymously, and in various periodicals, goes a long way toward explanation. Roellinger makes a good deal of Goethe's confusion

as to the authorship of "State of German Literature" in
the 1827 *Edinburgh*.[43] Of course Goethe's inability to dis-
criminate among the styles of English reviewers need
hardly puzzle us. Goethe's English was, after all, not nearly
so good as Carlyle's German. It is much more remarkable
that Goethe inquired of Carlyle about it than that he was
not certain of the authorship. It shows the extent of his
recognition of Carlyle's role as interpreter of German
letters, and perhaps an awareness of Carlyle's distinctive
manner.

When we look at the "State of German Literature," we
are struck by those elements that mark it as Carlyle's alone,
so much so that it can stand as typical of Carlyle's review
manner. After a brief introduction dealing with Franz Horn
and the literary history allegedly under review, Carlyle
turns to the real business of his essay to say "a word or
two . . . on that strange Literature itself," and the essay
proper then begins. Carlyle commences by declaring the
opposite of what he wants to prove. He quotes the seventeenth-century Frenchman, Père Bouhours, who asked, "Si
un allemand peut avoir de l'esprit?" Carlyle's reply to this
impertinence is to hoist Bouhours with his own petard. He
observes that obviously the good father had neglected to
study the question he had so lightly raised, had not known
of "Gunpowder, Printing, and the Protestant Religion"
(perhaps this was Bouhours' very point!), had been ignorant of such works as the *Nibelungenlied, Reineke
Fuchs, Faust*, "and four-fifths of all the popular mythology,
humour, and romance to be found in Europe in the sixteenth and seventeenth centuries," and that Bouhours had
conducted his thought *in vacuo* and had succeeded merely
in escaping oblivion himself by having asked his question
in the first place: ". . . and now it is by this one *un*timely

[43] Roellinger, pp. 944, 951. One is tempted to ask whether the
readers of *Titus Andronicus* readily discern in the style of that
play the author of *Lear*. For Goethe's queries about the article
see *Correspondence between Goethe and Carlyle*, p. 45.

joke that the hapless Jesuit is doomed to live; for the blessing of full oblivion is denied him, and so he hangs, suspended in his own noose, over the dusky pool, which he struggles toward, but for a great while will not reach" (*Works*, xxvi, 29). Thus launched, the essay proceeds to a consideration of the central task facing the contemporary student of culture—to understand his neighbor in so significant an age, "an era of such promise and such threatening, when so many elements of good and evil are everywhere in conflict, and human society is, as it were, struggling to body itself forth anew, and so many *coloured rays* are springing up in this quarter and in that, which only by their union can produce *pure light*."[44]

It is interesting to observe that the two major parts of the essay, which follow the introductory portion posing the great question, are not merely contrived by Carlyle to suit some abstract, however much they happen to conform to the theories we have been investigating; for these two parts correspond to the two main objections that have been made to German literature. That is, the division grows out of the subject matter. The first objection is that the Germans are uncouth ("bad taste," Carlyle calls it); the second is that they are mystic. To the first objection Carlyle devotes some thirty pages, ranging over the history of German literature and the condition of German writers to the principles of modern German criticism, which he unhesitatingly affirms to be far in advance of comparable critical theories anywhere else. In his discussion of the new criticism in Germany he gives an outline of what

[44] *Works*, xxvi, 30 (italics in original). Elsewhere in this same essay Carlyle asserts his thoughts about this *Zeitgeist* and the Germans' transcendence of it: "The Nineteenth Century stands before us, in all its contradiction and perplexity; barren, mean, and baleful, as we have all known it, yet here no longer mean or barren, but enamelled into beauty in the poet's spirit; for its secret significance is laid open, and thus, as it were, the life-giving fire that slumbers in it is called forth, and flowers and foliage, as of old, are springing on its bleakest wildernesses, and overmantling its sternest cliffs" (*Works*, xxvi, 66).

criticism must concern itself with, in a passage exceedingly relevant to *Sartor Resartus:*

> The grand question is not now a question concerning the qualities of diction, the coherence of metaphors, the fitness of sentiments, the general logical truth, in a work of art, as it was some half-century ago among most critics; neither is it a question mainly of a psychological sort, to be answered by discovering and delineating the peculiar nature of the poet from his poetry, as is usual with the best of our own critics at present: but it is, not indeed exclusively, but inclusively of those two other questions, properly and ultimately a question on the essence and peculiar life of the poetry itself. The first of these questions, as we see it answered for instance in the criticisms of Johnson and Kames, relates, strictly speaking to the *garment* of poetry; the second, indeed, to its *body* and material existence, a much higher point; but only the last to its *soul* and spiritual existence, by which alone can the body in its movements and phases, be *informed* with significance and rational life.[45]

We cannot fail to be struck by the similarity in language between this 1827 critical pronouncement and the clothes metaphor of *Sartor*. The similarity is more than accidental, however, for Carlyle is setting forth his own procedure as a critic and also what became his procedure in the organization of *Sartor*. In "State of German Literature" the issue is the alleged bad taste of German writers. The defense of German criticism forms Carlyle's chief rebuttal, and he is then prepared to move to the next major objection.

To the second chief drawback of German literature—its mysticism—Carlyle addresses himself with equal vigor. He seeks to dispel the charge of mysticism entirely by arguing that the Germans have merely confronted the essential

---

[45] *Works,* xxvi, 51. Carlyle uses the same terminology in the essay on Werner, *Works,* xxvi, 143–144.

problems skirted, ignored, and even denied by British empiricist philosophy. In his defense he posits the distinction between visible and invisible worlds that informs so much of the purpose of his own writing:

> In the field of human investigation there are objects of two sorts: First, the *visible*, including not only such as are material, and may be seen by the bodily eye; but all such, likewise, as may be represented in a *shape*, before the mind's eye, or in any way pictured there: And, secondly, the *invisible*, or such as are not only unseen by human eyes, but as cannot be seen by any eye; not objects of sense at all; not capable, in short, of being *pictured* or imaged in the mind, or in any way represented by a *shape* either without the mind or within it. (*Works*, xxvi, 70–71)

Carlyle naturally goes on to state that the so-called mystic is one who is concerned with picturing in some way the invisible world, and one whose task is extremely difficult, subject to misunderstanding and misinterpretation, but nevertheless the most essential task any poet has to perform. The dichotomy of visible and invisible interests us in its own right, as a way of looking at things as characteristically Carlylean as the three-part pattern—garment, body, soul—set forth earlier. Further, Carlyle's whole approach is rhetorically designed to dispel objections by recasting the terms so as to persuade the reader that what he objected to is in no way objectionable. So earnest is Carlyle in his endeavor that he runs the risk of simplifying and distorting complex things. In so far as mysticism was loosely used to denominate anything strange, Carlyle is surely justified in clarifying the issues. But in so far as mysticism is, as in the case of Novalis, genuinely mystic, Carlyle is guilty of making the ineffable appear to be subject to conventional analysis and explication. Still, we can grant him this license when we bear in mind his well-placed conviction that some means must be found to bring the lessons of German literature home to the English reader. Of course, the task was not carried out solely by organizing the objections under two main categories and demolishing them. Hand in glove with Carlyle's organization is his style.

As previous citations must have suggested, Carlyle's style in "State of German Literature" is directed toward winning the reader's assent, not merely by logical argument, but by exhortation, suggestion, insinuation, and unabashed praise as well. The following thunderous conclusion to the essay was made possible only by an increasing intensity of tempo and language through the whole work:

> In any point of Space, in any section of Time let there be a living Man; and there is an Infinitude above him and beneath him, and an Eternity encompasses him on this hand and on that; and tones of Sphere-music, and tidings from loftier worlds, will flit round him, if he can but listen, and visit him with holy influences, even in the thickest press of trivialities, or the din of busiest life. Happy the man, happy the nation that can hear these tidings; that has them written in fit characters, legible to every eye, and the solemn import of them present at all moments to every heart! (*Works*, xxvi, 86)

One wonders how Carlyle's style reached this degree of Carlylese and whether the aesthetic and critical principles advanced in the essays really account for it. Perhaps no theory ever fully accounts for a style, but an examination of actual writing practice can show a style developing and pointing itself with a consistency that may be subject to theoretic formulation. Something of the sort has already been suggested in the examination of Carlyle's pre-essay and pre-*Sartor* writings. What these may have failed to illustrate should come clear from an inspection of the style of the essays.

Before looking at the essays, it is well to remind ourselves of the Sartorian aspects of Carlyle's style before *German Romance* in 1826. The first that comes to mind is the

Water of Milk—Kuhbach passage in its early form in the 1825 letter to Jane Welsh. But long before this Carlyle has revealed a tendency toward a fervid style. In 1822 he apologizes to Jane for what he calls his "heroics," for Jane always had a "wicked laugh" for his heroics.[46] In a letter from the following year he extols the joys of writing in a somewhat Sartorian manner: "And yet by *this,* our thoughts go from us to the utmost bounds of space and time; hearts that beat in the remotest borders of the world are fired by the sentiments that ours have conceived, they love us tho' unseen, and 'being dead we yet speak' " (*Love Letters,* I, 138). By 1823 Carlyle's reaction to the spurious London celebrity of his friend Edward Irving offered him an opportunity to exhibit his skill at antithesis:

> The fame of a genuine man of letters is like the radiance of another star added to the galaxy of intellect to shine there for many ages; the popularity of a pulpit orator is like a tar-barrel set up in the middle of the street to blaze with a fierce but very tarnished flame, for a few hours, and then go out in a cloud of sparkles and thick smoke offensive to the lungs and noses of the whole neighbourhood. (*Love Letters,* I, 299)

On an 1824 trip to France Carlyle wrote Jane some highly Carlylean exclamations about Paris and included an affecting description of a visit to the Paris morgue.[47] He

---

[46] *Love Letters,* I, 71. Obviously Jane had more than a wicked laugh for Carlyle's heroics, for in January 1822 she had criticized Carlyle's mixture of levity and seriousness and said of a letter from him: "Besides this there is about your Letter a *mystery* which I detest. It is so full of *meaning* words underlined; *meaning* sentences half-finished; *meaning* blanks with notes of admiration; and *meaning* quotations from foreign languages, that really in this abundance of meaning it seems to indicate, I am somewhat at a loss to discover what you would be at" (*Love Letters,* I, 21). Carlyle's letter must be read in its entirety to perceive the full force. It is printed in *Love Letters,* I, 17–20.

[47] "Yesterday I walked along the *Pont Neuf;* jugglers and quacks and cooks and barbers and dandies and gulls and sharpers were

spoke then, too, of writing a "wild letter" which he did
not send. In July of 1825, just after the letter with the
early Kuhbach passage, Carlyle writes to Jane:

> There is a spark of heavenly fire within us, an ethereal
> glow of Love and Wisdom, for it was the breath of
> God that made us living souls; but we are formed of
> the dust of the ground, and our lot is cast on Earth,
> and the fire lies hid among the ashes of our own fortune
> or burns with a fitful twinkle, which Chance, not we,
> can foster. It makes me sad to think how very small
> a part we are of what we might be . . . . Will affection
> also die at last in that inhospitable scene? Will the excel-
> lent become to us no better than the common, and the
> Spirit of the Universe with his thousand voices speak
> to us in vain? Alas! must the heart itself grow dull and
> callous, as its hopes one after the other shrink and
> wither? *"Armseliger Faust, ich kenne dich nicht mehr!"*
> (*Love Letters,* ii, 141)

He cites the passage as evidence that "my preaching faculty
is not a whit diminished, had I opportunity to give it
scope."

Although it would be false to equate it with the style
of *Sartor,* Carlyle's preaching faculty has indeed been there
from the very start. Until *German Romance* it appears
chiefly in the letters. The correspondence from Hoddam
Hill in 1825, over and above the Kuhbach passage, is

---

racketing away with a deafening hum at their manifold pursuits;
I turned aside into a small mansion with the name of *Morgue*
upon it; there lay the naked body of an old grey-headed artisan
whom misery had driven to drown himself in the river! His face
wore the grim fixed scowl of despair; his lean horny hands with
their long ragged nails were lying by his sides; his patched and
soiled apparel with his apron and *sabots* were hanging at his head;
and there fixed in his iron slumber, heedless of the vain din that
rolled around him on every side, was this poor outcast stretched
in silence and darkness forever" (*Love Letters,* ii, 28).

studded with passages reflecting Carlyle's "preaching faculty." At Hoddam Hill in 1825 he finally found opportunity to give it scope, and the style known as Carlylese begins to appear in the essays for *German Romance*. As it cast light on the development of Carlyle's style to see the transformations of the Kuhbach passage, so it illuminates the refinement of his style to examine it in the essays. A singularly appropriate sequence offers itself in Carlyle's Jean Paul essays between 1826 and 1829, for it is a curious circumstance that his chief effort in *German Romance* was the presentation of Jean Paul, that his maiden essay for the *Edinburgh* treated Jean Paul, and that his last major essay before *Sartor* was again a study of Jean Paul. In the very first essay the style is distinctively Carlylean; by the third essay features have accrued that mark the style as Carlyle's with a vengeance.

He begins the Jean Paul essay in *German Romance* with a familiar device—the citation of objections English readers are likely to raise against Jean Paul:

> The first aspect of these peculiarities [the structure of Jean Paul's novels] cannot prepossess us in his favour; we are too forcibly reminded of theatrical clap-traps and literary quackery; nor on opening one of the works themselves is the case much mended. Piercing gleams of thought do not escape us; singular truths conveyed in a form as singular; grotesque and often truly ludicrous delineations; pathetic, magnificent, far-sounding passages, effusions full of wit, knowledge and imagination, but difficult to bring under any rubric whatever; all the elements, in short, of a glorious intellect, but dashed together in such wild arrangement, that their order seems the very ideal of confusion. The style and structure of the books appear alike incomprehensible. The narrative is every now and then suspended to make way for some "Extra-leaf," some wild digression upon any subject but the one in hand; the language groans with indescribable

metaphors and allusions to all things human and divine; flowing outward, not like a river, but like an inundation; circling in complex eddies, chafing and gurgling now this way, now that, till the proper current sinks out of view amid the boundless uproar. (*Works,* xxii, 119–120)

The first sentence seems to be the start of an unfavorable judgment, but the second sentence gives the reader pause. What has been called "theatrical clap-trap and literary quackery" is said to have "piercing gleams of thought . . . singular truths . . . pathetic, magnificent far-sounding passages." Carlyle mixes praise with blame as preparation for the reversal to come. Even toward the end of the passage, where the criticism seems harsher, several important words mitigate its force: "their order *seems* the very ideal of confusion. The style and structure . . . *appear.* . . . indescribable metaphors and allusions to all things human and *divine.* . . ." Carlyle is planting the seeds of doubt even while seeming to state the case for the plaintiff. He continues in the next passage to argue that if the foregoing is true of Jean Paul, he is guilty of affectation, which is "the product of Falsehood, a heavy sin, and the parent of numerous heavy sins; let it be severely punished, but not too lightly imputed." But affectation is not a charge properly to be imputed to Jean Paul after all. The mists melt away, once we understand him, "and he stands revealed to us in his own steadfast features, a colossal spirit, a lofty and original thinker, a genuine poet. . . ." Carlyle then launches into an encomium that far eclipses the original denunciation:

His Imagination opens for us the Land of Dreams; we sail with him through the boundless abyss, and the secrets of Space, and Time, and Life, and Annihilation hover round us in dim cloudy forms, and darkness and immensity and dread encompass and overshadow us. . . . His very language is Titanian; deep, strong, tumultuous, shining with a thousand hues, fused from a thousand elements, and winding in labyrinthic mazes.

Among Richter's gifts, perhaps the first that strikes us as truly great is his Imagination; for he loves to dwell in the loftiest and most solemn provinces of thought; his works abound with mysterious allegories, visions and typical adumbrations; his Dreams, in particular, have a gloomy vastness, broken here and there by wild fire-darting splendour, and shadowy forms of meaning rise dimly from the bosom of the void Infinite. (*Works*, xxii, 122)

We can hardly direct too much attention to these passages written in July 1826. That the style represents a considerable intensification of Carlyle's "heroic" or "preaching" manner must be allowed. Carlyle himself was aware of this, for immediately after completing the Richter preface he wrote to Jane Welsh: "It is singular what a mockbird I am: I am writing here unconsciously in the very note of Jean Paul Friedrich Richter, on whose works I have been labouring for the last four weeks. I sent a most mad *article* on the man to *press* . . . this morning" (*Love Letters*, ii, 305). The specter of imitation immediately arises, but one must emphasize that Carlyle declares he has written *unconsciously* in the note of Jean Paul. Imitation is a rather different matter. If in discussing Carlyle's style one can harmonize Froude's arguments about native sources (the Annandale speech of Carlyle's father) and German influences (imitation of Jean Paul), here is the very passage to do it. Carlyle *is* writing to a large extent in the note of Jean Paul, but he is doing it unconsciously. The rush and force of the language, the power it holds in its native idiom for readers who have never read Jean Paul, argue that something other than calculated imitation is at work. Transmutation might be a better term.

Carlyle has his own purposes in his Jean Paul essay. He is deeply involved in the matter of persuasion. His initial statement blends praise with blame; it sets the reader up for the punch. His method involves taking a position contrary to the one he actually holds, a position he identifies with the reader's, stating the case, and then reversing his position to argue, triumphantly, the reverse. He has made use of the rhetorical device of prolepsis. The reversal has the greater impact for having been subtly prepared for in the indictment, so that the reader, who in any case senses the direction of the argument, is gratified by the outcome. Positive after negative becomes a Carlyle trademark.

What of the syntax, so wild, so abundant, so German? And the language? Some Carlylean hallmarks are here: he capitalizes for effect—Space, Time, Life, Annihilation, Titanian. In these examples his capitalization rests for the most part on abstract nouns, but later he will expand the practice. He also uses *and* extensively for clausal linkage: "we . . . sail . . . and . . . secrets . . . hover" are approximately equal in weight; but then follows a series of nouns linked by *and*. The effect is as of three weights, the third the heaviest of all:

> and darkness
> and immensity
> and dread.

Slight as it may appear, the use of *and* instead of commas alters conventional expectations. The effect is Biblical. Carlyle is also fond of constructing a two-part sentence, then adding yet a third part with a Biblical *and:*

> his works . . . abound
> his dreams . . . have
>   and
> shadowy forms . . . rise.

The first two parts are parallel, the third is a result rather than another parallel, so that the sentence does not close but leads on to another idea pregnant with suggestion.

When Carlyle takes up Jean Paul again in the first periodical essay (1827), there is, if anything, a further intensification of manner:

He is a phenomenon from the very surface; he presents himself with a professed and determined singularity: his language itself is a stone of stumbling to the critic; to critics of the grammarian species, an unpardonable, often an insuperable rock of offence. Not that he is ignorant of grammar, or disdains the sciences of spelling and parsing; but he exercises both in a certain latitudinarian spirit; deals with astonishing liberality in parentheses, dashes, and subsidiary clauses; invents hundreds of new words, alters old ones, or, by hyphen, chains and pairs and packs them together into most jarring combination; in short, produces sentences of the most heterogeneous, lumbering, interminable kind. Figures without limit; indeed, the whole is one tissue of metaphors, and similes, and allusions to all the provinces of Earth, Sea and Air; interlaced with epigrammatic breaks, vehement bursts, or sardonic turns, interjections, quips, puns, and even oaths! A perfect Indian jungle it seems; a boundless unparalleled imbroglio; nothing on all sides but darkness, dissonance, confusion worse confounded! Then the style of the whole corresponds, in perplexity and extravagance, with that of the parts. Every work, be it fiction or serious treatise, is embaled in some fantastic wrappage, some mad narrative accounting for its appearance, and connecting it with the author, who generally becomes a person in the drama himself, before all is over. He has a whole imaginary geography of Europe in his novels; the cities of Flachsenfingen, Haarharr, Scheerau, and so forth, with their princes, and privy-councillors, and serene highnesses; most of whom, odd enough fellows everyway, are Richter's private acquaintances, talk with him of state matters (in the purest Tory dialect), and often incite him to get on with his writing. No story proceeds without the most erratic digressions, and voluminous tagrags rolling after it in many a snaky twine. Ever and anon there occurs some "Extra-leaf," with its satirical petition, program, or other wonderful intercalation, no mortal can foresee on what. It is, indeed, a mighty maze; and often the panting reader toils after him in vain; or, baffled and spent, indignantly stops short, and retires, perhaps forever. (*Works*, xxvi, 11–12)

In this passage from the *Edinburgh* essay Carlyle has approached his subject much as he did in the *German Romance* essay. He cites the objections in even greater measure, interlarding substantial praise. Then he says, But stay, reader, things are not what they seem; affectation is not a charge properly levelled at Richter at all: "There are rays of the keenest truth, nay, steady pillars of scientific light rising through this chaos: Is it in fact a chaos; or may it be that our eyes are of finite, not of infinite vision, and have only missed the plan?" (*Works*, xxvi, 13) Carlyle is in full-blown Carlylese. The positive after the negative, then this intensified by an even more positive statement that follows upon a "nay." The next sentence then departs from the point reached in the climax of the nay clause, and once started on an upward progression he amasses a galaxy of lights to equal and surpass his inventory of sins:

Richter has been called an intellectual Colossus; and in truth it is somewhat in this light that we view him. His faculties are all of gigantic mould; cumbrous, awkward in their movements; large and splendid, rather than harmonious or beautiful; yet joined in living union; and of force and compass altogether extraordinary. He has an intellect vehement, rugged, irresistible; crushing in pieces the hardest problems; piercing into the most hidden combinations of things, and grasping the most distant: an imagination vague, sombre, splendid, or appalling; brooding over the abysses of Being; wandering through Infinitude, and summoning before us, in its dim

religious light, shapes of brilliance, solemnity, or terror:
a fancy of exuberance literally unexampled; for it pours
its treasures with a lavishness which knows no limit,
hanging, like the sun, a jewel on every grass-blade, and
sowing the earth at large with orient pearl. (*Works,*
xxvi, 14)

The method, as so often in Carlyle, is to make an initial
declarative statement and then to follow it with a string
of amplifying dependent participial clauses. Again and
again the subordinate parts (adjective groupings and
clauses) fall into clusters of three. Schematically arranged
the whole appears thus:

```
He has . . . an intellect
                      vehement
                      rugged
                      irresistible
             crushing . . . problems
             piercing into . . . things
        and grasping . . . most distant [things]
        [he has] . . . an imagination
                             vague
                             sombre
                             splendid
                          or appalling
                   brooding over . . . Being
                   wandering through . . . Infinitude
                   summoning . . . shapes of
                                        brilliancy
                                        solemnity
                                     or terror
        [he has] . . . a fancy
                          of exuberance
                for
        it          pours . . . treasures
                    hanging
                and sowing. . . .
```

The excess extends to sentence structure and words. By its very weight it works toward conviction, if not exhaustion. Moreover, the sentence lives by the reliance on present tense and present participle. The brilliance of these latter—crushing, piercing, grasping, brooding, wandering, summoning, hanging, sowing—is matched only by the glitter of the adjectives in the same sentence—vehement, rugged, irresistible, vague, sombre, splendid, appalling! Since the sentence comes from Carlyle's first review essay, it seems no longer very accurate to speak of his essay style as "impersonal."

The last substantial review essay before *Sartor* was again on Jean Paul. It is popularly known as "Jean Paul Friedrich Richter Again," despite the fact that "Again" did not appear in the original title in the *Foreign Review*. One might think the case for Jean Paul sufficiently proven by this time, but Carlyle knew otherwise; and, regrettably, today we must admit that even the labors of Carlyle failed to make Jean Paul the household word his advocate felt the name should become in English-speaking countries. Of Carlyle we cannot in all conscience ask more. If his efforts failed to bring Jean Paul into English hearts, the fault lies not in the sincerity or vigor with which he stated the case. The last Jean Paul essay is a distinguished example. In it Carlyle presents a brief for Jean Paul so extensive, so detailed, so sympathetic, so ingeniously constructed that, next to *Sartor*, there is nothing quite equal to it in his writings up to 1832.

"Jean Paul Friedrich Richter Again" is in many respects a miniature *Sartor Resartus*. A sixty-four page essay in the standard edition, it begins with an eight-page introductory section setting forth the author's intentions. There follow then thirty-six pages of biography, including substantial portions of translation from Jean Paul's autobiography. The essay concludes with twenty pages of criticism of Jean Paul's literary works. The structure in main outlines, then, is tripartite. In the style of the essay, we have on display most of the elements that mark *Sartor Resartus*. The situation and attitudes are those of Carlyle's role as the Voice of Germany, the role of editor-translator and advocate, the emphasis on biography in the central section, criticism by the threefold method, and even the stylistic traits that largely determine that most elusive of qualities, tone. These are foreign-language foregrounding, the expanded metaphor, and self-quotation.

First, the structure. The essay is divided into three parts. In the first Carlyle introduces through elaborate analogies the need for renewed consideration of Jean Paul, proceeding again to anticipate and answer objections raised against him. In part two he takes the reader deep into the biography of Jean Paul with abundant quotations from Jean Paul's autobiography, some of them almost as cryptic as the autobiographical notations left by Teufelsdröckh. They include translations of maxims from Jean Paul's *"Andachtsbuch* (Book of Devotion)" as well as from the autobiography, *Wahrheit aus Jean Pauls Leben,*[48] and even such matters as the "Advertisement" Jean Paul circulated on the conclusion of his "clothes martyrdom." In part three Carlyle examines Jean Paul's literary attainments and their application to contemporary problems. The three parts progress from consideration of the garment to the body and finally to the soul of the phenomenon Jean Paul and his works.

Carlyle makes his procedure plain early in the essay by pointing out just what his procedure is: "So much for the dress or vehicle of Richter's thoughts: now let it only be remembered farther, that the thoughts themselves are often of the most abstruse description." The externals are merely preliminary: "It does not appear that Richter's life,

---

[48] The title was intended by Jean Paul to mock Goethe's autobiography, *Dichtung und Wahrheit aus meinem Leben.* Carlyle appreciated the joke, for he knew *Dichtung and Wahrheit,* admired its frank, confessional tone, and had used it for the writing of his preface to *Wilhelm Meister.*

externally considered, differed much in general character from other literary lives." "Nevertheless in looking over those Sixty Volumes of his, we feel as if Richter's history must have another, much deeper interest and worth, than outward incidents could impart to it." Finally, still in part one: "He shows himself a man . . . in whom Philosophy and Poetry are not only reconciled, but blended together into a purer essence, into Religion." One of the telling and Sartorian features of the essay is the frequent pointing of direction, which always turns out to lie in deeper penetration. First the garment (dress or vehicle of Jean Paul's thought), then the body (the outer and the inner man), and lastly the soul (the purer essence). Carlyle's aesthetic and critical principles are being put into practice.

A number of stylistic devices aid in pointing the direction of the essay and in imparting a distinctively Carlylean flavor. He had in the essays already found ways of channelling his naturally metaphorical turn of mind into his style. In the 1828 "German Playwrights" he succeeded in sustaining an analogy between playwrights and "any other wright whatever" for an entire essay—or, more properly, sustaining an analogy between playwriting and mechanical construction. Thereby he hammered home the point that the playwrights under consideration—Grillparzer, Müllner, and Klingemann—are mere technicians, constructing their engines with a certain mechanical ingenuity but certainly not creating poetry.[49] A similar capacity to sustain analogy over an extensive prose passage distinguishes this final Jean Paul essay. Just as Carlyle begins *Sartor* by taking a metaphor, expanding, renewing, and ultimately exhausting it, so in the initial two pages of the Jean Paul essay he seizes upon the way in which the fame of a celebrated man moves from place to place. He contrasts the slow adoption of Jean Paul in England with the swifter

[49] *Works,* xxvi, 355–356. Carlyle has been roundly criticized for his underrating of Grillparzer in this essay. See John C. Blankenagel, "Carlyle as a Critic of Grillparzer," *PMLA,* xlii (1927), 1027–1035. The attack on mechanism also lies at the heart of "Signs of the Times."

acceptance won by men of science. The exceptions among literary men—Goethe, Cervantes—merely prove the rule. He concludes that slow acceptance is preferable to too-rapid—all the while keeping in the reader's mind the idea of transportation, conveyance from one place to another—and he depicts the horrors that lie in wait for the literary man who wins too easy an acceptance. For these are "Bacchus-festivals" that turn out to be "pseudo-Bacchanalia, and end in directly the inverse of Orgies! Drawn by his team of lions, the jolly god advances as a real god, with all his thyrsi, cymbals, phallophori, and Maenadic women; the air, the earth is giddy with their clangour, their Evohes: but, alas, in a little while, the lion-team shows long ears, and becomes too clearly an ass-team in lion-skins; the Maenads wheel round in amazement; and then the jolly god, dragged from his chariot, is trodden into the kennels as a drunk mortal" (*Works*, xxvii, 97). Much of the force of the foregoing is lost without the full density of its context, but this is part of the difficulty of ever detaching anything from a passage Carlyle wrote, because he wove his prose so tightly. The passage cited constitutes a metaphorical expansion subordinate to the central metaphor that dominates the passage of more than three thousand words. The whole passage plays on the idea of transport—conveying the fame of a literary man from one country to another. Secondarily Carlyle develops the picture of the factitious fame of an inferior literary figure drawn by a lion-team that proves to be an ass-team. The metaphors spin off from the main metaphor to circle satellite-like around the parent planet. Thus metaphor becomes analogy, as point after point is brought into play and correspondence after correspondence is made to cast its light, sometimes flattering, sometimes lurid, on the main subject.[50]

[50] For a conventional treatment of Carlyle's metaphors see Mary B. Deaton, "Thomas Carlyle's Use of Metaphor," *College English*, v (1944), 314–318; for a more suggestive discussion see Robert Louis Peters, "Some Illustrations of Carlyle's Symbolist Imagery," *Victorian Newsletter*, No. 16 (1959), pp. 31–34.

Equally Carlylean as a feature of the essay style as seen in "Jean Paul Friedrich Richter Again" is Carlyle's inveterate foregrounding. Much of what has been singled out for years as characteristic of Carlyle's style comes under the general heading of the useful term *foregrounding*. Foregrounding means heightened or intensified language; it is a common characteristic of poetry.[51] One reason Carlyle's prose approaches so nearly the condition of poetry is that it is heavily foregrounded, perhaps the most heavily foregrounded of English prose styles. Curiously, his poetry is very unforegrounded. Most of the numerous ways in which language can be foregrounded are employed by Carlyle: inversions, italics, punctuation, unusual word choice, and the like. They are not unique with Carlyle, although he relies very heavily on them. In the essays he developed yet another device of foregrounding all his own. We can call this device foreign-language foregrounding. The origin goes back to his earliest work, the essays for the *Philosophical Journal,* in which the nature of his task as editor-translator demanded from time to time the insertion of the foreign-language original as a means of clarifying his translation. It was a kind of inadvertent foregrounding. In the Joanna Baillie essay Carlyle amplified his method somewhat. In *Schiller,* both in the main text and in the appendices, he made yet greater use of foreign-language foregrounding, although still principally for explanation. In *Meister* and in *German Romance* the habit grows, although occasionally there he casts the explanation in the form of a footnote. But in the periodical essays

[51] I have borrowed the term *foregrounding* from Prague School linguistic theory without meaning to imply at the same time any special agreement with the theory as such. The term is used by Bohuslav Havránek, "The Functional Differentiation of the Standard Language," in *A Prague School Reader on Esthetics, Literary Structure, and Style,* ed. and trans. Paul L. Garvin (Washington, 1955), p. 10. Havránek defines foregrounding as "the use of the language in such a way that this use itself attracts attention and is perceived as uncommon." See also the articles in the same collection by Jan Mukarovský.

he sees the possibilities inherent in juxtaposing foreign-language terms with the translations, and he uses such juxtaposition to attain maximum foregrounding. Nowhere is this more evident than in the final Jean Paul essay, unless it be in Carlyle's glittering 1829 essay "Novalis." There foregrounding results in an orgy of parentheses, dashes, italics, and hyphens, for these are the inevitable (and no doubt to Carlyle not unwelcome) concomitants of extensive foreign-language foregrounding. Consider, for example, the following excerpts from "Novalis," in which Carlyle, happily for his foregrounding penchant, has before him the fragments and apophthegms of the man he called the "German Pascal":

[From the *Fragmente*]
"It depends only on the weakness of our organs and of our self-excitement (*Selbstberührung*), that we do not see ourselves in a Fairy-world. All Fabulous Tales (*Mährchen*) are merely dreams of that home world, which is everywhere and no where."
"Spinoza is a God-intoxicated man (*Gott-trunkener Mensch*)."

[*From Das allgemeine Brouillon*]
"[The Bible's] two main divisions, also, are genuine grand-historical divisions (*ächt gross-historisch*). For in every grand-historical compartment (*Glied*), the grand history must lie, as it were, symbolically re-created (*verjüngt*, made young again)." (*Works*, xxvii, 40, 42)

"Novalis" bristles with such passages, and whatever can be said for Carlyle's method aiding the reader, much more can be said by way of his method frequently confusing and inhibiting the reader. Either it is an error (and to some readers, I suppose, it unquestionably is), or Carlyle has adopted his method consciously for a particular effect. Need we inquire which is the case?

In the final Jean Paul essay Carlyle uses substantial

amounts of foreign-language foregrounding in conjunction, of course, with his frequent quotations, which in turn demand translation as well. One such is the following passage from Jean Paul's autobiography:

> "In the future Literary History of our hero, it will become doubtful whether he was not born more for Philosophy than for Poetry. In earliest times, the word *Weltweisheit* (Philosophy, *World-wisdom*),—yet also another word, *Morgenland* (East, *Morning-land*),—was to me an open Heaven's-gate, through which I looked-in over long, long gardens of joy." (*Works,* xxvii, 111)

Carlyle is no longer foregrounding titles only, which is after all a necessary and conventional device, but words and phrases he wishes to emphasize: "a divine genius (*Gottgenius*)," "bestowed on him (*aufdrückte*)," "evening meal (*Vesperessen*)," and many more. Any sort of foregrounding gives emphasis and intensity. When one foregrounds a foreign language, as Carlyle does, it gives in addition another light on meaning and paradoxically at the same time a suggestion of mystery and obscurity. It becomes in itself a symbol, standing for one thing, suggesting much more. Carlyle uses it as a means of uniting the proximate and the distant, the finite and the infinite. Although we see it here in conjunction with Jean Paul, it is different from anything Jean Paul himself did.[52]

Metaphor (with countermetaphor) and foreign-language foregrounding are two of the three most Carlylean stylistic elements discernible in the last Jean Paul essay. The third

[52] I do not think it is possible to argue that Carlyle cited the foreign language for purposes of reference, to supply his readers with documentation. Carlyle was not a scholar: he fails to identify sources more often than he supplies them. Moreover, scholarship does not explain a passage like the following in which only the last phrase is given in the original although all of the sentence is a translation: " '. . . and the pit applauds and demands with enthusiasm the repetition of these disgusting ineptitudes (*de ces dégoutantes platitudes*)' " (*Works,* xxvi, 454—"Voltaire").

is a feature I have called self-quotation. Its importance for style and structure can hardly be over-estimated, for it is a means of controlling point of view without which *Sartor Resartus* is unthinkable. Conventionally, point of view can be shifted by changing narrators, or by changing focus from one character to another, by including written materials theoretically outside the author's control, such as letters and diaries, by dialogue, and perhaps other means. Many of the conventional means of effecting a change in point of view are eschewed or only scantily explored by Carlyle in *Sartor;* and yet *Sartor* has a pronounced variety in point of view. The means Carlyle wholeheartedly embraces to change point of view is the use of theoretically extrinsic material. Since all the material of a novel is in fact the author's own, he is always quoting from himself when he introduces outside material. The difference between Carlyle and other writers is the extent to which he relies on citation from outside material, his inordinate quotation from documents. The closest parallel is, of course, Jean Paul, but Carlyle carries his use of quotation beyond Jean Paul's. As a structural and stylistic principle, self-quotation is developed in the periodical essays.

The earliest instance of Carlyle's self-quotation occurs, fittingly enough, in the first Jean Paul review essay. There Carlyle includes a sample of Jean Paul's style from his own translation of *Fixlein* in *German Romance*.[53] He does not identify the source of the translation, so it might appear that it had been done for the work at hand. By "State of German Literature" the process has become more sophisticated. There Carlyle includes portions of his *Meister* translation.[54] In his essay "Goethe" (1828) he includes portions of his translation of *Meister* and passages from his critical preface to *Meister*. Again the source remains unidentified, but this time he does not let it stand without comment. He speaks of the author of it, however,

[53] *Works,* xxvi, 23–24.
[54] Ibid., xxvi, 62–63.

in the third person, as though it were someone other than the present author:

"It [i.e. the passage to be quoted] is written by a professed admirer of Goethe; nay, as might almost seem, by a grateful learner, whom he had taught, whom he had helped to lead out of spiritual obstruction, into peace and light. Making due allowance for all this, there is little in the paper that we object to." Following the quotation, he comments: "Considered as a transient far-off view of Goethe in his personal character, all this, from the writer's peculiar point of vision, may have its true grounds, and wears at least the aspect of sincerity" (*Works,* xxvi, 246, 249).

Now this kind of self-quotation represents a development by Carlyle of far-reaching importance for *Sartor* and his entire subsequent writing. The man who could not create character in the conventional novelistic sense, whose dialogue is notably wooden, whose plots are little more than romantic claptrap, has nevertheless devised a means of altering pace, increasing dimensions, illuminating character, changing focus—all by the use of materials which he can truly control. Already in the treatment of his quotation from his earlier essay on Goethe the tone of the Editor is beginning to appear. The same applies to the most extensive instance of self-quotation in the essays, which occurs appropriately in the last Jean Paul essay. When Carlyle turns in the essay from Jean Paul's biography to an examination of his works, he makes the transition by quoting from his own writing on Jean Paul for no fewer than five pages. And he takes as quotation the very passage cited above from the Jean Paul preface in *German Romance:* " 'The first aspect of these peculiarities,' says one of Richter's English critics, 'cannot prepossess us in his favour' "; and so on, from the apparent denunciation of Jean Paul's style and structure to the encomia of these same that we have previously considered. To speak, therefore, of the style of the last Jean Paul essay is to speak in part of the style of the first, for the first is liberally contained in the last.

The effect of all this self-quotation is to engage Carlyle in a dialogue with himself. Most frequently he chooses an enthusiastic passage from his earlier writing, holding it out at arm's length as it were, offering it as a specimen of another man's opinion for the reader to consider. The method enforces two voices, the more impassioned being always that in the quoted material, the more sedate always that of the writer at hand. Editor and Teufelsdröckh are merely waiting to be born.

Although variety of viewpoint was Carlyle's primary purpose in self-quotation, there may have been a secondary purpose as well, having to do with Carlyle's mission as the Voice of Germany. By appearing to quote from a number of other authorities, Carlyle conveys the impression that the field of German studies is large. The reader assumes that the various translations and commentaries come from different hands and that there is a widespread interest among cultivated people in German letters. As though to confirm this view, Carlyle in his Goethe essay, after including the translation from his own *Wilhelm Meister*, comments: "Here, however, we must terminate our pilferings or open robberies, and bring these straggling lucubrations to a close." We can now smile with Carlyle, knowing that it was robbery from himself, but such intelligence was denied the bulk of his readers, and it was necessary for Carlyle's purposes that it be. Whatever his initial aim in creating his multiple voices, the method proved useful when he came to write *Sartor*.

What the examination of Carlyle as the Voice of Germany has shown can be briefly summarized. Most of the essays were on German topics; Carlyle conceived of himself as both scout and guard of things German for the British public.[55] In the essays the biography of authors

[55] The metaphor is close to Carlyle's own: "For not only are we stationed on the coast of the country, as watchers and spials,

looms large; and his own biographical precepts dictate his practice: he wants to reach the inner man. Carlyle's aesthetic convictions—art as the relevation of the Divine Idea–Open Secret, the poet as prophet and seer, the need for organic form, the nature of allegorical symbolism, and the special modern suitability of the *Märchen*—inform the essays and direct us to the aesthetic that underlies *Sartor.* The structural principles, especially the three-part division of the most accomplished essays, arise from aesthetic and critical convictions reinforced by the role he adopted—editor-translator of German works—and intensified by some far-reaching stylistic devices—the expanded metaphor, foreign-language foregrounding, and self-quotation. His syntax has become increasingly convoluted, although not obscure; the sentences release themselves outward with ever-increasing vitality. His language shows the effects of concentration on the German idiom and on German philosophy and the effects of the release of an energetically figurative and allusive turn of mind. The literary ingredients of *Sartor,* then, are at hand, awaiting only the opportunity to come together in a single work.

There is, of course, an essential difference between any of the essays and *Sartor,* even between the last Jean Paul essay and *Sartor.* That difference is that *Sartor* is fiction. Whatever methods, approaches, stylistic elements the essays have in common with *Sartor*—and they have a great many—they are, after all, essays on factual subjects: there was a Goethe, a Schiller, a Tieck, and a Jean Paul, and they did in fact write the works Carlyle reviews in the essays. This may appear to be both obvious and trivial, but it is an important critical point. Thus, in a recent listing of forthcoming books from an American publisher,

---

to report whatsoever remarkable thing becomes visible in the distance; but we stand there also as a sort of Tide-waiters and Preventive-service men, to contend, with our utmost vigour, that no improper article be landed" (*Works,* xxvi, 394—"German Playwrights").

Sartor Resartus appears under the heading "Essays and Belles Lettres." However much *Sartor* grows out of the essays, and however much of discursive essay-like material it contains, it is simply not an essay; and while it is literally *belles lettres* the genre term misleads. In another listing, this a study of books read in the nineteenth century, *Sartor* has been classified under "Miscellaneous," an improvement perhaps over "Essays," but only because it tells us nothing at all rather than telling what is untrue. The form and content of Sartor *is* dependent on Carlyle's essays and miscellaneous writings, but that dependence is the kind that any work of art has on the raw material of an author's experience and on the development of his writing skill. Writing is writing, but essays are still not novels. Yet *Sartor* is a work of fiction. I say this not in defiance of literary kinds, whatever residual force that concept may have, but indeed in support of it. Much as it may wrench the definition of the novel to include *Sartor,* even more does it violate definitions of other literary kinds to include *Sartor* there. More positively, there are clear affirmative reasons for calling *Sartor* a novel, and these will become apparent as we examine *Sartor* itself.

# III

Composition
1830–1831

To decipher and represent the *genesis* of this extraordinary Production, and what was the Author's state of mind in producing it; to *see,* with dim common eyes, what the [author], with inspired poetic eyes, then saw; and paint to oneself the thick-coming shapes and many-coloured splendours of his "Prospero's Grotto," at that hour: this were what we could call complete criticism and commentary; what D. T. is far from having done, and ought to fall on his face, and confess that he can never do.

—THOMAS CARLYLE

Circumstances immediately surrounding the composition of a work of literature, when known, frequently provide insights not otherwise available. The timely encounter with another work or idea, or a political event in the world at large, may be the impetus that sets an author writing and may dictate the direction his work takes. In other cases the circumstances at the time of composition may have only limited relevance. Possibilities of misestimation either way are legion. Overestimation of factors surrounding the composition of *Sartor,* for example, can lead to the notion that Carlyle's discussion with Francis Jeffrey on the latter's September 1830 visit to Craigenputtock issued in *Sartor,* or that Carlyle's reading of the June 1830 *Fraser's* gave him the whole idea for the book, or that John Carlyle's description of German life produced the "framework" for *Sartor*—all of these have been seriously advanced. By contrast, I have tried to show that Carlyle's methods and ideas in *Sartor* are to be sought in his work of the previous decade and that his successes in the essays as well as his failures in the early fiction were necessary undertakings in the disciplining of his literary skill and imagination before *Sartor* could be written. Still, the conditions under which *Sartor* was written have an undeniable relevance to the kind of book that emerged and to the very fact that Carlyle wrote it at all. Some of these conditions merely served to call to mind ideas and methods long familiar to Carlyle; others helped point the direction for Carlyle to take in writing *Sartor*.

JEFFREY, JOHN, AND "BLACKWOOD'S"

Carlyle's references to a *"Kunstwerk* of my own" up to 1827 must be taken, insofar as they are intended for a particular work, to apply to "Wotton Reinfred," the essential outline of which Carlyle drew up in 1822. In a broader sense, of course, allusions to a work of his own refer generally to Carlyle's desire to write something original, neither scientific and biographical hackwork nor even reviews, original as these latter were. When Carlyle laid "Wotton" aside in 1827, he did not also lay aside his desire to write a work truly on his own. Rather, with "Wotton" died the expectation that the work could be in the form of a romantic novel. From 1827 to 1830 Carlyle's allusions to an original work are not specific as to form. To his brother John he wrote in 1828 that, once the necessary work was done in fitting up Craigenputtock, "I shall have leisure to cease *reviewing* a little, and try to give Work for reviewing." At the same time he wrote to Goethe's secretary Eckermann: "I confess I begin to grow tired of *Reviewing;* but whether there is any force in me to produce an original work is a question which I am still agitating, and, I believe, shall ever [*sic*] leave at rest, till I have practically tried,—and too probably got answer in the negative."[1]

---

[1] *Letters*, I, 178; William A. Speck, "New Letters of Carlyle to Eckermann," *Yale Review*, xv (1926), 740.

Carlyle was still agitating the question of his talent for original work a year later, when he wrote of himself to Goethe: "I am still but an Essayist, and longing more than ever to be a Writer in a far better sense." A month later, in December 1829, he wrote to Goethe: "Were this 'Historical View' [the 'History of German Literature'] once off my hands, I still purpose to try something infinitely greater! Alas, alas! the huge formless Chaos is here, but no creative voice to say, 'Let there be Light,' and make it into a world."[2] Actually Carlyle must have had the first glimmerings of his course, for at almost exactly the same time he wrote to John Wilson, the "Christopher North" of *Blackwood's:* "I have some thoughts of beginning to prophesy next year, if I prosper; that seems the best style, could one strike into it rightly."[3]

With Carlyle's financial help John Carlyle had gone to Germany in the fall of 1827 for further medical study. Carlyle, who hoped to be able to visit Goethe in Weimar, followed John's adventures in his imagination:

> I am trying sometimes to follow you with my imagination, up the fair *Rheingau,* and through the *Krönungsstadt,* on to your home in München; but it will not do; for all that region is to me unpeopled space. Where art, thou, Jack, this very night? Surrounded by what aproned *Kellners,* or well-booted *Schwagers,* or whiskered *Mautbeamters,* or other men of strange speech, art thou living and looking even now while I write? (*Letters,* I, 86)

At Carlyle's urging, John sought out such distinguished men as Schlegel and Schelling, and presumably he responded to the many questions Carlyle asked him about Germany. Carlyle requested John to investigate the state of education in Germany; but above all he asked, "How does the social machine work?" John's letters may have

[2] *Correspondence between Goethe and Carlyle,* pp. 158, 163.

[3] Gordon, *"Christopher North,"* II, 151.

supplied Carlyle with some information on Germany that went into *Sartor*. After his return in 1829 he told Carlyle of his visits to the Schelling Club in Munich. He later immodestly claimed that "the framework of *Sartor* was suggested by what I used to tell him of my experiences in Germany." The inapplicability of John's claim to *Sartor* is demonstrated by his explanation of what those experiences were: "There was a Schelling Club, which Schelling himself used to visit (in Munich). It was devoted to beer, tobacco and philosophy. I used to amuse my brother remembering their free and often wild speculative talk; and *Sartor* recalls his comments and laughter."[4] Carlyle may well have used some of John's reminiscences for scenes and details in *Sartor,* but to conceive of the scenes in the *Grüne Gans* as the "framework of *Sartor*" is to let desire overpower reason. There are too many echoes in *Sartor* of Carlyle's extensive reading and writing on German subjects to credit John's adventures with more than a small share in forming Carlyle's picture of Germany.

While writing the "History of German Literature" in the first half of 1830, Carlyle entertained the idea of doing a book on Luther. On the proceeds from his "History" he hoped to go to Weimar to write "Luther," both because of the availability of materials in Germany and the presence of Goethe in Weimar. Carlyle coresponded frequently with Goethe, who was now sending him the final edition of his work as the volumes appeared. One interesting inclusion, which may have been suggestive to Carlyle, has not been noted. Goethe sent Carlyle a copy of his *Farbenlehre,* and he included instructions on how to read it and a description of its order.[5] The *Farbenlehre,* he said, was in two parts, the first didactic-polemic, the second historical. Goethe urged Carlyle to read the historical part first, then to turn to the didactic. The first

[4] Moncure Conway, *Thomas Carlyle* (New York, 1881), p. 71. See also Wilson, *Carlyle to "The French Revolution,"* pp. 183–184.
[5] *Correspondence between Goethe and Carlyle,* pp. 177–178.

draft of *Sartor,* containing the present Book One and some
of Book Two, could also be described as didactic-polemic
and historical. It too is a *Lehre,* or teaching—a *Kleider-
lehre.* Carlyle, the former student of science and thrice
unsuccessful applicant for university professorships, would
have examined Goethe's *Farbenlehre* sympathetically as a
learned work by a literary man. With equal sympathy and
possibly greater interest, Carlyle would have read two
works by Ludwig Wachler that Goethe sent him, a German
literary history and a monograph titled *Über Werden und
Wirken der Literatur.* From the monograph, as other commentators have noted, Carlyle borrowed the subtitle of
Teufelsdröckh's book, *Die Kleider, ihr Werden und
Wirken.*[6]

The initial successes Carlyle enjoyed with the leading
reviews had begun to wear thin by 1830. He felt the un-
desirable effects of being labeled a mystic. Moreover, the
first part of the 1830 he devoted to the "History of German
Literature," only to find himself in the summer without
a publisher and obliged to divide his text into articles
in order to realize any money from it. He professed to
his mother not to be overly concerned: "I could write
and will write, something infinitely better, ere long."[7] But
his financial situation was serious. Jeffrey in September
1830 offered to settle an annuity on Carlyle, an offer Carlyle
instantly rejected and always resented. John, now in
London and as destitute as ever, urged Carlyle to submit
material to the new heterodox Tory publication *Fraser's
Magazine.* One piece by Carlyle had already appeared
there in the first six months of 1830. Accordingly, Carlyle

[6] See Harrold's edition of *Sartor,* p. 8n. For Carlyle's use of other
German literary histories see Werner Leopold, "Thomas Carlyle and
Franz Horn," *Journal of English and Germanic Philology,* xxviii
(1929), 215–219. Leopold traces the expressions "Everlasting No"
and "Everlasting Yea" to Franz Horn. See also Leopold's *Die
religiöse Wurzel von Carlyles literarischer Wirksamkeit* (Halle a.
s., 1922).
[7] *Letters,* i, 226.

wrote John: "I have, at your suggestion, *sent* that miserable dud of 'Cruthers and Johnson' [*sic*] to Fraser, with two other Papers: certain abstruse 'Thoughts on History,' and a small scantling of my Fables and Rhymes (or rather one Rhyme 'What is Hope'): you are to correct the Proofs, if there be any printing: 'Cruthers and Johnson' is to be *forthwith* returned to you, if found unsuitable; and the *name* in any case kept *strictly* secret."[8] All of the items cited were eventually printed in *Fraser's.* Carlyle's caution must have stemmed from the fact that he was sending, not his usual essays, but fiction and poetry with which he was himself not altogether happy. But he knew that if any magazine would take it, *Fraser's* would.

At the same time that John Carlyle was offering his brother's early imaginative compositions to *Fraser's,* Carlyle himself sensed that the time had come for him to try something new. The repeated *Sartor*-like entries in the notebooks in 1829–1830 point to a fermentation of ideas that was bound to produce uncommon results. Sometime in the second part of 1829 Carlyle wrote that some day he would do a "good Essay on Metaphors." About March 1830 he entered in his notebooks: "I have now almost done with the Germans. Having seized their opinions, I must turn me to inquire *how* true are they?" In May he advised himself, *"Im Teufel's* [*sic*] *Namen,* get to thy work then!" In the summer of 1830 he asked in his journal what the "idle rich *do* for their wages?" His answer: *"Kill Partridges."* In August he asked, "What is man?" and replied as in *Sartor,* that he is a "Biped that wears Breeches."[9]

---

[8] *Ibid.,* p. 226.

[9] *Two Note Books,* pp. 141, 150, 156, 159, 162–163. Cf. *Sartor,* ii, ii, 99; ii, iv, 129. See Norton's notes throughout *Two Note Books* for further parallels. Entries in the *Note Books* are not always dated, so one can only indicate the approximate time of an entry as it appears between two dated entries.

Carlyle's preoccupation with the partridge-killing aristocracy probably has its origin in his reading of Voltaire. Cf. "Diderot," *Works,* xxviii, 215.

No better expression of what Carlyle was thinking can be found than a letter he wrote to Goethe at the end of August 1830:

> I must forthwith betake me to something more congenial and original: except writing from the heart and if possible to the heart, Life has no other business for me, no other pleasure. When I look at the wonderful Chaos within me, full of natural Supernaturalism, and all manner of Antediluvian fragments; and how the Universe is daily growing more mysterious as well as more august, and the influences from without more heterogeneous and perplexing; I see not well what is to come of it all, and only conjecture from the violence of the fermentation that something strange may come. (*Correspondence between Goethe and Carlyle,* pp. 210–211)

Jeffrey's visit to Craigenputtock in September 1830, with the consequent discussion and arguments Froude tells us Jeffrey and Carlyle had on politics and government,[10] did not so much inspire *Sartor* as confirm that it needed to be written; for Carlyle was clearly already on the verge of something new. Likewise, the importance of the arrival in early September of a "bundle of *Fraser's*" has been sorely misinterpreted and needs to be set right.[11]

In the June 1830 *Fraser's* there had appeared an article attacking the fashionable novels of Bulwer Lytton. Carlyle himself had once offered to Jeffrey a "sort of sally on Fashionable Novels." Basing his argument on the June *Fraser's* and Carlyle's earlier offer to Jeffery, S. B. Liljegren has fashioned a theory that the true germ and first version of *Sartor* was nothing other than what is now the chapter "The Dandiacal Body" in Book Three. While this theory deserves high marks for ingenuity, it collapses in the face

[10] Froude, II, 125–129.

[11] The overinterpretation appears in S. B. Liljegren, "The Origin of *Sartor Resartus,*" *Palaestra,* no. 148 (1925), pp. 400–433. Liljegren, p. 403, also makes the remarkable assertion that "Wotton Reinfred" went "wholly into *Sartor Resartus!*"

of the facts, which clearly argue that the first version was what is now the first third of *Sartor*.[12] Moreover, Liljegren's theory obscures the real importance of the receipt of copies of *Fraser's* on 8 September 1830. The significance of the receipt of *Fraser's* at a time when Carlyle was already contemplating something new lies not in a particular article but in the general nature of *Fraser's* and its spiritual progenitor, *Blackwood's*. The magazine put Carlyle in mind of a kind of writing not suitable for the great reviews. He saw an outlet for truly venturesome work, as his description of *Fraser's* style shows: "A certain quickness, fluency of banter, not excluding sharp insight, and Merry-Andrew Drollery, and even Humour, are available here: however, the grand requisite seems to be Impudence, and a fearless committing of yourself to talk in your Drink."[13]

Fraser's, in but six months, had shown itself to be as impudent and irreverent as *Blackwood's*. The publisher was a Scotsman from Inverness, James Fraser, who appropriately adopted a thistle as the emblem of the magazine he always called after its subtitle, "the 'Town and Country.'" But the guiding spirits behind *Fraser's* were William Maginn, the fiery Irishman formerly of *Black-*

[12] The weaknesses of Liljegren's theory can be quickly summarized: 1) There is no evidence that Carlyle actually wrote the proposed article for Jeffrey. 2) Liljegren does not account for—and even avoids considering—Carlyle's persistent use of "Teufelsdreck" to refer to his manuscript, but it is manifestly unsuitable for the section on dandies. 3) Liljegren does not account for Carlyle's description of the manuscript in the January 1831 letter to John (see below, p. 144). 4) Liljegren seems to believe that the parts of *Sartor* can be interchanged and rearranged with no damage at all to the structure. 5) Liljegren gives three different dates for the receipt of the copies of *Fraser's*, evidently misreading Wilson in two of the three cases, all of which suggests that he did not consult the *Note Books* in which Carlyle makes clear how the copies of *Fraser's* affected him.

[13] *Two Note Books*, p. 170. Carlyle adds: "Literature has nothing to do with this." Later in March 1831 (p. 259) he has a much harsher judgment of *Fraser's*, calling it "a chaotic, fermenting, dunghill heap of compost." At the time he was about to leave London after an unsuccessful attempt to market *Sartor*.

wood's, and Hugh Fraser (no relation to James), after whom it was named. Like *Blackwood's*, which became familiarly known as "Maga," *Fraser's* came to be called "Regina," presumably for its Tory proclivities. Maginn introduced into *Fraser's* a number of features similar to those in *Blackwood's*. *Fraser's*, for example, ran a series called "Horae Gallicae," a direct borrowing from *Blackwood's* "Horae Germanicae" and other "Horae" series. *Fraser's* published comic verse (like Carlyle's "Nimmo"); and it ran a "Gallery of Literary Characters" with text by O. Y. and drawings by Daniel Maclise. Carlyle himself was to be featured in the "Gallery" in 1833. From the start, everything about *Fraser's* suggested daring and experimentation, and, like *Blackwood's*, it was the direct antithesis of Carlyle's chief periodical outlet of the twenties, the *Edinburgh*, which was solid, sober, and very Whig. *Fraser's* was enough like *Blackwood's* to suggest to Carlyle in September 1830 a common paternity for the two. He noted that it was "such a hurly-burly of rhodomontade, punch, loyalty, and Saturnalian Toryism as eye hath not seen. This out-Blackwoods Blackwood. Nevertheless, the thing has its meaning—a kind of wild popular lower comedy, of which John Wilson is the inventor. It may perhaps (for it seems well-adapted to the age) carry down his name to other times, as his most remarkable achievement."[14]

To out-Blackwood Blackwood meant that *Fraser's* contained features as outrageous as *Blackwood's* "Noctes Ambrosianae," "Letters from the Lakes," and "Horae Germanicae," all of which originated in the early eighteen-twenties, and some of which were still appearing (the "Noctes" ran to 1835). It is well known that not long after Carlyle settled in Edinburgh he read all the back issues of the *Edinburgh* (founded 1802);[15] he also appears

[14] *Two Note Books*, p. 170. Carlyle's prediction has not really been borne out, but perhaps the *Fraser's* style has helped to carry down Carlyle's own name to other times.

[15] Shine, *Carlyle's Early Reading*, pp. 27, 67.

to have read *Blackwood's* from its beginning in 1817. There is record of his bemusement with the scandal of the "Chaldee Manuscript," an early foreshadowing of the manner of the "Noctes" and other series.[16] His own name appeared in the "Noctes" in 1824 as the translator of *Meister* and again in 1827 as a member of the assembled convivial group itself. He knew John Wilson well enough to appeal to him for a recommendation for a university position in 1828. The ramifications of Carlyle's familiarity with *Blackwood's* have never been explored, although some preliminary suggestions have been made. The sometimes overprotesting insistence by Froude that Carlyle's manner was entirely the product of "native sources" would have had a good deal to commend it had he pointed to the comic tradition of *Blackwood's* rather than to the Annandale speech of Carlyle's father. The *Blackwood's* manner has some remarkably suggestive points of similarity with *Sartor*.

The *Blackwood's* style came about as the result of group association rather than individual inspiration.[17] Wilson, Maginn, Lockhart, and Gillies were the chief participants in the Edinburgh social life that produced *Blackwood's*. Most of them were also members of the Dilettanti, a convivial drinking association that met in Young's Tavern in High Street, Edinburgh, and most of their *Blackwood's* efforts were essentially re-creations of their meetings. But what set the tone of *Blackwood's* for more than a decade was the publication of the "Chaldee Manuscript" in the 1817 forerunner of the magazine. The "Manuscript," which was purported, of course, to be genuine, was a scurrilous attack in Biblical language upon the Whigs. It rocked Edinburgh, and *Blackwood's* presses were stopped after two

---

[16] *Early Letters,* I, 130–131, 133–134.
[17] There is no single history of *Blackwood's Magazine,* although much valuable information appears in Mrs. [Margaret] Oliphant, *Annals of a Publishing House: William Blackwood and his Sons,* 2 vols. (London, 1897); A. L. Strout, *A Bibliography of Articles in Blackwood's Magazine,* 1817–1825 (Lubbock, Tex., 1959); and in the introduction to Mackenzie's edition of *Noctes Ambrosianae.*

hundred copies, but not soon enough to alter the direction in which *Blackwood's* moved. After the *succès de scandale* of the "Manuscript" the *Blackwood's* circle began a number of series that ultimately ran for years. The earliest of these was "Christopher in the Tent," the most significant of the ante-Noctes series. It began on 12 August 1819, a day of consequence for gentlemen because it was the first day for grouse-shooting under British game laws. The "Tent" featured most of the principals of the later more celebrated "Noctes Ambrosianae," including Dr. Morris, William Wastle, Morgan Odoherty, the "Ettrick Shepherd" (James Hogg), Timothy Tickler, the Sage Kempferhausen, and, after 1819, Christopher North himself. Pseudonymity was the hallmark of the *Blackwood's* series. More remarkable, and evident as early as the "Tent" series, is the frequency of invented characters that appear in company with actual persons. These fictitious people were sometimes composite figures that correspond to no single person, but often they were purely comic *personae,* such as Kempferhausen for R. P. Gillies and North for John Wilson. On inspired occasion they were actual persons who, however, bore no resemblance to their projections in *Blackwood's.* Such was Dr. Scott, the Odontist of Glasgow. The Odontist appears to have had no literary talents whatever, but the *Blackwood's* group repeatedly attributed literary works and brilliant sayings to him, so that he enjoyed a minor Edinburgh celebrity in defiance of any evidence of his merits. Christopher North took on larger dimensions, too, becoming the titular editor of *Blackwood's* and being used more or less indiscriminately by contributors, although John Wilson always used North more than the others and retained certain proprietary rights over him. Later the name came to be associated almost exclusively with Wilson. The names chosen for the imaginary figures were often ingenious, and frequently they were but half-concealed jokes in themselves. Kempferhausen is perhaps the least inspired, but Tickler and Wastle (Scots for a kind of bread) suggest more, and Dr. Berzelius Pendragon was justified in *Black-wood's* by the gloss of his surname as Pen-drag-on.

With the founding of the "Noctes Ambrosianae" series in March 1822, the *Blackwood's* series began adding other figures to the roster of visitors to Christopher North, who was conceived in the "Noctes" as holding court for Edinburgh wits. Feldborg, the Danish counterpart of the German Kempferhausen and a principal player in the "Horae Danicae," began appearing, as did Baron Frederick von Lauerwinkel and his companions from the "Letters from the Lakes" series, Dr. Ulrick Sternstare and Professor Gunthred Bumgroschen, who, in terms of *Sartor*, is perhaps the most intriguing of all. Bumgroschen wrote the "Urstoffe der Allgemeine [*sic*] Sparsamkeit, oder Einleitung zur ed-lere [*sic*] Wissenschaft der Aschensiebungslehre" ("The Original Materials of General Thrift, or Introduction to the Noble Science of the Study of Cinder Sifting").[18] The title, like the author Bumgroschen himself, was entirely fictitious. By the time of the "Noctes" the practice of creating authors and titles was firmly established. As early as "Christopher in the Tent" the *Blackwood's* authors showed a strong inclination to create not only comic characters but comic book titles as well. One of the most celebrated of these, from the "Tent" series, was *Peter's Letters to His Kinsfolk*, a book full of humorous observations on Edinburgh life, including a number of passages on dandyism that may have been suggestive to Carlyle.[19] The case

[18] These similarities are briefly noted in Alan Lang Strout, "Writers on German Literature in Blackwood's Magazine, with a footnote on Thomas Carlyle," *The Library*, ix, 5th s. (1954), 35–44. Earlier there was also a passing reference in Gilbert Macbeth, *John Gibson Lockhart: A Critical Study*, Univ. of Illinois Studies in Language and Literature, vol. xlii (Urbana, 1935), p. 151.

[19] *Peter's Letters to His Kinsfolk* (2nd. ed., Edinburgh, 1819). Carlyle's preoccupation with the Dandy would, of course, have received additional immediate stimulation from the article in the 1830 *Fraser's* on Bulwer Lytton. The phenomenon of the Dandy in the life of the times and later is ably explored by Ellen Moers, *The Dandy: Brummel to Beerbohm* (London, 1960).

of *Peter's Letters* is typical of *Blackwood's* sense of humor. The title first appears simply as a comic play on Scott's *Paul's Letters to His Kinsfolk* (1815), which described visits to the lowlands. The *Blackwood's* jesters invented a work published in Aberystwyth that contained humorous observations in the vein of *Paul's Letters*, but in this case on life in Edinburgh itself. Like other imaginary books it was duly reviewed in the pages of *Blackwood's*. Lockhart seems to have invented *Peter's Letters*, but in any case the response was so strong that he eventually wrote it, and then, to maintain the fiction, *Blackwood's* issued it in Edinburgh as a second edition! Other imaginary works abound in the various series in *Blackwood's*. The Sage Kempferhausen, in one of the "Tent" numbers, is said to have read an essay on the character and manner of the Tyrolese. The first of the "Letters from the Lakes" (January 1819) purports to be a translation from the German of Kempferhausen, and Dr. Sternstare also contributed letters alleged to be translated in *Blackwood's*.

The *Blackwood's* group, in addition to creating imaginary characters and imaginary literary works, developed a style of alluding to public figures by symbolic or suggestive names. Much of this humor was too parochial to survive, but Lockhart's jeering epithet "Cockney School" of poets has won a permanent place, even if we have all forgotten the "Leg of Mutton School." Carlyle readily adopted both the Cockney and the *Edinburgh's* Lake School terms and used them liberally in his letters and increasingly in his public writings.[20] *Blackwood's* also cre-

---

It is interesting to speculate on the possibility of influence on Carlyle of some of the now obscure Scottish novels and novelists of the period, especially John Galt, James Hogg, and D. M. Moir, the latter two members of the *Blackwood's* circle. There seems to have been a number of auto-biographical novels, some using interpolated documents such as Moir's *Life of Mansie Waugh, Tailor in Dalkeith* (1828); but there is scant record of Carlyle's familiarity with many of these.

[20] Cf. Teufelsdröckh's "Satanic School" in *Sartor*, II, vi–viii.

ated names for publishers and their friends, especially the transplanted Scotsmen in England like Murray (who was later to refuse to print *Sartor*), who was called the "Emperor of the West," and Longman (who was also to reject *Sartor*), who was known as "The Divan." These references were also connected with the publishers' London locations, centers of literary activity. The *Blackwood's* group possessed a considerable linguistic inventiveness, which shows itself in titles and jokes as well as in names and epithets. The obsession with Latin as a serio-comic language, which Carlyle shared, issued in such titles as "Metricum Symposium," "Carmen Diabolicum," adaptations such as "Nihil Germanici a se alienum" (said of Kempferhausen), and of course the "Noctes Ambrosianae" itself.

The points of similarity between *Blackwood's* and *Sartor* are striking, but there are some fundamental differences too. What distinguishes the *Blackwood's* manner from Carlyle's is the very diffuseness of it all. *Blackwood's* was always a group endeavor; it gained its whole impetus from the bantering good times of a group of Edinburgh wits. When that disintegrated, so did *Blackwood's*. Even at its best it condemned itself to oblivion by the intense personalness of the associations. The multiplicity of hands inevitably resulted in a multiplicity of styles; the pressures of monthly publication inevitably resulted in considerable variation, repetition, maundering, and inconsistency. At times the humor verges on the sophomoric and the tasteless. The *Blackwood's* series are truly an *olla podrida;* when the ingredients are right, it is a savory dish, but when wrong, it is the literal translation of that term.

Because of the transiency of much of the material and the fact that it stretches over a period of years, there is nothing in *Blackwood's* approaching the intensity of a single work. Nor does *Blackwood's,* for all its political concern, grapple very seriously with political or philosophic questions. Maginn's "Maxims of Odoherty," for example, are sometimes no better than his No. 6: "A Whig is an Ass." Carlyle was surely right in calling this manner a "kind of popular lower comedy"; but it does have occasional wit and brilliance. The parody of Wordsworth—"My heart leaps up when I behold / A bailiff in the street"—still amuses. And we have seen a number of comic features that Carlyle was not above employing on his own, whatever his source for them: the conception of the ludicrous German with his mystic lucubrations, the play on names, the fertile invention of titles of books and documents, and sometimes the creation of the books themselves, the *persona* of an editor—these are features of *Blackwood's* that found a loftier place in *Sartor Resartus* and that have no parallel in other contemporary writing, except of course for *Blackwood's*-inspired periodicals like *Fraser's*. *Fraser's*, with its "quickness, fluency of banter . . . sharp insight . . . and even Humour," took on the mantle of this aspect of *Blackwood's*, even though *Blackwood's* continued to be published—as it is today, a longevity record matched only by one of its sister publications, the *Quarterly Review*. But literary leadership was passing to London, as were Scottish writers and publishers themselves. Lockhart left *Blackwood's* in 1826 to edit the *Quarterly Review* and, in the words of a later editor of the "Noctes," "much of the personal sarcasm of *Blackwood's* left with him." Maginn, in turn, left in 1829 or 1830 and became the editor of *Fraser's*. In place of Christopher North, the "editor" of *Blackwood's*, Maginn invented "Oliver Yorke" as the "editor" of *Fraser's*, a *persona* used by other contributors to the periodical, including Carlyle, who introduced Yorke to good effect into "Peter Nimmo" and subsequently into his translation of Goethe's "*Märchen*," and even into *Sartor*.

When Carlyle received copies of the first six months of *Fraser's* in September 1830, its significance was not lost on him, both as an impudent and daring newcomer and as a perpetuator of the manner pioneered in *Blackwood's*.

Fraser's seemed to offer Carlyle freedom to speak his own mind in his own way. It is therefore not surprising to learn that *Sartor* was begun as an article for *Fraser's*.

"TEUFELSDRECK"

The earliest reference to *Sartor* appears in Carlyle's notebooks in an entry probably from the end of September 1830: "I am going to write—Nonsense. It is on 'Clothes.' Heaven be my comforter!" Rather more explicit is the reference in a letter to his mother written 10 October: "For the last three weeks I have been writing by taskwork again, and get along wonderfully well: what it is to be I cannot yet tell, whether a Book or a string of Magazine Articles; we hope the former; but in either case, it may be worth something."[21] Nine days later he wrote to John in London:

What I am writing at is the strangest of all things: begun as an Article for Fraser; then found to be too long (except it were divided into two); now sometimes looking almost as it would swell into a Book. A very singular piece, I assure you! It glances from Heaven to Earth and back again in a strange satirical frenzy, whether fine or not remains to be seen. . . .

Teufelsdreck (that is the title of my present *Schrift*) will be done (so far—fifty pages) tomorrow. . . . (*Letters*, I, 236–237)

On 28 October Carlyle noted in his journal: "Written a strange piece 'On Clothes' know not what will come of it" (p. 177).

[21] *Two Note Books*, p. 176; *Letters*, I, 235. Much later in his *Reminiscences*, Carlyle recalls the "genesis" of *Sartor*, but not the details of the period of composition. He wrote: "The first genesis of *Sartor* I remember well enough, and the very spot (at Templand) where the notion of astonishment at *Clothes* first struck me. The Book had taken me in all some nine months, which are not present now, except confusedly and in mass, but that of being wearied with the fluctuations of review work, and of having decided on London again, with *Sartor* as a *Book* to be offered there, is still vivid to me . . ." (*Reminiscences*, II, 190–191).

In Carlyle's references to *Sartor* there is from the start an air of excitement and portentousness not otherwise found in notes made while he was at work on a composition. Singular too is the frequency with which Carlyle talks of the work as a book or possible book. Often Carlyle writes as though the book were writing itself. He appears to have a feeling of wonder at his accomplishment. Such a feeling is not uncommon among creative artists, but it was evidently new to Carlyle with the writing of *Sartor*. It accounts, perhaps, for the strengthening in the early thirties of his doctrine of the unconscious in artistic creation.

By 12 November Carlyle told John that he had written to *Fraser's* about terms and about "that Teufelsdreck paper of mine which I have now resolved not to make a Book of; but, if I have opportunity, two *Articles,* and the germ of more." Shortly after this he sent the manuscript to *Fraser's.* Hardly had he sent the manuscript off but he regretted it. He wrote in his journal: "Sent away the Clothes; of which I could make a kind of Book; but cannot *afford* it. Have still the Book *in petto,* but in the most chaotic shape."[22] In any case, the first version of *Sartor* was written and dispatched. It amounted to approximately fifty manuscript pages, the length of Carlyle's small hand of Book One and about a third of Book Two in the final version. References Carlyle makes to it during the period indicate that it probably corresponded in substance as well as length to the first third of the final *Sartor.*

Carlyle did not write further at "Teufelsdreck" in December and January, once he had sent off the paper to *Fraser's,* but he continued thinking about it. He kept wishing he had made a book of it. In December he expressed to John his dissatisfaction with *Fraser's* for delaying in printing some of his articles: "Hang them! I *have* a Book in me that will cause ears to tingle; and one day out it must and will issue" (*Letters,* i, 242).

[22] *Letters,* i, 238; *Two Note Books,* p. 178.

In August 1830 Carlyle had received a communication from the Saint-Simonian Society in Paris, occasioned by his provocative article "Signs of the Times." In October Goethe had written his much-quoted advice about the Saint-Simonians: "Von der Société St. Simonienne bitte Sich fern zu halten." Carlyle had responded that the Saint Simonians "have discovered and laid to heart this momentous and now almost forgotten truth, *Man is still Man;* and are already beginning to make false applications of it."[23] Nevertheless, in the December letter to John, Carlyle wrote that he had translated Saint Simon's *Nouveau Christianisme,* and he asked John to see if he could find a printer who would issue it as a pamphlet. Saint-Simonian ideas of the rebirth of society have been found in *Sartor,* but it is more than likely that Carlyle originally acquired his similar concepts from German writers like Herder. The insistent use of phoenix imagery and palingenesis (*Palingenesie*) suggest German sources; and, in any case, Carlyle's point of view is not cyclic or evolutionary as was the Saint-Simonian but, as Wellek argues, individual, developmental, and intuitive.[24] As we shall see later, Carlyle is far from a religion of humanity. Of course, the timing of Carlyle's translation of Saint Simon argues that, where they coincided, Saint-Simonian ideas reinforced many of Carlyle's at a time of special importance for *Sartor.*

In December of 1830 and January of 1831 Carlyle busied himself with preparing an article on William Taylor's book *Historical Survey of German Poetry* for the *Edinburgh.*

[23] *Correspondence between Goethe and Carlyle,* pp. 225–258.

[24] Saint-Simonian influence on Carlyle's thought has been hotly contested. John Carlyle was personally acquainted with the brothers D'Eichthal, ardent Saint Simonians, as early as 1827; and Carlyle translated Saint Simon's *Nouveau Christianisme* in 1830. Nevertheless, Saint-Simonian doctrines did not genuinely appeal to Carlyle, despite the arguments of David Brooks Cofer, *Saint Simonism in the Radicalism of Thomas Carlyle* (College Station, Texas, 1931) and Hill Shine, *Carlyle and the Saint-Simonians* (Baltimore, 1941). See the convincing rebuttal by René Wellek, "Carlyle and the Philosophy of History," *Philological Quarterly,* xxiii (1944), 55–76.

Much of the material was reworked from the "History of German Literature." By January 1831 Carlyle gave in to his original impulse to make a book out of "Teufelsdreck," and wrote John to retrieve the manscript from *Fraser's:*

> Will you go to Fraser and get from him by all means my long paper entitled *Thoughts on Clothes:* I would not for above half a dozen reasons have it appear there so long as I have potatoes to eat. Get it from him unless it is absolutely printed: the rest he can keep, they will surely pay him: but of this (in addition to the above reasons) I have taken a notion that I can make rather a good *Book,* and one, above all, likely to produce some desirable impression on the world even now. Do thou get it, my dear Jack, read it well over thyself, and then say what thou thinkest. I can devise some more biography for Teufelsdreck; give a second deeper part in the same vein, leading through Religion and the nature of Society, and Lord knows what. Nay that very "Thoughts," slightly altered, would make itself a little volume first (which would encourage me immensely) could one find any Bookseller, which however I suppose one cannot. [You decide whether to show it to Fraser, who surely hasn't read it, or to] Edward Irving (whose friendliness and feeling of the True, widely as it differs from him, I know).[25]

Ten days later (31 January) Carlyle wrote to his mother that he was "hovering about the materials of a Book, which I have so long talked of: one day or other it *must* out." By mid-February he told John that his plan was "in the meantime to labour at my *Teufelsdreck* Book, and bring

[25] *Letters,* I, 249–250. The "him" of the last line refers, I believe, to Fraser, whom Carlyle is contrasting with Irving. In February 1831, in an entry in *Two Note Books,* p. 183, Carlyle said that he was "seriously thinking to make a Book of it: the thing is not right, not *Art;* yet perhaps a nearer approach to Art than I have yet made. We ought to try."

it up to London in my pocket as soon as it is ready."[26] Evidently John had obtained the manuscript without delay and dispatched it to Carlyle, who immediately set to work revising and expanding. At most, however, only three people other than Carlyle are likely to have read the first draft of *Sartor*—brother John, Edward Irving, and, presumably, Jane. Carlyle commented on John's verdict: "I am a little comforted by your view of *Teufelsdreck*, which agrees with my own . . . and I believe, myself, that possibly I may make something of the work, and therefore shall try. It is full of dross, but there is also metal in it, and the thing still lives and produces with me" (*Letters*, I, 262).

"SARTOR RESARTUS"

The book that Carlyle had from the start wanted to make out of "Teufelsdreck" occupied his attention during the spring and summer of 1831. In March he called it his "prodigal son" and said that in the fall he hoped to "find a publisher of Devilsdreck." He foresaw a busy summer: "*Teufelsdreck* I *hege und pflege* night and day. . . . [It] is not the right thing yet, but there is a kind of life in it, and I *will* finish it." In June he wrote to John: "I am daily busy with *Teufelsdreck*, which I calculate on finishing early next month. But . . . 'I write dreadfully slow.' It will be one of the strangest volumes ever offered to the English world, whether *worth* anything is another question. At all events, I determine to finish it, and bring it up to London in my pocket this very Session of Parliament (if I can)."[27]

In July Carlyle was almost finished with "Teufelsdreck," but rather pessimistic about its chances for success: "I am struggling forward with *Dreck*, sick enough, but not in bad heart. I think the world will nowise be enraptured with this (medicinal) *Devil's Dung;* that the critical re-

[26] *Letters*, I, 257, 261.
[27] Ibid., I, 268, 271, 289–90.

public will cackle vituperatively or perhaps maintain total silence."[28] On 19 July Carlyle wrote his mother that his "book is drawing to a close"; but, as though sensing the difficulties ahead, he assured her that he was "very high in the humor and defiant both of the Devil and the world. I think I have looked into the *worst* that is in them both; and, through God's grace, no longer fear it" (*Letters,* I, 302–303).

Carlyle set out for London on 4 August 1831 with the manuscript, still not named *Sartor Resartus,* but rather "Thoughts on Clothes." So began anew the sorrows of Teufelsdröckh. By the end of August Carlyle wrote to Jane that in resisting quackery "poor *Teufelsdreck* is well-nigh singular"; and by early September he could read the signs of the times: "The history of *Dreck* still sticks simply where it was. . . . That the poor book is worth something I feel more and more convinced; that it will ever bring us any money seems less and less likely."[29] He still had some hopes that by the time Jane arrived in London in September they would be able to see the book through the press together, but in October he wrote to John, now departed for the continent as private physician to a noblewoman:

> As to *Teufelsdreck,* I may conclude this first section of his history in few words. Murray on my renewed demand some days after your departure, forwarded me the Manuscript with a polite enough note, and a

[28] *Letters,* I, 229. Carlyle's term here, "medicinal devil's dung," makes clear that he intended the name to carry the connotations that John J. Parry has noted at greatest length. In his "A plea for Better Anthologies," *College English,* v (1944), 322–323, Parry points out that Diogenes Teufelsdröckh means not only "God-Born Devil's Dung," but that Teufelsdreck is also the German word for asafoetida, a medicine made from herbs, and that Carlyle meant that "his divinely inspired message, although it may prove unpleasant, will also prove salutary [for England]." Parry exaggerates the uniqueness of his reading. Wilson, *Carlyle to "The French Revolution,"* p. 183, notes the significance of asafoetida, as does MacMechan in his richly annotated edition of *Sartor* (Boston, 1925), p. 282. I have added further glosses below, pp. 205, 220–222.

[29] *Letters,* I, 319–325.

"Criticism" from some altogether immortal "master of German Literature," to me quite unknown; which Criticism (a miserable, Dandiacal *quodlibet,* in the usual vein) did *not* authorise the Publication in these times. . . . Thus *Dreck* may perhaps be considered as postponed *sine die:* with which result also I am perfectly contented. What I have written I have written: the reading of it is another party's concern. (*Letters,* I, 357–358)

What actually happened was a bit more complicated. Carlyle, on Jeffrey's advice, first tried the publisher Murray. Ten days later he retrieved the manuscript, unread by Murray. He took it to Longmans, where it was declined in a few days. Efforts by William Fraser, editor of the *Foreign Review,* to get other publishers to read the work failed. Fraser's brother James, a printer, agreed to print the book for Carlyle if Carlyle would advance *him* £150. Carlyle couldn't, and wouldn't. The reason for the unwillingness of editors and publishers to print *Sartor* resided in the nature of *Sartor* itself and the uncertainty of the times. Reform Bill agitation was so great in England in late 1831 that many believed a revolution was imminent unless Reform passed Parliament. No one wanted to undertake risky business ventures in the face of possible social upheaval. Carlyle described the stuation to Goethe:

I have come hither chiefly to dispose of the Piece which I lately described myself as writing. Whether, or how well, I shall succeed seems questionable: for the whole world here is dancing a Tarantula Dance of Political Reform, and has no ear left for Literature. Nevertheless, I shall do my utmost to get the work, which was meant to be a "word spoken in season," actually emitted: at lowest I shall ascertain that it cannot be emitted, and study to do what duty that situation also will call for.[30]

[30] *Correspondence between Goethe and Carlyle,* pp. 290–291. Cf. *Letters of Thomas Carlyle to William Graham,* ed. John Graham, Jr. (Princeton, 1950), pp. 53–57.

By way of doing his utmost, Carlyle at last took the manuscript back to Jeffrey, who read twenty-eight pages and said he "very much admired the scene of the sleeping city."[31] He promised to write to Murray about it, and soon Murray agreed to publish the book on the "half-profits" system, by which Carlyle paid and received nothing for the first 750 copies. Whatever might sell after that would go to Carlyle. Only a page or two had been printed, when Murray thought better of the arrangement. He used the pretext of Carlyle's having offered the manuscript to Longmans in the interval between the first and second deposition of it at Murray's to suggest that Carlyle had not acted honestly or sincerely with him, and that he, Murray, wished now to have the opportunity of submitting the manuscript to a specialist. Carlyle, ever proud, insisted that Murray should indeed obtain a specialist's verdict, with the result that Murray declined the manuscript and returned it with the opinion of the reader, whom Carlyle always believed to be John Gibson Lockhart, although there is some doubt that he was right. In a gesture that Froude called "pardonable malice" Carlyle reprinted the reader's opinion in the first book edition of *Sartor* as a communication from "Highest Class, Bookseller's Taster."[32] Murray's rejection of the work returned "Thoughts on Clothes" to the category of an unpublished manuscript.

Toward the end of the year Carlyle again made efforts to find a publisher for his book. He gave it to a few selected friends to read, and he tried other publishers;

[31] Wilson, *Carlyle to "The French Revolution,"* p. 248.

[32] Froude, II, 194; Wilson, *Carlyle to "The French Revolution,"* p. 253. The view that Lockhart did not write it is maintained by Francis Espinasse, *Literary Recollections and Sketches* (London, 1893), p. 230; and the opposite view is presented in Samuel Smiles, *A Publisher and His Friends* (London and New York, 1871), II, 353.

All but one of the other critical testimonies Carlyle added to the book form of *Sartor* are clearly identified and all but the "Bookseller's Taster" come from published documents. The other unidentified comment, called "New England Editors," was written by Emerson in his preface to the first edition of *Sartor* (Boston, 1836), pp. iii–v.

but by January 1832 he wrote to John, now in Italy, that while it really mattered not at all, "also is it not wholly a Lie that Lucubration of Dreck's; it can rest for twelve-months and will not wormeat."[33] As hope faded for the immediate publication of "Thoughts on Clothes," Carlyle consoled himself with the conviction that the book had permanent worth, which would not fade if publication took longer than expected.

The Carlyles returned to Scotland in March 1832. The book lay untouched for about a year. In January 1833 Carlyle wrote his brother Alexander: "My old Manuscript is lying by me quiet; there is no likelihood of its being printed this winter, for I have not the cash just ready, and it is a thing that can wait."[34] In the interval between the completion of *Sartor* and its first appearance in print Carlyle continued to write articles for a living. Most of them are heavily marked with the stamp of *Sartor*, although no reader at the time could have been aware of it. "Biography," the first part of a review of an edition of Boswell's *Johnson,* is typical of the kind of influence *Sartor* had on Carlyle's writing at this time. The essay set up the existence of a Professor Gottfried Sauerteig ("God's-Peace Sour-Dough"), author of a work entitled the *Aesthetische Springwurzeln,* "a Work, perhaps, as yet new to most English readers."[35] Carlyle uses Sauerteig again in 1833 in the two-part "Cagliostro," one of the essays most heavily impregnated with Sartorian elements. Indeed, the eccentric commentator obsessed Carlyle during the period in which *Sartor* lay waiting for a publisher: in "Biography" and "Cagliostro" he offers Sauerteig, in "Corn-Law Rhymes" a certain Smelfungus Redivivus ("Fault-Finder Revived"),

---

[33] *Letters*, I, 391.

[34] *Letters*, II, 90.

[35] *Works*, XXVIII, 49. The *"aesthetische Springwurzeln"* ("aesthetic mandrakes") may be an echo of Jean Paul, as Wellek suggested in his "Carlyle and German Romanticism," *Zvláštní otisk z Xenia Pragensia* (1929), p. 399; but Carlyle had already used the *Springwurzeln* in his literary history from German *Volksmärchen* sources. See Shine, *Carlyle's Unfinished History of German Literature*, pp. 43–45.

and, in "Goethe's Works" in the *Foreign Quarterly Review*,
Carlyle could evidently wait no longer to introduce his
favorite commentator to the British public: he offers more
than a half-dozen pages of quotations from "Herr Professor
Teufelsdröckh," whom he identifies as "a continental
Humorist . . . whose works are as yet but sparingly if
at all cited in English literature." He says he has written
a chapter in the manner of a "metaphysico-rhetorical
homiletic-exegetic rhapsody, on the *Greatness of Great
Men*." Following the first quotation, Carlyle footnotes its
source as none other than *Die Kleider: ihr Werden und
Wirken*.[36] The actual lines cited in "Goethe's Works" nowhere occur in *Sartor*, although the sentiments are pure
Teufelsdröckh. Carlyle apparently continued to generate
Teufelsdröckhisms so long as the book lay awaiting a publisher. To his translation of "Das Mährchen" Carlyle
added a running explanatory footnote commentary on the
allegory of the tale, which he ascribed to the "poor Translator, who signs himself 'D. T.' "[37] The preface and additional footnotes to the footnotes purported to be the work
of O. Y., Oliver Yorke, the fictitious editor of *Fraser's*.
At last in 1833, before *Sartor* had been contracted for
by *Fraser's*, Carlyle published in that magazine "On History Again," which is presented by O. Y. as a "singular
Fragment from an 'Inaugural Discourse' delivered by our
assiduous 'D. T.' at the opening of the *Society for the
Diffusion of Common Honesty*."[38] Of the thirteen essays

[36] *Works*, xxvii, 391. The Centenary edition has silently modified
the spelling to bring Teufelsdröckh into harmony with *Sartor*. In the
original essay the name appears as "Teufelsdreck."

[37] *Works*, xxvii, 448. German critics, aware of Goethe's conception
of the *Märchen* as an open, flowing, imaginative form have been
dismayed by Carlyle's heavy-handed allegorizing of "Das Mährchen."
Carlyle himself called his performance "cavalier," but it serves to
underline his absorption with allegory and the *Märchen* at the time
of *Sartor*. Further, Goethe's conception of the *Märchen* was not
entirely representative: Novalis said of Goethe's *Märchen*, "Goethe
wird und muss übertroffen werden." See Thalmann, *Das Märchen
und die Moderne*, p. 21.

[38] *Works*, xxviii, 167. Cf. Teufelsdröckh's "Oration," "On receiving
the Doctor's Hat," *Sartor*, ii, xi, 78.

and translations Carlyle wrote between the completion of *Sartor* in the summer of 1831 and its publication in 1833, seven involve the use of some eccentric observer of life and letters; three of the seven use material from the pen of "D. T."; all of the thirteen except "Novelle," a straight translation, make use of Carlyle's device of self-quotation. Eight of the thirteen essays were published in *Fraser's*, and these the most unorthodox ones; but the full name Diogenes Teufelsdröckh first appeared in the pages of the *Foreign Quarterly Review*.

While stylistic devices from *Sartor* were finding their way into Carlyle's essays between 1831 and 1834, ideas from *Sartor* also were emerging in the essays. Sauerteig in "Biography" carries Carlyle's ideas on the importance of biography far beyond the views expressed in the earlier essays. In "Characteristics," written at the end of 1831, there is no eccentric Carlylean commentator, for the essay was written for the staid *Edinburgh Review*, but the title is the same as that of chapter four of Book One of *Sartor*, and, of course, defining characteristics had occupied Carlyle's attention since his scientific days. "Characteristics" illustrates what C. F. Harrold means when he calls Carlyle a dualist who, when he reflects, is a monist.[39] Carlyle's dualism is the product of an imaginative faculty that constitutionally sees the world in terms of opposites. In "Characteristics" he contrasts the rhetorician with the orator, the conscious with the unconscious, material with spiritual. But the conflict between dualism and monism in Carlyle is more apparent than real. His monism is an ineffable concept, not a system; and the habitual dualism of his writings is designed to demonstrate an underlying inexpressible unity in all phenomena, not to posit a Manichaean universe.

One passage in "Characteristics" may safely be taken as a word from the heart—Carlyle's attack on reviewers, or "tasters" as he called them. He, who, even as he wrote,

[39] *Carlyle and German Thought,* p. 119.

had his luckless manuscript beside him, must have had a wry pleasure in demolishing reviewers and asking for real readers: "Sterne's wish for a reader 'that would give-up the reins of his imagination into his author's hands, and be pleased he knew not why, and cared not wherefore,' might lead him a long journey now" (*Works*, xxviii, 24).

During the time Carlyle was inventing Sauertieg Smelfungus, and a modified "D. T.," *Sartor* was lying presumably untouched, among his papers. In February 1833, however, Carlyle made the one known emendation on *Sartor* after its completion in 1831: he emended the name Teufelsdreck to the subtler form Teufelsdröckh;[40] but he

[40] Hitherto C. E. Norton in a note in *Letters*, ii, 104, has been the sole source for this dating, but it is confirmed by an unpublished Carlyle letter to John which Norton too had seen. Part of the letter was published by Froude, ii, 331–335, but the portion treating the name change was omitted. It reads:

. . . on the whole as I told poor Murray the other day while he was advising and encouraging me. "*Allah bis mallah,* God is great, we shall find means"! *Teufelsdreck* cannot see the light this summer, tho' I remain determined to spend a sixty pounds on him, when convenient: also, most probably, neither now nor at any other time will I treat again with Booksellers about such a matter. Suffering the skaith, we may at least go without the scorn: in the Bookseller, himself a condemned man, lies no help for us. Teufel[k] (whom, by the by, I mean to call Teufels-*dröckh*) is worth little, yet also *not* worth nothing. (From MS, NLS 523.11 [No. 20/2, 1300].)

I am grateful to the National Library of Scotland for permission to quote from this letter and to Professor Charles R. Sanders of Duke University, who permitted me to consult his copy.

Carlyle does not explain the change to John, but it seems clear that he was trying to subtilize the meaning of the name, to make it appear more like a possible name and less obviously a noun. Teufelsdröckh hovers on the borders of credibility. Berend, "Die Namengebung bei Jean Paul," p. 820, who is hostile to double meanings in Jean Paul's naming of characters, nods when he criticizes Carlyle for the name Teufelsdröckh: "Selbst ein so guter Kenner der deutschen Sprache wie Carlyle hat dem Helden seines humoristischen Romans Sartor Resartus den unmöglichen Namen Teufelsdröckh gegeben." Carlyle knew full well what he was doing in selecting the name, and in fact he makes it quite clear that the name is unique. See *Sartor*, ii, i, 86.

still frequently used the old form in reference. He was still convinced that the book should be published, for he believed "there are from four to five hundred young men in the British Isles whom he would teach many things; and sure enough *they,* and not the fire, shall have him." In May he wrote to John of his plan for the summer to "cut Teufelsdreck into slips, and have it printed in Fraser's Magazine," by which means he hoped to earn the sum of £200.[41] He blamed his want of diplomacy for failure to reach a successful arrangement with publishers in the past. Ten days later he wrote to *Fraser's,* offering the manuscript. The title, however, is still not the one we know:

The Book is at present named "Thoughts on Clothes; or Life and Opinions of Herr D. Teufelsdröckh, D.u.J."; but perhaps we might see right to alter the title a little; for the rest, some brief Introduction could fit it handsomely enough into its new destination; it is already divided into three "Books," and farther into very short "Chapters," capable in all ways of subdivision. Nay, some tell me, what perhaps is true, that taking a few chapters at a time is really the profitablest way of reading it. There may be in all some Eight sheets of *Fraser.* It is put together in the fashion of a kind of Didactic Novel; but indeed properly *like* nothing yet extant; I used to characterise it briefly as a kind of "Satirical Extravaganza on Things in General"; it contains more of my opinions on Art, Politics, Religion, Heaven, Earth, and Air, than all the things I have yet written. The Creed promulgated on all these things, as you may judge, is *mine,* and firmly *believed:* for the rest, the main Actor in the business ("Editor of these Sheets," as he often calls himself) assumes a kind of Conservative (though Anti-quack) character; and would suit *Frazer* perhaps better than any other Magazine. The ultimate result, however, I need hardly premise, is a deep religious specula-

41 Ms, NLS 523.11; *Letters,* II, 99.

tive-radicalism (so I call it for want of a better name), with which you are already well enough acquainted in me. (*Letters,* II, 105)

Carlyle adds that five persons have read the work by now: two liked it, two were astonished, and one disliked it. He was evidently discounting publishers and their readers and partial tasters like Jeffrey. Still, five is too modest a number. There had been at least seven readers by this time: Jane, John, Edward Irving, Henry Inglis, Charles Buller, a certain Mr. Glen (a disciple Carlyle had acquired on his 1831 London trip), and John Stuart Mill! None of them actually disliked the book, and most of them were, like Henry Inglis, "ecstatic."[42]

Carlyle's letter succeeded in not offending. *Fraser's* agreed to print the work, but not at the £200 Carlyle had expected; rather he received only £82 for the *Fraser's* serialization.[43] Part of the bargain was to have a set of the installments set aside and stitched into book form by *Fraser's* at the end of the run. Fifty-eight such copies were produced, which constitutes the first "edition" of *Sartor.*[44] Since these were not for sale but were all for Carlyle's personal use, bibliographically *Sartor* had not yet been published as a book. Before November, when the first installment appeared, Carlyle gave the work the name *Sartor*

[42] Wilson, *Carlyle to "The French Revolution,"* p. 253; Froude, II, 338.

[43] Wilson, *Carlyle to "The French Revolution,"* p. 327. Froude, II, 347–348, says that Carlyle expected 200 guineas (at 20 guineas a sheet), but got only twelve guineas a sheet for a total of 120 guineas. Sir Charles Gavan Duffy, *Conversations with Carlyle* (New York, 1892), p. 89, maintains that Carlyle received only £5 a sheet, for presumably a total of £50. But Carlyle himself is the authority for £82, or more precisely £82.1, in a letter to his brother John. The rate, thus, at ten sheets, comes out to a curious £8.4.1 and a fraction per sheet. Actually the rate must have been eight guineas a sheet, with the tenth sheet not quite full.

[44] Carlyle sent out 38 of these and retained the rest. Some of the presentation copies survive. For example, the copy Carlyle inscribed to John Stuart Mill's associate Harriet Taylor is now in the Pierpont Morgan Library in New York.

Resartus. Installments appeared from November 1833 through August 1834 in each monthly issue of *Fraser's*, with gaps in January and May. Aside from the favorable responses of Emerson and Father O'Shea, the reaction of *Fraser's* readers was more like that of the gentleman who went to James Fraser's shop to rage, "If there is any more of that damned stuff I will. . . ."[45] But *Sartor* had at least been printed and started on its career in English letters.

Regular book publication of *Sartor* did not take place until 1836, when Emerson arranged for publication in Boston and wrote an enthusiastic preface. The text was that in the *Fraser's* installments. Publication in England did not follow until 1838, when unbound sheets from America were bound with new title pages and sold in England. At last in 1840 a true English first edition was published under Carlyle's supervision. From 1840 on *Sartor* gained in popularity, eventually becoming one of the best selling books of the nineteenth century.[46] Even today, in the general neglect of Carlyle, *Sartor Resartus* is one of the two or three of his works still regularly in print.

The pertinence of Carlyle's writing experiences of the eighteen-twenties and of the immediate circumstances surrounding the writing of *Sartor* in 1830–1831 speaks for

---

[45] Emerson's enthusiasm is well known and it was vital for the subsequent fortunes of the book. Father O'Shea was an Irish priest whom Carlyle met years later without being very favorably impressed. See Duffy, *Conversations with Carlyle,* pp. 95–96.

There is abundant testimony as to the general disapprobation that greeted *Sartor* in *Fraser's.* See, for example, Wilson, *Carlyle to "The French Revolution,"* pp. 358, 362; *Letters,* II, 128; and *Correspondence of Carlyle and Emerson,* ed. Charles Eliot Norton (London, 1883), I, 21.

[46] In 1882 alone, almost fifty years after its first publication, *Sartor* sold 70,000 copies. See Richard D. Altick, *The English Common Reader* (Chicago, 1957), p. 243. Altick lists it as a best seller under "Miscellaneous" (p. 390). But *Sartor* did not begin making money for Carlyle until 1841. See *Letters of Thomas Carlyle to His Youngest Sister,* ed. C. T. Copeland (2nd. ed., London, 1899), p. 113.

itself: once Carlyle turned from reviewing to "give Work for reviewing," once he determined to be no longer an essayist but a "Writer in a far better sense," once he put himself in mind of *Fraser's* as an outlet, he was started in a direction that had determinative consequences for *Sartor*. First, the work would be bound to show the results of the kind of writing he had mastered—translation and the essay. Second, the work would be, nevertheless, neither a translation nor an essay but an original composition. Third, all of the impudence, sharp insight, "Merry-Andrew Drollery and even Humour" that was tossing about in Carlyle's mind would be given play. Small wonder that the result perplexed many readers. Yet ultimately *Sartor* prospered, for what Carlyle created out of the "Chaos . . . of natural Supernaturalism" within himself is an integrated work of art that combines its garments, body, and soul in "living union." To understand how that union lives will be the endeavor of the following pages.

IV

The Structure of "Sartor Resartus"

Hast thou not heard, that my Lord Jesus di'd
   Then let me tell thee a strange storie.
   The God of power, as he did ride
   In his majestick robes of glorie,
   Resolv'd to light; and so one day
He did descend, undressing all the way.

The starres his tire of light and rings obtain'd
   The cloud his bow, the fire his spear,
   The sky his azure mantle gain'd.
   And when they ask'd, what he would wear;
   He smil'd and said as he did go,
He had new clothes a making here below.

          —GEORGE HERBERT

The first version of *Sartor* did not satisfy Carlyle artistically. "The thing is not right, not *Art,* he wrote in February 1831, while waiting for John to return the manuscript. As he faced the task of rewriting "Teufelsdreck," he speculated on the problem of artistic unity:

What is a *Whole?* Or how, specially, *does* a Poem differ from Prose? Ask not a definition of it in words, which can hardly express common Logic correctly; study to create in thyself a *feeling* of it: like so much else it cannot be made clear, hardly even to thy Thought (?)—Alas, "white men know nothing."

I see some vague outline of what a *Whole* is: also how an individual Delineation may be "informed with the Infinite"; may appear hanging in the universe of Time & Space (partly): in which case is it a Poem and a Whole? Therefore, are the true Heroic Poems of these times to be written with the *ink of Science?*

Were a correct philosophic Biography of a Man (meaning by philosophic *all* that the name can include) the only method of celebrating him? The true History (had we any such, or even generally any dream of such) the true Epic Poem?—I partly begin to surmise so.[1]

Carlyle's problem of the "Whole" is in great part the problem of structure. To be sure, the totality of a work, its wholeness, embraces more than structure alone. There are considerations usually expressed by terms like "style," "texture," "theme," "meaning," and so on. But structure, broadly conceived, is surely one of the most vital aspects of unity; for structure does not operate apart from meaning, and as we examine structure, we perceive what kind of emphasis a work has, we discern its rhythm and, if our examination is penetrating enough, we apprehend its meaning. "Structure," then, is taken here to mean initially the arrangement of parts, the order of elements; but, beyond that, it is taken to mean the way in which parts affect each other, the kind of progression in a given work, and ultimately how the arrangement of the parts informs the content with meaning.

An inquiry into the structure of *Sartor Resartus* is especially needful because of the widespread conviction that *Sartor* lacks structural unity, that it is a chaotic jumble of Carlyle's opinions and fancies, suggestive but incoherent. Earlier defenses of *Sartor* rested content with statements about "seeming confusion," but did little to justify the use of "seeming."[2] Only in recent years have there been any at-

[1] *Two Note Books*, p. 187–188, entry of about February, 1831.

[2] Even Harrold sometimes inclines toward the "seeming confusion" view: "And Carlyle's frequent references to the chaos of Teufelsdröckh's papers and methods may be taken as roughly descriptive of the actual jumble which is *Sartor Resartus*. Yet there is more order than is apparent to the timid reader . . ." (*Sartor*, p. xxxii). Cf. also Bliss Perry, *Thomas Carlyle* (Indianapolis, 1915), p. 90.
  Outspokenly unfavorable judgments have been made by James Russell Lowell, *My Study Windows* (Boston, 1884), p. 126, when he accuses Carlyle of having "no artistic sense of form or rhythm";

tempts to examine the unity of *Sartor*, and these have generally erred on the side of simplification.[3] But *Sartor* is a complexly structured work. It is not the case that *Sartor* simply follows the life pattern of a man—what of the first and third books? Any account of the structure of *Sartor* must consider all of *Sartor*, not just that part which most readily adapts itself to conventional treatment. If we isolate Teufelsdröckh's story, for instance, and hang the rest of *Sartor* onto it, we have in fact violated the form and spirit of Carlyle's work. Our effort must be to do justice to the parts at the same time that we are doing justice to the whole.

When Carlyle wrote *Sartor* he had behind him the experience of writing scientific and scholarly articles, criticism, biography, poetry, and fiction. At the time of writing, the claims of all the forms in which he had written were in something close to balance. The material Carlyle used in *Sartor* also reflects a diversity of interests, a function in part of varied efforts to earn a living by his pen. Further, Carlyle was not hampered by an adherence to a concept of strictly defined genres. There had been a steady erosion in theories of literary kinds during the Romantic period, nowhere more strongly than in the German literature Carlyle knew so well. Carlyle's equation of literature and religion, his doctrine of the prophetic, and his reliance on

---

and by Augustus Ralli in his *Guide to Carlyle* (London, 1920), I, 140. Otto Baumgarten in *Carlyle und Goethe* (Tübingen, 1906), pp. 70–71, berates Carlyle for the "abtruse Unordnung der Komposition," and suggests that we dispense entirely with large portions of the book, retaining only Book Two and through chapter seven of Book Three.

[3] See Daniel P. Deneau, "Relationship of Style and Device in *Sartor Resartus*," and John Lindberg, "The Artistic Unity of *Sartor Resartus*," published together under the title "The Art of *Sartor Resartus*: Two Views," *Victorian Newsletter*, No. 17 (1960), pp. 17–23. The beginning of a criticism of Carlyle's variety of point of view in *Sartor* is seen in Alvan S. Ryan, "The Attitude Towards the Reader in Carlyle's *Sartor Resartus*," *Victorian Newsletter*, No. 23 (1963), pp. 15–16.

a concept of organic form all contributed to make him seek a new mode to express his views. The course of Carlyle's literary practice up to 1830–1831 is one of increasing daring and experimentation. *Sartor* is the culmination of his whole literary endeavor of the twenties, as well as the fruit of his developing aesthetic.

PRINCIPLES AND HERESIES

Carlyle asserted that once the poet had grasped the divine idea of the world, once he had a "genuine, deep, and noble" meaning, the means of bodying it forth, "the form best suited to the subject and the author," would "come of its own accord." As a principle this is unexceptionable, even if it is very specific. If we grant that in *Sartor* Carlyle has a "genuine, deep, and noble" meaning, how are we to know that the form in which it is bodied forth is truly suitable to it? The answer is that we do not know the meaning until we understand the form, for the form and meaning combine in "living union" and are not extricable—except, of course, in the critical act. It is this act we must perform, separating for purposes of criticism the meaning from the form. Neither form nor meaning will emerge from *Sartor* with any great clarity unless we are clear about the materials of the work and how they have been shaped. It has been an unwitting avoidance of some of the materials in *Sartor* that has made for confusion in the past in efforts to see the book steadily and whole.

What, then, are the materials of *Sartor*? First, we have an Editor, who through personal and professional interests comes into possession of a work by an old German acquaintance. Besides the Editor we have the work itself, *Die Kleider, ihr Werden und Wirken.* And we have the man Teufelsdröckh, with biographical and other documents relating to him. There are also ideas—about clothes, society, man, the natural and supernatural world—which rise out of the fragments of the book, the documents, and the life, and which must somehow be brought into meaningful order. We can put the question of materials another way by asking, what is the book about? The question is deceptive. That many have answered, "Diogenes Teufelsdröckh," constitutes one of the sources of confusion in assessing Carlyle's accomplishment. In the personal limited sense of psychology and conduct of character, *Sartor Resartus* is not in fact about Teufelsdröckh. Only in the sense that Carlyle meant when he spoke of a "correct philosophic Biography of a man (meaning by philosophic all that the name can include)" is *Sartor* about Teufelsdröckh. But Carlyle's is not a common definition of biography. It is better to avoid the biographical approach to *Sartor*, for in practice it quickly turns into exclusive concern with Book Two and degenerates thence into an explication of Carlyle's own biography. Whatever poetic justice may lie in such an approach, it obscures the organization of *Sartor*.

We should take the title as our guide: *Sartor Resartus* means "the tailor retailored," "the patcher patched," and the "clothes volume edited."[4] The subtitle helps: "The Life and Opinions of Herr Teufelsdröckh." To say the book is about Teufelsdröckh is to exclude part of the subtitle, for the argument that "opinions" are automatically included in any description of Teufelsdröckh is misleading. In a conventional novel the opinions of the characters are, of course, revealed to the reader as they operate in the action. But in Teufelsdröckh's case the opinions are not merely those expressed by or inferred from speech and action;

[4] There is no convincing argument for allowing only one reading of the title, as does Keith Rinehart, "Carlyle's *Sartor Resartus*," *The Explicator*, xi (1953), item 32. Rinehart opts for "patcher repatched," but he does not mention the reading "clothes volume edited," first suggested in Dyer's *Bibliography*, p. 585, and included by Harrold, *Sartor*, p. 301. R. S. Craig, *The Making of Carlyle* (New York, 1909), p. 423, is alone in thinking that the title *Sartor Resartus* was a blunder "and probably responsible for much of the hard fortune of the book." Since much of the hard fortune came in finding a publisher under the pre-*Sartor* title, Craig's notion appears to be misplaced.

they are also the opinions in the volume *Die Kleider*, which, child though it be of Teufelsdröckh's brain, has an independent existence in the volume *Sartor Resartus*. Carlyle, of course, takes pains to make Teufelsdröckh and his book inextricable: "*Call one Diogenes Teufelsdröckh, and he will open the Philosophy of Clothes.*" The two are by no means unrelated. Neither, however, must we let one part of the book obscure the other. *Sartor* is about a man and about a work and, beyond that, about the complex unity of the man and his work. When once we have stopped thinking of *Sartor* as either the story of Teufelsdröckh or as a synonym for *Die Kleider*—with each reading excluding the other—we are in a position to investigate the structural unity of the whole work.

We return, then, to the materials, to the subject matter of *Sartor Resartus*. We note that almost all of the material is fragmentary, so that part of the *donnée* is to make a unity of the fragments. How does Carlyle do this? How does he put the materials into an arrangement in which any one part is relevant to the rest and in which there is any necessary order? Differently phrased, does *Sartor* have an organic form? For two reasons the question is of the essence in examining *Sartor*. First, whatever inadequacies we may find in the concept of organic form, such a concept is still today the closest to a universally held critical principle. We may dislike the picture of a work of art as growth, with its implications of the unconscious and the unwilled, but whenever critics seek to determine whether structure complements meaning, whether the words in their existing order achieve their intended effect (not some other, perhaps worthier effect, but the one they were chosen to produce), whether a given point of view, seemingly so capricious, is not really careful chosen to underline the theme, they are paying respect to the theory of organic form. The principle of organic form still serves a worthy critical purpose. Second, Carlyle himself subscribed to a theory of organic form, with his insistence that form would come of its own accord once the poet had grasped a meaning and that all would then combine in living union. It thus serves both critical and historical interests to inquire whether *Sartor* has a structure suited to its materials and to an inner necessity in its meaning.

Carlyle, of course, spoke of organic form in the context and terminology of German Romantic theory.[5] He had no disposition to object to the strong emphasis on the unconscious. Indeed, he is remembered as the prophet of the unconscious, although to set the matter straight we should make clear that he was the prophet of unconscious *growth*.[6] Carlyle accepted the notion that works of art arise from the unconscious, mysterious, and even inscrutable depths of the psyche, but he believed also that works of art emerge with a congruence and form uniquely suited to their natures and that the form issues not in spite of but because of the unconscious origin of the work. Thus, by Carlyle's own theory, if *Sartor* is a work of art, it must possess a form in harmony with its nature. This kind of theory is naturally best expressed by analogy with plant life, and metaphors of plant life are a distinguishing feature of the organic theory of the Romantic period. An important result of genetic thinking about art is the abandonment of traditional literary genres and the consequent elevation of unique forms. Another is the emphasis on variety—Cole-

[5] Abrams, *The Mirror and the Lamp*, pp. 211–216.

[6] In actuality, the theory of the unconscious is inherent in the analogy with plant growth, so that it becomes a question of emphasis. The choice of plant metaphors rather than, say, animal metaphors makes acceptance of the role of the unconscious unavoidable, since plants are distinguished by lack of volition. Nor was there any desire to avoid the implications of the plant metaphor. Abrams points out that the organic theory was extended to include far more than works of art: "In a full-fledged organology, which exploits the detailed possibilities of living and growing things, any human product or institution is envisioned as germinating, without anyone's deliberate plan or intent, and as fulfilling its destiny through an inner urgency, feeding on the materials of its time and place in order to proliferate into its ultimate and living form" (pp. 218–219).

ridge's "Multëity in Unity"—by analogy with the assimilative powers of the plant. *Sartor* itself is impregnated with organicist metaphors and expressions. Even the recurring metaphor of clothing is frequently rendered in organic terms: looms continually weave as though by a force beyond the human, clothing and vesture grow secretly and mysteriously, and even ideas grow in the "seed-field" of time. One of Carlyle's most suggestive metaphors in *Sartor* may stand as a metaphor of the growth of *Sartor* itself: "Cast forth thy Act, thy Word, into the ever-living, ever-working Universe: it is a seed-grain that cannot die, unnoticed today (says one), it will be found flourishing as a Banyan-grove (perhaps, alas, as a Hemlock-forest!) after a thousand years."[7]

The banyan tree suggests the kind of growth I think we find in *Sartor Resartus*. The banyan is a tree of the Mulberry family, often called self-renewing because it sends down what are termed aerial-roots from its branches, which upon reaching the ground thicken and help support the tree by becoming additional trunks. Underground the roots extend deep and extremely far outward. Such is the form of *Sartor Resartus*. Carlyle begins with the book *Die Kleider* and its ideas; he begins, that is, with the simple tree. But, repeatedly, the clothes volume sends down aerial-roots which lead to the roots of the tree itself. These roots constitute Book Two, the life of Teufelsdröckh, for it is Teufelsdröckh from whom *Die Kleider* grew and who nourishes and sustains it. The aerial roots of the life of Teufelsdröckh become additional portions of the trunk, and the strengthened base is now capable of supporting the flowers and fruits of speculation which constitute Book Three.

It may be asked whether Carlyle's form can be called organic if we remove from the description the consciously organicist terms in which I have wrapped it. Even shorn

[7] *Sartor,* i, v, 40. Carlyle also compared the *Nibelungenlied* to a banyan; "Thus, though Tradition may have but one root, it grows like a Banian [sic], into a whole overarching labyrinth of trees" (*Works,* xxvii, 220).

of the metaphorical language, *Sartor* does not disappoint. The Editor obtains a curious manuscript, the more immediately comprehensible portions of which he presents to the reader. The Editor is understandably interested in how such a manuscript came into existence and in what he can learn about its author. He obtains biographical data, which he attempts to construe in such a way as to make meaningful the genesis and source of the clothes volume. Having examined the biography and determined its significance, the Editor is enabled to present the more abstruse portions of the clothes volume with greater insight. All of these events and the sequence of them grow out of the situation in which the Editor finds himself. Thus, Book One is the presentation of Teufelsdröckh's opinions as best the Editor can grasp them until the biographical documents arrive. Once these come, he sets about to make sense out of them, thus producing Book Two. When he has carried out that task as far as his materials allow, he turns with renewed vigor to the clothes volume and other documents to see if they will now reveal themselves more clearly, and he produces Book Three. The large divisions in the book are determined by the nature of the materials and by the sequence of their availability. Quite apart, then, from the banyan or plant metaphors in general, *Sartor* grows out of its materials, and these relate organically to each other. Moreover, to remove the curse of inertness suggested by the metaphor of organism, we can speak equally well of *Sartor* and dynamic form, a form that issues from the interplay of the Editor with his materials. In both cases, organic and dynamic, the book falls naturally into three divisions.

The question of organic form in *Sartor*, as it relates to the sequence and order of the parts, must be answered affirmatively. But Carlyle, we remember, demanded more. The form must grow, not simply out of the situation and the materials, but out of the very meaning that the poet has grasped. Is there such a meaning in *Sartor* that the ordering of the materials fulfills? When we look at *Sartor*

in the light of Carlyle's precept, the meaning emerges less
as a philosophic formulation than as an aesthetic perception. For Carlyle was more poet than philosopher, and
he thought habitually in analogy and symbol. With August
Wilhelm Schlegel he would have argued that metaphor
and symbol are the essence of poetry, just as with Friedrich
Schlegel he would have argued that a work of art must
be organic.[8] Thus the meaning with which Carlyle began
Sartor appears as the clothes metaphor itself; just as clothing covers the body, which in turn houses the soul, so
the visible world covers an invisible one, which has as
its animating spirit the mind of God. What gives *Sartor*
an organism to grow on also gives it a dynamism. *Sartor*
in operation is the expansion of the clothes metaphor to
analogy, the elaboration of an initial perception of *likeness*
to a detailed working out of similarities in *relations*. From
the comparison of clothing to the visible features of the
world, Carlyle goes on to discern limitless other comparisons—the relation of custom to society to the spirit of
man, the facts of history to the body politic to the collective
soul of humanity—and he works out the relations between
these similarities. Throughout *Sartor* there are repeated
subordinate analogies, from the threefold interpretation of
symbols to a threefold interpretation of the history of
Whiggery.[9] These are analogical wheels within wheels that

[8] René Wellek, *A History of Modern Criticism: 1750–1950,* (New
Haven, 1955), II, 5–73, ascribes these emphases to the frequently
interchanged Schlegels. Wellek also sagely points to the twin perils
of intellectualism and mysticism that attend any symbolist and
analogist view of the universe such as that held by August Wilhelm
Schlegel (II, 43). Both dangers are encountered by Carlyle in *Sartor,*
and the abundance of philosophic and mystical criticism the book
has engendered testifies to these inclinations in it.

[9] Still others are the three types of hero, the three kinds of
clothes that are examined, and of course the three stages of the
conversion experience. In a later essay on Goethe, Carlyle also
compares the three ages of Goethe to the three ages of modern
man: Despair-denial-doubt (*Werther*), Pagan or Ethnic (*Meisters
Lehrjahre*), and Reverential (*Meisters Wanderjahre*). See "Goethe's
Works," *Works,* XXVII, 431.

give *Sartor* much of its complexity and much of its momentum. To cite all of the analogies would be to exhaust *Sartor* itself, for, once begun on his course of analogizing, Carlyle sweeps forward, touching all things in heaven and earth. It is analogical vitality that sustains the initial, not especially startling or original, metaphor and that gives the metaphor a direction and a fertility that can support a whole book. But it is from this metaphorical perception that all the rest flows, and it operates much as Carlyle's critical dictum claims: the meaning has gathered a form seemingly of its own accord. The initial metaphor is three-fold: vesture, body, spirit. Its suitable formal expression is, therefore, also threefold. We have seen in Carlyle's early writing and thought a strong inclination to organize his material in three parts. The task of contemporary criticism is so expressed in "State of German Literature," and a similar division is applied to religion in "Life and Writings of Werner."[10] Carlyle conceived of the task of literature as both critical and religious, since he saw the destiny of literature in its replacement of organized religion. All this is remarkable enough and well supports the threefold design of *Sartor*. But Carlyle has made his method explicit by providing a commentator on the movement of the work in the person of the Editor. The analogical application of the clothes metaphor to the task of criticism gives *Sartor* an effect of double exposure, because the examination of the world on analogy with the clothes metaphor is paralleled throughout the book by a critical commentary that underlines the very procedure of analogy itself. It follows again from Carlyle's theory. Since the critic is one who follows the same course the artist took, his critical procedure will parallel the artist's creative one. To embody his aesthetic and critical perceptions in a single work,

[10] *Works*, xxvi, 51, 143. In the latter place Carlyle speaks also of putting off and on religious creeds "like a new suit of apparel." Carlyle's ideas on literature and religion anticipate in substantial measure the more celebrated theories of Matthew Arnold. See David J. DeLaura, "Arnold and Carlyle," *PMLA*, lxxix (1964), 123–124.

Carlyle offers not only the poetic insight of the clothes metaphor but simultaneously a critical commentary on that insight. Conveniently, the double exposure of art and criticism enables Carlyle to exploit all of the writing strengths he had developed in the eighteen-twenties.

The intertwining double function of art and criticism is essential to the meaning and form of *Sartor*. Taking the whole of the book, which is paradoxically both art and criticism of it, we find that the three major divisions correspond on both levels to the threefold relationship: vesture, body, soul. Book One, the introduction to the clothes volume and its author, is the vesture or garment of the material of *Sartor Resartus*. It is simultaneously an investigation by the Editor of that vesture or garment. Book Two, the life of Teufelsdröckh, is the body which the garment covers, and at the same time the Editor's attempt to discover and delineate the peculiar nature of the poet from his poetry. Book Three constitutes the soul or spiritual existence of the whole work, just as it comprises the Editor's laying bare that soul and spiritual existence.

At all times we are, with the Editor, examining the clothes volume as critic and experiencing it as art. The simultaneity of art and criticism in *Sartor* helps explain why the work has been so perplexing. Carlyle believed his threefold method to have application to all genuine works of art, but in the case of *Sartor* he did not trust critics or readers to apply the method; so he provided an application of it in the very work itself. The function of criticism in *Sartor* also makes clear why Carlyle did not simply present what could have purported to be a full translation of *Die Kleider,* and why he did not render, as omniscient author (as in "Wotton"), a full biography of Teufelsdröckh. He would have had no assurance that the clothes volume and the biography would be properly understood. Moreover, since the structural pattern of the work and the criticism of it are parallel, they continually illuminate each other and in the end coalesce. The fact that Teufelsdröckh's work is itself a criticism, based on the threefold analogy, deepens the significance of the overall pattern.

The function of the threefold analogy in *Sartor* could be indicated visually by a strand of three interlocking circles. When we add the continuous running critical commentary, we add a parallel strand of three additional interlocking circles. It appears as follows:

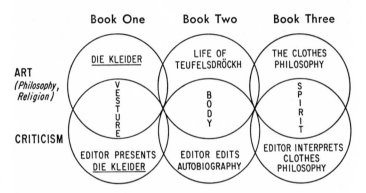

Within individual books occur analogical epicycles, the plotting of which would appear virtually Ptolemaic. Abiding with the larger units, however, we can see from the graph something of the way the three parts denominated "Art" interact with each other and with the parallel parts denominated "Criticism." Of course, only a forcible disjunction for critical purposes permits this kind of graphic presentation. Carlyle does not devote half of each book or each chapter to art and half to Criticism; he constantly mingles the two. There is no absolutely reliable way of separating even the Editor's comments from Teufelsdröckh's, but it may surprise many readers to learn that my calculations of distribution of words between Editor and Teufelsdröckh indicate close to one-half of *Sartor* to be composed of statements by the Editor, not translation, but his own commentary on translation and on his task as Editor. To give less than equal billing to the role of criticism in *Sartor* is to discard half the book, which too many critics have been all too willing to do. At the same time, it is clear from the way Carlyle modulates his material that the chief weight is to fall on the art, on the ideas and life of Teufelsdröckh. Therefore, art rightly stands above criticism in the graph.

By now it must be evident that Carlyle's threefold pattern is a matter of concept, not of imposition, that the concept and Carlyle's own literary experience dictated the materials and the form of *Sartor*. Even in terms of the larger relations in the book we have not exhausted the conceptual framework by examining the clothes analogy. There is yet the concept of natural supernaturalism, the culmination of *Sartor* and the "message" of the clothes philosophy. The explicit statement of the message belongs in the chapter of the same name, but the organizing influence of the concept brilliantly counterpoints the threefold clothes analogy. Carlyle's use of natural supernaturalism as an organizing principle calls to mind the Hegelian triad of thesis, antithesis, synthesis, although it probably does not indicate any debt to Hegel.[11] Carlyle was, however, familiar with a Goethean concept that epochs of creativity alternate with epochs of destruction, and with the more elaborate thought along these lines of the Saint Simonians. In his "History of German Literature" Carlyle presented his own version of the German idea. He divided the history of Europe into two grand movements, the supernatural (the world's youth) and the natural (the world's manhood), and he proposed the idea that Europe was on the verge of a synthesis of the two.[12]

[11] Carlyle mentions Hegel twice in *Sartor*: i, iii, 15; i, x, 69. Shine, in *Carlyle's Early Reading*, p. 266, suggests a possible reading of Hegel by December, 1831.

[12] Harrold, *Sartor*, p. 19n., suggests that Carlyle encountered the Goethean concept in the *West-Östlicher Divan*, note on "Israel in der Wüste." The reflection of Carlyle's division of European history into three stages appears in the essays developed out of his "History of German Literature." See *Works*, xxvii, 282–283 ("Early German

This synthesis was what Carlyle meant by natural supernaturalism. It is his attempt to resolve the polarities. Once
again it calls for a threefold development.

Book One of *Sartor* represents the natural world—the
world of Teufelsdröckh in Weissnichtwo, of Heuschrecke,
of the published scholarly treatise *Die Kleider*.[13] Book Two
represents the supernatural world of the pre-*Kleider* life
of Teufelsdröckh, as will become more obvious later. The
order of the books is the reverse of the historical order,
because we begin with the Now, the natural world we know
from our own experience and the stage of development
the world has now reached. Book Two, as supernatural
world, is the world of the past. Book Three represents
the world of tomorrow, or natural supernaturalism, a resolution of the polarities of the first two books, which constitute the conflict between the *temporalia* of the world
and the supernatural agency of Diogenes Teufelsdröckh.
A similar conflict can be seen operating on a smaller scale
with Books One and Two separately. Book Three resolves
the conflict, because the natural and supernatural worlds
are shown as aspects of one another, no longer in conflict
but joined in a new harmony.

Natural supernaturalism is, then, another concept demanding the same threefold division which the clothes

---

Literature"). Of the *Nibelungenlied* Carlyle wrote: "here too, a
supernatural world encompasses the natural" (*Works*, xxvii, 236).
In a rare definition of literature he stated: "Literature unites the
Past with the Present; and the scattered Present into one whole"
(Shine, *Carlyle's Unfinished History of German Literature*, p. 5).
For a full treatment of Carlyle's ideas on historical periodicity see
Hill Shine, *Carlyle and the Saint-Simonians* (Baltimore, 1941).

[13] "Natural" here is not intended to be the same as realistic or
everyday; but, in comparison to Book Two, there is in Book
One no defiance of the laws of nature as such. Improbable as
Weissnichtwo and Heuschrecke are, they are not of the supernatural
order of much of Book Two. The historical-descriptive portions
of *Die Kleider*, which appear only in Book One, are, of course,
allegedly undertaken in the spirit of modern scientific investigation,
distinctly a phenomenon of the "natural" world.

analogy, as art and as criticism, requires. We might legitimately add yet another chain of circles to the graphic rendition of the form offered previously, but the following can serve as well as schema for the whole:

Book I = Stem   Vesture   Natural World
Book II = Roots   Body   Supernatural World
Book III = Flowers   Soul   Natural Supernaturalism

Had Carlyle not indicated formal divisions in his work, one might be inclined to herald this division even more stridently than I have done. Still, in the face of Carlyle's careful indication of the major divisions, critics have persisted in rearranging it or announcing that no arrangement of any kind can be discerned.[14] Critics are, of course, at liberty to question the validity of Carlyle's philosophic stance or to give low marks for his metaphysics, but they should cease to charge Carlyle with faults of organization he did not have. His overall plan for *Sartor* is more than evident, it is persistent. To give his work a vitality absent

[14] There is a tendency in Carlyle to telescope the first two stages of his triad into one, making, for example, the garment and the body both a kind of single exterior covering. Cf. *Sartor*, I, xi, 73. Carlyle was also often impatient with the hindrances to penetration into the essence and when he is most confirmedly dualistic he posits a hostility between inner and outer that he does not resolve but seeks to leap beyond. At such time he is close to what William F. Lynch calls the "univocal imagination" (*Christ and Apollo* [New York, 1960], pp. 114–129); but he is not consistent in such matters, because they rest ultimately in a paradox. The illuminating argument here, however, is that conceptual unities do exist in *Sartor* even when subject to constant tensions. Modern studies have concentrated on the unity of relationships, but a few older studies touched on the question of conceptual unity. Wilhelm Streuli, for example, in *Thomas Carlyle als Vermittler deutschen Literatur und deutschen Geistes* (Zurich, 1895), p. 121, argues that *Sartor* has really only two parts and that the three-part division is purely external. He silently borrows Carlyle terms (and derivatively Goethe's) in calling the two parts "historisch-beschriebend" and "philosophisch-spekulativ"; but this obliges him to amalgamate Books One and Two and to ignore entirely the differences in time sequence and focus of the two books.

from pure philosophy and to insure that the reading of it would be an experience, an action as well as a thought, Carlyle also cast it in the form of a novel. Recognition of *Sartor* as a novel is long overdue. I have already touched upon the question in treating what I called its dynamic organization, but it deserves further exploration as a means of showing how the structural unity of *Sartor* is also a vital unity and that analogy and anagoge, which the conceptual framework gives us, are tied to a story that engages our interest sufficiently so that we want to reflect on the abstract concepts Carlyle is presenting.

"SARTOR" AND THE NOVEL

Most commentators are chary of denominating *Sartor Resartus* a novel: it seems to stretch the concept of that form too far. In taking a minimal definition, such as "extended piece of prose fiction," it is hard to see why *Sartor* is excluded. But most critics require more. Some relationships must be operative.[15] But even here *Sartor* may not be excluded. Carlyle himself put the case clearly when he said *Sartor* was "put together in the fashion of a kind of Didactic Novel; but indeed properly *like* nothing yet extant." And the fact is that *Sartor* is a novel but, of course, not *like* any other. Carlyle has somehow hoaxed us again. He has managed to write a novel that is also an anti-novel, years before anyone else thought of it. If Carlyle used the term *novel* for his book, and if we can readily see that it is an "extended piece of prose fiction," what hinders general recognition of *Sartor* as a novel? It is this question of human relationships and, more

[15] The minimal definition comes from Meyer H. Abrams, *A Glossary of Literary Terms* (rev. ed., New York, 1957), p. 58. An example of the concept of the primacy of human relations can be found in Walter Allen, *The English Novel* (New York, 1954), p. xvii: "Like any other artist the novelist is a maker. He is making an imitation, an imitation of the life of man on earth." Allen finds that his definition includes *Pilgrim's Progress* but not *Gulliver's Travels*.

covertly behind it, the tradition of the English realistic novel.

The real obstacle to seeing *Sartor* as a novel is, paradoxically, that portion of the book that critics have been willing to call a novel even while dispensing with the rest—Book Two, Teufelsdröckh's biography.[16] If Teufelsdröckh's biography is the novel in *Sartor,* then two other things follow: the rest of the book is not a novel but extraneous, and Teufelsdröckh's biography is not a very successful novel as such things are usually measured. But this is not the answer. The answer is that the whole of *Sartor* is a novel, with Teufelsdröckh's biography a substructure of the whole book. Further, Book Two is not conceived or executed in terms of the realistic novel of English tradition. This aspect will be treated subsequently. First, let us look at the whole of *Sartor* in novelistic focus, that is, from the point of view of a continuous story involving human relationships in a sustained illusion of a world. In such a light, *Sartor* focuses on the Editor; and the clothes volume and Teufelsdröckh are the main figures in the Editor's relationships. The kind of focus I am talking about is illustrated by the story of the lady who applied to the British Museum to see the documents from the paper bags that the Editor alleges to have deposited there

---

[16] That there is no magic in the term *novel* applied to *Sartor* is demonstrated by the fact that those who have claimed *Sartor* as a novel often have done so on the basis of Teufelsdröckh's biography. Such in part in Lindberg's basis, and it is exclusively that of Arthur Mämpel, *Thomas Carlyle als Künstler* (Göttingen, 1935), p. 62, who calls the work a "biographischer Roman." Evidence of a growing awareness that *Sartor* is a unified work of art can be seen in such recent studies as Morse Peckham's *Beyond the Tragic Vision* (New York, 1962), pp. 177–195. Peckham calls *Sartor* a novel, "such a novel as had never been written before" (p. 178). A valuable article on *Sartor* and fiction appeared after my study was completed: see George Levine, " 'Sartor Resartus' and the Balance of Fiction," *Victorian Studies,* viii (1964), 131–160. On form see also Leonard W. Deen, "Irrational Form in *Sartor Resartus,*" *Texas Studies in Literature and Language,* v (1963), 438–451.

upon completion of the biography of Teufelsdröckh.[17] The lady may have let herself be carried away by Carlyle's "ink of science," but she did not forget that our access to Teufelsdröckh is through the Editor. Or again we can turn to Carlyle, who, when he speaks of *Sartor* as a "kind of Didactic Novel," also identifies the "Editor of these Sheets" as "the main Actor in the business." The Editor, not Teufelsdröckh, is the protagonist of *Sartor* as a novel, although he is an unassuming one, who makes it appear that he is not in fact the protagonist at all. In a sense he is not, since his critical endeavors are less important than Teufelsdröckh's creative ones. It is one of those delicate arrangements that to discuss is almost to dispel. One does it more for understanding than for pleasure.

To see the Editor's role clearly in the novelistic structure of *Sartor*, we must avoid being misled, not only by Teufelsdröckh, but also by the presence of the clothes volume. It is a mistake to conceive of *Sartor* Resartus as synonymous with the volume *Die Kleider*. True, the work exists only in its pages, but *Sartor* is merely the editing of the work for British readers. *Sartor* presents only fragments of the original. Again, let the title be our guide: *Sartor Resartus* is both the retailoring of the tailor and the editing of the clothes volume. It is neither exclusively, and we cannot dispense with the process of the editing. Carlyle has contrived to exploit the typical interests of the novel—human relationships in a world we can recognize—for the purpose of engaging us in something quite different. In our day, when experimentation with the novel has reached the point of "novels" published in unattached nonsequential sheets, Carlyle's use and simultaneous nonuse of the novel should appear less surprising than it does, and his manipulation of the Editor should appear less alarming than *it* does.

As a novel *Sartor Resartus* operates through the conflict

[17] The story is told by Alexander Carlyle in *Love Letters*, II, 369n.

of the Editor with the refractory materials he uses to arrive at a completed picture of the man and his works, or "true philosophic Biography." To sidestep the role of the Editor to get at Teufelsdröckh's ideas is to sidestep the source of action in the novel. The Editor's is a normative voice in the presentation of the strange material. At the same time the Editor is an actor in the drama of the dissemination of Teufelsdröckh's views to England. The Editor's structural function constitutes also much of his meaning for the reader. Only by knowing what the purposes of the Editor's role are, can we understand how it provides a framework for the book, but one designed to be ultimately subordinated to interest in the ideas the Editor is presenting.

The Editor's story—his quest for the clothes volume and the man, for the complex of the life and opinions of Herr Teufelsdröckh—involves far more than the first and last chapters. In other words, the lesson of the underexploited frame of "Cruthers and Jonson" has been taken to heart. Approximately eight of the thirty-three chapters in *Sartor* belong primarily to the Editor—to his editorial difficulties, his observations on the material, his favorable and unfavorable reactions.[18] Moreover, virtually every chapter in the book begins with a statement by the Editor; and not a single chapter is free of his remarks and opinions. The Editor is, in fact, the only figure who appears in his own person in *every* chapter of *Sartor Resartus*. His presence simply cannot be dispensed with without doing away with much of the book itself.

We can see the Editor more clearly by a review of his role in the action. The Editor begins the book by paraphrasing some of Teufelsdröckh's ideas on the philosophy of clothes. After several pages it becomes evident that the sentiments expressed are original with someone else, and we now meet the actual Editor: "The Editor of these sheets, though otherwise boasting himself a man of con-

[18] Chapters devoted almost exclusively to the Editor and his relation to the materials are I, i, ii, iii, iv, xi; II, x; III, ix, xii.

firmed speculative habits, and perhaps discursive enough, is free to confess, that never, till these last months, did the above very plain considerations, on our total want of a Philosophy of Clothes, occur to him; and then, by quite foreign suggestion." The Editor is himself a speculative man and a former associate of Teufelsdröckh's, but he has a wholly British suspicion of the mystical meditations associated with German thought. He tells us in the next chapter that once he had been exposed to *Die Kleider* and the personality behind it, he resolved to present these altogether new ideas to the British public, but the difficulties in the way of such presentation appeared insurmountable: "Thus did the Editor see himself for the while, shut out from all public utterance of these extraordinary Doctrines, and constrained to resolve them, not without disquietude, in the dark depths of his own mind." Since the Editor is of a conservative bent, he is concerned that Teufelsdröckh's opinions might threaten existing institutions and "pervert our judgment"; so he announces that he will attempt to be a fair critic of them.

By assuming the role of critic the Editor sets the stage for the progression on the work in critical terms: and by establishing himself as a seeker after truth ("Teufelsdröckh is our friend, Truth is our divinity") the Editor sets the stage for his own involved encounter with the life and opinions of Teufelsdröckh, an encounter that will lead to the Editor's conversion. In the early part of *Sartor* the Editor repeatedly takes occasion to criticize the diction, metaphors, and sentiments of the original and to emphasize the detached, scientific nature of his own inquiry. By the end of Book One, however, the Editor is more involved in the question of the meaning of the sentiments, and he states that "the purport and promise of [the clothes philosophy] is becoming more and more important for us to ascertain." As he proceeds, the Editor's involvement increases and it includes more and more the reader himself. The arrival of the paper bags is occasion for redoubled effort by the Editor and for increased involvement. "Daily and nightly" the Editor sits with the scraps, attempting "to build a firm Bridge for British travelers," until he fears that "his whole Faculty and Self are like to be swallowed up." But the Editor is convinced that the struggle is worth the effort, and he urges the reader to join with him: "Forward with us, courageous reader; be it towards failure, or towards success! The latter thou sharest with us; the former also is not all our own."

The Editor is as hard at work in Book Two as he was in Book One. The construction of Teufelsdröckh's biography is fully as difficult an undertaking as the presentation of the clothes volumes—indeed greater, for the biography is constructed from scraps of paper in a state of immense disorder. Here the disjunction between Carlyle and the Editor is dramatically evident. Carlyle can create any materials he wants, but the Editor has no such power. The Editor must work with what he has. He is a victim of Carlyle's method and must not be confused with Carlyle himself.[19] Thus the Editor is not hypocritical (although he *is* frequently ironic). His difficulties are real, and they grow out of the relationships in the story. We are interested, or at least we are expected to be, in the Editor's task of making a coherent work out of Teufelsdröckh and the clothes philosophy, because the Editor's problem is also the reader's, and the extent to which the reader involves himself in the Editor's problem will affect his engagement with Teufelsdröckh and the clothes philosophy.

The Editor closes Book Two with the expectation that we will likely find in Book Three "some twinkling of a steady Polar star." He opens Book Three with praise for the "force of vision and of heart" with which Teufelsdröckh

[19] Use of the term *novel* at least renders this error less likely. Rinehart, in "Carlyle's *Sartor Resartus*," speaks of "Carlyle-Editor," and "Carlyle-Teufelsdröckh." We might equally well speak of "Carlyle-Heuschrecke" or "Carlyle-Blumine"; but if we think of *Sartor* as fiction, however unorthodox, we are unlikely to project Carlyle onto every figure.

"pierced into the mystery of the World." The Editor is gradually coming over to Teufelsdröckh's way of thinking, and he hopes his readers are with him: "We are to guide our British Friends into the new Gold-country, and show them the mines." In Book Three the Editor's cautions about Teufelsdröckh are no longer directed so much toward the very meaning and truth of what the philosopher says as they are toward warning the reader of Teufelsdröckh's irony: "Or has the Professor his own deeper intention; and laughs in his sleeve at our strictures and glosses, which indeed are but a part thereof?" There are, to be sure, in Book Three moments when the Editor's old suspicions and mistrusts come upon him again, especially in regard to Teufelsdröckh's political opinions. Characteristically, the Editor on the subject of politics reflects an uneasiness that the contemporary reader was likely to share. But the Editor reveals that he is won over against his will when he says, "It is our painful duty to announce, or repeat, that looking into this man we discern a deep, silent, slow-burning, inextinguishable Radicalism, such as fills us with shuddering admiration."

As the volume draws to a close, there is less criticism and more open admiration from the Editor. "Natural Supernaturalism" he calls "stupendous"; and those who have stayed with the investigation through that section are a "Happy few! little band of Friends!" The Editor himself in his own person writes the introduction to the Dandiacal Body, and it sounds very like Teufelsdröckh speaking, a stylistic influence of which the Editor is aware: "O, enough, enough of likenings and similitudes; in excess of which, truly, it is hard to say whether Teufelsdröckh or ourselves sin the more." By the final chapter the Editor's alignment with Teufelsdröckh appears more than stylistic. The Editor explains it as a case of the "lesser mind" having been "forced to become portion of the greater." Through the book the Editor has been something other than a passive recorder of the life and opinions of Teufelsdröckh. He

has endeavored to follow Carlylean critical precepts, and
in the very pursuit of the critical aim he has in large measure
become converted to the doctrines he presents. The Editor,
in revealing the soul of the poet and his works, has himself
become derivatively a prophet and a seer. Otherwise, why
did he undertake the task at all?

As a parallel to his increasing agreement with
Teufelsdröckh, the Editor's style approaches ever more
closely to Teufelsdröckh's. The few who have seen some
of the Editor's function in *Sartor* have complained that
there is not enough differentiation between the Editor's
voice and Teufelsdröckh's.[20] The Editor himself, however,
believes that the similarity has been progressive, that his
own British style has been colored by the powerful German
style of Teufelsdröckh. The Editor's conversion never takes
him so far as to applaud his absorption without qualifica-
tion; he always retains a measure of healthy British skepticism. He even promises the reader to work to erase the
harmful stylistic influences that have overtaken his writing.
To see how pervasive these have become, let us compare
two statements by the Editor, the first from the early part
of the book, the second from the final chapter:

> It were a piece of vain flattery to pretend that this
> Work on Clothes entirely contents us; that it is not,
> like all works of genius, like the very Sun, which, though
> the highest published creation, or work of genius, has
> nevertheless black spots and troubled nebulosities amid its
> effulgence,—a mixture of insight, inspiration, with dul-
> ness, double-vision, and even utter blindness. (I, iv, 28)

* * *

> Nevertheless, wayward as our Professor shows himself,
> is there any reader that can part with him in declared
> enmity? Let us confess, there is that in the wild, much-

[20] Thus Ryan, p. 16, but the differences between the Editor and
Teufelsdröckh are more pronounced than has generally been
supposed.

suffering, much-inflicting man, which almost attaches us. His attitude, we will hope and believe, is that of a man who had said to Cant, Begone; and to Dilettantism, Here thou canst not be; and to Truth, Be thou in place of all to me: a man who had manfully defied the "Time-Prince," or Devil, to his face; nay perhaps, Hannibal-like, was mysteriously consecrated from birth to that warfare, and now stood minded to wage the same, by all weapons, in all places, at all times. In such a cause, any soldier, were he but a Polack Scythe-man, shall be welcome. (iii, xii, 293)

The difference between the Editor early and late is not primarily a question of anything so transparent as sentence length. In fact, throughout the book the average sentence length of the Editor in his own voice is considerably greater than that of Teufelsdröckh.[21] It is certainly true that in many important respects the Editor's style and Teufelsdröckh's are both simply Carlylese. We can certainly see Carlyle's typical rhetorical strategy from the essays in the first example above. But there are some distinctions between the two passages. The Editor in the beginning maintains a considerably greater distance between himself and Teufelsdröckh than he does at the end. Toward the end the Editor is much more given to direct exhortation of the reader than at the beginning. The Editor therefore increasingly uses the imperative voice—surely a Teufelsdröckhism. Likewise, it is not until the end that the Editor uses the familiar *thou,* a form habitual with Teufelsdröckh. The Editor until Book Three never confesses himself moved by anything, although he frequently expresses other emotions: indignation, surprise,

[21] Spot counts in *Sartor* give the Editor an average sentence length of 40.1 words and Teufelsdröckh an average of 25.2 words. I based these counts on passages exclusively in one or the other voice, omitting the many passages that are composed of a mingling of Editor and Teufelsdröckh. The average for mingled passages—for example, the first 100 sentences of the book—is 38.2 words.

admiration, disgust, hesitation, and so on. All consciously-moving passages, all glories of nature and man, come from Teufelsdröckh. Yet we see the Editor at the end confessing that much in Teufelsdröckh "attaches us." Not that at any time the Editor becomes Teufelsdröckh. I do not believe that any reader of *Sartor* has, while reading, actually been confused as to who was speaking, although subsequent reference to the work may not distinguish between statements by Teufelsdröckh and the Editor or paraphrases by the Editor. This is understandable and as Carlyle would have wanted it. By the same token a critic may write, "Shakespeare says . . ." without specifying that it is Lear or Imogen or Mistress Quickly who really says it. But when one is examining the artistic organization of a work, then it does indeed matter who said what. In *Sartor* we must always make the distinction between the Editor and Teufelsdröckh to remind ourselves of the Editor's important mediating role.

It is in the role of the Editor, then, that *Sartor* has a kind of novelistic structure. In order to move into the ideas and story of *Sartor*, we need the mediation of the Editor. Thus the early statement from the Editor that the reader need pay no attention to him during the course of the book is paradoxically both disingenuous and sincere. Since the Editor is the critic building a bridge to the life and opinions of Teufelsdröckh, we must indeed use him to get at the life and opinions; but since the Editor is also present throughout the book, with his reactions helping condition our own and his selection determining our access to the materials, we cannot help being concerned with the Editor as a person. All this is not to say that the clothes volume and Teufelsdröckh are not of the essence of *Sartor Resartus* or that we can doubt that the author's intention is to emphasize Teufelsdröckh and his work. It is to say, however, that we must not overlook the way the material is presented and that we must not forget that Teufelsdröckh is, until the end, surrounded by the Editor. It is also to say that if we apprehend rightly the Editor's role in the movement of *Sartor*, we see in it the very unifying factor that those who seize upon Teufelsdröckh as subject fail to see. Viewed from the Editor's standpoint, the change in title is of central significance: the work is no longer "Teufelsdreck," or even "Thoughts on Clothes," but the "Clothes Volume Edited" and the "Tailor Retailored."

If the discussion of the Editor's central role has cast any light on the arrangement of parts in *Sartor*, it may seem to have done so only at the expense of the very meaning that I have alleged the structure was designed to reinforce. Have I not, by exalting the role of the Editor, violated the spirit of *Sartor*, which is, after all, to transmit the remarkable story of Diogenes Teufelsdröckh and his book, not to distract our attention with the editorial problems of a nameless figure of surely limited interest? The answer lies in our ability to use the Editor both as a figure in the larger novelistic structure and as a bridge to the materials of Teufelsdröckh and the clothes philosophy. Even as a bridge, of course, the Editor never entirely disappears, for it is the kind of access that the Editor provides to the materials that enables us to see them in proper perspective.[22] Critics customarily seize upon Teufelsdröckh's biography to discuss it out of context. If we bear in mind the Editor's placement of the biography, we see that, except for Teufelsdröckh, none of the characters in it intrudes into the contemporary world. Nor do the characters of the Editor's world have any function in Teufelsdröckh's biography. The

---

[22] This is not to say that the Editor is always right, for there are times when we are certainly going to disagree with him and when we are supposed to. Over the entire book plays the attitude of what Wayne C. Booth calls the "implied author" in *The Rhetoric of Fiction* (Chicago, 1961), pp. 70–76. In *Sartor* the implied author sometimes works to make the Editor appear overly reticent and too conservative in order, indeed, that our sympathy for Teufelsdröckh be intensified. But in general the Editor's role is that of a cicerone in Teufelsdröckh-land, and if we occasionally dwell longer here or there than the Editor does, we nevertheless follow his lead overall.

point of contact between the two groups is the town of Weissnichtwo, where contemporaries like the Editor and Heuschrecke know Teufelsdröckh. Still, neither one appears in the biography proper in Book Two. Teufelsdröckh's biography and *Die Kleider* are the two classes of materials that most need setting in proper perspective, and to these we must turn. First, however, let us note a peculiar feature of the time sequence which the Editor's mediation makes clear.

As a novel *Sartor* has three time sequences: the present, the immediate past, and the more distant past of Teufelsdröckh's life, although these do not correspond to the three books or diminish in any way the emphasis of Book Three on the future. The present is the world of the Editor, the inclusive novelistic framework. In the present world appear such figures as Heuschrecke, the nameless Hamburg booksellers who transmit material to the Editor, the reviewer of Teufelsdröckh's book in the *Weissnichtwo'sche Anzeiger,* and above all the clothes volume itself, for it is a character in the action as much as, say, the river in the story of Huck Finn. Then there is the immediate past of the Editor's reminiscences in Weissnichtwo. The Editor and Heuschrecke appear in both times. There is nothing remarkable about this in the novel, and I am not trying to make any special claims for it in *Sartor;* but it is necessary to make clear that there are time sequences in *Sartor,* to prevent confusing characters from one time sequence with those in another. Characters like Old Lieschen, Teufelsdröckh's housekeeper, and Jean Paul appear only in the immediate past of Editorial reminiscence. For one thing, Jean Paul died in 1825 and must be kept firmly in the past. For another, characters like Lieschen and Jean Paul in *Sartor* need the special aura that Teufelsdröckh casts on things to be at all acceptable in conjunction with rational figures like Heuschrecke and the Editor. Both the present and the immediate past involve the natural world, and they must be comprehensible in natural terms. The third time sequence, that of Teufelsdröckh's biography, is a world of the past, a supernatural world. About a dozen characters appear in Teufelsdröckh's biography, not counting historical figures. Except for Teufelsdröckh himself, none of these characters appears in any other time sequence. Their significance depends entirely on their function in Teufelsdröckh's biography. The time sequences are means of getting at the truth of Teufelsdröckh and his book, and it is these that must occupy our attention among the materials the Editor deploys in his critical capacity. Let us turn to these to see how *Die Kleider* and Teufelsdröckh function in *Sartor*.

"DIE KLEIDER" AND TEUFELSDRÖCKH

As a character in the action involving the Editor, the clothes volume provokes him to annoyance, amusement, suspicion, delight, awe, and numerous other reactions. Behind the volume the Editor sees the labyrinthine, complex, tumultuous mind of Diogenes Teufelsdröckh.[23] But we never really get all of the clothes volume: we get only those selections the Editor makes. That the clothes volume continually eludes the reader can be demonstrated by pointing to the impossibility of reconstituting that volume. We know that it is composed of two parts, that part one is "Historical-Descriptive," and part two "Philosophical-Speculative." The two parts correspond to the "Werden und Wirken" of the subtitle. We even know that the first chapter is about "Paradise and Fig-leaves," although it is not clear that this is the name of it. Chapter one is followed by an indefinite number of historical chapters, proceeding more or less chronologically. There is then the chapter on "Aprons," which is quoted from. Somewhat later, it seems, after addi-

---

[23] The very sentence to which this note refers offers an instance of the way in which the Editor's reactions affect us. Many commentators take the Editor's judgments, especially his early ones, as insights of their own and then use them to criticize Carlyle!

tional historical chapters, the Editor extracts from a chapter on medieval and renaissance clothing. Presumably, subsequent chapters bring the history of clothing up to the present time, that is, to the nineteenth century. Part two, the speculative-philosophical portion, is quoted from at greater length, and rightly so, for it gives us the *Wirken* of the clothes philosophy. First in Book One of *Sartor* the Editor quotes from the chapters "World out of Clothes" and "Adamitism," both from part two of *Die Kleider*. Then he gives portions of a chapter probably named "Pure Reason." He prefaces selections from all three of these chapters by saying that he is quoting "at random" from the speculative portion. In Book Three of *Sartor* the Editor quotes at greatest length from *Die Kleider,* and in that part there is somewhat more certainty about chapter titles, although, as always, the certainty is not absolute. "Perfectibility" appears to be the Editor's title for one of the chapters from the *Wirken.* It is followed by "Church-Clothes," and "Symbols"; then comes "Organic Filaments," which is apparently the Editor's own title. Finally there is "Natural Supernaturalism," which is evidently a chapter title from *Die Kleider. Die Kleider* as a volume is perceived only in fragments, only as the Editor sees fit to extract from it and translate for us. A table of contents assembled from *Sartor* would obviously be incomplete, but it would look something like this:

Die Kleider
Ihr Werden und Wirken

Part I. *Werden*
Chapter 1. "Paradise and Fig-leaves"
　Several historical chapters
c. Chapter 5. "Aprons"
　Several historical chapters
c. Chapter 8. Medieval and Renaissance clothing
　Several historical chapters up to nineteenth century

Part II. *Wirken*
Chapter 1. "World out of Clothes"

Such an abstract is clearly highly tentative. In a sense it does a disservice to *Sartor*, for it is part of the intention that we have the feeling that Teufelsdröckh's book is an inexhaustible German treatise, a vast encyclopaedic compilation into which the reader could dip without ceasing to find something new. By omitting precise details on chapters and lengths, the Editor communicates just such a feeling; Teufelsdröckh's book appears to be thoroughly typical of the type of book the Germans disarmingly call a *Handbuch*. And yet there is another reason that we never get the clothes volume steadily and whole.

In Book One the Editor offers samples of the *Werden* and *Wirken* of the clothes volume in an attempt to communicate its message, but without the aid of biography the attempt is doomed to failure. Barely launched on the speculative section in Book One, the Editor exclaims: "Would to Heaven those same Biographical Documents were come! For it seems as if the demonstration lay much in the Author's individuality; as if it were not Argument that had taught him, but Experience." In the final chapter of Book One the Editor declares that we have yet to ascertain the meaning of the clothes volume and expresses the pious hope that the biographical documents will provide a key to understanding the book. Book Two, which seems to be an interruption of the investigation of the *Die Kleider*, is, in fact, another phase of that investigation. It has, of course, its own movement and meaning, but this is related to the movement and meaning of the rest of the book. The climax of Book Two, the dramatic struggle with the Everlasting No and the affirmation of the Everlasting Yea, is not the climax of the book as a whole.[24] The Editor's selection and emphasis guide us to the greater climax in Book Three with the return to the clothes volume. This climax is "Natural Supernaturalism," of which the Editor says: "It is in his stupendous Section, headed Natural Supernaturalism, that the Professor first becomes a Seer; and, after long effort, such as we have witnessed, finally subdues under his feet this refractory Clothes-Philosophy, and takes victorious possession thereof." The Editor's purpose is clear at last: it is to emphasize the clothes *philosophy* even more than the clothes volume. Thus the final chapters are no longer selections from *Die Kleider,* but applications of the clothes philosophy to practical problems in a British context. The philosophy is actually moving out of the restrictions of Teufelsdröckh's book and even out of the Editor's book into the real world. But we miss this emphasis if we attempt to throw the Editor out and get right at Teufelsdröckh's book. Such a goal is in any case unattainable, as in Carlyle's view the whole truth of the universe is unattainable. Small portions of it we can read. The Editor is doing the duty nearest him in attempting to extract the essence of the clothes philosophy. We can never get the whole book in all its richness and detail, but we can grasp its essence, the Divine Idea of it, and that is what the Editor's selections and arrangement are designed to do.

What at last are we to make of the biography of Teufelsdröckh? Has the present schematization of *Sartor* reduced Teufelsdröckh's biography to triviality? By no means. I do not intend to minimize the legitimate interest in *Sartor* as the spiritual biography of a soul. The Editor's problem is not only to edit the clothes volume but to retailor the tailor. The reader's interest in Teufelsdröckh, in fact, sus-

---

[24] Lindberg, "Artistic Unity," p. 22, makes a similar point, although he differs from the present approach by insisting that *Sartor,* as a whole, is a biography.

tains much of the clothes material, so that Teufelsdröckh's story is called for not only on the grounds of the critical principle of delineating the peculiar nature of the poet from his poetry but also on the grounds of its inherent interest. But how are we to take the story? Why is it presented as it is?

We must first avoid the all-too-widespread error of confusing Carlyle's sources with the finished product—an error that leads us to extract Carlyle's own life from the biography of Teufelsdröckh as a kind of ultimate goal, or to identify Teufelsdröckh's laugh, for example, as unmistakably that of Dr. Johnson.[25] The greatest single disservice such an approach does to Teufelsdröckh is to suggest, however unintentionally, a kind of realism that spells death to the biography Carlyle wrote in *Sartor Resartus*. For if there is one thing Teufelsdröckh's biography is not, that thing is realistic.

Carlyle said later that nothing in *Sartor* is "fact." He called it "symbolical myth all."[26] Teufelsdröckh's biography

[25] The tendency toward the first type of criticism—*Sartor* as literal autobiography—is everywhere evident in Carlyle criticism; that toward the second—individual identifications—can also readily be found. The example given comes from D. L. Maulsby, *The Growth of Sartor Resartus* (Malden, Mass., 1899), p. 13. Others have argued that the laugh reflects Jane Welsh Carlyle's uncle Walter Welsh, and Carlyle seems to point to his friend Frank Dixon as the source of the laugh. Cf. *Reminiscences*, II, 63–64. Curiously, Maulsby argues at the same time that "it is probably mere coincidence that the circumstances of Schiller's parents were like those of young Diogenes." Yet these circumstances are surely more significant than Dr. Johnson's laugh.

[26] Although Carlyle excepts the incident in Leith Walk, even that has undergone a *märchenhaft* sea change, for he places it in *Sartor* in the Rue Saint-Thomas de l'Enfer in Paris—that is, he places the incident in the center of French rationalism and atheism on the Street of St. Thomas (The Doubter) of Hell. What is typically "factual" here is the quality of the experience itself and Carlyle's appropriations from various sources. There was in Paris truly a Rue d'Enfer (today there is an Impasse d'Enfer). For symbolic purposes Carlyle combined the street with St. Thomas. He appears to have encountered the Rue d'Enfer in his readings for "Cagliostro" and "The Diamond Necklace."

190 *Structure*

is indeed symbolical myth. It can justly be called a *Märchen.* We have repeatedly encountered Carlyle's interest and delight in the *Märchen* and the fact that it provided the ideal form for the free play of fancy and a kind of allegorical symbolism Carlyle liked.[27] In Teufelsdröckh Carlyle created his own version of a *Märchen* figure, and in Teufelsdröckh's biography Carlyle placed him in a *Märchen* world. From his first appearance Teufelsdröckh is presented as something other than a realistic figure: he lives in a tower on "Dream Lane" in the town of "Know-not-Where."[28] He is compared to the Wandering Jew and his one associate is a certain Councillor Grasshopper.[29]

---

[27] The only approximation of this idea heretofore appears in the intriguing but neglected work by Henry Larkin, *Carlyle and the Open Secret of his Life* (London, 1886). Larkin was responsible for the summaries of essays and chapters now printed in all editions of Carlyle's works. In 1857 he wrote an analysis of *Sartor* similar to Carlyle's allegorical exegesis of "Das Mährchen." He says that Carlyle called it a "poetical performance" but rejected it as too long and too difficult for readers to understand. See Larkin's "Carlyle and Mrs. Carlyle: A Ten Years' Reminiscence," *British Quarterly Review,* LXXIV (1881), 24–25. Larkin's summary now constitutes the first three chapters of *Carlyle and the Open Secret,* pp. 11–59. It is an ingenious reading of *Sartor* as an allegory of the rise and teachings of German transcendentalism. One can hardly agree with all of Larkin's interpretation, but his insistence on a not exclusively autobiographical approach and on an underlying consistency in *Sartor's* symbolic structure is both laudable and rare.

[28] Harrold gives "Dream Lane" or "Illusion Street" for *Wahngasse* (*Sartor,* p. 20n.). *Wahn* also carries the idea of madness. Harrold claims there was an actual *Wahngasse* in Munich which John mentioned to Carlyle. Weissnichtwo is evidently Carlyle's translation into German of Kennaquhair from Scott's *The Monastery.*

[29] I shall treat the Wandering Jew theme subsequently. Councillor Grasshopper is for some reason almost never "identified," but Hagberg, *Thomas Carlyle,* pp. 185–187, makes a very probable identification of Heuschrecke with Francis Jeffrey, whom Carlyle frequently referred to as a grasshopper. One might also argue for a certain Dr. Fyffe, a physician in Jane Welsh's home town of Haddington, whom Carlyle often called a cricket. But again such allusions would have been private jokes and virtually meaningless to early readers. The real meaning of Heuschrecke must reside in the fabric of *Sartor* itself. The image that a grasshopper evokes is the purpose of the name, with perhaps an implied criticism

When Heuschrecke dispatches the biographical documents, he inquires whether the conventional questions of biography can with any propriety be directed toward the life of such a figure as Teufelsdröckh. The life presented in Book Two is hardly conventional, although at the same time it is in certain important respects typical.[30]

The early part of Teufelsdröckh's life is organized around the contents of paper bags labeled with signs of the zodiac. As the turbulence in his life increases, so does the confusion in the bags (in the heavens).[31] Teufelsdröckh, we must re-

---

of magistrates as feeders on the crops of others; for *Heuschrecke* means also "locust" and translates literally as "hay terror." Regrettably, scholarship has been quicker at pointing out possible private allusions in *Sartor* than in examining their operation in terms of the relationships within the book itself.

[30] The typicality is reflected in the similarities between Teufelsdröckh's life and those of the many literary figures Carlyle was intimately familiar with, such as Schiller, Goethe, Jean Paul, Heyne, et cetera; but typicality is not intended to mean identity, since Teufelsdröckh is himself, not merely one or the other of these figures camouflaged. Although the representative quality of some of Carlyle's figures has been noted before, it has not been emphasized as a fundamental feature of the character Teufelsdröckh. See William Savage Johnson, *Thomas Carlyle: A Study of his Literary Apprenticeship, 1814–1831* (New Haven, 1911), pp. 78–81. Mämpel, *Carlyle als Künstler*, p. 63, also notes Carlyle's skill at amalgamating elements. He calls *Sartor* a "Schmelztiegel," and argues rightly that if Margaret Gordon is Blumine, nevertheless Novalis' "blaue Blume hat Pate stehen müssen."

[31] Alexander Carlyle in *Love Letters*, II, 369, makes something of the significance of the zodiacal signs. James L. Halliday in *Mr. Carlyle, My Patient* (London, 1949), p. 101, considers them highly significant, although for reasons which are scarcely acceptable to the student of literature—namely, as evidences of Carlyle's varied sexual neuroses. Halliday's book, in which Carlyle is called a "scoptophiliac," and the form of *Sartor* is said to be "anal," is an ironic fulfillment in advance of Julian Symons' less than charitable prediction that an American would someday do a study of the effect of chronic constipation on Carlyle (*Thomas Carlyle* [London, 1952], pp. 132–133)—ironic, because Dr. Halliday is British and had already done it. The American contribution, of course, was forthcoming and is represented by Gaylord C. LeRoy, *Perplexed Prophets: Six Nineteenth-Century British Authors* (Philadelphia, 1953).

member, was not born of man, but deposited by a mysterious stranger on an old couple symbolically named Futteral (cover all and feed all). His childhood and schooling are depicted by symbolic incidents. Blumine too is a fairy-tale figure. Even the name Blumine, it should be pointed out after all these years, is not really the girl's name. The Editor inquires whether we may assume from it that her real name was Flora. But the question admits no answer. She is young love, the flower of beauty, and she has no more reality than Cinderella. The Towgoods, or Toughguts, are also representative figures. They are the decadent aristocracy, shooting partridges, as the famous epitaph tells us. Teufelsdröckh wanders the earth with magical speed: it is "as if our Traveller, instead of limbs and highways, had transported himself by some wishing-carpet or Fortunatus' Hat." His spiritual crisis has, of course, been generally accepted not as a realistic depiction of events but as a reflection of a state of mind. But we customarily overlook the mechanics whereby Carlyle represents the states of mind he is describing. Yet the whole context of Teufelsdröckh's story depends on the symbolic, allegorical quality of names, places, and situations possible only in the *Märchen* world Teufelsdröckh inhabits.

The Editor puts the case squarely when he comes to comment on the just completed biography. He has, he says, a certain uneasiness about the facts of Teufelsdröckh's life, "a suspicion, in one word, that these Autobiographical Documents are partly a mystification! What if many a so-called Fact were little better than a Fiction; if here we had no direct Camera-obscura Picture of the Professor's History; but only some more or less fantastic Adumbration, symbolically, perhaps significantly enough, shadowing-forth the same!" (ɪɪ, x, 202)

In his essays Carlyle used much the same language to describe the function of *Märchen* in German literature, and as we recall the definitions of the *Kunstmärchen*, current today, we find it eminently suitable for Book Two:

". . . the *Kunstmärchen,* as the creation of an individual poet, appropriates narrative method and motifs from the *Volksmärchen* and shapes these with conscious artistry, but in so doing partly destroys the unconscious play of imagination by dressing it over with allegorical thoughts, tendencies, and meanings."[32] Put in a more favorable light, Carlyle has introduced a *Märchen* into his works much as Novalis did, a *Märchen* by no means separated from the work itself, but one that takes up and elaborates themes and images that appear in the story proper. In the *Märchen* of Book Two, *Sartor Resartus* comes to grips with that sur-reality that Marianne Thalmann recognizes as the distinctive dimension of the Romantic *Märchen.*

No form but the *Märchen* could have given Carlyle the latitude he needed to depict a figure who, like Teufelsdröckh, is a little more than human and less than divine. By freeing Teufelsdröckh from the requirements of conventional biography, Carlyle could invest his figure with symbolic significance impossible to overlook. And how else can we accept a figure with Teufelsdröckh's name and Teufelsdröckh history except on other than a realistic level? The movement of Teufelsdröckh's biography to its climax prepares us for the movement of the clothes philosophy to its climax. Teufelsdröckh, the symbolic figure, along with his symbolic philosophy, is in the end freed of the restrictions of *Sartor Resartus.* In the final chapter we find that Teufelsdröckh has disappeared from "Know-not-Where" and is even now abroad in the real world, perhaps "actually in London!" But only by following the Editor's arrangement of the materials can we appreciate the purport of Teufelsdröckh's life and opinions and their final emancipation into reality.

[32] Von Wilpert, p. 355.

V

The Texture of "Sartor Resartus"

Many careful readers of *Sartor* have declared that, while
it appears to lack unity, in truth it does not. Yet they have
often been at a loss to explain wherein this unity resides.
It is something felt, even though explanation seems to defy
logical argument. Part of the unity resides in the larger
components already examined, but the case for the artistic
integrity of *Sartor* does not stop there. Structure eventually
merges into style, but by degrees. Taken as extreme points
on a critical continuum, structure and style meet in an area
that I, adapting a term in general use, shall call texture.
By "texture" I do not of course mean that which distinguishes poetry from prose, as the term has sometimes
been used, for prose has texture as surely as poetry, if by

texture we mean the pattern of imagery, thematic inter-
weavings, the verbal surface, the very feel of a work.
Sartor is especially rich in texture, from persistent themes
that echo and revivify major ideas to specific qualities and
densities of words that condition the meaning and motion of
the book. Construed in this way, texture can show a good
deal that is easily overlooked in an examination of structure
or style: what helps knit the larger divisions together? are
there recurrent images? what thematic patterns lie below
the major structural ones?

If anything, *Sartor* is too rich in imagery, with an abundance of coruscating allusions that initially obscures the
pattern. But only initially. The reader caught up in Sartorian pyrotechnics is in large measure caught up by the very
images, themes, and allusions he has not consciously
perceived in pattern. Reflection leads us to agree with John
Holloway that Carlyle is much addicted to recurrent patterns of imagery. The problem lies in tracing these through
the lavish language of a Carlylean work. In this treatment
of texture I shall examine first the imagery in *Sartor*, then
themes or motifs. Subsequently I shall consider two aspects
of texture peculiar to *Sartor* alone, the use of fragments
and the nature of Carlyle's allusions.

IMAGERY AND THEMES

The central image of *Sartor Resartus* is clothing. This
follows, of course, from the initial metaphor, expanded, as
we have seen, into analogy. Teufelsdröckh's insight into
the world in terms of clothes permeates not only his
own extensively quoted writings but even the Editor's
mode of perception. From the title of the book flows a flood
of images relating to garments, commonplace and elegant,
quaint and fantastic. Much of what Carlyle is concerned
to do in the book is progressively to strip away coverings,
taking man down to the bare essentials, which prove
to be not merely the naked, unclothed human body
but the incorporeal, invisible human soul. Thus the

frequent imagery of visible and invisible—central in all of Carlyle—counterpoints the imagery of clothing. Likewise, the brilliant play on rags is a part of the overall clothing image; Teufelsdröckh talks of the tatters and rags of "super-annuated worn-out Symbols (in this Ragfair of a World)" and the Editor later echoes him. So much is clear. Without the clothing imagery *Sartor* as we know it would evaporate. But there are other important images too.

Beyond clothing, the most notable imagery in *Sartor* is that of light and, in dynamic opposition to it, darkness. Holloway makes a convincing case for light-dark imagery as the very basis of all Carlyle's imagery.[1] It is certainly true that a dichotomy of this sort is apparent from his earliest surviving work, the "Night-Moth" poem, and it appears again and again in later works. Light-dark imagery is an indispensable feature of *Sartor Resartus*. Like clothing, light and dark represent poles around which subordinate images gather—fire, planets, hope, and life to one, ashes, hell, despair, and death to the other, for with Carlyle light and dark are not merely visual but also moral qualities. Light symbolizes creativity, reason, power, heaven, and goodness; darkness stands for ignorance, nothingness, negation, hell, and evil. The associations are probably as old as time itself.[2] Carlyle's strength resides in the dexterity and variety of his use. The very first sentence of the book gives a taste of what Carlyle can do with light, fire, and torches:

> Considering our present advanced state of culture, and how the Torch of Science has now been brandished and borne about, with more or less effect, for five thousand

[1] John Holloway, *The Victorian Sage: Studies in Argument* (London, 1953), p. 28. For a recent brief treatment of an instance of Carlyle's imagery related to light and fire see Richard A. Levine, "Carlyle as Poet: The Phoenix Image in 'Organic Filaments,'" *Victorian Newsletter*, No. 25 (Spring 1964), pp. 18–20.

[2] Cf. Carlyle's own allusion in the first substantial quotation from *Die Kleider* to "*Nifl* and *Muspel* (Darkness and Light) of the antique North" (I, v, 37).

years and upwards; how, in these times especially, not only the Torch still burns, and perhaps more fiercely than ever, but innumerable Rush-lights, and Sulphur-matches, kindled thereat, are also glancing in every direction, so that not the smallest cranny or doghole in Nature or Art can remain unilluminated,— . . . (I, i, 3)

This first sentence is but the beginning of the play on light images in *Sartor*. It ranges from very slight allusions, such as the clothes volume becoming "lucid and lucent,"[3] to the grand apostrophe to light at the conclusion of the Everlasting Yea:

"But it is with man's Soul as it was with Nature: the beginning of Creation is—Light. Till the eye have vision, the whole members are in bonds. Divine moment, when over the tempest-tossed Soul, as once over the wild-weltering Chaos, it is spoken: Let there be Light! Ever to the greatest that has felt such moment, is it not miraculous and God-announcing; even as, under simpler figures, to the simplest and least. The mad primeval Discord is hushed; the rudely-jumbled conflicting elements bind themselves into separate Firmaments: deep silent rock-foundations are built beneath; and the skyey vault with its everlasting Luminaries above: instead of a dark wasteful Chaos, we have a blooming, fertile, heaven-encompassed World." (II, ix, 197)

In the following paragraph the reader is exhorted: "'Work while it is called Today; for the Night cometh,

[3] Carlyle was exceedingly fond of such alliterative doublets, and elsewhere in *Sartor*, he uses, among many others, "Tailors and Tailored," "Heaven-gate and Hell-gate," "Cloth-webs and Cob-webs" (pp. 56, 141, 254). Sterling berated him specifically for "lucid and lucent," insisting they have the same meaning, as perhaps they originally did; but Carlyle's sensitivity to the differences seems more defensible and is supported by modern usage. For Sterling's comment see *Sartor*, p. 310. On Carlyle's doubling and tripling see also Grace Calder, *The Writing of Past and Present* (New Haven, 1949), pp. 169–183.

wherein no man can work.'" The grand positive pole of
light stands ever in contrast to the dread negative pole of
darkness: God is light, the Devil is the "Prince of Lies and
Darkness." When in flight from the shattering experience
of Blumine, Teufelsdröckh takes comfort in "View-
hunting," and he gazes upon the superb panorama
of the mountains touched by the last gleam of the setting
sun: "'A hundred and a hundred savage peaks, in the last
light of Day; all glowing of gold and amethyst, like giant
spirits of the wilderness.'" A moment later Blumine and
Towgood pass in their Barouche-and-four, and the stricken
Teufelsdröckh quotes Richter: "*I remained alone, behind
them, with the Night.*"[4]

Light imagery spawns subordinate clusters. Fire imagery
is the most notable. Carlyle plays on the paradox of fire
as destroyer and renewer in such passages as that of the
Baphometic Fire-baptism in Book Two and in the "Phoenix" chapter in Book Three. In "Organic Filaments" he resumes the phoenix imagery:

> For us, who happen to live while the World-Phoenix
> is burning herself, and burning so slowly that, as Teufels-
> dröckh calculates, it were a handsome bargain would she
> engage to have done "within two centuries," there seems
> to lie but an ashy prospect. Not altogether so. . . . "Far
> otherwise! In that Fire-whirlwind, Creation and Destruc-
> tion proceed together; ever as the ashes of the Old are
> blown about, do organic filaments of the New mysteri-
> ously spin themselves: and amid the rushing and waving
> of the Whirlwind-element come tones of a melodious
> Deathsong, which end not but in tones of a more melodi-
> ous Birthsong." (III, vii, 244–245)

The progeny of darkness send forth their images too
in *Sartor*. The most prominent of these is the imagery
of Hell. When Teufelsdröckh has reached his lowest verge

[4] *Sartor*, II, vi, 150–151. The Jean Paul allusion is to *Quintus
Fixlein*, which Carlyle had translated in *German Romance*.

of despair in the Everlasting No, he writes: "'Doubt had darkened into Unbelief . . . shade after shade goes grimly over your soul, till you have the fixed, starless, Tartarean black.'" Significantly, only "a certain aftershine (*Nachschein*) of Christianity" holds him back from suicide. Then the double-pronged imagery of fire is employed to depict the agonies Teufelsdröckh suffered: "'The heart within me, unvisited by any heavenly dew-drop was smouldering in a sulphurous, slow-consuming fire.'" In such a mood he passes into the Rue Saint-Thomas de l'Enfer, over "pavements hot as Nebuchadnezzar's Furnace," and yet over and above that heat there suffuses a "stream of fire over [his] whole soul." With that image Carlyle is fighting fire with fire; the smoldering, sulphurous dark fire of hell is overcome by the fire that is light, that comes from Heaven.

Almost invariably Carlyle's imagery has two faces, the false and the true. There are false lights, like the rush lights and sulphur matches of science, and true lights, like the light of creation and of celestial luminaries. Even darkness has its favorable side. It sometimes pictures the unknown and the mysterious of which Carlyle was fond. So it is used, in conjunction with the glory of light, in the final passage in "Natural Supernaturalism" to suggest the transitoriness and illusion that is human life:

"So has it been from the beginning, so will it be to the end. Generation after generation takes to itself the Form of a Body; and forth-issuing from Cimmerian Night, on Heaven's mission APPEARS. What Force and Fire is in each he expends: one grinding in the mill of Industry; one hunter-like climbing the giddy Alpine heights of Science; one madly dashed in pieces on the rocks of Strife, in war with his fellow:—and then the Heaven-sent is recalled; his earthly Vesture falls away, and soon even to sense becomes a vanished Shadow. Thus, like some wild-flaming, wild-thundering train of Heaven's

Artillery, does this mysterious MANKIND thunder and flame, in long-drawn quick-succeeding grandeur, through the unknown Deep. Thus, like a God-created, fire-breathing Spirit-host, we emerge from the Inane; haste stormfully across the astonished Earth; then plunge again into the Inane. Earth's mountains are levelled, and her seas filled up, in our passage; can the Earth, which is but dead and a vision, resist Spirits which have reality and are alive? On the hardest adamant some footprint of us is stamped-in; the last Rear of the host will read traces of the earliest Van. But whence?—O Heaven, whither? Sense knows not; Faith knows not; only that it is through Mystery to Mystery, from God and to God."(III, viii, 266–267)

Light-dark imagery pervades everything in *Sartor*. It even touches names. Diogenes Teufelsdröckh, as has been long noted, signifies God-born Devil's-dung, suggesting at once the opposites of God and the devil, heaven and hell. But it also calls to mind the associations of light with goodness, for Diogenes is the man who took a lantern in the daytime looking for an honest man. At the same time the name is used in conjunction with the imagery of clothing in being, called by Teufelsdröckh "the earliest Garment you wrap round the earth-visiting ME; to which it thenceforth cleaves, more tenaciously . . . than the very skin" (II, i, 87).

These few examples merely suggest the pervasiveness of Carlyle's major images. Complete tracking is beyond the scope of the present study. But there are some image clusters that are strung together in such a way in *Sartor* that they constitute more than imagery; they operate as motifs, thematic images that knit the work together as though it were an epic or dramatic poem. These motifs are sometimes difficult to isolate, for they depend for their realization on more than a given number of images or allusions. They depend in large part on the sensitivity of the reader to Carlyle's method: once we see that Carlyle is picking up a thread of imagery or allusion and reintroducing it, we begin to perceive some of the artistic unity of *Sartor*. Three themes or motifs have been chosen to illustrate this aspect of the texture of *Sartor Resartus:* first, the Wandering Jew, or, perhaps better, the theme of Jewry in general; second, the water theme; and third, a cluster of images associated with the names Diogenes Teufelsdröckh and *Sartor Resartus*.

It has been justly claimed that Carlyle's language is heavily Biblical, and probably the theme of Jewry owes a good deal to the Biblical quality of Carlyle's prose.[5] But it is more than that; it is the result of a concerted selection of words and phrases. As the idea of Jewry is used in *Sartor*, it intensifies two central elements: one relates to the character and personality of Diogenes Teufelsdröckh, the other to the clothes philosophy. On the one hand, Carlyle's motif contributes to the picture of Teufelsdröckh as a man apart, a doubter and wanderer, and a spiritually disturbed soul. On the other hand, Jewry in connection with the clothes philosophy, in the ancient metaphor of the old versus the new, is depicted as a kind of old clothes in contrast to the new garments of the clothes philosophy. The two functions of the theme are not in any formal sense separated, although it will be necessary to separate them here for purposes of examination. Let us first examine the theme of the Wandering Jew, then the play upon Jews in general.

The story of the Wandering Jew occurs in European literature as early as the sixteenth century, and it seems to be linked to a mediaeval story told by Matthew Paris.[6]

[5] Holloway, pp. 23–26. In a cogent figure Holloway also speaks of the "marches and countermarches" of Carlyle's prose.

[6] Werner Zirus, *Ahasverus, der ewige Jude, Stoff-und Motivgeschichte der deutschen Literatur,* No. 6 (Berlin and Leipzig, 1930), pp. 1–2. There is an immense bibliography on this topic, most of the titles being German. The most recent study in English is Peter J. Thorslev, Jr., *The Byronic Hero* (Minneapolis, 1962), es-

But it did not become a favorite in popular literature until the Romantic period, when the Jew naturally appealed to a sensibility fascinated with brooding, mysterious, condemned figures. A number of English works comes to mind, such as Shelley's *Queen Mab,* and Wordsworth's "Song for the Wandering Jew."[7] But the most extensive use of the Wandering Jew theme occurs in German literature.[8] Goethe contemplated a poem in which Ahasuerus would

---

pecially the chapter "Cain and Ahasuerus," pp. 92–107. However, Thorslev does not discuss *Sartor Resartus.*

The Matthew Paris story differs in some important respects from the later legends of Ahasuerus. Paris gives his name as Cartaphilus, and the Jew is said to have become a priest in Armenia; while the later legends almost all use the name Ahasuerus, and the Jew is pictured as wandering endlessly. No direct linking of the mediaeval and modern stories has been made. The first modern treatment seems to have been a German chapbook of 1602, describing an encounter with the Jew alleged to have occurred in the previous century.

The kernel of the modern story is that of the Jerusalem shoemaker who refused Christ rest on the way to the cross, and who was therefore condemned to wander the earth forever, unappeasable and peregrine.

[7] Lesser-known English treatments before Carlyle are Maturin's novel *Melmoth the Wanderer* (1820), George Croly's *Salathiel* (1827), and Shelley's 1810 poem "The Wandering Jew," first published in 1829, and again in *Fraser's* in 1831. The most impressive French treatment of the legend did not appear until the series of stunning woodcuts executed by Gustave Doré in 1854.

There are also a number of English works which tell similar stories in different guises, such as Southey's *Curse of Kehama* (1810) and Coleridge's "Wanderings of Cain," which the author abandoned to write the story of another outcast, "The Rime of the Ancient Mariner." See Moncure Daniel Conway, *The Wandering Jew* (New York, 1881) pp. 225–248. Conway, who also wrote a biography of Carlyle, notes the presence of the Wandering Jew in *Sartor,* but he confines his few remarks to one passage, in which the idea is explicitly expressed (Conway, pp. 246–248). Zirus, p. 71, lists nine treatments in English before *Sartor,* which he does not include. Nor does he mention the appearance of the legend in Percy's *Reliques,* although this appearance was probably very influential in the Romantic period.

[8] Zirus, pp. 64–71, lists more than seven pages of bibliography for German treatments of the legend from 1602 to 1930. Some thirty-two entries are dated before the publication of *Sartor.*

have been treated as a Faust figure, although the fragment
he left is in a different vein.[9] Schubart, Schlegel, and Arnim
all wrote versions of the story. In 1816 Franz Horn, one
of Carlyle's authorities on German literary history, wrote
a novel about the Wandering Jew. Carlyle reviewed, un-
favorably, Klingemann's play *Ahasuerus* (1825) in the essay "German Playwrights"; the play was based on Horn's
novel.[10] The list indeed is far longer, and the flood of

[9] Zirus, pp. 9–10, 24. A more extensive treatment of Goethe's
preoccupation with the theme can be found in Johann Prost, *Die
Sage vom ewigen Juden in der neueren deutschen Literatur* (Leipzig,
1905), pp. 12–19; and J. Minor, *Goethes Fragment vom ewigen
Juden und vom wiederkehrenden Heiland* (Stuttgart and Berlin,
1904). Cf. also Goethe's comments in *Dichtung und Wahrheit*
(*Werke,* "Jubiläums-Ausgabe," xxiv, 228–231) with his fragment
"Der ewige Jude" (*Werke,* iii, 232–241). Carlyle could not have
known the fragment, first published in 1836, but he had read
Dichtung und Wahrheit. Goethe says that he considered the subject
at a time when he was concerned about the problem of original
sin and heresy. He intended, among other things, to trace the
history of Christianity through the story of the Jew. In an essay
reworked from material in the "History of German Literature" at
the very time of the writing of *Sartor,* Carlyle refers to a work
called *Faust and The Wandering Jew,* published in Leipzig in
1824. See "Early German Literature," *Works,* xxvii, 307.

The story continues to exert a certain attraction into our own
times: Paul Elmer More, in *Pages from an Oxford Diary* (Princeton,
1951), Sect, v, tells of his desire to write the story when under
the influence of German Romantics; George Sylvester Viereck's and
Paul Eldridge's novel *My First 2000 years* is subtitled "The Autobiography of the Wandering Jew" (London, 1929); and more
recently Pår Lagerkvist published his version in *The Death of
Ahasuerus* (New York, 1962).

[10] There is no evidence that Carlyle knew Horn's novel, although
he may well have. In "State of German Literature" he wrote of
Horn: "His novels, accordingly, to judge from the few we have
read of them, verge towards the sentimental" (*Works,* xxvi, 27).

The review of Klingemann's play appears in *Works,* xxvi, 370–372.
In his discussion of the play Carlyle makes the following arresting
comment: "Why do Klingemann and all the Germans call the man
Ahasuer, when his authentic Christian name is John; *Joannes a
Temporibus Christi,* or, for brevity's sake, simply *Joannes a Tempori-
bus?* This should be looked into." There is no trace of this idea
in *Sartor,* but earlier, in an appendix to the *Life of Schiller* (1825),
Carlyle noted Schubart's story and commented on *Joannes a
Temporibus;* see *Works,* xxv, 299–300.

Wandering Jew stories and plays in German literature raged into the eighteen-thirties and forties and beyond.

Carlyle's use of the Wandering Jew theme occurs during a period of widespread European interest in Ahasuerus; but in *Sartor* Carlyle is not retelling the Wandering Jew story or attempting to write his own version: he is simply exploiting certain of its aspects, sometimes satirically, to help define the character of Teufelsdröckh. Again we must not confuse Carlyle's sources with the finished product.[11] He who would know the story of the Wandering Jew should not look to *Sartor Resartus;* but he who knows that story will find that Carlyle has used some of its salient features to depict Diogenes Teufelsdröckh, and, further, that the idea of Jewry reverberates beyond the story of Teufelsdröckh to underline the prevailing clothes metaphor.

Annotated editions of *Sartor* customarily first identify the Wandering Jew when explicit reference is made to him in chapter three of Book One.[12] Actually Carlyle suggests the idea earlier. In chapter one the Editor transcribes the title page of Teufelsdröckh's book as follows: " '*Die Kleider, ihr Werden and Wirken* (Clothes, their Origin and Influence): *von Diog. Teufelsdröckh, J.U.D. etc. Stillschweigen, und Cognie. Weissnichtwo, 1831.*' " Annotations of this title explain everything but the pun in Teufels-

---

[11] Thus it is tempting to identify Carlyle himself with the Wandering Jew, but it is meaningful only as it casts light on *Sartor*. As early as 1824 he wrote to Jane: "My ideas cannot rest, for nothing about me or my fortunes rests. The Wandering Jew or Shoemaker of Jerusalem was but a type of me. From day to day my scene changes, my companions change, my hopes, my fears; nothing stays with me but my old friends Disease and *Tedium vitae,* kind followers, that at a closer or a wider distance never fail to trace my footsteps, turn me whither I may" (*Love Letters,* I, 383).

[12] *Sartor*, I, iii, 17, and n. Harrold's note, however, is in error. He calls the Ahasuerus legend mediaeval and distinguishes it from the legend of the shoemaker who refused Christ rest, but Ahasuerus was usually considered to be the same person as the shoemaker. The mediaeval legend, as stated, was that of Cartaphilus, the Armenian priest. Goethe, calling his character Ahasuerus, modelled him on an actual Dresden shoemaker.

dröckh's university degree. The usual explanation reads:
"Doctor of Civil and Canon Law, i.e., LL.D," which is, of
course, perfectly accurate as far as it goes. But at the same
time the university degree as Carlyle abbreviates it is designed to suggest the Jew, the German word for Jew being
Jud-e.[13] The title of *Sartor* when Carlyle offered it to
Fraser's in May 1833 was still "Thoughts on Clothes," and
the subtitle, "or Life and Opinions of Herr D.
Teufelsdröckh, D.u.J." In August Carlyle changed the title
to *Sartor Resartus.* Evidently, at the same time he altered
the conventional abbreviation D.u.J. (Doctor utriusque
Juris) to the unconventional J.U.D. No possible reason for
such a change exists except the play on the word for Jew.

By chapter three the association of Teufelsdröckh with
the Wandering Jew is made explicit: ". . . they called him
the *Ewige Jude,* Everlasting, or as we say, Wandering Jew."
The term Eternal Jew is the more common in Teutonic
countries, that of Wandering Jew in Latin countries.[14]
Carlyle plays upon both ideas. Before calling him the
Wandering Jew, the Editor explains that Teufelsdröckh
"was a stranger in Weissnichtwo, wafted thither by the
course of circumstances." And after identifying him as the
Wandering Jew, the Editor explains further that in Weissnichtwo Teufelsdröckh was more an accepted natural
phenomenon than a human being: "To the most, indeed,
he had become not so much a Man as a Thing: which
Thing doubtless they were accustomed to see, and with
satisfaction; but no more thought of accounting for than
for the fabrication of their daily *Allgemeine Zeitung,* or
the domestic habits of the Sun."

The Eternal and Wandering Jew theme provides

[13] For clarity I have indicated the stem. The word is a weak
noun, declined as an adjective, so that the only unchanging portion
of the word is the stem *Jud-.* Note, too, that many German-Jewish
surnames are taken from trees, plants, metals, etc.—another justification for asafoetida. Cf. below, pp. 220–222.

[14] Zirus, p. 2. Perhaps this neat division is an exaggeration. In
Dutch he is *de wandelende Jood,* in French *le juif errant,* in Italian
Ebreo errante, but in Spanish he is *Juan Espera en Dios.*

Teufelsdröckh with certain characteristics which coincide
with the role he is to play and with the nature of the
Märchen invented to depict his life.[15] In the "Sorrows of
Teufelsdröckh" explicit reference is again made to the
Wandering Jew: "Thus must he, in the temper of ancient
Cain, or of the modern Wandering Jew . . . wend to and
from with aimless speed." As the Wandering Jew, Teufelsdröckh is the man apart, the endless wanderer, restlessly
seeking rest, cut off from normal human enjoyments—*the*
Romantic figure. But at the same time there is a touch of
the ludicrous, as there is inadvertently in Klingemann's
treatment. In *Sartor*, however, the leaven of irony is at
work. The irony undercuts the histrionics of the "Sorrows
of Teufelsdröckh" and calls to mind not only the Wandering Jew but the spate of *Werther*-like stories that the
Romantic age produced. Werther and the Wandering Jew
are intimately connected in any case. Goethe's own plan
for the Wandering Jew story seems to have been
abandoned partly because he divested himself of the more
lurid feelings he associated with it by writing *Werther*.[16]

[15] A hitherto unnoted source for a famous Sartorian expression—
"Aesthetic Tea"—may have stimulated Carlyle's thinking about the
Wandering Jew. In Wilhelm Hauff's *Mitteilungen aus den Memoiren
des Satan* (1825–1826) the whole central section is devoted to
Satan's encounter with the Wandering Jew. After lengthy conversation with the Jew, Satan invites him to an "aesthetischen Tee,"
the description of which occupies some half-dozen pages. See
Wilhelm Hauffs Werke, ed. Felix Bobertag, *Deutsche National
Literatur*, ed. Joseph Kürschner (Stuttgart [1891–1892]), CLVII, pp.
61–102. See also Edwin Sommermeyer, *Hauff's "Memoiren des Satan"*
(Berlin, 1932). There is no record of Carlyle's having read this or
any work by Hauff, who also wrote numerous *Märchen*, but the
identity of terms is too striking to dismiss as coincidence.

[16] *Dichtung und Wahrheit*, *Werke*, XXIV, 231. *Faust* too seems
to have disposed of some of the impulse behind the original plan
for the story. Cf. Zirus, p. 24.
The variety of functions to which the Wandering Jew theme
has been put is the basis for the organization of Zirus' monograph:
Ahasuerus as restless wanderer, as believing admonisher, as critic
of the times, as a "weltschmerzlich" sufferer, as benefactor and
savior. Teufelsdröckh partakes of most of these roles in *Sartor*,
with perhaps chief emphasis on his roles as critic and benefactor.

Thus in *Sartor* the Editor, who is "Conservative" and "Anti-quack," dispels some of the aura of romantic doom and gloom that has been created around Teufelsdröckh by the events in "Romance" with the observation that to the less philosophical reader there are but three things for Teufelsdröckh to do now that he has lost Blumine: "Establish himself in Bedlam; begin writing Satanic Poetry; or blow out his brains. In the progress towards any of which consummations, do not such readers anticipate extravagances enough; breast-beating, brow-beating (against walls), lion-bellowings of blasphemy and the like, stamping, smitings, breakages of furniture, if not arson itself?" Thus does Carlyle disengage *Sartor* from the purely romantic treatments of the *Werther* type, only at the same time to continue using seriously those elements associated with the Wandering Jew that serve his purpose. The method is the familiar one of Carlylean paradox. Teufelsdröckh *is* a romantic figure, full of sound and fury, but he is also being subjected to counterinfluences best expressed by that favorite nineteenth-century term— *Bildung*.[17] In Teufelsdröckh, as intensified by the theme of the Wandering Jew, there is a conflict between finite and infinite, natural and supernatural, which must be resolved if a whole personality is to result.

Teufelsdröckh's response to the loss of Blumine is to set forth with his *Pilgerstab* to begin a "perambulation and circumambulation of the terraqueous Globe"—a response at once romantic and indicative of the start of inner *Bildung*, just as Meister's *Wanderjahre* follow upon the *Lehrjahre*. Throughout the remainder of the chapter we endeavor to follow the Wanderer's wanderings. Nor do they cease until "The Everlasting Yea." Carlyle may have known

[17] Roy Pascal has pointed out that the German emphasis on *Bildung* was a response to the problem of specialization and, more specifically, a consideration of the problems of the individual in contrast to the Scottish school concentration on the state. See his "*Bildung* and the Division of Labor" in *German Studies Presented to Walter Horace Bruford* (London, 1962). pp. 14–28.

the nineteenth-century version of the story that took the
Jew on his wanderings to the north pole, for in the "Centre
of Indifference" he sends Teufelsdröckh to the North Cape.
Thus the theme helps determine the structure. And the
Wandering Jew theme harmonizes with the *Märchen* world
of Diogenes Teufelsdröckh. As a *Märchen* figure Teufelsdröckh is everywhere; he travels by magic carpet and Fortunatus' Hat: "In figurative language, we might say he becomes, not indeed a spirit, yet spiritualised, vaporised."[18]
As the Wandering Jew he encounters a multitude of public
events: "Teufelsdröckh, vibrating everywhere between the
highest and the lowest levels, comes into contact with public History itself. For example, those conversations and relations with illustrious Persons, as Sultan Mahmoud, the
Emperor Napoleon, and others, are they not as yet rather
of a diplomatic character than of a biographic?"

By the end of "Sorrows of Teufelsdröckh" varying
strands come together in explicit statement by the
Editor:

> Thus must he, in the temper of ancient Cain, or of
> the modern Wandering Jew,—save only that he feels
> himself not guilty and but suffering the pains of
> guilt,—wend to and from with aimless speed. Thus must
> he, over the whole surface of the Earth (by footprints),
> write his *Sorrows of Teufelsdröckh;* even as the great
> Goethe, in passionate words, had to write his *Sorrows
> of Werter,* before the spirit freed herself, and he could
> become a Man. Vain truly is the hope of your swiftest
> Runner to escape "from his own Shadow"! Neverthe-
> less, in these sick days, when the Born of Heaven first
> descries himself (about the age of twenty) in a world
> such as ours, richer than usual in two things, in Truths
> grown obsolete, and Trades grown obsolete,—what can
> the fool think but that it is all a Den of Lies, wherein

[18] Carlyle couples the Jew and Fortunatus' Hat explicitly in "On
History Again," *Works,* xxviii, 168.

whoso will not speak Lies and act Lies, must stand idle and despair? Whereby it happens that, for your nobler minds, the publishing of some such Work of Art, in one or the other dialect, becomes almost a necessity. For what is it properly but an Altercation with the Devil, before you begin honestly Fighting him? (II, vi, 156)

The Wandering Jew theme has joined forces with *Werther* and has done further service in providing Teufelsdröckh with the kind of *Bildung* necessary for the man of sensibility and talent in the modern world if he is to come to grips with the multitudinousness of life. Throughout the following three chapters, the climax of Book Two, it is evident that Teufelsdröckh has reached his spiritual majority largely through what he learned in his wanderings, that indeed his wanderings, spanning as they do time and space in a way quite impossible for an ordinary mortal, symbolize as well the condition of European man after centuries of learning, wars, art, and religion. By exploiting some of the characteristics of the Wandering Jew, Carlyle has invested his hero with a representative quality designed to render his lesson applicable to a large number of men.

Besides helping to particularize and generalize Teufelsdröckh, the Wandering Jew theme is made to link up with another very important aspect of *Sartor*—the idea of old clothes, outworn beliefs. In the same chapter in which the Editor refers to Teufelsdröckh the Wanderer in preparation for the forthcoming biography, he quotes from Heuschrecke's letter about Teufelsdröckh's attainment of the clothes philosophy: " 'By what singular stair-steps, in short, and subterranean passages, and sloughs of Despair, and steep Pisgah hills, has he reached this wonderful prophetic Hebron (a true Old-Clothes Jewry) where he now dwells?' " Typically, this one short passage calls for four explanatory footnotes in the standard edition: one to note the echo of Bunyan in Slough of Despair; one to refer to Deuteronomy for the reference to Pisgah hills from which Moses viewed the promised land; one to explain that Hebron was the residence of King David and the burial place of the patriarchs; and finally, one to explain that Old-Clothes Jewry is an allusion to the former London ghetto, the Old Jewry, now a street of that name. But the allusions are also connected to Teufelsdröckh as the Wandering Jew and as a kind of spiritual Jew among Gentiles. For in the paragraph immediately following, Heuschrecke declares: " 'Certain only that he has been, and is, a Pilgrim, and a Traveller from a far Country; more or less footsore and travel-soiled; has parted with road-companions; fallen among thieves, been poisoned by bad cookery, blistered with bugbites.' " The New Testament echo in this passage has its purpose too, for Teufelsdröckh is one of the prophets, but he is also one of the apostles.

Throughout Book Two there are constant plays on the idea of the Jew, most of them connected with the Wandering Jew but some referring to Jewry in a broader sense. Teufelsdröckh is said, for example, to have in him "the old Adam," a common enough allusion to be sure; but it also echoes the chapter in Book One on "Adamitism," in which the fear is expressed that Teufelsdröckh is a "new Adamite," a fear the Editor is at pains to allay. Much of the purpose of the network of allusions to Jewry, to the Old and the New Testaments, is not so much to serve an explicitly Christian purpose (since existing creeds are outworn) as to make use of a familiar dichotomy to advance the idea that we need new creeds for new times.

The most sustained allusion to spiritual Jewry occurs in Book Three in the chapter appropriately titled "Old Clothes," in which Teufelsdröckh is quoted on the occasion of a visit to London when he walked in Monmouth Street. The passage is, of course, satiric, but it is also serious. Monmouth Street, the location of old-clothes shops, becomes for Teufelsdröckh a temple, and the Jewish hawkers of old clothes are likened to the Pope with triple tiara. These sellers of old clothes are also Wandering Jews. This time, however, they remind us of the phophets, not of the storm-tossed Werther figure. Teufelsdröckh writes of his excursion into Monmoth Street.

"Often have I turned into their Old-Clothes Market to worship. With awe-struck heart I walk through that Monmouth Street, with its empty suits, as through a Sanhedrim of stainless Ghosts. Silent are they, but expressive in their silence: the past witnesses and instruments of Woe and Joy, of Passions, Virtues, Crimes, and all the fathomless tumult of Good and Evil in 'the Prison men call Life.' Friends! trust not the heart of that man for whom Old Clothes are not venerable. Watch, too, with reverence that bearded Jewish High-priest, who with hoarse voice, like some Angel of Doom, summons them from the four winds! On his head, like the Pope, he has three Hats,—a real triple tiara; on either hand are the similitude of wings, whereon the summoned Garments come to alight; and ever, as he slowly cleaves the air, sounds forth his deep fateful note, as if through a trumpet he were proclaiming: 'Ghosts of Life, come to Judgment!'" (III, vi, 241)

For Carlyle's contemporaries the use of Field Lane and Monmouth Street must have been especially telling. Larkin, writing a half-century later, vividly describes the scene Carlyle had in mind: "Field Lane also has been swept from existence by the new times; but both it, and what where once called the 'Ou' Clo' men,' were once familiar enough to the inhabitants of London. The weird look of those Wandering Jews, and their bodeful perpetual cry—'Ou' Clo'—Ou' Clo','—through all the streets, seems to have stirred strange feelings of coming doom in Carlyle's mind."[19]

[19] Larkin, *Carlyle and the Open Secret*, p. 48. Larkin points out that Carlyle alludes again to the clothes merchants in *Latter-Day Pamphlets*. With the Jew and Jewry Carlyle may also have been alluding generally to chthonic powers and the forces of magic. See his allusions to Talmudic and cabbalistic lore, *Sartor*, I, iv,

Remarkably enough, Carlyle does not use the term Wandering Jew in the passage in question. Nor does Larkin show himself aware of the motif in *Sartor*. It would seem that the term Wandering Jew came to Larkin's mind as a natural descriptive term for the "bodeful" figures of Monmouth Street evoked by Carlyle's description and Larkin's own memory of the place.

When at the close of *Sartor* the Editor reports that Teufelsdröckh has disappeared from Weissnichtwo, there is in his mysterious vanishing once again a hint of the role of the Wandering Jew. The Jew seems always to have been present at the great moments in history: he had seen the sack of Rome, witnessed the Crusades, and, like Teufelsdröckh, he had appeared at decisive Napoleonic battles. Now Teufelsdröckh, with his portentous comment on the Paris Revolts of 1830, "*Es geht an*," has departed Weissnichtwo to witness the new birth of society. Perhaps, Heuschrecke speculates, he has left behind him in his archives the long-awaited *Palingenesie*, wherein the new birth itself is set forth.

Jewry in *Sartor* has more than merely verbal significance. It is a means of delineating the struggle in Teufelsdröckh's soul and of portraying the course he follows to resolve his conflict. It links Teufelsdröckh with history and the phenomena described in the clothes volume. It is a way of capitalizing on the contrast between old and new and on the prophetic element of the Old Testament as well as on the emphasis on regeneration in the New Testament. The linking of the Wandering Jew Motif with the Old-Clothes Jewry motif shows on a small scale what is continually going on in Carlyle's prose. An image or metaphor begets an idea, which is then expanded and explored, let drop from sight, brought forward again later, allowed to submerge again only to re-emerge slightly altered or recolored, joined to another image, and so on. The resulting density is something quite staggering. Thus in the very passage in which the two valences of Jewry merge, in "Sorrows of Teufelsdröckh," they touch upon another pattern of imagery that has reverberations throughout the book— water imagery.

Teufelsdröckh's unrequited love sets him forth on a "circumambulation of the terraqueous Globe," and shortly thereafter we learn that he viewed the entire love affair as "a Calenture . . . whereby the Youth saw green Paradise-groves in the waste Ocean-waters." The fact is that Teufelsdröckh's whole progression through life is related to water, to the movement of water itself, and to passage of the wanderer over bodies of water. His wanderings upon the loss of Blumine are reported in scattered fragments in Capricornus and, above all, in Aquarius, the water-bearer. But the imagery has begun before this. Let us go back to the childhood of little Gneschen.

He was deposited upon the Futterals in the village of Entepfuhl ("Duckpond"). Gneschen's childhood was sheltered, as he tells us later in his autobiographical fragments: "The young spirit has awakened out of Eternity, and knows not what we mean by Time; as yet Time is no fast-hurrying stream, but a sportful sunlit ocean, years to the child are as ages: ah! the secret of Vicissitude, of that slower or quicker decay and ceaseless down-rushing of the universal World-fabric, from the granite mountain to the man or day-moth, is yet unknown." Time, for the young, is a calm sea, but it will become both a turbulent stream and an ocean of sorrow. Here we can begin to see the significance of the much misunderstood Kuhbach ("cow brook"), the "little Kuhbach" that gushes "kindly by, among beech rows, through river after river into the Donau, into the Black Sea, into the Atmosphere and Universe." The flow of its waters forms a parallel with life. The Kuhbach passage that has previously been examined in its several versions finds its proper place in the context of *Sartor* as it never did in "Wotton." With the idea of a water theme in mind we can look again at the passage in its final form:

"It struck me much [Teufelsdröckh reminisces], as I sat
by the Kuhbach, one silent noontide, and watched it
flowing, gurgling, to think how this same streamlet had
flowed and gurgled, through all changes of weather and
of fortune, from beyond the earliest date of History.
Yes, probably on the morning when Joshua forded Jordan;
even as at the mid-day when Caesar, doubtless with
difficulty, swam the Nile, yet kept his *Commentaries*
dry,—this little Kuhbach, assiduous as Tiber, Eurotas
or Siloa, was murmuring on across the wilderness, as
yet unnamed, unseen: here, too, as in the Euphrates
and the Ganges, is a vein or veinlet of the grand World-
circulation of Waters, which, with its atmospheric
arteries, has lasted and lasts simply with the World."
(II, iii, 102)

Teufelsdröckh the sojourner takes his voyage on the
metaphorical sea of life, as does each individual man. The
waters of the Kuhbach are part of the waters of the world,
in times past and in the future, part of a vast unity of
being of which Carlyle's awareness is so profound that it
can only be called mystic. The commentators who seize
upon Entepfuhl and the Kuhbach as nothing more than
Carlyle's way of referring (presumably for some private
joke) to the duckpond in Ecclefechan fed by a meandering
"burn," or brook,[20] have not merely missed the larger
significance of these two aspects of the "World-circulation

[20] See *Sartor* pp. 81n., 91n. Carlyle may well have had personal
allusions in mind for both Entepfuhl and the Kuhbach, including
a rarely noted play on the Dumfriesshire stream the "Water of
Milk," but such allusions must remain secondary in a consideration
of the art of *Sartor*. A good example of how some have remained
happily undetected is provided by Teufelsdröckh's reminiscences
of the yearly-returning Swallows (II, ii, 96), unglossed in editions
of *Sartor*. It is possible that Carlyle had in mind the returning
Craigenputtock swallows that he wrote of in the poem "To a Swallow
Building under Our Eaves," *Love Letters*, II, 358–59, although that
is hardly the point of the passage in *Sartor*.

of Waters," but they have misled countless readers into believing that Carlyle's purpose here was to depict his own life in quasi-realistic terms, terms moreover that no more than a half-dozen contemporary readers could have appreciated; whereas any reader can appreciate the water imagery if he gives up the reins of his imagination to Carlyle, especially because Carlyle rarely lets his references stand without gloss.

Changes in the water imagery indicate Teufelsdröckh's progress in life. At first it is Entepfuhl, the little duckpond, and Gneschen merely speculates on the destination of the Kuhbach. But after Teufelsdröckh has been to the university and passed his auscultatorship he must leave the paternal nest, although scarce-fledged: "Already has the young Teufelsdröckh left the other young geese; and swims apart, though as yet uncertain whether he himself is cygnet or gosling." When his sorrows overwhelm him, and he sets off on his wanderings, it becomes, the Editor tells us, increasingly difficult to follow his course:

> The river of his History, which we have traced from its tiniest fountains, and hoped to see flow onward, with increasing current, into the ocean, here dashes itself over that terrific Lover's Leap; and, as a mad-foaming cataract, flies wholly into tumultuous clouds of spray! Low down it indeed collects again into pools and plashes; yet only at a great distance, and with difficulty, if at all, into a general stream. To cast a glance into certain of those pools and plashes, and trace whither they run, must, for a chapter or two, form the limit of our endeavour. (II, vi, 153)

From Teufelsdröckh's arrival in the world through his early manhood Carlyle has depicted his life in terms of water—in still ponds, in tiny rivulets, in swift currents, in mighty rivers, at last pouring itself into the ocean, into the ultimate element of the world. At length the Editor contents himself with discerning the general flow of Teufelsdröckh's biography without being able to trace its specific outward course; for at the end of the biography he says:

> His [Teufelsdröckh's] outward Biography, therefore, which, at the Blumine Lover's-Leap, we saw churned utterly into spray-vapour, may hover in that condition, for aught that concerns us here. Enough that by survey of certain "pools and plashes," we have ascertained its general direction; do we not already know that, by one way and other, it *has* long since rained-down again into a stream; and even now, at Weissnichtwo, flows deep and still, fraught with the *Philosophy of Clothes*, and visible to whoso will cast eye thereon? (ii, x, 204)

In view of the frequent comparison of Teufelsdröckh's biography to a stream flowing into the ocean, the significance of the Editor's constant references to his own task as a "bridge" becomes considerably deepened; likewise the "pontoons" the Editor is continually throwing out are apt figures in the context. Immediately after the passage cited above the Editor says: "To speak in that old figure of the Hell-gate Bridge over Chaos, a few flying pontoons have perhaps been added, though as yet they drift straggling on the Flood; how far they will reach, when once the chains are straightened and fastened, can, at present, only be matter of conjecture" (ii, x, 205). If it were merely a question of vivifying Teufelsdröckh's life and progress, the water imagery in *Sartor* would still be worth noting. But things are never so simple in Carlyle. His images serve to give particular point to his thought as well. As must have been evident from the Kuhbach citation, water imagery, like light and dark, heat and cold, is designed to communicate Carlyle's total vision. Therefore, it is not dropped when the biographical portions are completed. In the climatic chapter of *Sartor*, "Natural Supernaturalism," water imagery is one of the means by which the unity of all things is conveyed. Teufelsdröckh, writing on nature, compares it to water and man to the smallest creature in the water:

"To the Minnow every cranny and pebble, and quality and accident, of its little native Creek may have become familiar: but does the Minnow understand the Ocean Tides and periodic Currents, the Tradewinds, and Monsoons, and Moon's Eclipses; by all which the condition of its little Creek is regulated, and may, from time to time (*un*miraculously enough), be quite overset and reversed? Such a minnow is Man; his Creek this Planet Earth; his Ocean the immeasurable All; his Monsoons and periodic Currents the mysterious Course of Providence through Aeons of Aeons." (III, viii, 258)

The wealth of imagery, themes, and motifs in *Sartor* can hardly be overemphasized and certainly not exhausted. Carlyle's use is a little like the orchestration of leitmotifs: now this one, now that one is brought forth in the score, modulated, transposed, let sink back into the main body of the music while another is drawn forward. The process takes place on a smaller scale too, with certain images peculiar to specific portions of the books and others dispersed but only sparingly used. Two such are the play on the zodiac and the name Diogenes Teufelsdröckh.

All of the biographical information about Teufelsdröckh comes from what the Editor is able to piece out of the scraps of paper jammed into six bags, each marked with a zodiacal sign. The notes being in Teufelsdröckh's own hand result in our having a biography that is paradoxically also an autobiography. Critical comment about the peculiar means of preserving the scraps of paper in the six paper bags is almost entirely wanting, except, of course, for the notation that Jean Paul frequently uses similar devices to account for the acquisition of his manuscripts, the chief example being *Hesperus*.[21] But one wonders why Carlyle chose to mark the bags with the signs of the zodiac. We must remember that we are, in the biography, in a *Märchen* world where meanings are adumbrated and allegorized. Teufelsdröckh is, first of all, brought to Entepfuhl by a mysterious stranger, nameless, unidentifiable. The stranger is obviously an emissary of heaven, so that Diogenes is quite literally born of God, is heaven-sent. The number of occasions on which terms like "Heaven-sent," the "born of Heaven," and the like are used to describe Teufelsdröckh is so vast that Carlyle's method begins to resemble the Homeric epithet. But for the born-of-heaven what more appropriate receptacles for biographical notes than bags marked with the signs of the heavens? Since Teufelsdröckh comes from heaven, heaven guides his destiny. But why these particular zodiacal signs? Biographical criticism is entirely at a loss to explain them, for Carlyle himself was born in December, in Sagittarius, not, like Teufelsdröckh, in Libra. Further, Teufelsdröckh's "birthdate," or deposit date, may be calculated as having taken place as early as 1775, not as late as 1795 like Carlyle's.[22] As so often in *Sartor*, the explanation of these

---

[21] *Hesperus* (1798) is divided into 45 "Hundposttage" (Dogpost days), which signify the delivery of installments of the book to the editor by a Spitz. See Carlyle on this device in *Works*, XXII, 119; XXVI, 12. J. A. S. Barrett's note, quoted by Harrold, *Sartor*, p. 78, that "The bags seem to cover about five years of the hero's life," is clearly erroneous. The bags take Teufelsdröckh from birth to young manhood.

[22] Carlyle is intentionally vague as to the date, but Andreas Futteral is described as a veteran of the Battles of Rossbach (1757), Hochkirch (1758), and Kunersdorf (1759) in the Seven Years' War (1756–1763) under Frederick the Great. Now retired from the military and "verging towards old age," Andreas, if he retired after the Seven Years' War, even at age forty, would be in his sixties in the seventeen-eighties, certainly "verging towards old age," and by 1795 he would be seventy-five. In order to place Teufelsdröckh's birth in 1795, we would have to assume Andreas to have been only twenty at the outbreak of the Seven Years' War, which is also possible, though rather less likely. Carlyle's own father, quite unlike Andreas as a person, was born in 1757.

mysteries is not biographical and literal, but typical and figurative.

As the sun enters the southern zodiacal signs, the northern hemisphere turns toward winter. At time of entry the sun is in the Balance, in Libra. Six months later, in Aries, the sun tilts again toward the northern hemisphere. The paper bags cover the winter months of the year. But Teufelsdröckh's life is measured not by months, but by years. Facts relating to his birth and early childhood are in Libra, when his life is in balance. As he grows and voyages further into life, he enters more hostile signs. Thus his early schooling falls in Scorpio, the scorpion. Biographers have hastened to point out that Hinterschlag is Annan Academy and that Carlyle bitterly jeers at his school experiences in the name Hinterschlag—"strike behind." No doubt he does. In terms more meaningful to the reader who is not acquainted with Carlyle's biography, the name has a double meaning. It means to strike behind and it calls to mind not merely Carlyle's but many a schoolboy's anguish from excessively severe discipline. It means also to strike back as a spirited boy does in rebellion at harsh and spiritually empty pedagogy. The scorpion, of course, strikes by raising its hindquarters over its back, so that it strikes behind and strikes back.

Teufelsdröckh's university years are reported in the bag Sagittarius, the Archer. At the transition point between Scorpio and Sagittarius the Editor glosses for the reader the meaning of these signs. It is, he says, "as if, in the Bag *Scorpio*, Teufelsdröckh had not already expectorated his antipedagogic spleen); as if, from the name *Sagittarius*, he had thought himself called upon to shoot arrows." With such a clear correspondence posited by the Editor, it can hardly be surprising then to find that subsequently, during the period of Teufelsdröckh's *Sturm und Drang*, there is tremendous confusion even as to the order of the paper bags, for the confusion of the Heaven-sent is imaged in the confusion in the heavens. The events surrounding

Teufelsdröckh's agitated disappointment in love with the Flower-Goddess are scattered in almost hopeless disorder in Capricornus and Aquarius. These are the months of deepest winter and least light. In short, Carlyle has taken the zodiac as another means of symbolizing events. The winter of Teufelsdröckh's discontent has also the same moral quality attributed in *Sartor* to two concomitants of winter, cold and darkness.

In the final analysis, Carlyle in his choice of zodiacal signs is also making a comment on the age. Teufelsdröckh's youth and early manhood span the winter. He was born in the late eighteenth century, in the winter of Rationalism, the sere and yellow leaf of Unbelief. As Teufelsdröckh at the end of the book emerges into present time, he does so as one who has survived and triumphed over the winter of the eighteenth century and one who hopefully looks forward to a new spring and new summer of faith and belief.

As a final example of Carlyle's play with imagery and motif, let us look at what he has done with the name Diogenes Teufelsdröckh. Earlier it was noted that the name means God-born Devil's-dung, and that Teufelsdröckh is a modified spelling of the German word *Teufelsdreck*, the word for asafoetida. Further, Wilson has pointed out that Scots for asafoetida is *Deil's dirt*, giving thus a Scots-German appropriateness to the word similar to Weissnichtwo, which reflects Sir Walter Scott's Kennaquhair in *The Monastery*.[23] Parry emphasized that Carlyle also had in mind the idea of asafoetida as an emetic and quotes Carlyle's statement that with Teufelsdreck he hoped to give a medicinal Devil's-dung to the pudding stomach of England.[24] All of these glosses together indicate the depth of meaning Carlyle put into a single word. And yet there is more.

Diogenes, as we have seen, calls to mind Diogenes the

[23] *Carlyle to "The French Revolution,"* p. 183. Cf. MacMechan's edition of *Sartor*, p. 282.

[24] Parry, pp. 322–323.

Cynic. It also suggests Diogenes Laertius, the second-century biographer of the philosophers. Carlyle quotes him in *Sartor*, referring to him as Diogenes the First, and he it was who attributed the expression "Cor ne edito" to Pythagoras, an expression that is sprinkled throughout Carlyle's early letters and notes and directed to Teufelsdröckh as well. Teufelsdröckh is a latter-day Diogenes the Cynic, looking with his own light for an honest man, as well as a latter-day Diogenes Laertius chronicling the life of a philosopher in a manner that ironically echoes the fragmentary and anecdotal character of Laertius' *Lives of the Philosophers*. The name Teufelsdröckh also has a greater complexity than that indicated by the established glosses, little known as they are. *Teufelsdreck*, of course, means asafoetida, which is an aloetic plant and an anti-spasmodic medicine made from the gum resin of the middle-eastern ferule. It appears almost certain that Carlyle's idea of the word was suggested by a hitherto unnoticed passage in Jean Paul's *Titan* (1800–1805) in which Jean Paul speaks of "Teufelsdreck, den sie aus Persien holen";[25] for Carlyle describes the advent

[25] Jean Paul, *Werke,* ed. Norbert Miller (Munich, 1959–1963), III, 63:

> Der gegenwärtige *Titan* benutzt noch den andern Vorteil, dass ich gerade den väterlichen Hof bewohne und schmücke und mithin als Zeichner gewisse Sünden recht glücklicherweise näher und heller vor dem Auge zum Beschauen habe, wovon mir wenigstens der Egoismus, die Libertinage und das Müssiggehen gewiss bleiben und sitzen; denn diese Schwämme und Moose säete das Schicksal so weit, als es konnte, in die höhern Stände hinauf, weil sie in den niedern und breitern zu sehr ausgegriffen und sie ausgesogen hätten—welches das Muster derselben Vorsicht gewesen zu sein scheint, aus der die Schiffe den Teufelsdreck, den sie aus Persien holen, stets oben an den Mastbaum hängen, damit sein Getsank nicht die Fracht des Schiffraums besudle.

One can only speculate as to whether Carlyle himself had taken doses of asafoetida to stimulate his digestion, for which purpose the herb has long been used medicinally. And it remains an even more abstruse speculation as to whether Carlyle was aware that the fire Prometheus stole from Zeus was supposed to have been enough to make smoulder the pith of the stalk of a giant fennel, a plant closely allied to asafoetida.

of Teufelsdröckh as having occurred when the Stranger removed from his mantle "what seemed some Basket, overhung with green Persian silk." Teufelsdröckh later reveals that " 'the little green veil . . . I yet keep; still more inseparably the Name, Diogenes Teufelsdröckh. From the veil can nothing be inferred: a piece of now quite faded Persian silk, like thousands of others.'" The insistence that the visible garment which clothed the infant Teufelsdröckh is Persian silk has the purpose of associating Teufelsdröckh with Persia, the land of asafoetida. The allusion is obscure, but not private. For those familiar with the epithet "Western-Oriental" applied to Jean Paul and the frequent associations of the Orient with mysticism made by contemporary German writers, it is especially fitting that Teufelsdröckh should have a mysterious oriental heritage. It even suits the name Diogenes, of which Teufelsdröckh says: " 'Again, what may the unchristian rather than Christian "Diogenes" mean?' " But how *could* Teufelsdröckh, born in the Atheistic Century, be a Christian? Moreover, Persia is the home of astrology and the zodiac. Teufelsdröckh would naturally label his autobiographical notes with Persian signs.

From this compacting of allusions the following picture of Teufelsdröckh emerges: Diogenes Teufelsdröckh is child of both God and the devil, he comes from heaven to base earth, his voyage on the sea of life is ruled by the stars, his name becomes more inseparable a garment to him than the Persian silk in which he is swaddled in infancy as a hint of the mystic Orient, the home of astrology, and the land of the emetic asafoetida which his teachings will prove to be for the English public. Much later when the Editor says (banteringly?) that he found Heuschrecke's paper lying "dishonourably enough (with torn leaves, and a perceptible smell of aloetic drugs), stuffed into the Bag *Pisces*," readers alive to the associations know at once that all about the document (literally in the margins) there is hell and heaven, purgation and salvation, for it has been touched by Diogenes Teufelsdröckh.

FRAGMENTS

While the texture of *Sartor Resartus* is determined in part by the brilliant display of verbal dexterity in the use of imagery and the interweaving of themes, it is further shaped by some aspects that are unique to *Sartor* alone. Of these the most startlingly original is Carlyle's use of fragments.

There are two kinds of fragment to consider in *Sartor*. First there is the conventional fragment—the jotting and the incomplete or unfinished work. While fragments of this sort can be found throughout the history of literature, they are especially plentiful in the Romantic period. Romantics constitutionally left fragments, in part because they so often died young, but also because inspiration sometimes faded before a work was done. It was as though, once having themselves grasped the insight, it was no longer necessary to communicate it. There is scarcely a Romantic figure who did not leave incomplete literary works behind: Novalis, the Schlegels, Wackenroder, Tieck, Hölderlin, Goethe, Schiller, and many more in Germany; Blake, Wordsworth, Shelley, Keats, and above all Coleridge in England. While fragments in the sense of jottings and incomplete works are eminently Romantic, there is another sense in which fragments are uniquely associated with the nineteenth century—the fragment as a literary mode in itself.

The Fragment as a mode in itself may be considered a contribution of German Romantics. To be sure, there is a history extending back to antiquity of works in the larger category in which fragments fall, the category that has been called "wisdom literature." In more modern times the apophthegms of Erasmus and the maxims of LaRochefoucauld come to mind, as do the works of the immediate eighteenth-century predecessors of the Romantics, Lichtenberg and Chamfort. But it remained for the Romantics themselves to make the Fragment a mode of thinking; for the principle of the Fragment is not that it offers a polished truism or even a surprising, often cynical insight into human behavior, but that it suggests something ultimately ineffable. The proverb, the maxim, the apophthegm, the epigram, all offer some sort of prudential wisdom, polished and pointed by time, use, or wit. The Fragment, however, offers a glimpse of the Truth. Friedrich Schlegel is one of the first writers of fragments in the Romantic sense. His contemporary Novalis is another. Novalis, who probably wrote more Fragments than anyone else, also left fragments in the conventional sense of incomplete works. Carlyle was, of course, extraordinarily fond of Novalis and was influenced by him and by both the Schlegels. As we saw earlier in his essay on Novalis, Carlyle quoted a number of Novalis' *Fragmente,* and these give some of the flavor of the Fragment as a type.[26]

Robert Preyer has traced the development of the fragment as a Victorian form and noted the especial fondness for it on the part of such writers as the brothers Hare, Augustus and Julius, whose *Guesses at Truth* appeared in 1827.[27] Carlyle's association with the Hares postdates *Sartor,* but it is still worth noting that the Hares were closely associated with John Sterling, the earliest literary critic of *Sartor,* the close friend of Carlyle and the subject of one of Carlyle's finest biographies. The Fragment as a mode was very much in the air in England during the Romantic and Victorian periods. Coleridge's dicta are cast substantially in the form of the Fragment, and consequently Coleridge's ideas are subject to endless dispute, for the Romantic Fragment is the very opposite of a closed form. It is rather a form in which all things

[26] See above, p. 119, and *Works,* xxvii, 40.
[27] Robert J. Preyer, "Victorian Wisdom Literature: Fragments and Maxims," *Victorian Studies,* vi (1963), 245–262. I have relied on Preyer's study for much of the background of the Fragment, but see also Wellek, *History of Modern Criticism,* ii, 35. Wellek distinguishes two literary types perfected by Friedrich Schlegel, the "Charakteristik," and the Fragment. Neither Wellek nor Preyer feels the need to distinguish orthographically, as I do, the fragment from the Fragment.

are possible, all things suggested. It may be considered the Victorian equivalent of the literature of meditation, for it was invariably taken up by persons of immense sincerity and usually by persons of pronounced religious inclinations.

The Romantic Fragment is used as a mode in *Sartor,* while the conventional fragment is used as the raw material from which *Sartor* is pieced together. Teufelsdröckh's utterances are cast almost entirely in the form of the Romantic Fragment. Since they purport to come from a full-length complete work, the mode of the Romantic Fragment is possible only because the Editor persistently quotes from portions and pieces of Teufelsdröckh's writings rather than presenting a complete translation. The fragmentary nature of the quotes is necessary in order for the style to be that of the Fragment. In the biographical portions the Editor has literally nothing more than fragments, both the conventional and the Romantic kind. The multiplicity of fragments has led many to believe that *Sartor* is a thing of shreds and patches. But the proper comparison would better be a coat of many colors or a patchwork quilt. There is every imaginable kind of cloth, every piece and snippet of material, but they all relate to the whole, which constitutes a wild, kaleidoscopic unity unlike that in any other literary work. As Preyer observes, "Carlyle found a way of converting these devices of melodrama to the purposes of high art in *Sartor Resartus.*"[28]

Let us look first at the conventional fragment in *Sartor.* The idea of the fragment not only suited a mystic German Romantic like Teufelsdröckh, but it satisfied Carlyle's almost obsessive need in a literary work for documents from which he could quote. The careless reader is apt to think of *Sartor* as composed of some comments by the Editor and extensive quotation from *Die Kleider.* Such an impression is not entirely amiss, for it does place the emphasis

---

[28] P. 251. A typical Fragment by the Hares cited by Preyer is: "Man without religion is the creature of circumstances. Religion is above all circumstances, and will lift him up above them."

on Teufelsdröckh's opus and, one hopes, on the clothes philosophy itself. But it will not do for anything more than a casual impression. What makes *Sartor* so fragmentary is the huge number of documents invented by Carlyle for citation by the Editor. Consider the following fictional documents which are quoted from in the text:

> *Die Kleider, ihr Werden und Wirken*
> Review of *Die Kleider* in the *Weissnichtwo'sche Anzeiger*
> Letter from Heuschrecke about *Die Kleider*
> The "University Program" (i.e. catalogue)
> Letters from Heuschrecke about biographical documents
> The Six Paper Bags, containing:
>> "Miscellaneous masses of Sheets, and oftener Shreds and Snips," bills, essays, and "perhaps the completest collection extant of Street-Advertisements."
>> "Discourse on Epitaphs"
>> Program of the "Society for the Conservation of Property"
>> Heuschrecke's "Institute for Repression of Population" with marginalia by Teufelsdröckh
> Letter from Heueschrecke about Teufelsdröckh's disappearance

All of the fictional documents are quoted from in *Sartor;* further, there is substantial quotation from actual works. The following titles represent the real works quoted from at some length in *Sartor:*

> Paullini's *Zeit-Kürzende erbauliche Lust*
> *Fraser's* article on fashionable novels
> Bulwer's *Pelham*
> Bulwer's *The Disowned*
> Bernard's *Retrospections of the Stage.*

There are, in all, more than a dozen documents real and fictional quoted from in *Sartor*, not counting, of course, the hundreds of allusions and paraphrases from established works, which constitute another dimension entirely of

Carlyle's esemplastic style. In some cases the documents themselves are incomplete, and in others, even where they are full-scale works, the quotations are fragmentary. There is yet another considerable list of works not actually quoted from in *Sartor* but invented by Carlyle as part of the atmosphere of documents and fragments ready to hand. They are:

> *Allgemeine Zeitung* of Weissnichtwo
> Documents from the Paper-Bags not quoted from:
>> "On Receiving the Doctor's-Hat" (inaugural address)
>> "Detached Thoughts on the Steam-Engine"
>> "The Continued Possibility of Prophecy"
> *Palingenesie der menschlichen Gesellschaft* (the second volume of the clothes philosophy)

Sartor is studded with literal fragments of every imaginable kind of writing. The very feel of the book depends on these fragments, the titles, the passages taken from here and there, the works unfinished or stopped in mid-passage. Even visually the book reflects the abundance of fragments for the text is bestrewn with titles (italicized and in quotations), with double and single quotation marks for passages cited, and editorial interpolations in the midst of quotations to clarify and comment. All of this is only compounded by Carlyle's foreign-language foregrounding. While the typesetter despairs, the reader may be encouraged to think of chaos. But the fragments are there precisely for the variety of effect, precisely to make the business of grouping and understanding them a joint endeavor that issues ultimately in an understanding of their underlying unity.

Amidst all these literal fragments the Romantic Fragment is thoroughly at home. And it is everywhere evident, because it is Teufelsdröckh's habitual mode of expression. The Editor calls *Die Kleider* a "very Sea of Thought . . . wherein the toughest pearl-diver may dive to his utmost depth, and return not only with sea-wreck but with true orients." Immediately as we meet Teufelsdröckh in his watchtower room in Weissnichtwo, we meet also his oracular utterances in the form of the fragment: " 'That living flood, pouring through these streets, of all qualities and ages, knowest thou whence it is coming, whither it is going? *Aus der Ewigkeit, zu der Ewigkeit hin.* From Eternity, onwards to Eternity!' " Thus Teufelsdröckh, to say that men are mortal. Shortly thereafter he exclaims: " 'Oh, under that hideous coverlet of vapours, and putre-factions, and unimaginable gases, what a Fermenting-vat lies simmering and hid! The joyful and the sorrowful are there; men are dying there, men are being born; men are praying,—on the other side of a brick partition, men are cursing; and around them all is the vast, void Night.' " The Editor calls these "extraordinary Night-thoughts," and we may also call them Fragments.

Examples multiply throughout *Sartor*. In the first citation from *Die Kleider* we encounter such a Fragment as the following:

"Reader, the heaven-inspired melodious Singer; loftiest Serene Highness; nay thy own amber-locked, snow-and-rose-bloom Maiden, worthy to glide sylphlike almost on air, whom thou lovest, worshipped as a divine Presence, which, indeed, symbolically taken, she is,—has descended, like thyself, from that same hair-mantled, flint-hurling Aboriginal Anthropophagus! Out of the eater cometh forth meat; out of the strong cometh forth sweetness. What changes are wrought, not by Time, yet in Time! For not Mankind only, but all that Mankind does or beholds, is in continual growth, re-genesis and self-perfecting vitality." (I, v, 39–40)

Again, when the Editor undertakes to quote from the *Wirken* of *Die Kleider*, he offers the reader fragments and Fragments:

"Sure enough, I am; and lately was not: but Whence? How? Whereto? The answer lies around, written in all colours and motions, uttered in all tones of jubilee and wail, in thousand-figured, thousand-voiced, harmonious Nature: but where is the cunning eye and ear to whom that God-written Apocalypse will yield articulate meaning? We sit as in a boundless Phantasmagoria and Dream-grotto; boundless, for the faintest star, the remotest century, lies not even nearer the verge thereof: sounds and many-coloured visions flit round our sense; but Him, the Unslumbering, whose work both Dream and Dreamer are, we see not; except in rare half-waking moments, suspect not." (ɪ, viii, 53–54)

Even in the biographical portion of *Sartor*, where the Editor is concerned chiefly to piece out of the notes in the paper bags a coherent external biography for Teufelsdröckh, the Fragment cannot be avoided. In "Genesis" Teufelsdröckh speaks of his early growth in the tone of the Fragment:

"To breed a fresh Soul, is it not like brooding a fresh (celestial) Egg; wherein as yet all is formless, powerless; yet by degrees organic elements and fibres shoot through the watery albumen; and out of vague Sensation grows Thought, grows Fantasy and Force, and we have Philosophies, Dynasties, nay Poetries and Religions!" (ɪɪ, i, 88)

Likewise, when Teufelsdröckh later discourses on his childhood, he rhapsodizes in the quasi-oracular, quasi-religious tones of the Fragment:

"Happy season of childhood!" exclaims Teufelsdröckh: "Kind Nature, that art to all a bountiful mother; that visitest the poor man's hut with auroral radiance; and for thy Nurseling hast provided a soft swathing of Love and infinite Hope, wherein he waxes and slumbers, danced-round (*umgaukelt*) by sweetest Dreams!" (ɪɪ, ii, 90)

Finally, "Natural Supernaturalism" is cast in the form of an imaginary dialogue, or even argument, in which the telling points are made in answers that are also Fragments. Teufelsdröckh himself poses the questions, attributing them to disbelievers; then he provides the answers as Fragments. Thus, such questions as " 'But is not a real Miracle simply a violation of the Laws of Nature?' ask several," and " 'But is it not the deepest Law of Nature that she be constant?' cries an illuminated class," are countered with such Fragments as:

> "What are the Laws of Nature? To me perhaps the rising of one from the dead were no violation of these Laws, but a confirmation; were some far deeper Law, now first penetrated into, and by Spiritual Force, even as the rest have all been, brought to bear on us with its Material Force." (III, viii, 256)

and:

> ". . . I, too, must believe that the God, whom ancient inspired men assert to be 'without variableness or shadow of turning,' does indeed never change; that Nature, that the Universe, which no one whom it so pleases can be prevented from calling a Machine, does move by the most unalterable rules. And now of you, too, I make the old inquiry: What those same unalterable rules, forming the complete Statute-Book of Nature, may possibly be?" (III, viii, 256)

The problem, indeed, is not to find examples in Teufelsdröckh's writings that are characteristic of the Fragment, but to find those that are not. All readers of *Sartor* have noted the rhapsodic, oracular, and lyric tone, but few have seen its rationale. It lies in the Fragment as a mode suited to the mystic, mantic Teufelsdröckh, to the sage and the seer, the poet and the prophet. The Fragment is the ideal way of communicating the Divine Idea and the Open Secret. For the seer's capacity to read, or, in Carlyle's term, *rede*,[29] the mystic alphabet is never unremitting; it is always a matter of sustaining for longer or shorter periods; it is always in some sense a matter of inspiration. The poet is more likely to be inspired for a short swallow-flight of song than for an entire book. Indeed, the Romantics are associated not only with Fragments but with the lyric rather than with the novel, even though German Romantic theorists continually praised the novel as *the* Romantic form. The lyric in poetry or Fragment form is not long: the poet cannot sustain it, the reader cannot endure it. Carlyle solves the problem of sustaining the lyric by citing only fragments and these usually Fragments.

ALLUSION

From pervasive imagery, such as that of clothing and light and dark, to recurring motifs of varying degrees of complexity, the texture of *Sartor* ranges to literal fragments and Romantic Fragments. The area normally termed "style" is plainly close at hand. Indeed the final aspect of texture to be examined might easily be called a part of style. I refer to Carlyle's habit of allusion, specifically his allusion to material objects. We may call this the "things of *Sartor Resartus*," or the concreteness of Carlyle's style. Part of the confusion about the artistic unity of *Sartor* lies in a misunderstanding of the intent and effect of the various physical objects that appear throughout the book, a misunderstanding that readily runs to the hoary charges of confusion and chaos.

Conventional novels are often distinguished by the extent to which they render the things of the visible world. Some are extremely rich in portrayal of these things. For their varying purposes a Dickens or a James can devote long passages to descriptions of physical objects. At the opposite

[29] Carlyle's preference for this form appears to be more than a matter of dialect, although *rede* is peculiarly Scots. It means both "to advise and counsel" and "to explain or interpret." In this second sense Carlyle uses it habitually. Like *read*, the word derives from OE *rǣdan*, "advise, read."

extreme a novelist like Kafka often presents a shadowy
world in which even the characters have only initials for
names. To the extent that one can generalize, the more
"realistic" the novel, the greater the abundance of things.
The more the novel approaches fantasy, the less extensive
the incidence of objects. Now *Sartor Resartus* is certainly a
kind of fantasy, and yet things abound. It would be hard to
imagine a work richer in allusion to concrete everyday
things. It is the way in which Carlyle uses things that
distinguishes *Sartor* from the conventional novel. They are
not in *Sartor* presented as part of the atmosphere of the
real world, the backdrop or setting for action; they are
not designed to create verisimilitude. The things in *Sartor*
arrest our attention because of their very presence in an
alien atmosphere. Thus in the paper bags there are "fragments of all sorts; scraps of regular Memoir, College-Exer-
cises, Programs, Professional Testimoniums, Milkscores,
torn Billets," and more. Thus Teufelsdröckh says, "My
breakfast of tea has been cooked by a Tartar woman, with
water of the Amur, who wiped her earthen kettle with
a horse-tail. I have roasted wild-eggs in the sand of the
Sahara"; and the objects continue to mount up.

In an earlier connection we looked at the very first
sentence of *Sartor* as typical. It is also typical of Carlyle's
way of introducing allusion to physical objects:

> Considering our present advanced state of culture, and
> how the Torch of Science has now been brandished
> and borne about, with more or less effect, for five
> thousand years and upwards; how, in these times es-
> pecially, not only the Torch still burns, and perhaps
> more fiercely than ever, but innumerable Rush-lights,
> and Sulphur-matches, kindled thereat, are also glancing
> in every direction, so that not the smallest cranny or
> doghole in Nature or Art can remain unilluminated,—it
> might strike the reflective mind with some surprise that
> hitherto little or nothing of a fundamental character,

whether in the way of Philosophy or History, has been
written on the subject of Clothes. (I, i, 3)

In one, admittedly lengthy, sentence Carlyle has managed
to refer to such concrete objects as torches, rush lights,
and sulphur matches, not to mention the references to
such abstracts as science, nature, art, philosophy, and history. The abstracts are important indeed, but they take
their coloration from the concrete words. Carlyle's philosophy has appealed to many because his diction is so often
unphilosophic. It is interesting to trace how Carlyle gets
so much concreteness into a statement that by rights seems
to be largely concerned with the abstract. A good deal
of what gets into the sentence was suggested by the
metaphor "Torch of Science." In other hands the expression
might well have remained what it usually is, a fossilized
metaphor. When we speak of the torch of science, the
arm of the law, the jaws of hell, or any of a thousand
originally vivid phrases, we are usually content to let the
metaphor lie dormant. Much of the individuality of
Carlyle's style manifests itself precisely in his unending
revivification of such moribund metaphors. Carlyle's torch
of science is "brandished and borne about," so that it becomes quite literally a real torch. From it are kindled
rush lights and sulphur matches of science. The metaphor
has come to life with a vengeance.

If we turn to the final chapter of the book, we find that
Carlyle has not ceased enlivening dead metaphors:

So have we endeavoured, from the enormous, amorphous Plum-pudding, more like a Scottish Haggis,
which Herr Teufelsdröckh has kneaded for his fellow-
mortals, to pick out the choicest Plums, and present them
separately on a cover of our own. (III, xii, 292)

The metaphor of the plum pudding is rather like that
of the torch of science. The pudding is enlivened initially
by the descriptive adjectives that precede it—enormous,

amorphous—but, most of all, it is thrown into grotesque relief by the immediately following comparison of it to a Scottish Haggis, which is, as the annotation tells us, another kind of pudding, "made by boiling the heart, liver, and lungs in the maw of a sheep or calf, with suet, oatmeal, etc." On reflection we see the aptness in the comparison, even if initially a plum pudding does not make us think of a haggis. It is an aptness enforced by the self-consciousness of the comparison. The reader's imagination is taxed.

Readers of *Sartor* know that the examples given could be duplicated from almost any page in the book. Nor is the presence of allusion to objects conditional only on the practice of enlivening dead metaphors. Things occur in every possible context, in every kind of rhetorical figure, and in every type of sentence. Repeatedly the most concrete of objects appears in juxtaposition to the most abstract of qualities or ideas. The variety of things in *Sartor* becomes almost monstrously vast, and the total effect can appear rather like an enormous amorphous plum pudding, the more so if we conceive of the objects in terms of mere enumeration. But an examination of any passage in *Sartor* will reveal that the appearance of a given object is in fact related imaginatively to the passage in question. Carlyle does not assemble disparate objects with no sense or meaning. The physical objects in *Sartor* relate to the larger aims of the book. Carlyle's natural supernaturalism is a perception of the ultimate unity and meaning of all things physical and spiritual. Since any explanation of the world—and *Sartor* is that among other things—must account for physical phenomena, the allusion to objects in *Sartor* is a phase of that accounting. Physical objects in Carlyle's view are not only actual phenomena of the real world but also symbols, representations of a reality that lies beyond the physical. The inclusion of vast numbers of objects serves both to delineate the real world of contemporary nineteenth-century life in what Carlyle called "all its contradictions and perplexity; barren, mean, baleful" and to disclose the significance that lies behind objects, their subtle and sometimes surprising relationships, so that the age is "enamelled into beauty in the poet's spirit; for its secret significance is laid open . . . " Therein lies the modernity of *Sartor*. The countless objects represent an almost explosive increase in knowledge of the physical world. Few persons had been so closely connected with so many manifestations of modern knowledge as had Carlyle. He had studied and written about science and literature, philosophy and history, language and poetry. *Sartor* is an attempt to bring the innumerable facets of modern life together in a meaningful order, an attempt that had engaged Carlyle's energies from the time he turned from religion to science.[30]

The immediate verbal level of the relations of things in *Sartor* is clear. There is a level beyond. When, for example, in the previously quoted passage about the old-clothes men, the multiple hats piled on top of the peddler's head are made to suggest humorously the Pope's triple crown, the point lies not merely in the wit of the perception but in the revelation of what is, in the world of *Sartor,* a truly meaningful relationship. When C. F. Harrold notes in his edition that the passage is a satiric one, he is in fact abiding with an immediate verbal level and ignoring a deeper level of meaning.[31] Satiric of course the passage is; but at the same time it is absolutely serious. Teufelsdröckh has entered Monmouth Street to worship, not to mock. One is struck by the uncommon acuity of

[30] The breakdown of faith, both in Carlyle personally and in the age in general, is a prime cause for the effort to make meaning out of the phenomena of existence. In an age in which faith is secure, all things have their place. One of Carlyle's great strengths was his recognition of the spiritual crisis of his time, as well as his ability to depict its manifestations. The uncommon form of *Sartor,* with its wide-ranging content, is a reflection of Carlyle's effort to comprehend modern life.

[31] *Sartor,* p. 241n. Harrold may not have been entirely impartial in such passages. His note on Luther in Wittenberg (p. 248) is a good example.

perception that sees tiaras in Jewish vendors' hats, but the point is that the arresting of attention achieved by this verbal play is designed to lead to a thoughtful and serious consideration of the actual meaning and similarity between these seemingly disparate objects.[32] The paradox is, like that in the treatment of the Wandering Jew theme, an occasion for mockery of Teufelsdröckh as a *Schwärmer* and for praise of him as a seeker after truth.

The physical objects in *Sartor* seize our attention. Coupled with the rhetoric they serve to make us stop, look, and think. Moreover, by obliging the reader to move through the density of the objects and allusions in *Sartor*, Carlyle preserves the work equally from the dryness of philosophy and the factitious ease of self-help. Through the objects, much of the imaginative effect of *Sartor* is obtained. Our response to the whole is conditioned by

[32] Jean Paul alludes briefly to the triple tiara in *Titan, Werke,* III, 17–18:

> Will hingegen ein Literator, ein Kleinstädter, ein Zeitungsträger oder Zeitungsschreiber einen grossen Kopf zu Geischt bekommen und ist er auf einen grossen Kopf ebenso ersessen wie auf eine Missgeburt mit drei Köpfen—oder auf einen Papst mit ebensoviel Mützen—oder auf einen ausgestopften Haifisch—oder auf eine Sprach- und Buttermaschine: so tut ers nicht, weil ein warmes, seinen *innern Menschen beseelendes* Ideal von einem grossen Manne, Papste, Haifische, Dreikopfe und Buttermodelle ihn drängt und treibt sondern weil er frühmorgens denkt: "Es soll mich doch wundern, wie der Kauz aussieht," und weil ers abends bei einem Glase Bier berichten will.

There are a number of similarities between *Titan* and *Sartor,* at least in vocabulary, that have not been noted even in the voluminous Carlyle-Jean Paul scholarship.

For further light on the Carlyle-Jean Paul relationship see, among many works on the subject, Hermann Conrad, "Carlyle und Jean Paul," *Die Gegenwart,* XXXIX (1891), 309–311; Paul Hensel, *Thomas Carlyle* (Stuttgart, 1901); Henry Pape, *Jean Paul als Quelle von Thomas Carlyles Anschauung und Stil* (Rostock, 1904); Theodor Geissendoerfer, "Carlyle und Jean Paul Friedrich Richter," *Journal of English and Germanic Philology,* XXV, (1926), 540–553, and Geissendoerfer's "Carlyle und Jean Paul," *Hesperus,* No. 16 (1958), pp. 44–47; and J. W. Smeed, "Carlyles Jean Paul-Übersetzungen," *Deutsche Vierteljahrsschrift,* XXXV (1961), 262–279.

the plum puddings, the six paper bags, the triple tiaras, and the Hyperborean Stranger, not to mention the untold examples of various kinds of clothing. These objects are surely not out of place in the "factual" portions of the book; and who can deny them suitability in the *Märchen* world of Teufelsdröckh? The things of *Sartor* are not blemishes but beauties, not weaknesses but strengths. Through the things of the book, *Sartor* becomes a vast reticulation of allusions. Remove them, and *Sartor* disintegrates: as they stand, they are the organic filaments uniting the vision of *Sartor* into a whole.

VI

The Style of "Sartor Resartus"

. . . a style resembling either early architecture or
utter dilapidation, so loose and rough it seemed;
a wind-in-the-orchard style, that tumbled down here
and there an appreciable fruit with uncouth bluster;
sentences without commencements running to abrupt
endings and smoke, like waves against a sea-wall,
learned dictionary words giving a hand to street-
slang, and accents falling on them haphazard, like
slant rays from driving clouds; all the pages in a
breeze, the whole book producing a kind of elec-
trical agitation in the mind and the joints.

—GEORGE MEREDITH

Flee Carlylese as the very devil.

—MATTHEW ARNOLD

Yes, the Carlylese, Ruskinese, Meredithese, and
every other *ese*, past, present, and to come.

—FREDERIC HARRISON

THE MATTER OF MANNER

The first to appear of many terms relating to Carlyle's
style was *Carlylism*. The *OED* defines it in two senses:
"The characteristic literary manner or teachings of Carlyle";
and "A mannerism of Carlyle (chiefly in language or
style)." That the style was initially conceived of as a vehicle for a certain substance is indicated by the way
Fraser's reviewer in 1841 used the term: "It is Carlyleism
in manner, but not in matter." But the *Fraser's* comment
also shows the distressing ease with which imitators detached Carlyle's manner from his matter. Later terms often
have reference to manner alone. By 1858 there was
Carlylese, "the literary style or dialect of Carlyle," and

then came *Carlylite* (1865) *and Carlylesque* (1866). Finally in 1878 the Sage of Chelsea was dignified with the more neutral *Carlylean* (*-eian, -ian*), "of, pertaining to, or like Carlyle."[1]

But it is the pejorative coinage in *-ese* that has gained the widest currency and spread the conviction that with Carlyle style is affection. Yet, as F. L. Lucas observed, to limit the term *style* to "affected writing" is an unnecessary restriction, and we would do better to conceive of style first as the way a man writes, and second as good writing.[2] So I have taken it here. Carlyle's style, Carlylese, is first the way Carlyle writes, and second what is effective in his writing. For, as Carlyle, like everyone else, was fond of quoting from Buffon, "the style is the man." If the style is the man, or even if the style is the way a man writes, where are we to draw the line in an examination of style? After all, everything in *Sartor* is in some sense the way Carlyle writes. So it is, and by treating of such matters as structure and texture, I have already dealt with some aspects of style. But style customarily deals with more intimate matters than overall structure: it is concerned with syntax, sentences, and words, and finally with the quality of all these in concert.

Carlyle's style overall is distinctly a nineteenth-century phenomenon. Walter Pater's 1889 essay on style helped give much-needed respectability to the kind of prose that in the hands of Carlyle and others in the nineteenth century was developed into high art. Wordsworth had recognized the essential issue with his distinction between imaginative and unimaginative writing. DeQuincey pinpointed the difference more memorably with his "literature of power" and "literature of knowledge." Pater pays due respect to these early rebellions against what he called the "arbitrary psychology of [the eighteenth] century," and he offers the best phrase of all, "the literature of the imaginative sense

[1] *OED*, ii, 122.
[2] F. L. Lucas, *Style* (London, 1955), p. 16.

of fact."[3] Carlyle's style communicates this imaginative sense of fact, and *Sartor* especially conveys it as strongly as any prose document in the nineteenth century. Yet the means Carlyle uses have been censured as often as applauded. They have also mystified more than one reader of *Sartor*.

John Sterling started the criticisms of *Sartor* in 1835 when he wrote to Carlyle, criticizing "that headlong self-asserting capriciousness, which . . . is yet plainly to be seen in the structure of the sentence, the lawless oddity, and strange heterogeneous combination and allusion."[4] He objected to the language, a good deal of which he claimed was "positively barbarous," citing, to the surprise of later generations, "environment," "stertorous," and "visualised," among others, as words without authority, and registering his weariness with repetitions of words "in a quaint and queer connection" such as "quite," "nay," "manifold." Apart from specific words (which Sterling distinguished from style) his objections were levelled chiefly at the frequency of Germanic compounds ("snow-and-rosebloom maiden" was his scarifying example), the ubiquity of inversion, and in general at the "heightened and plethoric fulness of the style." Most subsequent criticisms of Carlyle's style have moved along similar lines without really improving very much on Sterling's strictures, and without evidencing the understanding that Sterling brought along with his objections. For Sterling recognized much of the purpose behind the style of *Sartor*. "It certainly gives emphasis and force," he wrote of Carlyle's inversions, "and often serves to point the meaning." At the same time he made the most telling objection yet raised against an emphatic style: "But a style may be fatiguing and faulty precisely by being too emphatic, forcible and pointed; and so straining the attention

[3] Walter Pater, *Works*, ("Library Edition"; London, 1910), v, 8.
[4] Sterling's letter is reprinted in Harrold's edition of *Sartor*, pp. 307–316. Carlyle's reply also appears, pp. 316–318. For Sterling's 1839 *Westminster Review* essay on Carlyle see his *Essays and Tales*, ed. Julius Charles Hare (London, 1848), I, 252–381.

to find its meaning, or the admiration to appreciate its beauty."

Sterling's criticism points to the stylistic issues that must be grappled with in *Sartor:* Carlyle's sentences and syntax, with their problems of inversion, repetition, and imbalance; and his language, with its problems of compounding, neologisms, and Germanisms. Carlyle himself was not unaware of the peculiarities of his style, and he did not affect to believe his style was classical. He replied to Sterling with an appeal to the nature of the times:

> But finally, do you reckon this really a time for Purism of Style; or that Style (mere dictionary Style) has much to do with the worth or unworth of a Book? I do not: with whole ragged battalions of Scott's-Novel Scotch, with Irish, German, French, and even Newspaper Cockney (when "Literature" is little other than a Newspaper) storming in on us, and the whole structure of our Johnsonian English breaking up from its foundations,—revolution *there* as visible as anywhere else! (*Sartor*, p. 317)

Carlyle implicitly contrasts his own style with that of Dr. Johnson, and most subsequent treatments of Carlyle's style have done the same. It is a natural and perhaps inevitable contrast to make. Johnson's style, while peculiar to him, is also especially neoclassic, characterized by balance, gravity, and composure. W. K. Wimsatt singles out for particular attention parallelism, antithesis, and a diction that is general, abstract, and "philosophick." Secondarily he notes Johnson's lengthy sentences, his use of inversion and chiasmus.[5] Carlyle too has lengthy sentences, and he is no stranger to inversion. But, in general, Carlyle's style is not balanced, grave, and composed. It is characterized by imbalance, excess, and excitement. Both Carlyle and Johnson tend to write long sentences, but the quality of

[5] *The Prose Style of Samuel Johnson* (New Haven, 1941), esp. pp. 15–37, 63–71.

their sentences is extraordinarily different. Nothing reveals more forcefully the uselessness of mere sentence-length computations than the fact that Carlyle's average sentence length in *Sartor* is almost the same as Johnson's in the *Rambler* and far above Johnson's in *Rasselas!*[6] For purposes of contrast, then, Johnson's style is a good one to use; but the results tend to appear unduly negative. The question must be what *is* Carlyle's style, not what is it not.

Carlyle's style exhibits a vast range of peculiarities once carefully denominated in classical rhetoric. One could call it paratatic, periphrastic, parasynthetic, hypotypotic, paraenetic, paraleptic, parenthetic, paradoxical, occasionally paralogic, and no doubt more. Many would be content to add paralytic. But it is doubtful that most of these terms would really clarify the issue even for the academic reader. *Para* as a Greek prefix means "along side of," "beside," and also "amiss," "against." The predominance in the list of terms beginning with that prefix suggests something about Carlyle's style: that it is strung out rather than subordinated and that it is often in conflict or opposition to

[6] Wimsatt, p. 64, gives Johnson's *Rambler* average as 44.03, whereas *Rasselas* reaches only 30.78. An average from spot checks that I made throughout *Sartor* yields a sentence length of no less than a weighty forty words. In general Johnson's sentences, according to Wimsatt, become shorter as Johnson ages. But the fact is that sentence length, like the more complex computations for clausal weight and for substitution of clauses by participial constructions and the like, affords interesting but not especially illuminating statistics. Invariably such computations reveal that writers in earlier periods wrote longer sentences with more clauses than later writers. Caxton, for example, averages 5.26 clauses and 65.07 words per sentence; and even Dryden, who contributed to reducing the sentence length in English, comes out with 60.76 words per sentence. It seems hard to do anything with this kind of information except to say that Caxton's sentences are longer than Carlyle's, and Carlyle's in turn longer than Hemingway's. But was there ever any doubt of it? For sentence length studies of English authors see Stuart Pratt Sherman, *Analytics of Literature* (Boston, 1893), pp. 256–262. By another means of computation, the Fog-Index, I have calculated Carlyle's rating at 23, as contrasted with Macaulay's 22, Bacon's 28, and DeFoe's 68! See Robert Gunning, *The Technique of Clear Writing*, (New York, 1952), pp. 34–39.

balance. We can get at the style more effectively by seeking its source. Carlyle himself speaks of revolution and breakup of style in defending *Sartor;* and he probably had both ideological and linguistic aspects in mind when he wrote his poem on *Sartor:* "He wrote a Revolution / Book without its like." Considered as a positive contrast to a style of ease and gravity, Carlyle's style might be the subject of the following paragraph:

> Expressiveness rather than formal beauty was the pretension of the new movement. . . . It disdained complacency, suavity, copiousness, emptiness, ease, and in avoiding these qualities sometimes obtained effects of contortion or obscurity, which it was not always willing to regard as faults. It preferred the forms that express the energy and labor of minds seeking the truth, not without dust and heat, to the forms that express a contented sense of the enjoyment and possession of it. In a single word, the motions of souls, not their states of rest, had become the themes of art.[7]

The subject of the preceding sentences is actually the baroque style of the seventeenth century. Its applicability to Carlyle's style, however, suggests that we should look beyond the Addison-Johnson tradition for antecedents of Carlyle's style.

The distinguishing feature of the baroque style is looseness. The earlier search for balance through the classical concept of *numerus* (in sixteenth-century England epitomized by "like members and like sounds") stands at the

[7] Morris Croll, "The Baroque Style in Prose," *Studies in English Philology: A Miscellany in Honor of Frederick Klaeber,* ed. Kemp Malone and Martin B. Ruud (Minneapolis, 1929), p. 428. The nineteenth-century prose of the imaginative sense of fact stands generally to the eighteenth-century neoclassic style as seventeenth-century prose does to sixteenth-century classicism. Perhaps this is symptomatic of what Germans call a systole and diastole of classic and romantic. See esp. Fritz Strich, *Deutsche Klassik und Romantik; oder Vollendung und Unendlichkeit* (Bern, 1949).

opposite pole from the Attic or Senecan style that dominated in the seventeenth century. So pronounced is the
looseness of the baroque style that Croll speaks of the
typical baroque sentence as the "exploded period," a
sentence that structurally appears to have suffered an inward explosion. By way of further discrimination, Croll
identifies two basic patterns of sentence organization, both
of which have their antecedents in philosophic positions,
but both of which in the seventeenth century came into
general use by prose writers. They are the *stile coupé*
(or *stile serré*) or curt style, and the loose or linked style.[8]

These two patterns can also be found in Carlyle, and
they may owe something to his abiding admiration for
seventeenth-century prose, a Carlyle preoccupation that
has been but slightly explored.[9] In any case, his style has
a tortuous syntax, one that breaks and alters course, one
that seems to have suffered an inward explosion. Consider
the following early quotation from Teufelsdröckh:

> "All visible things are emblems; what thou seest is not
> there on its own account; strictly taken, is not there at
> all: Matter exists only spiritually, and to represent some
> Idea, and *body* it forth." (I, xi, 72)

The sentence provides a good example of the curt style.
It strings together a series of curt statements, each of
which amplifies rather than rounds off the idea, and each

[8] Croll, p. 430. See also some of Croll's other studies of seventeenth-century style, " 'Attic Prose' in the Seventeenth Century,"
Studies in Philology, XVIII (1921), 79–128; " 'Attic Prose': Lipsius,
Montaigne, Bacon," *Schelling Anniversary Papers* (New York, 1923),
"Muret and the History of 'Attic Prose,,' " *PMLA*, XXXIX (1924),
254–309; and George Williamson, *The Senecan Amble: A Study
in Prose Form from Bacon to Collier* (London, 1951).

[9] Carlyle's reading as recorded by Shine reflects his seventeenth-
century interest to some extent, but it appears so overshadowed
by his German reading that it is easy to overlook. More revealing
are Carlyle's comments in *Two Note Books*, pp. 23–31, 67–70,
85–89, 98–99. Of seventeenth-century literature Carlyle wrote:
"*There*, in that old age, lies the *only* true *poetical* literature of
England."

of which is connected only by the most tenuous of syntactical relations. The statements are almost independent of each other grammatically, but they relate as expansions and modifications of the same idea. The idea Teufelsdröckh is expressing is a Carlyle favorite: all visible things are symbols of more important invisible ideas or forces. The sentence, with its three independent clauses, states this idea from several vantage points, turns, as it were, the jewel to different lights. First, and typically, Carlyle offers a forceful assertion, cast in simple, declarative form: "All visible things are emblems; . . ." Then he turns the thought around and casts it as a negative with the addition of a new thought: "What thou seest is not there on its own account; . . ." To this he appends, semi-independently, a more emphatic, farther-reaching phrasing of the first idea: ". . . strictly taken, is not there at all: . . ." Then he changes his counters by substituting, and capitalizing, "Matter" for "all visible things," and revealing at last what it is that visible things are emblems of, on what account they are there, i.e., to represent an idea: "Matter exists only spiritually, and to represent some Idea, and *body* it forth." By the conclusion of the sentence Carlyle has moved to a philosophic (and contemporary German) vocabulary—Matter, Idea—which lends authority to the statement that began with common language. Moreover, Carlyle, by the end of the sentence, has made a more inclusive statement than the one he began with. There is a progression, but it is not a logical one: it is emotional or, dare I say, poetic. Rather than a syllogism—which would have to state rather laboriously: All visible things are emblems; Clothes are visible things; Therefore clothes are emblems; . . . and then move on to the next syllogism—rather than all this, which would still be open to attack on basic propositions (in any case, one can ask, and argue, *are* all visible things emblems?), Carlyle conveys his idea by assertion and insinuation, by exhortation and repetition. One either accepts the proposition that visible things are emblems, or one does not. That is the key issue. If visible things are emblems, then much of what Teufelsdröckh has to say about them is worth the hearing. But Carlyle must persuade the reader that visible things are indeed emblems, and this is the purpose of his kind of statement. We are disposed to accept it for a number of reasons. For one thing, he insists so. For another, he shares the insight with the reader, enabling him to enter imaginatively into his thought, rather than presenting the thought neutrally for each man to weigh as he sees fit. Carlyle conveys what it feels like to think as he does. That is why some readers are not merely unconvinced, but actively repelled and other readers carried off with enthusiasm. Carlyle's kind of statement grasps and entwines, and we struggle as the fly in marmalade.

Note, further, a thoroughly Carlylean peculiarity. When he reaches the end of his sentence, he capitalizes for emphasis—Matter, Idea—and then he italicizes for further emphasis: *body*. Finally, he has the best of both worlds on matter, as he moves his thought forward rather than rounding it, when he adds the final phrase, "and *body* it forth." He declared initially that matter does not exist; now he declares that matter *bodies* forth the idea. There is a point here that will play into his later purpose, for he is about to speak of clothing as the *embodiment* of ideas, and then of matter as a kind of clothing, which in turn means that it too embodies ideas. This has to do with Carlyle's rhetorical strategy in the passage as a whole. But what I want to emphasize is that within the single sentence Carlyle maintains an outward movement, even in the last phrase. At the same time he attributes body to matter, which he had just denied the existence of. Logically if matter does not exist, to speak of it as a body is misleading. But again, logic is not the point. Carlyle's concept of matter, which has been called "shifting," is instead paradoxical; and we should no more balk at paradox in *Sartor* than we do in religion, for it is religion that Carlyle is dealing with.

But let us return to the syntactic issue. Carlyle structures his sentences as progressive, outward-moving statements. The sentences have exploded, as in the baroque, and they carry the reader with them, if he but permit himself that willing suspension of disbelief that he gives to poetry. Moreover, Carlyle is not above seeming to use rational argument (sometimes, of course, he actually does), and he will sprinkle his sentences with terminology from science, logic, and philosophy as a means of lending authority; further, he will frequently follow assertions with conclusions and words that appear to introduce conclusions: *hence, therefore, consequently, so, thus.* All of this is especially well adapted to the form of the Fragment, and Teufelsdröckh's meditations are, as we have seen, Fragments. The form itself encourages the loose sentence, the outward-flowing infinite statement; it demands the mystic, orphic utterance. It is thus fitting that the style of Teufelsdröckh's Fragments be that of the exploded period of the baroque, and especially that the parts be curt periods, the *stile coupé,* strung together in loose syntactic arrangement.

The Editor, on the other hand, conservative though he be, writes almost consistently lengthier sentences than Teufelsdröckh. These are sometimes even cast in something that approaches the classic style, but the asides and subordinate clauses usually obscure the basic balance of the sentences. More often, in any case, the Editor composes in the "loose" or "linked" style.

Hofrath Heuschrecke, in a too long-winded Letter, full of compliments, Weissnichtwo politics, dinners, dining repartees, and other ephemeral trivialities, proceeds to remind us of what we knew well already: that however it may be with Metaphysics, and other abstract Science originating in the Head (*Verstand*) alone, no Life-Philosophy (*Lebensphilosophie*), such as this of Clothes pretends to be, which originates equally in the Character (*Gemüth*), and equally speaks thereto, can attain its

significance till the Character itself is known and seen;
"til the Author's View of the World (*Weltansicht*),
and how he actively and passively came by such view,
are clear: in short till a Biography of him has been
philosophico-poetically written, and philosophico-poetically read." (ɪ, xi, 75)

We can reduce the preceding statement to a much more
workable one: "We cannot understand the clothes philosophy until we have a biography of the author." But obviously much is lost. For one thing, we lose the agreement
of the Editor with Heuschrecke (modified at the same
time by the Editor's criticisms of the Hofrath). For another,
we lose the contrast between metaphysics and life-philosophy (foregrounded as it is with the German terms in
parentheses). And we lose the definition of the kind of
biography necessary for right understanding, as well as the
emphasis on the proper reading of such a biography. It can
seriously be maintained that Carlyle's sentence is in its
way economical, if we allow that the vastness of the ter-
ritory he wants to take in deserves being included. And
that is the philosophical position involved. Carlyle wants
to touch on everything in heaven and earth. He wants to
bring the whole world, visible and invisible, into his
scope. The net is cast very wide. Only the adventurous
fisherman will want to pull it in.

In terms of sentence organization we should note that
Carlyle's sentence occupies just over thirteen lines in the
Harrold edition. Three and a half lines take care of the
subject and verb; the remaining twelve and a half are
devoted to the predication. These twelve and a half lines
actually hold in suspension the real goal of the sentence,
the word *Biography* and the clause relating to it. We
proceed through parenthetic observations about metaphysics, life-philosophy, the head and the character, and so
on, building to the climax of the philosophico-poetical
Biography and reading thereof. Here Carlyle differs from

the seventeenth-century loose style: he is always tantalizing the reader, leading him on through thicket and byway, so that the reader is both participant and pursuer. Carlyle's style thereby attains some of its intensity. We are always engaged in a movement forward; we feel that we are progressing to some momentous conclusion. It is Carlyle's version of the periodic sentence. In *Sartor* this kind of periodic sentence especially marks the Editor's style, of which the following example is typical: "The Editor will here admit that, among all the wondrous provinces of Teufelsdröckh's spiritual world, there is none he walks in with such astonishment, hesitation, and even pain, as in the Political" (III, vii, 249).

A wag once observed that the reason Germans listen so intently to conversation is that, of couse, they are waiting for the verb. In Carlyle's case we are often waiting for the verb and the noun. In the following sentence the Editor has delayed the arrival of both:

> Directly on the first perusal, almost on the first deliberate inspection, it became apparent that here a quite new Branch of Philosophy, leading to as yet undescribed ulterior results, was disclosed; farther, what seemed scarcely less interesting, a quite new human Individuality, an almost unexampled personal character that, namely, of Professor Teufelsdröckh the Discloser. (I, ii, 10)

To italicize in the foregoing sentence to demonstrate the point is quite impossible, for Carlyle himself has used so many devices of emphasis that additional ones would only obscure. But let us go over the sentences carefully. A "stylist" would perhaps recast it thus: "It became immediately apparent that here was a new branch of philosophy." Carlyle, however, inverts, placing the adverbial phrase first. Not content with that, he puts another such phrase directly after it in apposition. Then he makes his main statement: "it became apparent that here a quite new Branch of Philosophy . . . ," and the reader knows by the capitals that he has arrived at an important portion of the sentence. But then Carlyle modifies the substantive by a typical absolute participial construction before permitting "was disclosed" to appear. Once it does, the reader must pause with the semicolon that follows. Then comes another noun clause with "that" omitted. The new clause, syntactically related to the previous one, is nevertheless an entirely new idea, fraught, of course, with asides and appositional phrases: "farther, what seemed scarcely less interesting, [it became apparent that] a quite new human Individuality [was disclosed], an almost unexampled personal character, that, namely, of Professor Teufelsdröckh the Discloser." Verbally, Carlyle is playing on the *disclosure* of a new branch of philosophy and of the *disclosure* of Teufelsdröckh, who is at the same time the *discloser* thereof. Again the sentence is in Carlyle's way periodic, but it lacks full parallelism because Carlyle has suppressed the necessary parallel phrases which I have supplied in brackets. Carlyle's sentences rarely have the Ciceronian desideratum of equal number through equal members, but they frequently share with oratory the delay of full meaning until the end. By breaking up the balance, Carlyle seems to make his sentences rush headlong to their goals; yet he also impedes progress by the introduction of numerous parenthetical and appositional observations, so that the sentences both rush and hover. There is, however, always the sensation of *motion,* underway or incipient. The style has an unexampled vitality, a quite individual energy.

If the baroque style has its origins in latitudinarian and skeptical thought, Carlyle's energetic style has its origins in his disposition and outlook. His style is a function of his thought, of a mind restless with ideas, seeking and probing, a mind entirely other than at ease. The restlessness of Carlyle's mind manifests itself in his loose sentence structure. The periodicity of Carlyle's style is a manifestation of the predilection of Carlyle's mind for the emphatic.

To find a style more emphatic than Carlyle's would require another Diogenes. Even to chart what Carlyle has done is no easy task, but we can isolate the most significant devices he uses for emphasis. These are: parallelism, exclamation, interrogation, inversion, visual devices, and of course, his overall diction. These devices, or practices, grow out of the loose style of Carlyle's sentences, although they lend his style a febrile quality not often found in the baroque.

Carlyle's use of parallelism is directed toward the goal of fuller understanding, but it goes far beyond conventional parallelism. We may call Carlyle's parallelism "progressive apposition"—that is, his purpose is not merely to add further particulars as in most appositional constructions, but to extend the application of a statement by adding appositional phrases that include a wider area of reference than the original noun. Frequently he is moving up a hierarchy in an effort to show the immensity inherent in the slightest phenomenon. A good example of Carlyle's progressive apposition appears in the minnow passage already cited in another context.[10] Let us look at it with the parallels emphasized:

To the Minnow every cranny and pebble,
      and quality and accident,
            of its little native Creek
   may have become familiar:
but does the Minnow understand the Ocean Tides
               and periodic Currents,
               the Tradewinds,
               and Monsoons,
               and Moon's Eclipses;
by all which the condition of its little Creek is regulated, and may from time to time (*un*miraculously enough), be quite overset and reversed?

[10] See above, p. 217. The passage comes from *Sartor*, III, viii, 258.

Such a minnow is Man;
>   his Creek this Planet Earth;
>   his Ocean the immeasurable All;
>   his Monsoons and periodic Currents the mysterious
>   Course of Providence
>   through Aeons of Aeons.

Now it may strike the reader that the so-called parallels and appositions here are not that at all, but catalogues, for parallelism refers to structure, and Carlyle constantly suppresses parts of the parallel, and apposition is normally an adjunct that particularizes, whereas these expand.[11] But that is precisely the point. In the first place, the differences in the first set of appositions—cranny and pebble, quality and accident—are deceptive. The crannies of the creek *are* its qualities, the pebbles its accidents. Even the second lengthy set of appositional statements is not so very different. All have to do with the operation of extra-terrestrial forces on the currents and climates of the earth. All in fact are influenced by the phases of the moon. The apposition is progressive in that Carlyle moves from what the minnow would perceive (but not understand)—the ocean tides—to what would be beyond both understanding and perception—the moon's eclipses—by apposing words at least close in meaning to each other. Nor is this all, for the issue of all the apposition emerges in the second sentence, in which Carlyle draws his kind of conclusion from what has preceded. It is an analogy drawn between man in his habitat and the minnow in his. Metaphor and analogy are so fundamental to Carlyle's thought that his tendency to apposition can be seen to arise from his metaphorical cast of mind. His appositions are comparisons as much as particularizers, which is why they move ever farther afield: he is forever expanding the scope of the comparison.

---

[11] For a more conventional treatment of Carlyle's parallelism see Calder, *The Writing of Past and Present*, pp. 169–183.

Because Carlyle's appositions progress and expand, they are also fundamentally different from the Johnsonian or classical parallelism which they sometimes resemble, as in the doublets "cranny and pebble," "quality and accident," or in the parallel clauses of the second sentence cited above. Wimsatt observes that any writer who "dwells upon, elaborates, or emphasizes any point" will inevitably become involved in parallelism.[12] And Carlyle qualifies. But Carlyle's parallels are constructed not for balance but for movement, so that in the sentence comparing man to the minnow, while each clause is parallel in basic structure, each clause is also longer than the preceding, and each one moves forward to advance a new thought rather than settling into balanced repose. "Such a minnow is Man" is concise enough, and so perhaps is "his Creek this Planet Earth," although already the phrase is beginning to extend. "His Ocean the immeasurable All" is drawn out by the sound of *ocean* and *immeasurable*. Finally comes a much longer and unbalanced clause toward which the others have moved: "his Monsoons and periodic Currents the mysterious Course of Providence through Aeons of Aeons." The structure is basically the same as that of the preceding clauses, but it has been vastly lengthened and even unbalanced by the weight and number of its words. These words are, however, necessary to Carlyle's purpose. The sentence remains open-ended because it closes on the prepositional phrase rather than the predicate adjective on which the other clauses close. Carlyle has also effected a change here in points of reference which, disruptive as it is of balance, is an essential part of his method. His analogy is initially based on a perception of physical similarities, i.e., man stands in relation to his environment as the minnow to his. But through the stages of his analogy Carlyle is busy expanding, not merely the points of comparison and the structure of the sentence, but the very

[12] Wimsatt, p. 18.

meaning itself (of which, indeed, the expanding structure is the reflection). He suggests his direction by alluding to the minnow's almost certain ignorance of such distant influences as the moon's eclipses, but not until the final clause of the second sentence is the full force of the analogy clear; for there we see that he is speaking not only of man's relation to his physical surroundings but of his relation to the mysterious dimension of time. Man is not only infinitesimal on this earth, as the minnow in his creek; man is not merely moving through the vast spaces of the universe ("the immeasurable All"), but man's monsoons and periodic currents are likened to the "Course of Providence," which is not a physical object at all. The course of providence, which works on man as the currents on the minnow, works "through Aeons of Aeons," that is, it works *in* time, a dimension far more complex than the physical one. Carlyle's sentences are not only regularly irregular; they also move the reader from the particular to the universal. The appositions and parallels begin with the homeliest of everyday objects—crannies and pebbles—and move to the least understood and most mysterious of forces—providence and time. By such means does he communicate his mystic intuition of the world's oneness simultaneously with an acute awareness of the world's particularity. Style, as has often been said, is meaning.

Apposition and parallelism are aspects of emphasis. Another is the exclamation, and the exclamatory question. Carlyle employs both frequently. One of the reasons that Teufelsdröckh's sentences on the average are shorter than the Editor's is that Teufelsdröckh repeatedly exclaims. The Professor's Fragments abound with ejaculations like the following, all taken from the same chapter ("Natural Supernaturalism") "What are the Laws of Nature?" "Alas, not in anywise!" "System of Nature!" "To read it!" "What is Madness, what are Nerves?" "O Heaven!" "Fool!" "But whence!—O Heaven, whither?" Carlyle also gives

Teufelsdröckh extended exclamations, sometimes, as in the following example, one after the other:

> Were a Hatter to establish himself, in the Wahngasse of Weissnichtwo, and make felts of this sort for all mankind, what a world we should have of it! Still stranger, should, on the opposite side of the street, another Hatter establish himself; and, as his fellow-craftsman made Space-annihilating Hats, make Time-annihilating! Of both would I purchase, were it with my last groschen; but chiefly of this latter. To clap-on your felt, and, simply by wishing that you were Any*where*, straightway to be *There!* Next to clap-on your other felt, and, simply by wishing that you were Any*when*, straightway to be *Then!* This were indeed the grander: shooting at will from the Fire-Creation of the World to its Fire-Consumation; here historically present in the First Century, conversing face to face with Paul and Seneca; there prophetically in the Thirty-first, conversing also face to face with other Pauls and Senecas, who as yet stand hidden in the depth of that late Time! (III, viii, 261)

Six sentences, five exclamations. Small wonder that we never get Teufelsdröckh unmediated.

Exclamation in *Sartor* is oratory. The reader hears as much as he reads. But it is also colloquial. What the reader hears is couched in forceful, concrete language. Most of the time, indeed, the reader is being called a fool. Whether he likes it or not, the reader is compelled into involvement, and much of the distinctiveness of Carlyle's style lies in that involvement of the reader. In addition to exclamation Carlyle's use of tense and mood conspire to involve the reader. Were there ever so many questions? Were there ever so many exhortations? The imperative and interrogative moods are among Carlyle's favorites. Teufelsdröckh in "Natural Supernaturalism" uses, by actual count, almost three-fourths as many interrogative sentences as declarative ones.[13] Teufelsdröckh seems always to be either exclaiming or questioning, and at times he seems to contrive to do both at once. The effect is to compel the reader into participation (or in some cases to repel him from reading at all), and the advantage Carlyle gains by such frontal assault is sustained by his use of tense. The dominant tense in Carlyle is the present.[14]

Writing in the present tense is a feature Carlyle acquired from writing essays. Since Teufelsdröckh is writing a kind of extended essay or philosophic treatise, he quite properly uses the present tense. Deviations are few, and these are chiefly sentences, usually questions, cast in the future tense. The past is but little used except, of course, for Book Two. The Editor, as has been noted, is engaged in the act of making sense out of the clothes volume and the biography of Teufelsdröckh. He speaks habitually of his undertaking in the present tense, except at those few points when the Editor pauses for a backward and summary look at the ground already traversed. In such cases the tense is the present perfect, as referring to an undertaking only just completed or begun at a time in the past and continuing up to the present. Consider, for example, the Editor in "Prospective": "The Philosophy of Clothes is now to all readers, as we predicted it would do, unfolding itself into new boundless expansions, of a cloudcapt, almost chimerical aspect . . . ," "Is that a real Elysian brightness . . . ," "Our Professor . . . gives an Editor enough to do." By contrast, in "Circumspective," the Editor writes:

[13] By actual count there are 62 declarative sentences from Teufelsdröckh in the chapter, and 45 interrogative ones. It must, of course, be remembered that the abundance of questions also reflects the dialogue or dramatized nature of "Natural Supernaturalism" commented on previously; but in addition to the many questions that Teufelsdröckh puts into the mouth of "an illuminated class," there are many that Teufelsdröckh himself utters. These are often interrogative only in a technical sense, and could just as easily be called exclamatory.

[14] See also "Vernon Lee" [Violet Paget], "Carlyle and the Present Tense," *Contemporary Review*, LXXXV (1904), 386–392.

"Have many British Readers actually arrived with us at the new promised country?" Then he shifts into the present: "In a word, do we at length stand safe in the far region of Poetic Creation?" And he concludes with the future: "As will perhaps abundantly appear to readers of the two following Chapters." It is always the present that dominates, for the time in *Sartor* is now; the gaze in *Sartor* is toward the future.

Stylistically, there is a striking parallel between the books and the tenses Carlyle uses in each. We have already noted that the books fall into the three phases of the history of European man, with Book One representing the present, Book Two the past, and Book Three the future. Book One is cast chiefly in the present tense. Book Two, however, is cast chiefly in the past. Teufelsdröckh himself is looking back, and the Editor repeatedly intervenes, in the present, to comment on the events described and the continuing difficulties he faces. Book Three returns us to the present in terms of tense, albeit a present that looks toward the future. The initial effect of the reliance on the present tense is to engage the reader in the act of comprehending and pursuing the clothes philosophy. Another purpose is, by example as it were, the annihilation of time itself, the making of everything an everlasting Now. It is perhaps as close as we can hope to come to Teufelsdröckh's yearned-for time-annihilating hat. Only the present tense suits the discussion of those things that forever *are*—the unchanging truths and realities of all existence: "'O Heaven, it is mysterious, it is awful to consider that we not only carry each a future Ghost within Him; but are, in very deed, Ghosts!'" As much as it is the inevitable tense of lyric poetry, it is also the inevitable tense of Carlylean vatic prose.

Simultaneous with the use of the present tense appears an archaizing feature of the style—the extensive use of the second person singular familiar, *thou*. Surely the least justification for the frequent *thou*'s and the corresponding

258 *Style*

archaic verb form is the illusion of translation from a language that retains those forms in active use, although it is a justification of sorts. More pertinent, I think, is the Biblical association. Apart from Quakers, most people associate *thou* chiefly with the Bible, and the word trails some of the awesome authority of the Gospel. Carlyle, playing on the obvious Biblical associations of *thou*, uses it for Teufelsdröckh's dialogue with himself and in direct address to the reader, who, if he was not before, soon becomes conditioned to expect after it a statement of profound significance.

The Biblical echoes in *thou* and other archaic tendencies in Carlyle's style call to mind the question of the rhythm of Carlyle's prose, but there is little profit in pursuing the *ignes fatui* of cadence, *clausula,* and "prose rhythm."[15] Of course, the countless classical allusions in Carlyle's prose and the record of his wide reading bear sufficient witness that Carlyle knew classical writers and consequently the classical concern for cadence and the like. One can even isolate a few sound patterns in Carlyle's prose—his abundant alliteration, his fondness for like-sounding doublets, perhaps even a tendency for him to begin paragraphs on a trochaic or spondaic foot. But these are never enough to capture what may be, after all, Saintsbury's "indefinable."[16] Considerably more verifiable is the question

[15] To prove this point, Lucas, p. 257, offers several examples of *clausula* with cursus from the columns of the daily newspaper. See also Wimsatt, pp. 6–8. But for a contrasting view see Paull Franklin Baum, *The Other Harmony of Prose* (Durham, N.C., 1952).

[16] The most frequently mentioned classical writers in Carlyle's early reading are (in order) Homer, Virgil, Aristotle, and Horace. See Shine, *Carlyle's Early Reading,* passim. In J. A. K. Thomson's *Classical Influences on English Prose* (New York, 1962), no English author is referred to more often than Carlyle except for Johnson; and there are as many references to Carlyle as to Burke or Gibbon.

Saintsbury's "indefinable" appears at the end of a considerable catalogue of Carlylean peculiarities: "Its characteristics, like those of nearly all great styles, are partly obvious, partly recondite, or altogether fugitive, even from the most acute and persevering in-of diction, and it is to Carlyle's diction that we must now direct our attention.

THE LANGUAGE OF "SARTOR"

Just as Carlyle's syntax shows the effects of what he called "revolution," his language reveals revolutionary (some would say nihilistic) forces at work. In Carlyle we seek in vain for the lofty, philosophic diction of Dr. Johnson, and we are no better off if we hope to find Wordworth's "language of common men." Carlyle's language is as much Carlylese as his syntax. For the rebellion against the poetic, general diction of the eighteenth century has been carried further in Carlyle; the whole area of specialized, technical, distinctively "modern" language has been added to the range of literary English. As Carlyle wrote to Sterling, "If one has thoughts not hitherto uttered in English Books, I see nothing for it but that you must use words not found there, must *make* words . . . ."[17] The effects of Carlyle's convictions on this matter are evident, not merely in his choice of words, but in his coinages and inventions, and perhaps most impressively of all in the way he makes existing words work for him. The question here, however, is not, say, the number of coinages in -*dom* but the general purpose and effect of the language of *Sartor* overall, and, by extension, of Carlyle's language in general.

Even the casual reader of *Sartor* has been struck by

---

vestigation. In the lowest place come the mechanical devices of capitals. . . . Next may be ranked certain stenographic tricks as regard grammar. . . . Next and higher come exotic, and specially German, construction. . . . Farther still from the mechanical is the art of arrangement in order of words and juxtaposition of clauses, cadence and rhythm of phrase, all of which go so far to make up style in the positive. And beyond these again comes the indefinable part, the part which always remains and defies analysis." (George Saintsbury, *A Short History of English Literature* [London, 1898], pp. 761–762.)

[17] *Sartor*, p. 316.

Carlyle's use of words in what Sterling called "a quaint and queer connection." It might well be debated which aspect of Carlyle's use of language is the most striking and the most revealing. Many would plump for his persistent compounding, remembering such "un-English" coinages as "cabalistico-sartorial," "philosophico-poetical," "humano-anecdotical," "gaseous-chaotic," and "diabolico-angelical" among the adjectives; and "World-Mahlstrom," "Attorney-Logic," "Motive-Millwrights," "World-Phoenix," "Flesh-Garment," and "God-effulgences" among the nouns.[18] Others might cite his coinages in *-dom, -hood, -ity,* or even his Biblical *ands.*[19] John Holloway has claimed that Carlyle's tendency to borrow and paraphrase Biblical passages constitutes a fundamental element of his style.[20] One could profitably add Goethe, Shakespeare, Jean Paul, Milton, Swift, Sterne, and the seventeenth-century divines; for

[18] Caryle also used neologisms with considerable freedom. His use of *aesthetic* and *romantic* and related forms of those words, for example, antedates the entries in the *OED,* although Coleridge also has claims here. Carlyle certainly far precedes Arnold in his use of *philistine* as word and concept.

[19] Carlyle has been found to be the source for more than half of the coinages in *-dom* in the first forty years of the nineteenth century. The suffix enjoyed a kind of revival in the period, apparently sparked by Carlyle. See Robert M. Estrich and Hans Sperber, *Three Keys to Language* (New York, 1952), pp. 107–108. I cannot, however, agree with the authors' suggested explanation for Carlyle's linguistic inventiveness as residing in the severe schooling he received as a youth.

The most extensive treatment of Carlyle's coinages overall is in Otto Schmeding, "Über Wortbildung bei Carlyle," *Studien zur englischen Philologie,* v (1900), 1–352. Schmeding's monograph shows that Carlyle lavished his chief gifts on substantives, adjectives and adverbs in that order, and chiefly through suffix coinages like *-dom, -hood, -ness, -ship* and virtually every other suffix known in English. Among verbs he made far fewer coinages, although still a considerable number, chiefly through suffixes, verbs made out of other parts of speech, and through the prefix, *be-.* He also, not surprisingly, contributed a large number of negative expressions, especially with prefixes like *un-, in-, non-, dis-,* and the like. See also Otto Lincke, *Über die Wortzusammensetzung in Carlyles "Sartor Resartus"* (Berlin, 1904).

[20] Holloway, *Victorian Sage,* pp. 24–26.

Carlyle paraphrases and echoes wherever he goes. His style is intensely allusive. If, as seems likely, Biblical echoes are more pervasive than any other kind, one is probably justified in emphasizing the formative influence of the Bible on Carlyle's style. But it is possible to examine something even more comprehensive—Carlyle's theory of language itself.

True, Carlyle, in the matter of language as in other things, left no comprehensive treatise. But he left enough comments before and during the period of the writing of *Sartor* for us to see clearly the direction in which his thought tended at that time. In *Sartor* itself the essence of Carlyle's ideas on language is presented through Teufelsdröckh:

"Language is called the Garment of Thought: however, it should rather be, Language is the Flesh-Garment, the Body of Thought. I said that imagination wove this Flesh-Garment; and does not she? Metaphors are her stuff: examine Language; what, if you except some few primitive elements (of natural sound), what is it all but Metaphors, recognized as such, or no longer recognized; still fluid and florid, or now solid-grown and colourless? If those same primitive elements are the osseous fixtures in the Flesh-Garment, Language,—then are Metaphors its muscles and tissues and living integuments. An unmetaphorical style you shall in vain seek for: is not your very *Attention* a *Stretching-to?*" (i, xi, 73).

Apart from the stylistic peculiarities of the passage itself, which succeeds in exemplifying the theory it expounds Carlyle gives us the essence of his deepest convictions about language: all language is in origin metaphorical, except the few necessary primitive sounds that language reduces to. Since Carlyle's aesthetic theory also holds that metaphor is the essence of poetry, it becomes clear that language is by its very nature poetic. Therefore, since all styles are metaphorical, one can hardly object to a given style as too metaphorical; for such a style would merely be one that exploited the resources of languages more completely than others, would be in fact a style that was more poetic, more deeply attuned to the genius of language. As Carlyle noted as early as 1822, the "metaphorical talent . . . is the first characteristic of genius," and later in 1829: "All language but that concerning *sensual* objects is or has been figurative. Prodigious influence of metaphors!"[21] In his *Note Books* as well as in *Sartor* Carlyle records curious metaphorical names or intriguing etymologies.[22]

What is remarkable about Carlyle's speculations on language and metaphor is that he appears to have arrived at an idealist theory of language without having any acquaintance with the English idealist theorists of the eighteenth century, men like Harris and Monboddo.[23] Instead, he shows a great familiarity with such a complete nominalist and sensualist as Horne Tooke.[24] But whereas Tooke finds all words reducing themselves to certain sensible perceptions as grounds for opposing any postulation about the divine origin of language and as support for a thoroughly rationalist and skeptical philosophy, Carlyle finds in the same facts occasion for wonder and mystic speculation

---

[21] *Two Note Books,* pp. 30, 141–142.

[22] Ibid., pp. 168–169, 184–185, 260–263. The most arresting of these is that on tribulation: "Tribula was a kind of threshing-machine; a chest roughened with wood-bars, or iron or flint notches on the bottom, and so trailed by cattle back and forward over the ears of corn till the grain was hustled out of them. The driver sat on it; and (as among the modern Turks) might have a *ladle wherein to catch the dung!*"

"*Tribulatio* is from this word; and so originally signifies something like what we Scotch mean by a *Heckelling* (hatchelling); use has made it honourable" (*Two Note Books,* p. 260). Cf. also *Sartor,* III, vii, 249; ix, 270.

[23] For a history of their theories and opposing ones see Otto Funke, *Englische Sprachphilosophie im späteren achtzehnten Jahrhundert* (Bern, 1934), esp. pp. 1–84.

[24] John Horne, later John Horne Tooke (1736–1812), politician and student of language, philosophically a follower of Locke, set forth his linguistic and other speculations in *The Diversions of Purley* (1786–1805), rev. ed. (London, 1857).

on the divine hieroglyphs. The case is best illustrated when we compare what the two men do with the same etymology.

Hooke posited an elaborate, and now in part discredited, etymology for the word *true*. He traced it, as etymologists do today, to Old English *trow*, "believe," and he explained that it meant "simply and merely—that which is TROWED. And instead of being a rare commodity upon earth, except only in words, there is nothing but TRUTH in the world."[25] Tooke used the word to cast doubt on the idea that there could in fact be any such thing as abstract truth. But he also claimed the word was related to Latin *versus*, which he said also meant "trowed" and nothing more. His etymology went: "Res, a thing gives REOR, i.e., I am *thing-ed*; Vereor, I am strongly thing-ed; for *ve*, in Latin composition, means valde, i.e., valide. And versus, i.e., strongly impressed upon the mind, is the contract participle of vereor."

It matters little that modern etymologists find no connection between *true* and *versus*. The point is that Tooke saw in this word, as in every other, an occasion to assert the ultimate sensible origin of all words (truth is merely a thing) and to deny the subsequent abstract accretions a word may have taken on. He argued that the true meaning of words was the original meaning that arose out of sense impressions. In this respect he went even further than Locke in tracing ideas back to perceptions. Now when Tooke's speculations reach the hands of Dugald Stewart, the Scottish philosopher finds that Tooke's revelation of the metaphorical origin of words hinders abstract speculation, as indeed it does if one accepts Tooke's insistence that the original meaning only has validity. On *truth* and *versus*, for example, Stewart argues that we cannot any longer restrict the words to their original meanings, and that with these, as with other words, we must in fact do our utmost to avoid recalling the origins. In cases where the metaphorical origins are still close at hand, the writer

[25] Tooke, pp. 604–611.

would do best, Stewart argues, to so vary his language that no one metaphorical idea takes dominance and destroys the abstract. In short, Stewart does not dispute Tooke's general theory or his specific etymologies, but he thinks we had best forget about all of it as soon as possible in order not to clutter our minds with metaphors when we should be thinking in abstracts.[26]

Carlyle, of course, opposes Tooke's nominalism, but as early as "Wotton Reinfred" he shows himself disposed to accept the etymologies that Tooke unearthed. He has Williams, one of the guests at the House in the Wold, offer Tooke's explanation of the word *truth*. After the Kantist Dalbrook has asserted that what is measurable is not truth, but only the "ephemeral garments of truth," Williams interjects:

> "Truth!" interrupted Williams in his gay voice, "Horne Tooke's is the best of all definitions: *Truth* is simply *troweth*, or that which is *trowed*, or believed. In this way we have many troweths, and my troweth is very different from thy troweth, and the only rule is that the one should let the other live in peace."[27]

Now Williams, secondary as he is to Dalbrook in insight and profundity, is not an unsympathetic character in "Wotton." Although the product of a "rational university," he

---

[26] Dugald Stewart, *Works*, ed. Sir William Hamilton, (London, 1855), v, 162. Stewart also provides us with an especially fitting illustration of the dangers of the half-forgotten metaphorical significance of words leaping all too readily to the fore when the author least desires it. He quotes from Addison: "This much I thought fit to premise before I resumed the subject I have already handled. I mean the naked bosoms of our British ladies" (p. 184).

[27] *Last Words*, p. 87. The same etymology is referred to more fleetingly in the post-*Sartor* "On History Again," an essay that purports to be a fragment from an "Inaugural Dissertation by D. T." There Carlyle has D. T. manifest his impatience with the Tooke approach: "But again, Truth, says Horne Tooke, means simply the thing *trowed*, the thing believed; and now, from this to the thing *itself*, what a new fatal deduction have we to suffer!" (*Works*, xxviii, 171)

is a professed enemy of cant; he is in most respects the Wottonian equivalent of the Editor of *Sartor*. And Dalbrook does not call him to account for his definition of truth: so some approval attaches to it. But again Carlyle's manner does not make clear how much approval and why.

By *Sartor* Carlyle has learned how to use Tooke's etymologies for his own purposes. What he does, in effect, turns the tables on Tooke. But he does not confine himself to that end. Indeed Tooke's understanding, or misunderstanding, of etymology does not as such concern him, for he has a positive goal in sight: he makes etymology serve the very reverse of a sensualist philosophy. Nor does he want any part of Dugald Stewart's abstractness. Carlyle takes a stand different from that of either Tooke or Stewart. While using Tooke's etymologies for purposes quite at variance with Tooke's, he nevertheless disproves Stewart's objections to Tooke. Early in *Sartor*, in "The World in Clothes," Teufelsdröckh takes up the question of the real significance of the metaphorical origins of words. His example is the word *pecunia*, and his interpretation effectively discredits Stewart's contention, directed against Tooke, from whom the etymology stems, that we are not at all helped in our understanding of the functions of money by knowing that the word *pecunia* derives from certain Roman customs. On the contrary, Teufelsdröckh's treatment of the metaphorical meaning of the word makes us uncommonly aware of what the functions of money are—in retort to Stewart—and at the same time makes us start with wonder at the mystery of even commonplace things. Let us examine how Carlyle does this.

Teufelsdröckh has just paid tribute to the profound consequences in human history of the invention of printing and the invention of gunpowder. What, he asks, will the last blast of gunpowder accomplish? "Achieve the final undisputed prostration of Force under Thought, of Animal courage under Spiritual." By a paradox Carlyle has asserted that the invention of gunpowder was thought over force, or spiritual over animal courage. And perhaps, upon reflection, we can see it to be. The device in any case is that of investing the commonplace with new significance, and Carlyle repeatedly uses it. But now, immediately after exalting the invention of gunpowder, Teufelsdröckh turns to money and shows what he can do with metaphors from sensible objects:

> "A simple invention it was in the old-world Grazier,—sick of lugging his slow Ox about the country till he got it bartered for corn or oil,—to take a piece of Leather, and thereon scratch or stamp the mere Figure of an Ox (or *Pecus*); put it in his pocket, and call it *Pecunia*, Money. Yet hereby did Barter grow Sale, the Leather Money is now Golden and Paper, and all miracles have been out-miracled: for there are Rothschilds and English National Debts; and whoso has sixpence is sovereign (to the length of sixpence) over all men; commands cooks to feed him, philosophers to teach him, kings to mount guard over him,—to the length of sixpence." (I, v, 40–41)[28]

That should be answer enough for Dugald Stewart. It also illustrates Carlyle's fundamental concern with metaphor. What metaphor does for Carlyle is to *illuminate relationships*, to reveal connections between things not at first evident, and thus to suggest some vast and meaningful scheme in the universe. Since metaphor is, etymologically, "a carrying over" or "beyond," it is for Carlyle the carrying over of various kinds of meaning. Thus, too, symbol is

[28] Note, too, that in shouting his hosannas to the miracle of money, Carlyle also lets Teufelsdröckh undercut himself with the ironic asides on the uses to which money nowadays is put ("English National Debts") and the scarcity of money for some ("to the length of sixpence"). But that is secondary to the fact that Carlyle has used the very etymology Tooke cited for *pecunia* to prove the very reverse of Tooke's nominalism, and also the reverse of Stewart's abstractness—for we are shown that the transfer of Ox to leather has "out-miracled" all miracles.

intimately connected with metaphor. For when a meaning has been carried over, the word or thing which now bears that meaning stands for something else: it is a symbol. Thus *pecunia* is metaphorical in that it carries the meaning of ox to the piece of leather. It is also a symbol of the ox; it stands for the grazier's goods that he will barter. Ultimately, it comes to stand for goods of other kinds, and so on to money as we know it. Far from leading him to skepticism and nominalism, the metaphorical nature of language leads Carlyle, and then the reader, to an understanding of relationships obscured when the metaphor is not understood. And in the process of the reanimation of dead metaphors, a fresh insight is obtained into the abstractions they now represent. Carlyle's style, therefore, is most concrete when it is most abstract. It exists in and by metaphor and symbol.

The highly original "Symbols" chapter in *Sartor* does for symbols what earlier in the book had been done for metaphor, and provides further insight into Carlyle's theory of language:

"In the Symbol proper, what we can call a Symbol, there is ever, more or less distinctly and directly, some embodiment and revelation of the Infinite; the Infinite is made to blend itself with the Finite, to stand visible, and as it were, attainable there. By Symbols, accordingly, is man guided and commanded, made happy, made wretched. He everywhere finds himself encompassed with Symbols, recognised as such or not recognised: the Universe is but one vast Symbol of God; nay if thou wilt have it, what is man himself but a Symbol of God; is not all that he does symbolical; a revelation to Sense of the mystic god-given force that is in him; a 'Gospel of Freedom,' which he, the 'Messias of Nature,' preaches, as he can, by act and word?" (III, iii, 220)

In symbols, as in metaphors, Carlyle sees the mystery that reveals and conceals, the paradox in the heart of things.

268 *Style*

Taken for granted, a symbol is commonplace; once looked into, it has a meaning that transcends itself. Carlyle's style is grounded in his paradoxical insight into symbol and metaphor: he makes the reader see. He makes him see, as he has never seen before, what is actually there, and what it stands for.

Carlyle sees so much in every metaphor and symbol that he is able to see metaphor and symbol in everything. A passage cited earlier in illustration of Carlyle's exploded syntax also illustrates Carlyle's thought on a matter that conditions style: "'All visible things are emblems; what thou seest is not there on its own account; strictly taken, is not there at all: Matter exists only spiritually, and to represent some Idea, and *body* it forth.'" With this conviction Carlyle escapes from the sensationalism of the school of Locke. For Carlyle is arguing that, not only all language, but all objects exist to represent some idea, so that all things are metaphors and symbols. They carry across (from the infinite into the finite) ideas for which they then stand as symbols. The sentiment corresponds with Carlyle's known contempt for matter (although without it there would be presumably no glimpses at all into the infinite) and, further, with the distinction Carlyle makes between time and eternity: "Speech is of Time, Silence is of Eternity."[29]

[29] But Carlyle generally curbs his tendency to leap beyond the temporal: "For man lives in Time, has his whole earthly being, endeavour and destiny shaped for him by Time: only in the transitory Time-Symbol is the ever-motionless Eternity we stand on made manifest" (II, iii, 112). C. F. Harrold's cavil over Carlyle's shifting use of time appears to me to have missed the point of the Carlylean paradox, which is a feature of both his style and meaning. Time is used in *Sartor* in four distinct ways, as Harrold notes (pp. 87n., 112n., and 128n.), but that is the paradox of the time-eternity relationship. Time is therefore not, as we might logically desire, either good or bad, but both good and bad. Thus the fact that time is of the Devil and that it shuts us out from eternity is paradoxically countered by the equally important fact that time is our seedfield, wherein we can do good works, and our point of contact with eternity, through which we perceive the real meaning of existence. Time, then, like so much else in *Sartor*, is both metaphor and symbol.

Style 269

All of this has to do with Carlyle's words. The by now no-torious compounding has its roots in Carlyle's theory of language as well as having a further justification in that *Sartor* purports to be a translation from the naturally highly compound-prone German of Teufelsdröckh. There is, in fact, in the German associations of Carlyle and Teufelsdröckh a felicitous joining of idea and actuality: there is a need and an appropriateness in the Germanism of the style of *Sartor*. Students of language may be aware of the prodigious influence of metaphors in the making of English words, but Dugald Stewart was right in noting that many of these originally metaphorical meanings are now quite obscured. In German, however, the case is entirely different. Where English borrowed whole word complexes from Latin and the Romance tongues, German was much more likely to make loan-translations. Take, for example, the word *translation* itself. A desk dictionary discloses that it comes from the Latin *translatus*, the form used as the past participle of *transferre*—"transfer," or more literally, "carry across." Most of us, however, are not especially conscious of this etymology when we use the word. In German the corresponding verb is *übersetzen*, a typical German loan-translation; the form was borrowed from Latin, but the actual words used were Germanic. Had English done the same, we would have perhaps *overset* rather than *translate* —which is what the German actually has. Now, if one were to use the terms *overset* and *oversetting* instead of *translate* and *translation*, one would be much more conscious of the etymology, and consequently of the metaphor, that lies behind the word. In German, of course, one *is* conscious of the metaphor, in *übersetzen* and in a multitude of other words.[30] Carlyle was certainly

[30] Examples abound, and anyone who knows German could supply his own, but here I add a few with their literal German meaning to point up the contrast: *Vorlesung*, lit. "reading forth" Eng. "lecture"; *ausschliessen*, lit. "close out," Eng. "exclude"; *Einkauf*, lit. "in-buy," Eng. "purchase." In many cases if we trace the English word back to its origins, it will be found to have arisen from the selfsame metaphor as the German word, but the significance

attracted to this feature of the German language, and he seized it and made it his own in English. John Holloway has called attention to Carlyle's persistent claims to be revealing the real meaning, the true significance of a word, as one of the means whereby he directs and controls the reader's response.[31] To be sure, it can be illustrated on almost any page Carlyle wrote. What is additionally arresting is the fact that Carlyle generally *was* calling the reader's attention to the original meaning of the word, at least as far as etymology then allowed, and that his arguments were not in the least disingenuous. He found the true significance of a word in its metaphorical meaning, and, by illuminating it for the reader, he was able to make the reader think about things he had hitherto taken for granted. Moreover, the German language, with its metaphors close to the surface, provided the perfect material for Carlyle to exploit.

In *Sartor*, as opposed to many of Carlyle's later works where the practice is nevertheless the same, Carlyle had the excuse of "translation" from German. Frequently the Editor justifies a compound or an unusual use of a word by citing the German original from whichever Teufels-dröckh work he is translating: "doing and driving (*Thun und Treiben*)," "tool-using Animal (*Handthierendes Thier*)," "Devil's-smithy (*Teufelsschmiede*)," "Life-Phi-

---

is now obscured. It does not take much linguistic sophistication for an English-speaking person to realize that *unicorn* means "one horn," but it takes some. By contrast the German says *Einhorn*, which, without any obscurity at all, is quite literally "one horn." I must hasten to add that English, and many other languages, still have many words that are obviously metaphorical—*coverall, shoehorn, railroad, pigheaded*, to cite a few that occur at random. But in general, the more one approaches abstract diction, the greater the frequency of Romance-derived terms and the more obscure the metaphorical origin. It is precisely with abstracts that the difference between German and English is pronounced. These were the very words that Carlyle delighted in finding the metaphorical origins of: *attention, tribulation*, etc.

[31] Holloway, pp. 42–44.

losophy (*Lebensphilosophie*)," "humano-anecdotical (*menschlich-anekdotisch*)." While this citation method relieves the Editor of the responsibility for the term, it also foregrounds it for renewed emphasis. Again and again the terms are metaphors of an uncommon sort. They link together concepts not customarily associated or not associated so closely. Carlyle can thus praise or blame, and to that end he coins such constructions as "Motive-Millwrights," "Attorney-Logic," "World-kennel," "Hero-Divinity," and "Demon-Empire." He can also establish contrasts and paradoxes: "Heaven-gate" and "Hellgate," "City-builder" and "City-burner," "Self-worship" and "Demon-worship," and "cabalistico-satirical," "philosophico-poetical," "Prophetico-satiric," "humoristico-satirical," and "diabolico-angelical." All of these compounds are more than Sterling's merely Germanic compounds; they are precisely attempts to represent "some Idea and *body* it forth." They are all designed to blend finite and infinite, so that the language of *Sartor* itself stands as a symbol, according to which man is "guided and commanded, made happy, made wretched." The issue is not to catalogue Carlyle's adverbs, although that has been done, but to see that the pervasive heterodoxy of his language issues from his linguistic (and ultimately metaphysical) convictions. His syntax is the reflection of his conviction that revolution is everywhere, that the old forms no longer do service. His diction is the reflection of his conviction that the nature of language is metaphorical and symbolic, and that we need to reanimate the old and create the new, showing in both cases the infinite through the finite. Emphasis and insight go hand in hand.

Emphasis and insight also inform Carlyle's notorious visual devices. While these are initially the most arresting features of his style, they are also the most readily explained. Clearly they emphasize, much as the emblematic poems of a Herbert or a Quarles do. But neither in seventeenth-century poetry nor in Carlyle's prose is the manipulation of visual effects entirely adscititious. As I pointed out earlier, Carlyle's practice grows out of his writing experience. It is not hard to see that his inventiveness in applying it in the late essays and in *Sartor* is of a piece with his attitude about revolution in language.

Carlyle's linguistic inventiveness, indeed, is not confined to visual devices or the coinages of nouns and adjectives. He infuses every part of speech with his own distinctive fervency. Consider the passage cited earlier to illustrate Carlyle's use of the exclamatory sentence:

> "Still stranger, should, on the opposite side of the street, another Hatter establish himself; and, as his fellow-craftsman made Space-annihilating Hats, make Time-annihilating! Of both would I purchase, were it with my last groschen; but chiefly of this latter. To clap-on your felt, and, simply by wishing that you were Any*where* straightway to be *There!*" Next to clap-on your other felt, and simply by wishing that you were Any*when*, straightway to be *Then!*"

Space-annihilating and *Time-annihilating* are arresting enough constructions in themselves, but Carlyle tops them with his manipulation of the adverbs *where, there, when,* and *then.* Not until Joyce is there a comparable inventiveness in English prose.

When Carlyle is not coining new words or compounding others, he is juxtaposing words in new and unusual combinations. The result is what I have called the allusiveness of Carlyle's style. Its relation to his theory of language is self-evident: the abundance of allusion is another means of embodying the infinite in the finite. It serves as well to give the style much of its celebrated concreteness. The allusiveness of *Sartor* has already been examined as an aspect of texture, and it is necessary here only to recall how much this allusiveness is a feature of what is conventionally called style as well. The seeming breakdown in syntax and language originates in Carlyle's concept of revolution in language and in his attempt to reconstitute meaningful relationships. The seriousness of his endeavor is matched only by the humor of it. Carlyle sees all things under a dual aspect, that of the ridiculous and that of the sublime. The style of *Sartor,* is, therefore, not only that of earnest oratory, but also that of irrepressible comedy.

THE HUMOR OF "SARTOR"

It is hard to tell at first whether the ridiculous or the sublime holds the upper hand in *Sartor.* The judgment of history, of course, has given the nod to the sublime, and Carlyle's own moral earnestness has appeared to ratify this judgment. There seems to be scant likelihood that Carlyle will be mistaken for an exclusively comic figure, but in some areas there seems scant likelihood that he will be thought comic at all. It is, therefore, not out of place to consider, in an investigation of style, the humor of *Sartor Resartus.* For *Sartor* is a funny book. The fact must be stated thus baldly because many whose chief acquaintance with the work comes from an excerpt in a prose anthology find *Sartor* turgid, perplexing, pompous, and extraordinarily unfunny. Wherein lies the humor of *Sartor?* a reader might ask. Certainly not in the inflated moralizings or the lugubrious posturings of Teufelsdröckh. But if not there, where else?

Carlyle spoke of *Sartor* as offering an emetic to the "pudding-stomach of England." He meant the work to be perfectly serious, but he could not forbear a smile at the means by which he conveyed his message. Consequently *Sartor* both mocks and affirms the world. Its very outrages on conventional writing and conventional thought are meant to provoke amusement as well as reflection. He who has never laughed at *Sartor* has missed a substantial part of its appeal.

Caryle's theory of humor comes as no surprise to anyone familiar with his theory of language. Nor, given Carlyle's

long-time interests, is it surprising to find that his theory
has much in common with Jean Paul's and with German
Romantic theory generally.[32] In examining Carlyle's methods of allusion to material objects, I cited his striving to
unite the infinite and the finite in a single object. Later
we saw that this represented Carlyle's concept of the symbol. The idea recurs in Carlyle's and Jean Paul's theory
of humor. In the *Vorschule der Aesthetik* Jean Paul defines
wit: "On the lowest level . . . the first, simplest comparison
of two ideas is wit in its broadest sense, whether the objects
of the ideas be perceptions or other ideas, or mixed of
perceptions or ideas. . . . Therefore the word wit is
the power of *knowing*, of making wise. . . ."[33] Wit, then,
is primarily an intellectual attribute. It is the perception
of similarities and is therefore likely to issue in metaphor,
that is, in comparison. The less immediately relevant the
points of comparison, the greater the intellectual demand

[32] I am not attempting to assess the degree of so-called influence
on Carlyle either of German theorists or of Jean Paul as a stylist.
Affinities there clearly are, even elective ones, but the German
theorists offer chiefly the advantage of having explicitly theorized,
where Carlyle did not. Whenever possible I cite Carlyle's own
statements on theoretical matters.

The "influence" of Jean Paul as a stylist is still harder to determine,
but it seems clear to me that Carlyle is not the "English Richter"
insofar as that term means "echoer," "reflector," and the like. The
latest attempt to measure Carlyle by Jean Paul standards seems
to me as misplaced as the many earlier ones. It is J. W. Smeed's,
"Carlyle's Jean Paul-Übersetzungen," *Deutsche Vierteljahrsschrift,*
xxxv (1961), 262–279. For a comprehensive view on the latest
theories on influence see Dietrich Gerhardt, "Stil und Einfluss" in
Stil- und Formprobleme in der Literatur, ed. Paul Böckmann
(Heidelberg, 1959), pp. 51–65.

[33] Jean Paul, *Vorschule der Aesthetik,* ix, sect. 43; *Werke,* ed.
Norbert Miller (Munich, 1959–63), v, 171. The difficulties in translating Jean Paul are manifold even in his nonfiction. The passage
cited turns in part on a pun: "Auf der untersten Stufe . . . ist
das erste, leichteste Vergleichen zweier Vorstellungen—deren
Gegenstände seien nun Empfindungen, oder wieder Vorstellungen, oder
gemischt aus Empfindung oder Vorstellung—schon Witz, wiewohl
im weitesten Sinn . . . daher kommt das Wort Witz, als die Kraft
zu wissen, daher 'witzigen'. . . ."

on the reader, but the greater, too, the illumination, once he has perceived the meaning of the comparison. A certain premium is thus placed on the farfetched comparison.

Now humor to Jean Paul goes beyond this perception of similarities, for humor is the *contrast* of the finite (perceived by the Understanding) with the Infinite (perceived by Reason), so that the finite is annihilated.[34] Jean Paul calls humor the inverse of the exalted ("das umgekehrte Erhabene"), and he stresses that the individual object itself is not annihilated, but rather the finite, finiteness, is annihilated by its contrast with the ideal. In the annihilation of the finiteness (not the definiteness) of things resides Jean Paul's humor—in the precarious balance between the individual and the infinite.

Carlyle's notion of humor stands close to Jean Paul's, although it is not perhaps identical. When, during the composition of *Sartor*, Carlyle speaks of what constitutes a Whole, he states that it is "an individual Delineation . . . 'informed with the infinite.' "[35] The terminology is strikingly similar, although Carlyle is speaking not merely of humor, but of any kind of artistic unity. As to humor specifically, he gives an intimation of his sympathies in *Sartor* when he explains the cause of

[34] Cf. *Vorschule*, vii, section 31, 32: "Der Verstand und die Objektenwelt kennen nur Endlichkeit. Hier finden wir nur jenen unendlichen Kontrast zwischen den Ideen (der Vernunft) und der ganzen Endlichkeit selber." "Der Humor, als das umgekehrte Erhabene, vernichtet nicht das Einzelne, sondern *das Endliche* durch den Kontrast mit der Idee" (*Werke*, v, 124).

There has been substantial and informative treatment in recent years of Jean Paul's works, with special emphasis on the annihilation of the finite. See Wolfdietrich Rasch, *Die Erzählweise Jean Pauls* (Munich, 1961), esp. pp. 31–43. Rasch penetratingly points out that Jean Paul's purpose is not to disclose an invisible unity in the *world*, but a harmony in a superreality, in God. See also Peter Michelsen, *Laurence Sterne und der deutsche Roman des achtzehnten Jahrhunderts* (Göttingen, 1962), esp. pp. 319–325. These writers seem to me, however, to overemphasize the annihilating aspect of Jean Paul's play with metaphor.

[35] *Two Note Books*, p. 187.

Teufelsdröckh's one recorded laugh: "It was of Jean Paul's doing: some single billow in that vast World-Mahlstrom of Humour, with its heaven-kissing coruscations, which is now, alas, all congealed in the frost of death.[36] Teufelsdröckh was provoked to laughter by Jean Paul himself, specifically by an "'extra-harrangue,'" or what appears in Jean Paul as an *Extra-Blatt*. These numberless *Extra-Blätter* in Jean Paul are in fact the very substance of his work, to which the story itself merely appertains. From the title of the one which evoked Teufelsdröckh's laugh, "On the Proposal for a Cast-metal King," we can infer that it was a typical Jean Paul production, mocking both kingship as it is commonly and falsely understood, and mechanism as it is commonly revered—in short, a disquisition that would have pointed sharply at the contrast between the finite and the infinite. Note too the language Carlyle uses to describe Jean Paul's humor; it has "heaven-kissing coruscations." The flashes of light that emerge from Jean Paul's *Witz* at its best reach upward to heaven, kissing, as it were, the infinite through the comparison of individual objects or perceptions.

We can gain further insight into Carlyle's theory of humor by adverting to the discussion of humor in his first Jean Paul periodical essay. Carlyle reveals that for him humor is at bottom profoundly serious, which is why *Sartor* can be at one and the same time a serious and a comic work. Carlyle's treatment of humor in the 1827 Jean Paul essay is cast in the familiar terminology of a triple division, and it also reflects Goethe's concept of the three reverences from *Wilhelm Meister*:

> True humour springs not more from the head than from the heart; it is not contempt, its essence is love; it issues not in laughter, but in still smiles, which lie far deeper. It is a sort of inverse sublimity; exalting, as it were,

---

[36] *Sartor*, I, iv, 33. Jean Paul died in 1825. He is the only historical figure to appear as any kind of "character" in *Sartor*.

into our affections what is below us, while sublimity draws down into our affections what is above us.[37]

It is easy to substitute here Jean Paul's "finite" and "infinite" for Carlyle's "what is below" and "what is above." And Carlyle's expression "inverse sublimity" is an excellent translation of Jean Paul's "das umgekehrte Erhabene." Humor in Carlyle, then, as in Jean Paul, goes beyond the mere perception of similarities, although it is likely to start there. It goes from that which is beneath us to that which is above. As an example of what the theory means in Carlyle's practice, we have only to look at the subject of *Sartor Resartus*—Diogenes Teufelsdröckh. Diogenes, born of God, is linked with Teufelsdröckh, devil's dung. The juxtaposition must be comic if it is not blasphemous—or perhaps it is both at once.

Carlyle's juxtaposition of unlikes has often been called his dualism or his polarization of ideas. Double vision would be a better term for it, since ultimately the dualism resolves into a unity and the poles are subsumed in one. Upon reflection it is possible to see that the following passage poses not merely two widely separated extremes, but an indissoluble unity of those same extremes:

"Society," says he, "is not dead: that Carcass, which you call dead Society, is but her mortal coil which she has shuffled off, to assume a nobler; she herself, through perpetual metamorphoses, in fairer and fairer development, has to live till Time also merge in Eternity. Wheresoever two or three Living Men are gathered together, there is Society; or there it will be, with its cunning mechanisms and stupendous structures, overspreading this little Globe, and reaching upwards to Heaven and downwards to Gehenna: for always, under one or the other figure, it has two authentic Revelations, of a God and of a Devil; the Pulpit, namely, and the Gallows." (iii v, 236)

[37] *Works* xxvi, 17.

The perception of the likenesses of unlikes, of the necessary relations of the objects of the world to each other and
to the idea behind them, is at once a fundamental aspect
of the humor of *Sartor Resartus* and of its intense earnestness. G. K. Chesterton expressed it superbly when he wrote,
"The profound security of Carlyle's sense of the unity of
the Cosmos is like that of a Hebrew prophet; and it has
the same expression that it had in the Hebrew
prophets—humor. A man must be very full of faith to jest
about his divinity."[38]

There is a department of humor under which the Jean
Paul and Carlyle conceptions fall—irony. Carlyle's irony
throughout *Sartor* makes the book truly funny. The German
Romantic terminology of finite and infinite, annihilation and
sublime, can easily obscure the fact that what the theorists
are talking about is irony. In the example of the name
Diogenes Teufelsdröckh there is an immediate verbal joke
of the sort that Jean Paul would call *Witz*. And there is
humor in irony. The linkage is not funny merely because
it is unexpected, but also because the meaning it expresses
hits in two directions at once. More is implied than stated.
Is Carlyle mocking the traditional picture of man standing
just below the angels? Or is he turning the tables on
atheistic despair, man as a contemptible clod in the universe? He is doing both and assuming both together. He
is dissembling.

The *eiron* in Greek tragedy is a dissembler in speech who
comes forth saying untruths for the purpose of provoking
the antagonist. The Latin *ironia* means thence a dissembling, an utterance that deceives if we take it literally, be-

---

[38] G. K. Chesterton, *Varied Types* (New York, 1903), p. 111.
Chesteron adds a superb appraisal-cum-encomium of Carlyle's
achievement: "His supreme contribution, both to philosophy and
literature, was his sense of the sarcasm of eternity. Other writers
had seen the hope or the terror of the heavens, he alone saw the
humour of them. Other writers had seen that there could be something elemental and eternal in a song or statute, he alone saw that
there could be something elemental and eternal in a joke."

cause it means something other than it appears to mean on the literal level. In terms of the drama, irony is customarily revealed in action, but it, too, involves a discrepancy between what is believed to be and what is in actuality the case. This need not be humorous. Dramatic irony is frequently tragic enough: Claudius appearing to be at prayer, so that Hamlet refrains from dispatching him, only minutes later to run through meddling Polonius on the assumption that the lecher rather than the dotard is behind the arras. Irony takes its turn toward the humorous when the discrepancy is seen to be absurd, too vast for human acceptance, although there is even a kind of grim humor in tragic irony as such (some of it is caught when Hamlet says, "I'll lug the guts into the neighbour room"). Comic irony also customarily makes its appeal to the intellect, although Carlyle, for one, would object to leaving the heart out of it.

Comic irony is one of the subtlest and most elusive of literary modes. There are those who thought that Swift's modest proposal was far from modest because they took it to be serious. But Swift, of course, meant the opposite of what he said. He was dissembling in the purest sense of classical irony; he meant to provoke an antagonist. He wanted to bring thought about Ireland back to a rational basis, so that those responsible for Irish policy would recognize the waste in human resources which their treatment of Ireland had caused. Much the same kind of irony, adapted from Swift, is used by Carlyle when he lets Teufelsdröckh comment on Heuschrecke's Malthusian tract, "On the Institute for the Repression of Population":

"The old Spartans had a wiser method; and went out and hunted-down their Helots, and speared and spitted them, when they grew too numerous. With our improved fashions of hunting, Herr Hofrath, now after the invention of fire-arms, and standing-armies, how much easier were such a hunt! Perhaps in the most thickly-peopled country, some three days annually might suffice to shoot all the able-bodied Paupers that had accumulated within the year. Let Governments think of this. The expense were trifling: nay the very carcasses would pay it. Have them salted and barrelled; could not you victual therewith, if not Army and Navy, yet richly such infirm Paupers, in workhouses and elsewhere, as enlightened Charity, dreading no evil of them, might see good to keep alive?" (III, iv, 229–230)

Such is an instance of Carlyle's Swiftian irony. In such passages he differs not at all from classical irony.

Elsewhere, however, Carlyle employs an irony that involves another sort of dissembling. It comes back again to his double vision. He repeatedly lets Teufelsdröckh make statements that are ironic and that the Editor seeks, vainly for the most part, to dismiss. Teufelsdröckh's utterances enjoy a freedom from restraint, because of the perspective of the book, that enables him to say whatever he wants. Accordingly, Teufelsdröckh can urge the most radical measures, to the extreme annoyance of the Editor. But all the while Carlyle is building the conviction in the reader that what Teufelsdröckh says is what is truly consequential and deserves our hearing. The Editor habitually warns the reader against Teufelsdröckh, cautioning him not to be taken in by radical notions, or he throws up his hands in despair over Teufelsdröckh's incomprehensibility. At the same time, the Editor excerpts in such a way that Teufelsdröckh's ideas are given prominence, and the Editor himself is at last won over. All this is an irony of situation: the Editor sets himself up as the thoroughgoing British critic, mindful of the dangers to British sensibilities of seditious doctrine, and zealous to protect the reader from Teufelsdröckh's theories, when all the while he is also presenting them to the reader and contributing to his own and the reader's capitulation.

But this is not all. Once the reader catches on to Carlyle's game that Teufelsdröckh, not the Editor, is the man of insight—and the reader does this soon enough—he has to cope with Teufelsdröckh himself, a far more slippery character than the Editor. What, after all, *is* Teufelsdröckh up to? When is he serious and when not? Curiously enough, he is both serious and irreverent at the same time, all of the time. It is the special irony of *Sartor*. Teufelsdröckh's high-flown diction in the passage repeated below is clearly designed to provoke our amusement. It is almost a burlesque of the stock German professor, such as we might encounter in *Blackwood's*:

> "Reader, the heaven-inspired melodious Singer; loftiest Serene Highness; nay thy own amber-locked, snow-and-rose-bloom Maiden, worthy to glide sylphlike almost on air, whom thou lovest, worshippest as a divine Presence, which, indeed, symbolically taken, she is,—has descended, like thyself, from the same hair-mantled, flint-hurling Aboriginal Anthropophagus! Out of the eater cometh forth meat; out of the strong cometh forth sweetness." (I, v, 39–40)

No one could parody Carlyle better than Carlyle. And yet, he is absolutely serious. In Swift it would be as though Swift meant not only to show how grossly inadequate the Irish policy was, but at the same time meant genuinely to urge the massacre and eating of children!

In the matter of the humor of *Sartor* we might do well to remember *Blackwood's* and the strain of Scottish humor that always operates in Carlyle. First of all, *Sartor* is a hoax, much in the manner of the "Chaldee Manuscript" that launched *Blackwood's*. Part of the irate response from *Fraser's* readers came from the realization, as successive portions of *Sartor* appeared, that there was, after all, really no Professor Teufelsdröckh, no Weissnichtwo, no clothes volume, or any of the rest—in short, that someone was having a laugh at their expense. Thus, the *North-American Review* of 1835 concluded ponderously that none of the persons or places in the work really existed and that *Sartor* failed to provide the promised instruction about clothing. What better illustration of Carlyle's love of irony than his tongue-in-cheek inclusion of this very review in later book editions of *Sartor?* If we remember that one of the hallmarks of so-called romantic irony is the wilful breaking by the author of the illusion he has created, we can see how easy it was for Carlyle to wed his German preoccupations to his Scottish gifts.

Coincident with Carlyle's irrepressible love of hoax and irony is his sense of the ludicrous, much aided by the hyperbolic language Froude said he owed to his father and to Annandale. One of the more celebrated instances of ludicrous humor in *Sartor* is Teufelsdröckh's picture of the sudden flying-off of all clothing at a pompous ceremonial. The hitherto august proceedings become suddenly laughable "'*Ach Gott!* How each skulks into the nearest hiding-place; their high State Tragedy (*Haupt- und Staats-Action*) becomes a Pickleherring-Farce to weep at'" (I, ix, 61). Carlyle cannot resist pricking the bubbles of pomposity whenever he finds them. Teufelsdröckh himself is an absurdly laughable creature, with his impossible constructions, his outlandish diction, his wildly farfetched comparisons. And what is funniest of all, he is entirely in earnest. John Sterling perceived this when he wrote: "The noblest images are objects of a humorous smile, in a mind which sees itself above all Nature and throned in the arms of an Almighty Necessity; while the meanest have a dignity, inasmuch as they are trivial symbols of the same one life to which the great whole belongs."[39]

We are brought full circle, back to Sterling's justly celebrated criticism of *Sartor*. Sterling, as we know, objected to the style of *Sartor*. His objections ultimately come to rest on the principle that the style is simply *too* original, too demanding of the common reader, and too little grounded in common life—in short, too deviant from con-

[39] *Sartor*, p. 313.

ventional English usage. But underneath it all Sterling recognized, even if he did not approve, that the style of *Sartor* was no accident. He confesses that the "marvellous combinations" can hardly be considered a consequence of the style, "for the style in this respect coheres with, and springs from, the whole turn and tendency of thought." When all is said and done, that must be the final test of the style of *Sartor Resartus:* does it spring from and cohere with the whole turn and tendency of the thought? If we can answer that question in the affirmative, as I believe we can, we have a style uniquely suited to the work. We can ask for no more.

VII

Sartor Called *Resartus*

Mysticism has a language of its own and cannot be
directly translated into the language of theology.

—NICOLAS BERDYAEV

"Frères, je vous trompais: Abime! abime! abime!
Le dieu manque à l'autel où je suis la victime . . .
Dieu n'est pas! Dieu n'est plus!" Mais ils
dormaient toujours! . . .

—GÉRARD DE NERVAL

When the morning stars sang together and the sons
of man shouted for joy.

—JOB

DOUBLE VISION: THE SOUL AND THE AGE

"The work . . . was meant to be a 'word spoken in season,'" Carlyle said of *Sartor,* by which we can take it
that *Sartor* was addressed to the age. But in speaking
his word Carlyle had no real models; so he applied his
experience in reviewing and essay-writing to the task of
the novel. The review essay offered a ready-made format
that Carlyle was able to expand and adapt for imaginative
purposes, a mode whereby he could speak to the age and
speak for himself.[1] It was a habit that he never abandoned,

[1] The mode itself suggests bifurcation, and a divided sensibility
for the age as a whole has been persuasively argued by various
students of the period. See E. D. H. Johnson, *The Alien Vision
of Victorian Poetry* (Princeton, 1952); Jerome H. Buckley, *The
Victorian Temper* (Cambridge, Mass., 1951); Walter E. Houghton,
The Victorian Frame of Mind, 1830–1870 (New Haven, 1957);
Morse Peckham, *Beyond the Tragic Vision* (New York, 1962), pp.
87–160; William A. Madden, "The Victorian Sensibility," *Victorian
Studies,* VII (1963), 67–97.

although(nowhere did he find a more perfect embodiment
for the turbulences of the age and the insights of his own
mind than in the interchange and struggle of the com-
monsense Editor with the life and mind of the mystical
Teufelsdröckh.) For here Carlyle was able to embody his
own double awareness that everything has two aspects,
the spiritual and the material, or as he put it, "two authentic Revelations, of a God and of a Devil; the Pulpit,
namely, and the Gallows" (III, v, 236) If in *Sartor* the
material side is condemned, abused, and frequently violated, it is because the need to show that there is a genuine
spiritual life in the universe was far greater than the need
to call the attention of society to the material world, which
is in any case too much with us. Thus the style often
operates to annihilate the finite world entirely, and structurally Teufelsdröckh always threatens to swallow up the
Editor; but this serves the moral purpose of leaving no
doubt as to which is superior, finite or infinite, material
or spiritual. The structure and style of *Sartor* join in leading
us to use the material world as a window onto the divine.
But both ineluctably are, and our task is to see them in
proper perspective.

If there is a single aim toward which the double vision
of structure and style is directed, that aim is to make one
see. Indeed, the metaphor of vision and blindness stands
behind even the pervasive imagery of light and dark, investing it all with a moral dimension. *Insight* may be the
key word to *Sartor* after all: Carlyle has had an insight into
the nature of man and society; *Sartor* leads the reader
to the same insight. The assertion properly is, not either
finite or infinite, but both. Man and society are still man
and society. Furthermore, both are organisms; both live.
The feeling of pulsating, onrushing life conveyed by Carlyle's prose enlists the reader's support for Carlyle's beliefs
in a way that no amount of discursive reasoning can do.

By now everyone knows what the clothes metaphor
stands for, that clothes are figuratively the institutions, be-

liefs, customs, and conventions of man and society. Yet a further purpose of the painstaking identification of clothing with the practices of society is to strip the clothes off. Carlyle fashions the clothes metaphor less to apparel society than to denude it. Swift creates his clothes metaphor in *A Tale of a Tub* to comment on a particular set of beliefs, Christianity, and to show that one set of beliefs is superior to its rivals, that one suit of clothes fits man better than any other. Carlyle's metaphor is both more intensive and more extensive. All of society's old clothes are ill fitting and must be removed. *Sartor* abounds in allusions to nakedness, stripping away, disrobing—all designed to make us look at the fundamental object, man, so that we too see that he and his society are wearing tatters in this "Ragfair of a World." The time has come, Carlyle argues, to divest society of its clouts and deposit them where they belong—in the Monmouth Street Old Clothes market. There is no specific record that Carlyle was familiar with the fact that tearing off one's clothes is a "ritual gesture of revulsion against blasphemy,"[2] but the correspondence between the ancient Hebrew gesture and what Teufelsdröckh does for society is astonishingly close. The blasphemy, of course, resides in the decay into which divine institutions have been let fall and the hypocritical lip service those institutions continue to receive while the meaning they once symbolized is no longer operative. Let us, cries Teufelsdröckh, have new finite embodiments of the eternal truths that are ever there underneath the "adventitious wrappages," in the very nature of the organism that is the human being.

The insight that man is an organism applies with equal force to society. If we can but peer beneath the outer coverings, the "hulls," "husks," and "garnitures," and other

[2] Eric Voegelin, *Wissenschaft, Politik und Gnosis* (Munich, 1959), p. 71. Voegelin cites the gesture in connection with mediaeval golem legends. See Gershon Scholem, "Die Vorstellung vom Golem in ihren tellurischen und magischen Beziehungen," *Eranos-Jahrbuch*, XXII (1953), 261.

pejorative terms Carlyle employs to make these externals appear contemptible, we will see that a living unity lies revealed. The perception of organic life in man and society is one of the most important, although not the most original, of Carlyle's insights. The clothes metaphor dovetails with this insight at the most crucial point because clothes, in themselves lifeless, nevertheless presuppose a body. Machines are not clothed; society is, and man is. Even nature becomes the "living garment of God." Once the clothes metaphor in its widest extension is firmly planted in the reader's mind, Carlyle is able to play on the contrast between outer and inner, material and spiritual, real and ideal, dead and living, as on an instrument of which he is the designer and sole performer.

All of this is there in germ in Book One of *Sartor Resartus:* the double vision of material and spiritual, the stripping away of old clothes, the irreducible mystery and divinity of man. In "Pure Reason" the message is explicitly stated several times:

"To the eye of vulgar Logic," says he, "what is man? An omnivorous Biped that wears Breeches. To the eye of Pure Reason what is he? A Soul, a Spirit, and divine Apparition. Round his mysterious ME, there lies, under all those wool-rags, a Garment of Flesh (or of Senses), contextured in the Loom of Heaven; whereby he is revealed to his like, and dwells with them in UNION and DIVISION; and sees and fashions for himself a Universe, with azure Starry Spaces, and long Thousands of Years. Deep-hidden is he under that strange Garment; amid Sounds and Colours and Forms, as it were, swathed-in, and inextricably over-shrouded: yet it is sky-woven, and worthy of a God. Stands he not thereby in the centre of Immensities, in the conflux of Eternities?" (I, x, 65–66)

And again in "Prospective," where the Editor looks ahead to the task he has undertaken: "'Nay, if you consider it, what is Man himself, and his whole terrestrial Life, but an Emblem; a Clothing or visible Garment for that divine ME of his, cast hither, like a light-particle, down from Heaven?'" (I, xi, 73) Finally, in Book One, the extension of the insight to cover all things: "'Thus in this one pregnant subject of CLOTHES, rightly understood, is included all that men have thought, dreamed, done, and been: the whole External Universe and what it holds is but Clothing, and the essence of all Science lies in the PHILOSOPHY OF CLOTHES'" (I, xi, 74).

Carlyle recognized that the essence of his insight lay already in Book One, and he originally proposed to stop there and publish it as a long article. Then he realized that the development of the ideas in Book One was not extensive enough. The demands made on the reader are too radical for the full impact to be felt by a reading of Book One alone. In the context of the three books, Book One succeeds chiefly in introducing the reader to the terms necessary for an investigation of man and society, and above all in posing again and again the fundamental and ancient question to which *Sartor* as a whole is addressed: what is man that God is mindful of him? None of the contenders for the honor of being Carlyle's "source" for the clothes metaphor pose this same question with the force and violence of *Sartor*.[3] For a parallel we can look outside the accepted canon of works that anticipate the clothes philosophy. In *King Lear* we find a work that

[3] I have treated these "sources" only incidentally in this study, since there is generally less material there than at first seems apparent. The works most often cited in this connection are the Song of the *Erdgeist* from *Faust*, Swift's *Tale of a Tub* (both because of the clothing imagery), the Reineke Fuchs fable (because of Carlyle's own statement), and Jean Paul's *Quintus Fixlein* (because of alleged plot and character similarities). On this latter see Berenice Cooper, "A Comparison of *Quintus Fixlein* and *Sartor Resartus*," *Transactions of the Wisconsin Academy of Science, Arts, and Letters*, XLVII (1958), 253–272. Of all of these *A Tale of a Tub* most repays study as an influence on *Sartor*, both because of Swift's pervasive imagery and allegory of clothing and his "Occasional Satyr upon Dress and Fashion" in Section II.

deals with the fundamental question by a procedure that is sometimes strikingly similar to Carlyle's in *Sartor.*

Kenneth Muir calls *Lear* a work that attempts "to provide an answer to the undermining of traditional ideas by the new philosophy that called all in doubt."[4] How needful a similar attempt must have appeared to Carlyle can be appreciated when we consider the addition of the "Enlightenment" and the Industrial Revolution to the "New Philosophy." Both *Lear* and *Sartor,* in attempting to reaffirm eternal verities, go back to the nature of man rather than to existing dogma to construct a moral and meaningful order in the universe. The two image clusters that dominate *Lear* are that of the naked human body and that of clothing. Muir identifies the encounter on the heath between Lear and Poor Tom as, in one sense, the central moment of the play: "The poor Bedlam beggar provides him with a living example of the poverty he has been pitying; and by tearing off his clothes he identifies himself with unaccommodated man, the 'poor bare, forked animal.'"[5] It is just this phrase that Teufelsdröckh echoes (misattributing it) when he envisions the world out of clothes, the *Orbis Vestitutus:* "'Nevertheless there is something great in the moment when a man first strips himself of adventitious wrappages; and sees indeed that he is naked, and, as Swift has it, "a forked straddling animal with bandy legs"'"; and Carlyle cannot forbear adding his own essential conditions: "'yet also a Spirit; an unutterable Mystery of Mysteries'" (I, viii, 57).

As the Old Lear dies in the storm and the New Lear is born, so the Old Teufelsdröckh dies in a "Fire-baptism" on the Street of the Doubter from Hell one sultry Dog-day and from thence dates his "Spiritual Newbirth." What did he learn in that searing death and rebirth? "'Perhaps I directly thereupon began to be a Man.'" And so society

[4] Kenneth Muir, ed. *King Lear* (Arden ed.; Cambridge, Mass., 1959), pp. lv-lvi.
[5] *Ibid.,* p. liv.

must also die, casting its old clothes into the Monmouth Street ragfair, before it can be reborn. Man and society must examine themselves, go back to the fundamentals to build up belief from the elementary qualities of existence. Both *Lear* and *Sartor* cope with the problem of constructing a meaningful morality out of the breakdown of a world order; both insist that the morality is there in the very nature of human existence. *Sartor's* message to man and society is, like St. Paul's, to put off the old man and put on the new, although paradoxically in *Sartor* the new man has been there all along beneath the old.

In *Lear* Shakespeare creates a theology out of the raw materials of life itself, but its application to the contemporary situation must be perceived implicitly. In *Sartor*, however, Carlyle feels obliged as much to attack false conceptions as to inculcate right ones. He wants his message to be applied to the contemporary scene; thus its relation to contemporary problems is made quite explicit. Carlyle, too, has a strong sense of the dramatic and is quite capable of constructing miniature dramas throughout. He continually personifies, investing abstracts with qualities one likes or dislikes. But the overall rhythm of *Sartor* is not dramatic, even while that of Book Two may well be. In *Lear* the theology lies embedded in the dramatic moment, in the tension and gesture and passion of the situation. *Sartor* is closer to being a sermon: the text is enunciated in Book One, and Book Two is the *exemplum*. As if to confirm the homiletic nature of *Sartor*—though confirmation is hardly necessary when we consider the whole drift of Carlyle's efforts from 1814 on—Carlyle wrote in his journal in October 1831:

What an advantage has the Pulpit, when you address men arranged to hear you, and in a vehicle which long use has rendered easy: how infinitely harder when you have all to create, not the ideas only and the sentiments, but the symbols and the mood of mind! Nevertheless in all cases, where man addresses man, on his spiritual interests especially, there is a *sacredness*, could we but evolve it, and think and speak in it. . . .

—Is *Art* in the old Greek sense possible for man at this late era? Or were not (perhaps) the Founder of a Religion our true Homer at present?—The *whole Soul* must be illuminated, made harmonious: Shakespeare seems to have had no religion, but his Poetry.—[6]

At that time Carlyle was in London trying to market his manuscript. Back in Scotland the following spring, *Sartor* still with him and unpublished, he wrote in his journal: "Every man that writes is writing a new Bible; or a new Apocrypha; to last for a week, or for a thousand years: he that convinces a man and sets him working is the doer of a *miracle*."[7]

Carlyle's intention at any rate is clear: *Sartor*, like a sermon, addresses man's spiritual interests and as such is possessed of a *sacredness*. The question is merely how accurately the undertaking has been received by its audience, whether the author and reader have evolved the sacredness. We generally consider it one of the more eccentric characteristics of the Victorian age that any reader ever saw in *Sartor* a pattern for faith. Yet, from the nature of the work itself and Carlyle's explicit statements, that is obviously what *Sartor* was designed to offer. Book Two, as the *exemplum* of the sermon, provides the pattern for the individual. The application of Book Two is primarily tropological; it offers us the spiritual development of a man coming to right understanding in times as turbulent as the present. The symbolic and allegorical nature of the *Märchen* that is Book Two has been sufficiently emphasized. Let us concentrate on the spiritual dimension of the allegory as a means of seeing the kind of pattern that

[6] *Two Note Books*, p. 215.
[7] Ibid., p. 264.

Carlyle devises for Teufelsdröckh and that became in turn the classic pattern of Victorian doubt, denial, and affirmation.)

In keeping with the suggestion of denuding society, Carlyle also posits a denuding of the individual. Teufelsdröckh is another Adam; yet he is set down not in Eden but in the barren desert of modern life. Beyond that, he is fatherless, an important Christian allusion that is not forgotten when affirmation is reached. In the early part of Book Two Teufelsdröckh is fitted out with the current clothes of society, but they are simply inadequate. The Editor, as always, glosses Teufelsdröckh's spiritual development at crucial points. Up to his university years the situation is as follows: "So much we can see; darkly, as through the foliage of some wavering thicket: a youth of no common endowment, who has passed happily through Childhood, less happily yet still vigorously through Boyhood, now at length perfect in 'dead vocables,' and set down, as he hopes, by the living Fountain, there to superadd Ideas and Capabilities" (ii, iii, 108).

Ideas and capabilities are not forthcoming from a "Rational University," and Teufelsdröckh begins to fall into doubt. Even friendship is denied him, although he experiences a pale shadow of it in his association with Herr Towgood. In "Getting Under Way" the Editor's gloss makes clear that the situation is extremely grave:

> We see here, significantly foreshadowed, the spirit of much that was to befall our Autobiographer. . . . A young man of high talent, and high though still temper, like a young mettled colt, "breaks-off his neck-halter," and bounds forth, from his peculiar manger, into the wide world; which, alas, he finds all rigorously fenced-in. Richest clover-fields tempt his eye; but to him they are forbidden pasture: either pining in progressive starvation, he must stand; or, in mad exasperation, must rush to and fro, leaping against

sheer stone-walls, which he cannot leap over, which only lacerate and lame him; till at last, after thousand attempts and endurances, he, as if by miracle, clears his way; not indeed into luxuriant and luxurious clover, yet into a certain bosky wilderness where existence is still possible, and Freedom, though waited on by Scarcity, is not without sweetness. In a word, Teufelsdröckh having thrown-up his legal Profession, finds himself without landmark of outward guidance; whereby his previous want of decided Belief, or inward guidance, is frightfully aggravated. (II, iv, 120–121)

The turn to the lady known as Blumine is the last hope of a desperate man. His motivation is, as ever, spiritual: "A visible divinity dwelt in [women]; to our young friend all women were holy, were heavenly." Repeatedly in the autobiographical notes dealing with the love affair the Editor seeks in vain for items of "psychological" (i.e. novelistic) interest, but concludes: "To all which questions, not unessential in a Biographic work, mere Conjecture must for the most part return answer." The reason is that psychology is not at issue; spirituality is. (Blumine is the agency through which Teufelsdröckh reaches despair.) Accordingly, when Blumine parts with him, " 'thick curtains of Night rushed over his soul, as rose the immeasurable Crash of Doom; and through the ruins as of a shivered Universe was he falling, falling, towards the Abyss' " (II, v, 145–146).

Carlyle's celebrated portrait of the soul of modern man despairing will re-engage our attention later. For the moment, let us stress that the experience strips Teufelsdröckh of every external covering with which education and society have provided him. He becomes the prototype of the "poor forked animal." (Just as his low point is a denial of God, so the way back begins with a denial of the devil.) At the central moment in Teufelsdröckh's drama he too sees himself alone in the universe, and he defies hell. But as he does so, he gains strength from outside: " 'And as I so thought, there rushed like a stream of fire over my whole soul.'" The experience is characteristic of mystics at the moment of conversion. What gives Carlyle's its particular depth and relevance is that he proceeds from that point to carry his protagonist all the way back.

Carlisle Moore has pointed out that a subsequent "prolonged period of doubt . . . delays and modifies" the original mystic experience.[8] In Teufelsdröckh's case it is the Centre of Indifference. During this period Teufelsdröckh is far from spiritually secure; there are still times of misery and doubt; but there are signs of regeneration: "In a word, he is now, if not ceasing, yet intermitting to 'eat his own heart'; and clutches round him outward on the Not-me for wholesomer food." Teufelsdröckh himself glosses the whole meaning of his experience in spiritual terms:

> "Has not thy Life been that of most sufficient men (*tüchtigen Männer*) thou hast known in this generation? An outflush of foolish young Enthusiasm, like the first fallow-crop, wherein are as many weeds as valuable herbs: this all parched away, under the Droughts of practical and spiritual Unbelief, as Disappointment, in thought and act, often-repeated gave rise to Doubt, and Doubt gradually settled into Denial! If I have had a second-crop, and now see the perennial greensward, and sit under umbrageous cedars, which defy all Drought (and Doubt); herein too, be the Heavens praised, I am not without examples, and even exemplars." (II, ix, 184–185)

The feeling of understanding the world, the perception of truths previously hidden, and the positive out-going grip

---

[8] Carlisle Moore, "Faith, Doubt and Mystical Experience in 'In Memoriam,'" *Victorian Studies*, VII (1963), 159. Moore makes the telling point, which might well be applied to *Sartor* and other Victorian testaments of faith, that our belief in the persuasiveness of the doubt in *In Memoriam* and in the weakness of its faith says more about us than about the work.

of life are the final result of the conversion experience. Unlike some subsequent Victorian mystics, notably Tennyson, Teufelsdröckh experiences something like a second trance-like state, less intense than that moment on the Rue de l'Enfer, but nevertheless of considerable consequence in ascertaining the extent of the mysticism involved. It follows immediately upon Teufelsdröckh's exclamation: "'Or what is Nature? Ha! why do I not name thee God? Art not thou the "Living Garment of God"? O Heavens, is it, in very deed, HE, then, that ever speaks through thee; that lives and loves in thee, that lives and loves in me?'" (II, ix, 188). Immediately that Teufelsdröckh brings himself to name God as the real meaning of nature, he experiences his second moment of mystic oneness with the divine, and at last Teufelsdröckh recognizes that he has a Father:

> "Fore-shadows, call them rather fore-splendours, of that Truth, and Beginning of Truths, fell mysteriously over my soul. Sweeter than Dayspring to the Ship-wrecked in Nova Zembla; ah, like the mother's voice to her little child that strays bewildered, weeping, in unknown tumults; like soft streamings of celestial music to my too-exasperated heart, came that Evangel. The Universe is not dead and demoniacal, a charnel-house with spectres; but godlike, and my Father's!" (II, ix, 188)

The "Everlasting No" was the turning-point in the spiritual development of Teufelsdröckh's soul; the "Everlasting Yea," however, is the climax. If it were plotted in terms of dramatic action, the line would run as follows:

The difference is that it really involves a descent into the depths of the soul; and the turning point is what starts the soul on the way back up. Thus:

"Descend, so that ye may ascend" is an Augustinian injunction figuratively followed by Teufelsdröckh,[9] for his chthonic descent stops only in Hell (Rue de l'Enfer), and then he begins the ascent which takes him to an alpine peak ("'Beautiful it was to sit there, as in my skyey Tent, musing and meditating; on the high table-land, in front of the Mountains; over me, as roof, the azure Dome, and around me for walls, four azure-flowing curtains,—namely, of the Four azure Winds, on whose bottom-fringes also I have seen gilding.'"), where he experiences the softer, gentler "fore-splendours of Truth." The language of the experience itself is calculated to win the reader's emotional assent to what Teufelsdröckh has undergone. And it recalls, even to the imagery, the assertions in "Pure Reason" in which man is called "himself a Universe, with azure Starry Spaces, and long Thousands of Years."[10]

The soul has found such assurance as there is to find in the world. For all Carlyle's dogmatism this assurance is not presented as all-sufficient; mystery remains and will ever remain. But the degree of conviction attained trans-

---

[9] St. Augustine, *Confessions,* IV, xii.

[10] Carlyle's prose is notably free of colors; it tends rather to chiaroscuro. On this basis Logan Pearsall Smith compared Carlyle to Rembrandt. See his "Thomas Carlyle: The Rembrandt of English Prose," *Victorian Literature: Modern Essays in Criticism,* ed. Austin Wright (New York, 1961), 113–127, originally published in Smith's *Reperusals and Recollections* (New York, 1936). Carlyle's chiaroscuro is also alluded to by Basil Willey, *Nineteenth Century Studies* (London, 1949), p. 104. The one consistent exception to Carlyle's sparing use of color is the word *azure,* which occurs fairly frequently, always in a positive context, especially in connection with heaven and eternity.

forms Teufelsdröckh, producing in him at once a feeling of sympathy and love for his fellow-man (" 'O my Brother, my Brother, why cannot I shelter thee in my bosom, and wipe away all tears from thy eyes!' ") and an acceptance of the world as it is (" 'Truly, the din of many-voiced Life, which, in this solitude, with the mind's organ, I could hear, was no longer a maddening discord, but a melting one; like inarticulate cries, and sobbings of a dumb creature, which in the ear of Heaven are prayers' "). The experience is then generalized into a principle: *"The Fraction of Life can be increased in value not so much by increasing your Numerator as by lessening your Denominator"*—that is, *Entsagen.* And the principle becomes an exhortation: " 'Love not pleasure; love God. This is the EVERLASTING YEA, wherein all contradiction is solved: wherein whoso walks and works, it is well with him.' " Following that, there are practical, social, and ethical inferences to be drawn, which indeed are immediately embarked on, with the exhortation to *"Do the Duty which lies nearest thee."* All of this is part of the grand climax of Book Two, with its paean to light and order and its exhortation to produce:

> "I too could now say to myself: Be no longer a Chaos, but a World, or even Worldkin. Produce! Produce! Were it but the pitifullest infinitesimal fraction of a Product, produce it, in God's name! 'Tis the ulmost thou hast in thee: out with it, then. Up, up! Whatsoever thy hand findeth to do, do it with thy whole might. Work while it is called Today; for the Night cometh, wherein no man can work." (II, ix, 197)

Carlyle is not content to exemplify the problem of society through one man; he does the same thing for society itself. Book Three tells the tale. All that has been shadowed forth in Book One about the symbolic nature of clothes and all that the soul undergoes in Book Two is hammered home in Book Three in respect to Society. The analysis

of society's maladies is inherent and foreshadowed in Book
One. The moment we begin to look at institutions as clothing, and the moment we begin to look at society without
its clothing, we begin to see things in a new light. The
first part of Book Three is devoted to establishing the
fact that society is dead: its church clothes are out at
elbow, its symbols superannuated, its respect for the dignity of the individual vanished utterly away, and its aristocracy busy "Preserving their Game!" "Teufelsdröckh,"
says the Editor, "is one of those who consider Society,
properly so called, to be as good as extinct." The powerful
group of chapters that follows the depiction of society's
dead or at least moribund state forms Teufelsdröckh's prescription for the improvement of society promised in Book
One. The section also parallels on the social scale the personal experience of Teufelsdröckh from the biography of
Book Two. The fire and phoenix imagery of this climactic
section of *Sartor* echoes the fire imagery of Teufelsdröckh's
death and forms further a subdivision of the light imagery
of the whole book:

> "The Soul Politic having departed," says Teufelsdröckh,
> "what can follow but that the Body Politic be decently
> interred, to avoid putrescence? Liberals, Economists,
> Utilitarians enough I see marching with its bier, and
> chanting loud paeans, towards the funeral-pile, where,
> amid wailings from some, and saturnalian revelries from
> the most, the venerable Corpse is to be burnt." (III, v,
> 233)

Combustion and clothing imagery meet in "The Phoenix"
and "Old Clothes" to depict a society in its final tottering
moments:

> "The World," says he, "as it needs must, is under a
> process of devastation and waste, which, whether by
> silent assiduous corrosion, or open quicker combustion,
> as the case chances, will effectually enough annihilate

the past Forms of Society; replace them with what it may. For the present, it is contemplated that when man's whole Spiritual interests are once *divested,* these innumerable stript-off Garments shall mostly be burnt; but the sounder Rags among them be quilted together into one huge Irish watch-coat for the defence of the Body only!" (III, v, 234–235)

As Teufelsdröckh's old man was destroyed in the fire-consummation in Hell, so society will burn away: "'When the Phoenix is fanning her funeral pyre, will there not be sparks flying! Alas, some millions of men, and among them such as a Napoleon, have already been licked into that high-eddying Flame, and like moths consumed there'" (III, v, 236–237). As we survey the history of the time since Carlyle wrote, we should be more inclined to acknowledge his prophetic gifts than we have been.

As society smolders and as old clothes are cast away, we have an accumulation of ideas and beliefs that Teufelsdröckh delights to study, for his sojourn in the Old Clothes Market is a declaration of the beauty of the study of history. Society's old clothes are objects of reverence when once they have been removed, for in them one sees "'the whole Pageant of Existence [passing] awfully before us; with its wail and jubilee, mad loves and mad hatreds, church-bells and gallows-ropes, farce-tragedy, beast-god-hood,—the Bedlam of Creation!'"

But the parallels with the experience of the individual soul are clear: society lies dying—not in quite the same blaze of glory the Old Teufelsdröckh died in, for there are thousands of contingencies that mitigate against a rapid destruction of even worn-out symbols. But society is dying all the same, and it too must pass through a center of indifference, or more properly is even now passing through such a period, an age of transition, if Carlyle's reading of the *Zeitgeist* is right. "Organic Filaments" is to society what the Centre of Indifference was to Teufelsdröckh:

For us, who happen to live while the World-Phoenix is burning herself, and burning so slowly that, as Teufelsdröckh calculates, it were a handsome bargain would she engage to have done "within two centuries," there seems to lie but an ashy prospect. Not altogether so, however, does the Professor figure it. "In the living subject," says he, "change is wont to be gradual: thus, while the serpent sheds its old skin, the new is already formed beneath. Little knowest thou of the burning of a World-Phoenix, who fanciest that she must first burn-out, and lie as a dead cinereous heap; and therefrom the young one start-up by miracle, and fly heavenward. Far otherwise! In that Fire-whirlwind, Creation and Destruction proceed together; ever as the ashes of the Old are blown about, do organic filaments of the New mysteriously spin themselves: and amid the rushing and the waving of the Whirlwind-element come tones of a melodious Deathsong, which end not but in tones of a more melodious Birthsong. Nay, look into the Fire-whirlwind with thy own eyes, and thou wilt see." (III, vii, 244–245)

The fire-death of society is like the continued but diminished ravings of Teufelsdröckh's "old inward Satanic School" in the Centre of Indifference. During this period the organic filaments are mysteriously fashioning new clothes for Teufelsdröckh's soul. At the end of the Centre of Indifference, Teufelsdröckh's soul is described as follows: "We should rather say that Legion, or the Satanic School, was now pretty well extirpated and cast out, but next to nothing introduced in its room; whereby the heart remains, for the while, in a quiet but no comfortable state" (II, viii, 181). So in "Organic Filaments" the modern age is described: "'Or what if the character of our so troublous Era lay even in this: that man had forever cast away Fear, which is the lower; but not yet risen into perennial Reverence, which is the higher and the highest?'" But hope is at hand: "'If, in the most parched season of Man's

History, in the most parched spot of Europe [i.e. eighteenth-century Paris], when Parisian life was at best but a scientific *Hortus Siccus*, bedizened with some Italian Gumflowers, such virtue could come out of it; what is to be looked for when Life again waves leafy and bloomy, and your Hero-Divinity shall have nothing apelike, but be wholly human?'" (III, vii, 251, 252)

(Society, having passed through its Everlasting No in the atheistic eighteenth century, and passing now in the nineteenth through its Centre of Indifference, is slowly approaching its own Everlasting Yea. This will be "Natural Supernaturalism," the affirmation of a positive force in society just as the Everlasting Yea is Teufelsdröckh's personal affirmation. Only after the procedure of denial and destruction has been completed, only after the thousands of unseen forces in society gather new forms about them, can the soul of society, like the soul of man, attain a positive grasp on the divine. In all which speculation Teufelsdröckh is engaging in prophecy, the poet's highest calling; for at the moment society is yet in its death throes. By way of pointing the path for society, Teufelsdröckh urges the reader to pierce through both space and time, which are merely "Forms of Thought" that "hide from us the brightest God-effulgences." With the aid of Teufelsdröckh's mantic space and time-annihilating hats, the reader can pierce through to the future, to the "Fire-Consummation" of society, and see what Teufelsdröckh already saw in his skyey tent, the "fore-splendours" of Truth.

That Carlyle's formulation of the society of the future is blessedly free from the programmatic earthly paradise of many nineteenth-century planners is attested to by the mystery-haunted conclusion of "Natural Supernaturalism":

"Thus, like some wild-flaming, wild-thundering train of Heaven's Artillery, does this mysterious MANKIND thunder and flame, in long-drawn, quick-succeeding grandeur, through the unknown Deep. Thus, like a God-created,

fire-breathing Spirit-host, we emerge from the Inane; haste stormfully across the astonished Earth; then plunge again into the Inane. Earth's mountains are levelled, and her seas filled up, in our passage: can the Earth, which is but dead and a vision, resist Spirits which have reality and are alive? On the hardest adamant some footprint of us is stamped-in; the last Rear of the host will read traces of the earliest Van. But whence?—O Heaven, whither? Sense knows not; Faith knows not; only that it is through Mystery to Mystery, from God and to God."
(III, viii, 266–267)

The final chapters of *Sartor* stand as a coda to the biography and the clothes philosophy, perhaps even marring the symmetry. The Editor, professing himself exhausted by the demands of Natural Supernaturalism, but thoroughly persuaded of its profundity, turns to its practical applications. If we can see Book Two as an *exemplum* of the clothes philosophy introduced in Book One, the chapters dealing with the Dandiacal Body and tailors are *exempla* of the further text enunciated in Book Three. From an architectonic point of view, Book Three might well have been concluded with a chapter from the Editor following "Natural Supernaturalism," but the excursion into the practical realm was made to satisfy Carlyle's immense concern with practical social problems.

"The Dandiacal Body" attacks the do-nothing aristocracy that has failed to provide leadership and warns that the two nations, the rich and the poor, are headed for irreversible conflict. "Tailors" utters a paean to poets and artists and an admonition to the world to heed its prophets.[11]

[11] It reminds us too that Teufelsdröckh as a kind of tailor is also the artist par excellence. Book Two, with Teufelsdröckh as representative man and as the artist in society, stands as Carlyle's *Portrait of the Artist* and calls to mind some substantial points of kinship between Carlyle and Joyce. The subject has remained largely unexplored, but see Lindberg, "The Artistic Unity of *Sartor Resartus*," p. 20.

Then, his work done, the Editor lays down his pen, and Teufelsdröckh emerges into the present, perhaps to the Paris Revolution of July 1830, or, as the Editor surmises, "actually in London."

Carlyle's measure of the needs of the age was essentially accurate; but he may have miscalculated the extent to which his prescription for solution would or could be acted upon. For it was the way of a soul in Book Two that most completely fastened itself on the Victorian imagination. The social applications in Book Three were, in Carlyle's view, never really grasped. The tailor has certainly been retailored, but has he also given society a new suit of clothes that it will happily wear?

TRIAL OF THE CENTER

When Teufelsdröckh is "made immortal by a kiss" from the faithless Blumine, three things happen in quick and significant succession: light vanishes, the universe "shivers," and Teufelsdröckh falls "towards the Abyss." C. F. Harrold's annotation wisely calls attention at this point to a similarity in phrasing between Carlyle and Jean Paul in the latter's "Rede des toten Christus."[12] The parallel merely begins at this point, to continue in more striking manner for the next two chapters of *Sartor*, "The Sorrows of Teufelsdröckh" and "The Everlasting No." While similarities in language between Jean Paul and Carlyle are in themselves notable, they are more important as pointers to what is essentially the same experience undergone by the two men. This experience became central to the nineteenth-century response to the world, and to our own, even though Carlyle's treatment is unique in English at this time. It is the modern version of the experience of despair. In Jean Paul it is overcome by the force of a securely held Christianity. In Carlyle it is conquered by a fundamental but no longer dogmatic Christian orientation. In most later

[12] *Sartor*, p. 146n.

nineteenth-century figures, however, the traditional forces
are no longer sufficient, and the experience of despair leads
away from God and even to madness.

Despite Carlyle's inclusion of a translation in a Jean
Paul essay, the "Rede des toten Christus" remains little
known in English.[13] A familiarity with its central elements
is helpful in understanding the depths of Carlyle's own
experience of despair, an experience too often summed
up in the facile formulation, "He read Gibbon and lost
his faith." Jean Paul casts his vision in the form of a dream
in which he finds himself awakening in a churchyard at
eleven at night:

All the Graves were open, and the iron doors of the
charnel-house were swinging to and fro by invisible
hands. On the walls flitted shadows, which proceeded
from no one, and other shadows stretched upwards in
the pale air. In the open coffins none now lay sleeping,
but the children. . . . The Church wavered up and
down with two interminable Dissonances, which strug-
gled with each other in it; endeavouring in vain to mingle
in unison. At times, a grey glimmer hovered along the
windows, and under it the lead and iron fell down mol-
ten. The net of the mist and the tottering Earth brought
me into that hideous Temple; at the door of which,
in two poison-bushes, two glittering Basilisks lay brooding. I passed through unknown Shadows, on whom ancient centuries were impressed.—All the Shadows were
standing round the empty Altar; and in all, not the heart
but the breast quivered and pulsed. . . . Above, on the

---

[13] Carlyle's translation, which I have used in the following pages,
appears in "Jean Paul Friedrich Richter Again," (1829) the third
of the Jean Paul essays, *Works*, XXVII, 155–158. The "Rede" was
the first *Blumenstück* in *Siebenkäs* (1791–1797), and it was widely
translated. Jean Paul criticized the translation in Mme. de Stael's
De l'Allemagne. See Carlyle's translation of the criticism, "Jean
Paul Friedrich Richter's Review of Madame de Stael's 'Allemagne,'"
Works, XXVI, 485.

Church-dome, stood the dial-plate of *Eternity,* whereon no number appeared, and which was its own index: but a black finger pointed thereon, and the Dead sought to see the time by it.[14]

At last Christ appears to those assembled from the graves. They ask Him:

"Christ, is there no God?" He answered, "There is none!" Christ continued: "I went through the Worlds, I mounted into the Suns, and flew with the Galaxies through the wastes of Heaven; but there is no God! I descended as far as Being casts its shadow, and looked down into the Abyss and cried, Father, where art thou? But I heard only the everlasting storm which no one guides, and the gleaming Rainbow of Creation hung without a Sun that made it, over the Abyss, and trickled down. And when I looked up to the immeasurable world for the Divine *Eye,* it glared on me with an empty black, bottomless *Eye-socket;* and Eternity lay upon Chaos, eating

---

[14] *Works,* XXVII, 156. The portion quoted reads in the original:

Alle Gräber waren aufgetan, und die eisernen Türen des Gebeinhauses gingen unter unsichtbaren Händen auf und zu. An den Mauern flogen Schatten, die niemand warf, und andere Schatten gingen aufrecht in der blossen Luft. In den offenen Särgen schlief nichts mehr als die Kinder. . . . Die Kirche schwankte auf und nieder von zwei unaufhörlichen Misstönen, die in ihr miteinander kämpften und vergeblich zu einem Wohllaut zusammenfliessen wollten. Zuweilen hüpfte an ihren Fenstern ein grauer Schimmer hinan, und unter dem Schimmer lief das Blei und Eisen zerschmolzen nieder. Das Netz des Nebels und die schwankende Erde rückten mich in den Tempel, vor dessen Tore in zwei Gift-Hecken zwei Basilisken funkelnd brüteten. Ich ging durch unbekannte Schatten, denen alte Jahrhunderte aufgedrückt waren.—Alle Schatten standen um den Altar, und allen zitterte und schlug statt des Herzens die Brust. . . . Oben am Kirchengewölbe stand das Zifferblatt der *Ewigkeit,* auf dem keine Zahl erschien und das sein eigner Zeiger war; nur ein schwarzer Finger zeigte darauf, und die Toten wollten die *Zeit* darauf sehen. (Jean Paul, *Werke,* ed. Norbert Miller [Munich, 1959–63], II, 268)

it and ruminating it. Cry on, ye Dissonances; cry away
the Shadows, for He is not!"[15]

(When Teufelsdröckh sees the world without meaning,
he too flies madly to and fro, first to his "native Entepfuhl,"
where he perceives quickly no help is to be found, then
to nature and the mountains, where he feels momentarily
that nature is "One, that she was his Mother and divine."
Then Blumine and Towgood appear grotesquely in their
barouche-and-four, and night closes in again. Teufelsdröckh
realizes at once that the old romantic escape into nature will
no longer do.)The language again recalls Jean Paul's vision:
("That Basilisk-glance of the Barouche-and-four seems to
have withered-up what little remnant of a purpose may
have still lurked in him: Life has become wholly a dark
labyrinth; wherein, through long years, our Friend,
flying from spectres, has to stumble about at random, and
naturally with more haste than progress." Teufelsdröckh
must nevertheless press on: " 'A nameless Unrest,' says he,
'urged me forward.' " " 'Yet forward must I; the ground
burnt under me; there was no rest for the sole of
my foot. I was alone, alone!' "[16])Teufelsdröckh's procedure, though unsystematic and vague, is that of Christ
in the "Rede des toten Christus": he is looking for God,

---

[15] *Works*, XXVII, 157.

"Christus! ist kein Gott?"
Er antwortete: "Es ist keiner."
Christus fuhr fort: "Ich ging durch die Welten, ich stieg in
die Sonnen und flog mit den Milchstrassen durch die Wüsten
des Himmels; aber es ist kein Gott. Ich stieg herab, soweit das
Sein seine Schatten wirft, und schauete in den Abgrund und
rief: 'Vater, wo bist du?' aber ich hörte nur den ewigen Sturm,
den niemand regiert, und der schimmernde Regenbogen aus Wesen
stand ohne eine Sonne, die ihn schuf, über dem Abgrund und
tropfte hinunter. Und als ich aufblickte zur unermesslichen Welt
nach dem göttlichen *Auge,* starrte sie mich mit einer leeren
bodenlosen *Augenhöhle* an; und die Ewigkeit lag auf dem Chaos
und zernagte es und wiederkäuete sich.—Schreiet fort, Misstöne,
zerschreiet die Schatten; denn Er ist nicht!" (*Werke,* II, 269)
[16] II, vi, 152, 154.

for the "lost mean." Not merely in an imaginary vision does Teufelsdröckh find chaos; he finds it in the world at large. The world has ceased to be an organism. There is a shifting of perceptions whereby the inorganic and the organic cease to be distinguished, and, as in nightmare, inanimate objects terrify and take on a malevolent life. "In strange countries, as in the well-known; in savage deserts, as in the press of corrupt civilisation, it was ever the same: how could your Wanderer escape from—*his own Shadow?*" Hope of any kind has vanished: "Alas, shut-out from Hope, in a deeper sense than we yet dream of! For, as he wanders wearisomely through this world, he has now lost all tidings of another and higher." So the Editor glosses Teufelsdröckh's condition. As Christ looks into the divine eye and finds only an "empty, black, bottomless *Eye-socket*," so Teufelsdröckh shouts "question after question into the Sibyl-cave of Destiny," and receives "no answer but an Echo" (II, vii, 154, 159, 161).

Both Jean Paul and Carlyle reserve the ultimate horror for the depiction of a world that has lost its organic unity with the divine. To say that Carlyle was first and foremost the enemy of the machine, as many have said, is sometimes to mislead, for Carlyle's opposition was not that of an opponent of progress, as it may at first sound, but of one who cherished, above all, organic life. The machine becomes to him the great enemy, because it dehumanizes; it severs the organic relation of man to nature and God. Thus, when Jean Paul describes the worst that his vision can show, he describes the universe as an emotionless instrument:

> And as he saw the grinding press of Worlds, the torch-dance of celestial wildfires, and the coral-banks of beating hearts; and as he saw how world after world shook off its glimmering souls upon the Sea of Death, as a water-bubble scatters swimming lights on the waves, then majestic as the Highest of the Finite, he raised

308 *Sartor* CALLED *Resartus*

his eyes towards the Nothingness, and towards the void Immensity, and said: "Dead, dumb Nothingness! Cold, everlasting Necessity! Frantic Chance! Know ye what this is that lies beneath you? When will ye crush the Universe in pieces, and me? Chance, knowest thou what thou doest, when with thy hurricanes thou walkest through that snow-powder of Stars, and extinguishest Sun after Sun, and that sparkling dew of heavenly lights goes out, as thou passest over it? How is each so solitary in this wide grave of the All! I am alone with myself! O Father, O Father! where is thy infinite bosom, that I might rest on it? Ah, if each soul is its own father and creator, why cannot it be its own destroyer too?"[17]

And so Carlyle even more explicitly:

"A feeble unit in the middle of a threatening Infinitude, I seemed to have nothing given me but eyes, whereby to discern my own wretchedness. Invisible yet impenetrable walls, as of Enchantment, divided me from all living: was there, in the wide world, any true bosom I could press trustfully to mine? O Heaven, No, there was none! I kept a lock upon my lips: why should I

---

[17] *Works,* XXVII, 157–158.

Und als Christus das reibende Gedränge der Welten, den Fackeltanz der himmlischen Irrlichter und die Korallenbänke schlagender Herzen sah, und als er sah, wie eine Weltkugel um die andere ihre glimmenden Seelen auf das Totenmeer ausschüttete, wie eine Wasserkugel schwimmende Lichter auf die Wellen streuet: so hob er gross wie der höschte Endliche die Augen empor gegen das Nichts und gegen die leere Unermesslichkeit und sagte: "Starres, stummes Nichts! Kalte, ewige Notwendigkeit! Wahnsinniger Zufall! Kennt ihr das unter euch? Wann zerschlagt ihr das Gebäude und mich?—Zufall, weisst du selber, wenn du mit Orkanen durch das Sternen-Schneegestöber schreitest und eine Sonne um die andere auswehest, und wenn der funkelnde Tau der Gestirne ausblinkt, indem du vorübergehest?—Wie ist jeder so allein in der weiten Leichengruft des Alles! Ich bin nur neben mir—O Vater! O Vater! wo ist deine unendliche Brust, dass ich an ihr ruhe?—Ach wenn jedes Ich sein eigner Vater und Schöpfer ist, warum kann es nicht auch sein eigner Würgengel sein?" . . . (*Werke,* II, 269–270)

speak much with that shifting variety of so-called Friends, in whose withered, vain and too-hungry souls Friendship was but an incredible tradition? In such cases, your resource is to talk little, and that little mostly from the Newspapers. Now when I look back, it was a strange isolation I then lived in. The men and women around me, even speaking with me, were but Figures; I had, practically, forgotten that they were alive, that they were not merely automatic. In the midst of their crowded streets and assemblages, I walked solitary; and (except as it was my own heart, not another's, that I kept devouring) savage also, as the tiger in his jungle. Some comfort it would have been, could I, like a Faust, have fancied myself tempted and tormented of the Devil; for a Hell, as I imagine, without Life, though only diabolic Life, were more frightful: but in our age of Downpulling and Disbelief, the very Devil has been pulled down, you cannot so much as believe in a Devil. To me the Universe was all void of Life, of Purpose, of Volition, even of Hostility; it was one huge, dead, immeasurable Steam-engine, rolling on, in its dead indifference, to grind me limb from limb. O, the vast, gloomy, solitary Golgotha, and Mill of Death! Why was the Living banished thither companionless, conscious? Why, if there is no Devil; nay, unless the Devil is your God?" (II, vii, 163–164)

Jean Paul recoils in horror from his vision of the Dead Christ, for it is about to end in destruction:

And as I fell down, and looked into the sparkling Universe, I saw the upborne Rings of the Giant-Serpent, the Serpent of Eternity, which had coiled itself round the All of Worlds,—and the Rings sank down, and encircled the All doubly; and then it wound itself, innumerable ways, round Nature, and swept the Worlds from their places, and crashing, squeezed the Temple of Immensity together, into the Church of a Burying-ground,—and all

grew strait, dark, fearful,—and an immeasurably extended Hammer was to strike the last hour of Time, and
shiver the Universe asunder, . . . WHEN I AWOKE.[18]

Awake, Jean Paul cries for joy that he could "still pray
to God." Terrifying as his vision was, it was after all a
dream. Carlyle makes his experience an essential part of
the growth of Teufelsdröckh's soul. The dreadful question,
Is there no God, has been posed when the questioner is
fully awake; the palpitating dread, the fear that the universe is a vast, meaningless machine has been perceived
by a contemporary man: " 'Is there no God, then; but
at best an absentee God, sitting idle, ever since the first
Sabbath, at the outside of his Universe, and *seeing* it go?' "
(II, vii, 159) Perhaps Jean Paul's picture, with its shadowy
surreality more chillingly poses the question of a world
without meaning, but the frame of the dream places the
issue in a safer perspective for the reader. Carlyle brings
the question closer, although he attributes it to the
märchenhaft Teufelsdröckh, separated from the reader by
the Editor. Yet in both cases, Jean Paul's and Carlyle's,
the authors have depicted the horror of what a recent
critic has identified as the *experimentum medietatis*.[19]

Augustine named the turning away from God to the beast
the *experimentum medietatis*, the trial of the center.[20] It

[18] Works, XXVII, 158.

Und als ich niederfiel und ins leuchtende Weltgebäude, blickte:
sah ich die emporgehobenen Ringe der Riesenschlange der
Ewigkeit, die sich um das Welten-All gelagert hatte—und die
Ringe fielen nieder, und sie umfasste das All doppelt—dann wand
sie sich tausendfach um die Natur—und quetschte die Welten
aneinander—und drückte zermalmend den unendlichen Tempel
zu einer Gottesacker-Kirche zusammen—und alles wurde eng,
düster, bang—und ein unermesslich ausgedehnter Glockenhammer
sollte die letzte Stunde der Zeit schlagen und das Weltgebäude
zersplittern . . . als ich erwachte. (*Werke*, II, 271)

[19] Walther Rehm, *Experimentum Medietatis* (Munich, 1947), pp.
1–95.
[20] St. Augustine, *De trinitate*, XII, xi. *Pat. Lat.* XLII, 1006. Cited
in Rehm, pp. 7, 240.

results from the substitution of one's own ego for God, the desire to relish one's own power. For a time one's own ego becomes the center, the mean, but the assertion of the ego is short-lived. Overburdened by its own weight the soul loses its holiness and sinks toward evil. The trial of the center is an act of *superbia* that cannot be sustained. Augustine associated it in Christian tradition with Lucifer and in pagan tradition with Prometheus. These figures are common enough as heroes in Romantic and later literature; they indicate the direction in which modern thought has moved. There are, for that matter, signs of a similar kind as early as the Renaissance. Walther Rehm notes that Pascal saw signs of the turning away from God in Descartes, whom he despised because his philosophy did not concern itself with God.[21] Significantly, both Jean Paul and Carlyle echo Descartes in the promulgative terms by which they define being: Jean Paul's "Ich bin ein Ich," and Carlyle's incorporation and expansion of a similar Jean Paul speculation: "'Who am *I*; the thing that can say "I" (*das Wesen das sich* ICH *nennt*)?'" And shortly thereafter; "'Who am I; what is this ME? A Voice, a Motion, an Appearance; —some embodied, visualised Idea in the Eternal Mind? *Cogito, ergo sum*.'"[22] From such questioning one could make a case for both Jean Paul and Carlyle as being what it is fashionable to call existential writers. In part Teufelsdröckh recreates himself, asserting his own being as the basis for a system of morality. But only in part.

Jean Paul lets his imagination take him to the abyss. He envisions not merely the world without God—that indeed is the reason he is driven to his vision at all; no, Jean Paul envisions something much worse—the eternal without God. The linkage, however, is clear: the finite world has

[21] Rehm, p. 9. The departure of God evident in the work of several eminent Victorians is explored by J. Hillis Miller, *The Disappearance of God: Five Nineteenth Century Writers* (Cambridge, Mass., 1963).

[22] *Sartor*, I, viii, 53, Cf. Carlyle in the essay on Jean Paul in which he translates the "Rede," *Works*, XXVII, 111.

let its churches and its beliefs decay; the infinite is therefore denuded of its meaning. As Rehm points out, there
is a ghastly irony in Jean Paul's placing the announcement
of the emptiness of all being on the lips of Christ, of
him who, infinite, yet became finite precisely to announce
the infinite. Thus Christ, who manifested eternity in the
finite world, is the agent by which Jean Paul learns that
there is no eternity at all. One of the reasons Christ gives
for the disappearance of God is that men have let their
churches go empty, have lost their faith. God has therefore
departed—*Deus absconditus.* Carlyle likewise notes the
same phenomenon: " 'The whole world is, like thee, sold
to Unbelief; their old Temples of the Godhead, which
for long have not been rainproof, crumble down; and men
ask now: where is the Godhead; our eyes never saw him?' "
(II, vii, 161).

Carlyle's experiment is theologically dangerous. One
would indeed expect it to commend him more than it
has to those who abuse him as a proto-Nazi. To be sure,
once we appreciate Carlyle's demonic drive to the *Abgrund,*
he appears as a highly modern artist, one who travelled
a road subsequently travelled by the most daring minds
in nineteenth-century Europe. But to stop there is to read
only half of *Sartor* and miss another kind of modernity
altogether. To see *Sartor* only as the trial of the center
and the loss of the mean obliges us to interpret the Everlasting No as ego-glorification, the ultimate substitution
of man for God in the center of the universe. There are
passages in *Sartor* which might support such a view, and
for those who have a less compelling need for a God-
centered universe than Carlyle, the road he travelled will
surely lead to what has been termed the "Revolt against
God."[23] In the "Everlasting No" Teufelsdröckh is indeed
made to say, " 'I shook base Fear away from me forever.
I was strong, of an unknown strength; a spirit, almost
a god.' " The lines are crucial in determining just how

[23] Voegelin, pp. 44–51.

far Carlyle pushed his trial of the center. There can be no doubt that historically Carlyle belongs to that phase of modern thought that leads ultimately to what Eric Voegelin has stigmatized as modern Gnosticism. Put another way, once God has been separated from man and made identical with the universe, the divorce becomes total, and "it is into the universe that [God] disappears."[24] Carlyle's thought seems often to lead in this direction, perhaps because his negative feelings are frequently more convincing than his positive ones. He was, to be sure, no eudaemonist. Although it would be intemperate to agree with a recent critic who said that Carlyle turns everything to gall,[25] it is true that his depiction of a godless world and his invective against those he thought responsible for it proved more powerful than his paeans to a God re-found and his proposals for human betterment. The fault may lie, however, as much with us as with Carlyle, and it would be unfair to Carlyle to ignore what he attempted to do in a positive direction.

In the passage cited in illustration of Carlyle's "revolt against God" I would emphasize the expression "almost a God." A great deal resides in the "almost." The statement, in any case, follows and is a part of the mystic rebirth on the Rue de l'Enfer: " 'And as I so thought, there rushed like a stream of fire over my whole soul; and I shook base Fear away from me forever.' " It is, in the final analysis, Carlyle's mysticism that keeps him from gnosticism, from the pursuit of knowledge rather than wisdom, *gnosis* rather than *sophia*.

It used to be more fashionable than it now is to debate the question of Carlyle's mysticism. Was it genuine? Was he properly a mystic at all? Such questions are less

[24] Hans Sedlmayr, *Art in Crisis: The Lost Center,* tr. Brian Battershaw (New York, 1958), p. 175. Sedlmayr, p. 205, also interestingly points to an increase in caricature and "a secret demoniac element" in the visual arts between 1830 and 1840.

[25] Ian Jack, *English Literature, 1815–1832* (Oxford, 1963), p. 368.

frequently raised today, but not because they have been permanently settled. The questions simply do not arise, because there is not enough interest in either Carlyle or mystic experience to make them seem very important. But it is the validity of Carlyle's mysticism that determines whether or not his Everlasting No is merely a glorification of his own ego. Perhaps the question must ever depend on the weight we give to Carlyle's personal statements about Leith Walk and to the conviction carried by Teufelsdröckh's Baphometic Fire-baptism. C. F. Harrold has repeatedly confirmed Carlyle's credentials as a genuine mystic.[26] By any standard that seeks to establish what qualities mystic experience traditionally has had, Carlyle's experience qualifies. What Carlyle was not, is a contemplative, especially as that term applies to mediaeval Christian mystics who systematically worked toward states of religious *contemplatio,* attaining them only after years of the most austere and selfless meditation.

The mystical experience Carlyle translated into *Sartor,* however, conforms to the seven characteristics F. C. Happold says distinguish mystical states: ineffability, noeticism, transiency, passivity, consciousness of Oneness, sense of timelessness, and the ego as "not the real I."[27] The last feature is perhaps a function of the first stage of the mystical act, purgation of the self, which all mystics consider essential to attaining mystical insight. Carlyle echoes Novalis and the whole tradition of Christian mysticism

[26] See above, pp. 40–41, n. 27.

[27] F. C. Happold *Mysticism* (Baltimore, 1963), pp. 45–48. It is simple enough to discern these qualities in the three chapters spanning the experience (II, vii, viii, ix). One need only stress the noeticism of the experience as a reinforcement of Carlyle's doctrine of the unconscious and as a contributing cause for such Carlylean statements as that thought is "thaumaturgic art" (II, iv, 118). Teufelsdröckh's passivity too has not often been emphasized, but it is a cardinal feature of his spiritual makeup. Cf. *Sartor,* II, iii, 104; vii, 158; ix, 195; x, 205.

On mystic states and conversion see also William James, *Varieties of Religious Experience* (London, 1902), pp. 189–258, 300, and A. D. Nock, *Conversion* (Oxford, 1933), pp. 1–16.

when he asserts: " 'The first preliminary moral Act, Annihilation of Self (*Selbst-tödtung*), had been happily accomplished; and my mind's eyes were now unsealed, and its
hands ungyved.' " The fact that Carlyle writes "moral act"
where Novalis wrote "philosophical thinking" shows the
stress that Carlyle laid on his favorite Aristotelean precept:
"The end of Man is an Action, and not a thought"; and
it shows why Carlyle could never become a contemplative,
for his concern with action, ethics, and social issues was
too great. But mysticism of a spontaneous and non-scholas-
tic sort is clearly there.

Once we concede that Carlyle's mysticism was genuine,
we have to modify our description of his trial of the center.
Carlyle's mystic experience preserved him from the revolt
against God. It made his message, however revolutionary
its presentation, a conservative one. Jean Paul wakes up
and cries for joy that he can still pray to God. Teufelsdröckh comes back from the Abyss to announce, "He lives!"
From that the rest follows. But one can see how close Carlyle comes to the opposite point of view, namely, "He is
dead," how indeed he held such a view until force outside intervened. What does the man do who has experienced no such intervention? He conceives of man as the absent God:

> *The Madman.*—Have you ever heard of the madman
> who on a bright morning lighted a lantern and ran to the
> market-place calling out unceasingly: "I seek God!
> I seek God!" . . . "Where is God gone?" he called out. "I
> mean to tell you! *We have killed him,*—you and I! We
> are all his murderers! But how have we done it? How
> were we able to drink up the sea? Who gave us the sponge
> to wipe away the whole horizon? What did we do when
> we loosened this earth from its sun? Whither does it
> now move? Whither do we move? Away from all suns?
> Do we not dash on unceasingly? Backwards, sideways,
> forwards, in all directions? Is there still an above and

below? Do we not stray, as through infinite nothingness?
Does not empty space breathe upon us? Has it not become colder? Does not night come on continually, darker
and darker? Shall we not have to light lanterns in the
morning? Do we not hear the noise of the grave-diggers
who are burying God? Do we not smell the divine putre-
faction?—for even Gods putrefy! God is dead! God remains dead! and we have killed him! How shall we
console ourselves, the most murderous of all murderers?
The holiest and the mightiest that the world has hitherto
possessed, has bled to death under our knife,—who will
wipe the blood from us? With what water could we
cleanse ourselves? What lustrums, what sacred games
shall we have to devise? Is not the magnitude of this
deed too great for us? Shall we not ourselves have to
become Gods, merely to seem worthy of it? There never
was a greater event,—and on account of it, all who are
born after us belong to a higher history than any history
hitherto!"[28]

---

[28] Friedrich Nietzsche, *The Joyful Wisdom*, Aphorism 125, in *The
Complete Works*, ed. Oscar Levy, tr. Thomas Common (Edinburgh,
1910), x, 167–169. The portion I have cited reads in the original:

Der tolle Mensch. Habt ihr nicht vom jenem tollen Menschen gehört,
der am hellen Vormittage eine Laterne anzündete, auf den Markt lief
und unaufhörlich schrie "Ich suche Gott! Ich suche Gott" . . . . .
. . . . "Wohin ist Gott?" rief er, "ich will es euch
sagen! *Wir haben ihn getötet*—ihr und ich! Wir sind alle Mörder!
Aber wie haben wir dies gemacht? Wie vermochten wir das Meer
auszutrinken? Wer gab uns den Schwamm, um den ganzen Hori-
zont wegzuwischen? Was taten wir, als wir diese Erde von ihrer
Sonne losketteten? Wohin bewegt sie sich nun? Wohin bewegen
wir uns? Fort von allen Sonnen? Stürzen wir nicht fortwährend?
Und rückwärts, seitwärts, vorwärts, nach allen Seiten? Gibt es
noch ein Oben und ein Unten? Irren wir nicht wie durch ein
unendliches Nichts? Haucht uns nicht der leere Raum an? Ist es
nicht kälter geworden? Kommt nicht immerfort die Nacht und
mehr Nacht? Müssen wir noch nichts von dem Lärm der Toten-
gräber, welche Gott begraben? Riechen wir noch nichts von der
göttlichen Verwesung?—Auch Götter verwesen. Gott ist tot! Gott
bleibt tot! Und wir haben ihn getötet! Wie trösten wir uns, die
Mörder aller Mörder? Das Heiligste und Mächtigste, was die Welt

We cannot fail to note the Diogenes imagery in both Carlyle and Nietzsche.[29] Nor should we forget Nietzsche's preoccupation elsewhere with Diogenes Laertius. It is perhaps also significant that Nietzsche's "Der tolle Mensch" and his Diogenes Laertius writings fall in his "aphoristic" middle period, that is, during the period in which his habitual form of expression is the aphorism and the Fragment. But the similarities are not endless. Carlyle, too, strayed "through infinite nothingness," conceived of the universe as dead and deadening, and, as Nietzsche writes at the end of "Der tolle Mensch," saw churches as "the tombs and monuments of God." The echoes of Jean Paul in all of this are equally arresting. But Carlyle does indeed find God, and with his discovery the universe is re-illumined and re-animated, not with a new godless reality but with a revitalized godlike one. *Selbsttötung,* an act of humility that destroys the Old Adam, is not *Gottesmord.* The fore-splendors of Truth assure Teufelsdröckh that

---

bisher besass, es ist unter unsern Messern verblutet—wer wischt dies Blut von uns ab? Mit welchem Wasser könnten wirs uns reinigen? Welche Sühnefeiern, welche heiligen Spiele werden wir erfinden müssen? Ist nicht die Grösse dieser Tat zu gross, für uns? Müssen wir nicht selber zu Göttern werden, um nur ihrer würdig zu erscheinen? Es gab nie eine grössere Tat—und wer nur immer nach uns geboren wird, gehört um dieser Tat willen in eine höhere Geschichte, als alle Geschichte bisher war!" (*Nietzsches Werke,* ed. Gerhard Stenzel [Salzburg, 1952], II, 599–600)

Nietzsche himself felt only contempt for Carlyle's search for faith and dispensed with him as an "atheist who makes it a point of honor not to be so." See Nietzsche, *Works,* XVI, 69–70.

[29] Eugen Biser, *Gott ist tot* (Munich, 1962), pp. 42–48, calls attention to three symbolic motifs in the aphorism (the imbibed sea, the dissolved horizon, and the unfastened earth) that echo language found in Hölderlin, Novalis, and Jean Paul. Voegelin, p. 76, says of the Diogenes imagery: "Der hintergründige Sinn der Diogenes-Symbolik wird sichtbar. Der neue Diogenes sucht Gott—aber nicht den Gott, der tot ist, sondern den neuen Gott in den Menschen, die den alten ermordet haben—er sucht den Übermenschen." Neither Biser nor Voegelin mentions Carlyle, and it is well to emphasize the different conclusions Carlyle reached despite the similarities in language.

God lives: " 'The Universe is not dead and demoniacal, a charnel-house with spectres; but godlike, and my Father's!' "

Because Carlyle conceived of a higher force outside space and time, his orientation remained basically Christian. The double vision of style and structure serves to remind us that *Sartor* is poised eternally between the finite and the infinite, that there is a profound difference between time and eternity which can never be bridged (even as the Editor confessed to having built but a poor and contorted bridge between Teufelsdröckh and the English reader). The imagery of light and dark, the metaphor of vision and blindness, assert that God *is:*

"But it is with man's Soul as it was with Nature: the beginning of Creation is—Light. Till the eye have vision, the whole members are in bonds. Divine moment, when over the tempest-tossed Soul, as once over the wild-weltering Chaos, it is spoken: Let there be Light! Ever to the greatest that has felt such moment, is it not miraculous and God-announcing; even as, under simpler figures, to the simplest and least. The mad primeval Discord is hushed; the rudely-jumbled conflicting elements bind themselves into separate Firmaments: deep silent rock-foundations are built beneath; and the skyey vault with its everlasting Luminaries above: instead of a dark wasteful Chaos, we have a blooming, fertile, heaven-encompassed World." (II, ix, 197)

Carlyle was doctrinally no Christian, but spiritually he was perhaps a better Christian than most of the writers and artists of the age.

THE UNEARTHLY PARADISE

The misinterpretation of *Sartor* that sees Teufelsdröckh's Everlasting No as the center of the book is precisely that which depreciates the mystic illumination on the Rue de l'Enfer in favor of a view that Teufelsdröckh glorifies his own ego, and that which ignores the affirmative illumination in the Everlasting Yea, and that which fails to see that Natural Supernaturalism is the climax of the book as a whole. It comes from not letting the imaginative terms of the book direct our reading and thus missing the rhythm and the aesthetic and consequently moral stress of the entire work. When our attention turns to Book Three, we are supposed to see that Natural Supernaturalism boldly asserts that society, mankind, is involved in a divine plan, the full details of which can never be known, but revelations of which are vouchsafed to poets and prophets. The plan and its origin stand outside space and time: they are merely manifested in space and time. The mysticism of *Sartor Resartus* touches society as well as the individual.

Book One poses the question, What is man that God is mindful of him? Book Two provides an answer in a specific, yet typical, instance. Book Three generalizes the whole to apply to society. Carlyle's answer to the question is deceptively simple. It is the Open Secret, the Divine Idea. But lest we do Carlyle a disservice we must emphasize in as un-Carlylean terms as possible what this answer is; for the way we perceive Carlyle's answer ultimately determines what the whole of *Sartor* adds up to, and what we say to such seemingly distant issues as Carlyle's alleged proto-Fascism. What, then, is *Sartor*'s answer to the perennial question?

Book Two asserts that God still lives. This insight from individual experience is generalized onto the social plane in Book Three. Just as Carlyle's trial of the center has many features in common with typical nineteenth-century speculations, so his social observations in Book Three display affinities with the social speculations that arose from the displacement of God. But Carlyle's trial of the center was tempered by his mysticism, and so was his critique of society. It would be superfluous to rehearse the same points in the social arena that have been examined in the personal one, especially when we realize that for Carlyle society, as an organism, was essentially like man and thus susceptible of the same kind of analysis. It is necessary only to be clear on his view of man, for Book Two is chiefly about God, Book Three about man.

When Carlyle wrote to Goethe during the brief period around 1830 in which he flirted with the Saint Simonians, Goethe, as is well known, admonished him: "Von der Société St. Simonienne bitte Sich fern zu halten." Goethe was right, but Carlyle on his own soon discontinued his association with the Saint Simonians. He made an illuminating criticism of them, which is, however, more charitable than it need have been: "I should say they have discovered and laid to heart this momentous and now almost forgotten truth, *Man is still Man;* and are already beginning to make false applications of it."[30] Carlyle repeated this opinion often enough to make it clear that he held it very strongly. It tells us also a good deal about Carlyle's view of man: *Man is still Man.*

Sartor is studded with Carlyle's attempts at a definition of man, which establish the basis for Carlyle's view of society. Here are some:

"two-legged animals without feathers" (ɪ, iii, 23)

"Man is a Tool-using Animal" (*Handthierendes Their*) (ɪ, v, 41)

" 'a forked straddling animal with bandy legs'; yet also a Spirit, and unutterable Mystery of Mysteries."(ɪ, viii, 57)

"*Man is a Spirit,* and bound by invisible bonds to *All Men . . . he wears Clothes,* which are the visible emblems of that fact." (ɪ, ix, 60)

" 'A Forked Radish with a head fantastically carved.' " (ɪ, ix, 62)

[30] *Correspondence between Goethe and Carlyle,* pp. 225, 258.

"To the eye of vulgar Logic," says he, "what is man? An omnivorous Biped that wears Breeches. To the eye of Pure Reason what is he? A Soul, a Spirit, and divine Apparition." (I, x, 65)

" 'the true SHEKINAH is Man'; where else is the GOD's-PRESENCE manifested not to our eyes only, but to our hearts, as in our fellow-man?" (I, x, 66)

"The great Herr Minister von Goethe has penetratingly remarked that 'Man is properly the *only* object that interests man.' " (I, xi, 75)

"Wilt thou know a Man, above all a Mankind, by stringing-together beadrolls of what thou namest Facts? The Man is the spirit he worked in; not what he did, but what he became." (II, x, 203)

"What is man himself but a Symbol of God?" (III, iii, 220)

"Is he not a Temple, then; the visible Manifestation and Impersonation of the Divinity?" (III, vi, 239)

"Yes, truly, if Nature is one, and a living indivisible whole, much more is Mankind, the Image that reflects and creates Nature, without which Nature were not." (III, vii, 246–247)

"Find Mankind where thou wilt, thou findest it in living movement, in progress faster or slower." (III, vii, 248)

"A God-created, fire-breathing Spirit-host." (III, viii, 266)

Finally, Teufelsdröckh defines the matter at the close of the book in the same words and on the same provocation (the Saint Simonians) that Carlyle had used earlier to Goethe: " 'Here also are men who have discovered, not without amazement, that Man is still Man; of which high, long-forgotten Truth you already see them make a false application' " (III, xii, 296).

Man in *Sartor* is still man. He stands, as ever, poised
between Heaven and Hell, a God-born Devil's-dung.

(The trial of the center leads customarily to the loss of
the center. In its place man sets himself.) Jean Paul cries,
"Ah, if each soul is its own father and creator, why can
it not be its own destroyer too?" Such is precisely the
course of so many modern gnostic movements, most clearly
Naziism and Communism. The horrors to which such
movements lead have been demonstrated with sufficient
clarity in our time. Their alleged benefits all reside in
a forthcoming earthly paradise. All such movements endeavor to struggle out of the paradox of time and eternity
and end by denying eternity altogether. Paradise is taken
out of the infinite and brought into the finite world. History
is the only reality. If man is his own creator, then he
is capable of attaining perfection in this world. What repelled Carlyle in the Saint Simonians is this very direction
in their thinking, the proclamation of an earthly paradise.
Yet in the nineteenth century the earthly paradise became
an obsession not only of political thinkers, but of writers
and artists as well:

> The time when man was in "direct communication with
> heaven" had passed. In the nineteenth century faith lost
> the extra dimension that took it into another world and
> transferred heaven and hell into the present one. The
> prospect offered by a religion of life after death gave
> place to an ambition that could be satisfied on
> earth. . . . Though he no longer had a place in a world
> beyond, man was still determined not to have lived in
> vain. The hope of an earthly paradise went hand in
> hand with the fear that life should prove wholly without
> meaning.[31]

[31] Werner Hofmann, *The Earthly Paradise: Art in the Nineteenth
Century*, tr. Brian Battershaw (New York, 1961), p. 363. I have
omitted from the quotation one sentence which in the English version
rudely violates the original. Battershaw writes: "But although the
nineteenth century hoped again and again for an earthly fulfillment,

Students of the earthly paradise have found the telltale
signs of it in all areas of nineteenth-century life—in the
World Exhibitions, most dramatically in the "artificial paradise" of the 1851 Crystal Palace, in the visual arts in
works like Ingrès' "Golden Age" (1843), in the social
thought of the Saint Simonians, of Fourier, of Comte, and
in literary works like William Morris' *Earthly Paradise*
(1868–1870). The earliest signs are said to lie in the late
eighteenth century in writers like Novalis.[32] Yet again there
is a similarity of language and imagery that can obscure
differences in thought; for one can indeed trace the antecedents of the nineteenth-century earthly paradise back
through the whole history of utopias. The important
distinction rests on whether the vision of a golden age
is conceived of as likely to be realized in time or as being
an imaginative projection or vision of heaven. Precisely as
with the trial of the center, the conception of an earthly

---

and looked forward with frantic enthusiasm to the coming of the
Kingdom of God, in doing so it did not make a pseudo-religious
act of faith as in Büchner's 'comfortable religion,' adapted to a
collective desire for happiness; it merely sought to give human life,
from which God's presence had been removed, abundance, a mission,
significance and justification, in an earthly paradise existing now."
However, the original German reads: "Wenn das 19. Jahrhundert
immer wieder auf die irdische Vollendung hofft und die Heraufkunft
des Reiches Gottes mit schwärmerischer Begeisterung beschreibt,
so vollbringt es darin *nicht nur* eine pseudoreligiösen Glaubensakt—
im Sinne einer dem Kollektiven Glücksbedürfnis angepassten 'com-
moden Religion' (Büchner), es will dem menschlichen Dasein, aus
dem Gottes Gegenwart gewichen ist, im irdischen Paradies eine dies-
seitige Fülle, Auftrag, Sinn und Rechtfertigung geben." (My italics.)
The German, in short, reads precisely the opposite of the translation.
See Werner Hofmann, *Das irdische Paradies: Kunst im neunzehnten
Jahrhundert* (Munich, 1960), p. 331.
[32] See Hofmann, passim. See also Christopher Dawson, *Progress
and Religion* (London, 1945), esp. 196–201; and Holbrook Jackson,
*Dreamers of Dreams: The Rise and Fall of Nineteenth-Century
Idealism* (London, 1948), which contains a valuable chapter on
Carlyle; and *Ideas and Beliefs of the Victorians* (London, 1950),
pp. 33–93. For an arresting comparison of Carlyle's approach with
that of Karl Marx see Kenneth Burke, *A Grammar of Motives
and a Rhetoric of Motives* (Cleveland, 1962), pp. 638–647.

paradise is in itself symptomatic of attitudes in society that are strongly secular. Nevertheless, one man's earthly paradise may continue to remain another's vision of eternity, and it would be unfair, except in the grossest kind of survey, to equate the two. We can be sure of one thing. If Carlyle in *Sartor* is preaching a doctrine of man as intrinsically different from the poor unaccommodated man of traditional thought, he is likely to project, and certain to suggest, an attainable earthly paradise as a human goal. Let us see if he does.

The first chapter of Teufelsdröckh's treatise, we are told, turns on "Paradise and Fig-leaves." The paradise in question is, of course, Eden, and it finds its proper place at the commencement of the historical-descriptive portion of *Die Kleider*. But Eden is the lost paradise, not the paradise of nineteenth-century obsession; and of it in *Sartor* we learn little, since the Editor quickly gives the matter "an unconcerned approval" and soon quits "this twilight region" (i, v, 37). Nor, in Book Two, can we conceive of Teufelsdröckh, although another Adam whose beginning is called a Genesis, as living in a paradise. On the contrary, the allusions to Teufelsdröckh as Adam are ironic. Modern life is anything but a paradise, and Teufelsdröckh's Adamism (and Adamitism) serves to underline the misfortunes of birth in the Atheistic Century and adulthood in the Age of Transition. But Teufelsdröckh is a new man, and we are entitled to suppose that he may lead us to a paradise of some kind. Hence we may still find the earthly paradise in *Sartor*.

If there is to be an earthly paradise in *Sartor*, it must appear in Book Three, the book of the future, and it must result from a despair of a transcendental reality and a consequent rejection of God. It must issue from a substitution of man for the lost mean and a conviction that "all who are born after us belong to a higher history than any history hitherto!"—that is, a history no longer bound by the traditional imperfections attributed to man. But, as we have seen, Carlyle is painfully aware of the nature of man; his view is quite traditional. Because of it he does not fashion in Book Three what we should expect if his view of man were not traditional, if his conversion were not a real conversion but the glorification of his own ego—he does not fashion an earthly paradise.

To the extent that Book Three seems to promise some such apotheosis of mankind, Carlyle may have been more a "Son of Time" than he realized; but it is hard to find any passages truly supporting belief in an earthly paradise. Neither the "fire-consummation" of society nor the "Communion of Saints" projects a final state of perfection in time. They have to do with the shedding of old clothes and the fashioning of new ones to symbolize perennial religious truths, with new temples to the Godhead:

"But thou as yet standest in no Temple; joinest in no Psalm-worship; feelest well that, where there is no ministering Priest, the people perish? Be of comfort! Thou art not alone, if thou have Faith. Spake we not of a Communion of Saints, unseen, yet not unreal, accompanying and brother-like embracing thee, so thou be worthy? Their heroic Sufferings rise up melodiously together to Heaven, out of all lands, and out of all times, as a sacred *Miserere;* their heroic Actions also, as a boundless everlasting Psalm of Triumph. Neither say that thou hast now no Symbol of the Godlike. Is not God's Universe a Symbol of the Godlike; is not Immensity a Temple; is not Man's History, and Men's History, a perpetual Evangel? Listen, and for organ-music thou wilt ever, as of old, hear the Morning Stars sing together." (III, vii, 253–254)

God remains forever outside of time. The Kingdom of Heaven is not in any physical sense at hand, nor are we proffered any promise that it will be realized in what we call time. A man who could conceive, as Carlyle genuinely did, of the "Course of Providence through Aeons of Aeons,"

who could wish for a time-annihilating hat to transport
him to the thirty-first century, is not very close to envision-
ing the Earthly Paradise.

It is, of course, Carlyle's mysticism that makes him conservative, even though radical.[33] And radical he surely is.
His pursuit of being to the abyss is radical in the etymologi-
cal sense of the word. Many of his social ideas are also
highly radical: he would sweep away the idle, game-pre-
serving aristocracy, discard the old clothes of religion, acknowledge the presence of industrialism, attempt to cope
with the "Condition of England." But what he wants in
place of these anachronisms and burdens is not a religion
of man, not the earthly paradise, but a moral new birth
in the social order, the recognition of a true aristocracy,
and new clothes for old truths.

Perhaps the conservative equivalent to the earthly paradise is the nineteenth-century vision of the organic and
harmonious society of the Christian Middle Ages, the vision
Novalis projected in *Die Christenheit oder Europa,* the
vision Carlyle contrasted with the ugliness of modern-day
materialist England in *Past and Present.* But one must
distinguish such a vision in its very kind from the utopian
schemes of the Comtists and others, and the paradise of
the future foreseen by William Morris, although in Morris
a kind of fusion seems to be at hand. The mediaeval
vision (or for that matter the modern utopian one)
is realistically unattainable, but it is not in fact projected
as attainable by its formulators. What such mediaeval conceptions are designed to do is to help effect a change of
heart. They are parables of the spiritual life of mankind
that demand as much as they promise, with both demands
and promises being, first and foremost, spiritual conditions.

---

[33] The terms are used here without reference to modern political
ideas or groupings. I have avoided entirely the word *liberal,* since
it appears today, at least in American usage, to mean the reverse
of what it meant in nineteenth-century England. Thus, Carlyle,
who was opposed to what he called "the goddess Utilitaria" and
therefore to liberal economics, would in that area today perhaps be
regarded as an American "liberal."

We are, however, offered a paradise of sorts by Teu-felsdröckh. Only it is not earthly, but unearthly. It is the spiritual paradise that comes not from the love of pleasure but the love of God. It is Milton's "Paradise within thee, happier far." In such a paradise we may hear, as of old, the "Morning stars sing together":

". . . glance, if thou have eyes, from the near moving-cause to its far-distant Mover: The stroke that came transmitted through a whole galaxy of elastic balls, was it less a stroke than if the last ball only had been struck, and sent flying? O, could I (with the Time-annihilating Hat) transport thee direct from the Beginnings to the Endings, how were thy eyesight unsealed, and thy heart set flaming in the Light-sea of celestial wonder! Then sawest thou that this fair Universe, were it in the meanest province thereof, is in very deed the star-domed City of God; that through every star, through every grass-blade, and most through every Living Soul, the glory of a present God still beams." (III, viii, 264)

Chesterton was right when he spoke of the "profound security of Carlyle's sense of the unity of the Cosmos."[34] In that security resides the positive side of *Sartor Resartus,* the retailoring of the tailor. First, look at clothes and see that they are transient things of time; next, remove the outworn apparel; then fashion new clothes. The models lie in eternity, and we are ever symbolizing the same truths known fully only to the same God. *Sartor* does not deny God to seek salvation in an earthly paradise. Thus, of Carlyle's works, *Sartor* in any event does not offer a jus-tification for reading Carlyle as a Nazi,[35] since National So-

[34] Chesterton, p. 111.
[35] The most cogent arguments for Carlyle's Naziism are set forth in Eric Bentley, *A Century of Hero-Worship: Carlyle and Nietzsche* (2nd. ed., Boston, 1957). See also the strident attack in Norwood Young, *Carlyle: His Rise and Fall* (New York, n. d.). A valuable assessment can be found in H. J. C. Grierson, *Carlyle and Hitler* (Cambridge, Eng., 1933). See also Paul West, "Carlyle's Creative Disregard," *Melbourne Critical Review,* No. 5 (1962), pp. 16–26.

cialism is precisely a philosophy that arises out of the denial of God and the belief in an earthly paradise.

To argue that Carlyle would have approved, or indeed somehow even before the fact *did* approve, of Hitler, is an irresponsible calumny on Carlyle. It also rests on a mistaken equation of Hitler with Prussianism, but that is another story. The fact is that the effort at posthumous nazification of Carlyle is an effort to escape the implications of Carlyle's most fervently argued beliefs. What Carlyle asks his readers to do is far more difficult than submitting to what he would probably have identified as a sham-hero: he asks his readers to effect an inner change, a change of heart. Only then will man realize that he is a spirit and the *imago Dei*. Those who profess a distaste for Carlyle on the grounds of his incipient Naziism have seen only the Devil's-dung in *Sartor* and have shut their eyes to the fact that it is God-born. The most enduring strength of *Sartor Resartus* may lie in that, original, imaginative, and daring as it was, Carlyle resolutely did not push it beyond good and evil.

The reason above all others that confirmed Carlyle in his veneration of Jean Paul was that Jean Paul believed in the immortality of the soul. As did Carlyle, who also believed in life. In the final entry in his notebooks (dating from May 1832, or about the time of the completion of *Sartor*), Carlyle wrote:

> Joy and sorrow; irreparable losses; toils fruitless or fruitful: a share of all lies noted in this little tome. Onwards are we going, ever onwards: Eternity alone can give back what Time daily takes away. . . . Improve, cherish, laudably work with whatever Time gives and leaves. *Gedenke zu leben.* Farewell ye loved ones! I have still *zu luben.* (*Two Note Books,* p. 278.)

APPENDIX

APPENDIX

Chronologies of Composition for the Works of Thomas Carlyle
1814–1833

Although there exists in Dyer's *Bibliography* an excellent chronology of Carlyle's writings by date of publication, there has never been a chronology of his writings by date of composition.[1] A composition chronology is, however, needful, especially for Carlyle's apprentice years, because of the frequent lengthy intervals between composition and publication. Neglect of the gaps between composition and publication can lead to misunderstandings in an examination of Carlyle's development. Further, since interpretations in the present study have been colored by the date by which Carlyle wrote a given work, it appears useful to assemble a composition chronology to provide at a glance a guide to Carlyle's development.

The following table is designed chiefly to indicate the year of composition for all that Carlyle wrote through the time of the completion and publication of *Sartor*, that is, through 1833.[2] Within each year I have indicated the month, the work and its kind, sources for date of composition, and year of publication. Works for which there is no evidence for composition date have been assigned to the time of publication. For every item I have tried to cite Carlyle's own testimony, but in some cases the testimony of others was all that was available. Sources cited do not necessarily exhaust all possible confirmations. Since most dates are amply attested to by letters and other documents, I have merely indicated some of the sources when the

[1] Many of the composition dates are included in Shine's compilation, *Carlyle's Early Reading*, but their inclusion is an incidental aspect of Shine's work, and it is necessary to extract the entries relating to composition from the far greater number of entries relating to works read.

[2] *Sartor*, of course, continued appearing in *Fraser's* into 1834, but I have taken the end of 1833 as the terminal date for any work on *Sartor* as such, for by that time the whole manuscript was in the hands of the publishers.

matter is not one of controversy. I have included non-extant
works in order to give a general picture of the kind of writing Carlyle was engaged in at any given period. For the
sake of space I have adopted a set of abbreviations for
source works. A key appears opposite.

It has sometimes proven impossible, even when the year
is certain to fix the month of composition. Moreover, Carlyle
was often engaged in writing more than one piece at a time.
I have listed the compositions in what seems to me their
most probable order within a given year, but it is possible
that of two compositions undertaken almost simultaneously,
the first one to gain mention in letters and memoirs may
not have been the first one written. The error in any case
would be very slight. I am chiefly concerned to present
the general trend of Carlyle's literary activities and to correct the kind of gross misrepresentation engendered by
such things as the appearance of "Cruthers and Jonson"
in *Fraser's* almost ten years after its composition. The dates
of publication are designed as a check. For full details
of publication see Dyer's *Bibliography*.

The second, briefer chronology schematizes what is
known about the composition dates of the articles Carlyle
wrote for the *Edinburgh Encyclopaedia*. A separate chronology seemed called for because composition of the articles spans three years and presents dating problems of
special complexity.

KEY TO ABBREVIATIONS OF WORKS CITED AS
SOURCES IN THE CHRONOLOGY

Archiv	Richard Garnett, "Eight Unpublished Letters of Thomas Carlyle," *Archiv*, CII (1899), 317–330
CG	*Correspondence between Goethe and Carlyle*, ed. C. E. Norton (London and New York, 1887)
DAW, I & II	David Alec Wilson, *Carlyle till Marriage, 1795–1826* (London, 1923); *Carlyle to "The French Revolution," 1826–1837* (London, 1924)
Dyer	Isaac Watson Dyer, *A Bibliography of Thomas Carlyle's Writings and Ana* (Portland, Me., 1928)
EL, I & II	*Early Letters of Thomas Carlyle, 1814–1825*, ed. C. E. Norton (2 vols., London, 1886)
Froude I & II	J. A. Froude, *Thomas Carlyle, a History of the First Forty Years of His Life, 1795–1834* (2 vols., London, 1882)
L, I & II	*The Letters of Thomas Carlyle, 1826–1836*, ed. C. E. Norton (2 vols., London, 1888)
LL, I & II	*The Love Letters of Thomas Carlyle and Jane Welsh*, ed. Alexander Carlyle (2 vols., London, 1909)
L Mill	*Letters of Thomas Carlyle to John Stuart Mill, John Sterling, and Robert Browning* (London, 1923)
Leslie	John Leslie, *Elements of Geometry* (Edinburgh, 1817)
Masson	David Masson, *Edinburgh Sketches and Memories* (London, 1892)
MLR	Marjorie King, "'Illudo Chartis': An Initial Study in Carlyle's Mode of Composition," *Modern Language Review*, XLIX (1954), 164–175
Napier	*A Selection from the Correspondence of Macvey Napier*, ed. Macvey Napier (London, 1879)
Rem	*Reminiscences*, ed. C. E. Norton (2 vols., London, 1887)
Scribner's	"Unpublished Letters of Carlyle," *Scribner's Magazine*, XIII (1893), 416–425
TNB	*Two Note Books of Thomas Carlyle*, ed. C. E. Norton (New York, 1898)
Yale MS	Autograph manuscripts of twenty-four poems by Thomas Carlyle, now in the Yale University Library

NOTE: The list of abbreviations also serves as a key for Part II of this appendix dealing with the chronology of the encyclopaedia articles.

A CHRONOLOGY OF COMPOSITION
FOR CARLYLE'S WORK

1814–1833

Time of Year	Work	Source	Publication
	1814		
By Dec.	"Before I was afflicted I went astray" (sermon)	Rem, II, 20	Lost
	1815		
March–Dec.	"Num detur religio naturalis" (sermon)	EL, I, 30 Rem, II, 20	Lost
	1816–1817		
?	Problem in Leslie's *Elements of Geometry*	DAW, I, 144 Leslie, 340	1817
	1818		
Summer[1]	"Tragedy of the Night Moth" (poem)	LL, I, 94 & n.	1831
?	Travel piece on Annandale (article)	Rem, II, 235	Lost
	1818–1824		
?[2]	"Peter Nimmo" (poem)[3]	Masson, 285	1831
	1819		
Feb.–March	"Examination of some Compounds which depend upon very weak Affinities" (translation)	EL, I, 220, 227	1819

[1] Although Carlyle very clearly dates the work in the source cited, the presence in the poem of the name Goethe makes 1818 a suspiciously early date. However, the Goethe reference could have been a later addition.

[2] Greater precision in dating this piece is impossible, although I incline toward 1822 as the most likely year. Masson is the only source for a date earlier than time of publication.

[3] I am referring here only to the poem, not the prose preface, which I date 1830. For further detail on Carlyle's early poetry see my "Carlyle's Poetry to 1840," *Victorian Poetry* I (1963), 161–181.

Appendix 333

Time of Year	Work	Source	Publication
	1819–1820		
Dec. 1819– Jan. 1820	Review of Pictet's *Gravitation* (article)	EL, I, 262, 266–268 & n. Rem, II, 233–235	Lost
	1820		
May–June	"Remarks on Prof. Hansteen's 'Inquiries Concerning the Mag- netism of the Earth'" (article)	Archiv, CII, 320 Scribners, XIII, 416–417	1820–1821
June	"Outline of Prof. Mohs's New System of Crystallography and Mineralogy" (article)	Scribners, XIII, 416–417	1820–1821
By Dec.	Portion of *Thirty- Years' War* (transla- tion)	EL, I, 311	Lost[4]
	1820–1823		
Feb. 1820– Jan. 1823	Articles for *Edinburgh Encyclopaedia* (20 articles)[5]	EL, I, 276, 281, 301, etc.	1821–1830[6]
	1821		
Feb.	Portion of Malte Brun's *Geography* (translation)	EL, I, 328	Lost
Spring– Summer	"Baillie's *Metrical Legends*" (essay)	EL, I, 335	1821
	1821–1822		
Dec. 1821	Legendre's *Geometry* (translation)	EL, II, 15, 54, 79–80, 103 LL, I, 58	1824[7]

[4] As suggested above, this translation may not have been lost.
It may be the material that Carlyle appended to his *Life of
Schiller*.

[5] The chronology and special problems of the encyclopaedia contributions will be discussed in the following portion of this appendix.

[6] The encyclopaedia was in progress and appearing by volume
from 1809 to 1830, but its publication is customarily dated 1830,
by which time all the volumes had appeared.

[7] Shine, *Carlyle's Early Reading*, p. 86, writes that there was
an 1822 edition of this work, although he has not seen it. DAW,
I, 233, appears to be the source for this idea.

Time of Year	Work	Source	Publication

1822

Jan.	"Faustus" (essay)	EL, II, 25–26 LL, I, 17	1822
May ?	"Lines on Napoleon" (poem)	LL, I, 45, 48	Lost
May–June	"The Wish" (poem)	EL, II, 78	Posthumous
	"Lines on the Bass" (poem)	LL, I, 58 & n.	Lost
Summer	"Morgarten" (poem)	EL, II, 126	Posthumous
	"Address to the Kirk of Durisdeer" (poem)	LL, I, 72	Lost
Oct. ?	"Faust's Curse" (translation)	LL, I, 79 LL, II, 351	1830
Nov.–Dec.	Epistolary novel (no title known)	EL, II, 136–139 LL, I, 122–124	Lost
	"Cruthers and Jonson" (short story)	EL, II, 140 LL, I, 124–135 & n.	1831

1823

March–April	"Schiller," pt. 1 (essay)	LL, I, 184, 194, 204 EL, II, 191–192, 199–201	1823
June–Oct.	*Meister's Apprenticeship* (translation)	EL, II, 182, 219, 223–224 LL, I, 189, 229, 281, 289	1824
Oct.–Nov.	"Schiller," pt. 2 (essay)	EL, II, 230–236, 245 LL, I, 289	1824
Dec.	*Meister's Apprenticeship* (translation)	EL, II, 247, 252	1824
By Dec.	"To Miss Welsh"[8] (poem)	LL, I, 316n. LL, II, 353	Posthumous

1823–1825

?	"Where shall I find thee?" (poem)	Yale MS[9]	Posthumous

[8] Also known as "They Chide Thee" and "To Miss Jane B. Welsh."
[9] As far as I know, the only copy of this poem is in the Yale MS. Notes on the manuscript by J. A. S. Barrett assign it to 1823–1825. Presumably Barrett's notations had the sanction of Alexander Carlyle.

Time of Year	*Work*	*Source*	*Publication*
	1824		
By Jan.	"College Library" (article)	Inferential[10]	1824
Jan.	"Schiller," pt. 3 (essay)	EL, II, 256, 263 LL, I, 321, 332	1824
Feb.–May	*Meister's Apprenticeship* (finished)	EL, II, 265–266, 270–271 LL, I, 333–334, 346, 363, 371	1824
	1824–1825		
Sept. 1824– Jan. 1825	Revision of *Schiller* for book publication	LL, II, 19, 92 EL, II, 284, 297	1825
	1825		
June–Dec.	*German Romance*, approx. vols. I & II (translation)	EL, II, 313, 339 LL, II, 200, 205	1827
Sept.	"To Jane" (poem)	LL, II, 354	Posthumous
By Oct.	"The Village" (poem, translation)	Inferential	1825
Nov.	"Das Mährchen" (translation)[11]	LL, II, 188 & n., 194	1832
By Dec.	"Thunder-Storm" I (poem)	Inferential	1825
	1826		
Jan.–Aug.	*German Romance*, approx. vols. III & IV (translation)	LL, II, 210–214, 297, 305, 308 EL, II, 352–353, 355, 362	1827
By Feb.	"Thunder Storm" II (poem)	Inferential	1826
March	"The Sower's Song" (poem)	LL, II, 258	1831
? Nov.–Dec.	"Illudo Chartis" (unfinished novel)	MLR, XLIX, 175	Posthumous

[10] The date is inferred from publication in January 1824. I have not yet seen a copy of the article. Masson is the only authority for Carlyle's authorship, but Dyer accepts Masson's ascription. See Dyer, pp. 4, 61.

[11] At this time Carlyle translated only the story. Before publication in 1832 he wrote the footnote commentary in the *Sartor* manner. The translation was undertaken in connection with *German Romance*.

Time of Year	Work	Source	Publication
	1827		
Jan.–June	"Wotton Reinfred" (unfinished novel)	L, I, 27, 31, 44, 59, 62, 65	Posthumous
By June	"Cui Bono" (poem)	Inferential[12]	1830
June	"Jean Paul Friedrich Richter" (essay)	L, I, 62–63, 67, 69	1827
Aug.–Oct.	"State of German Literature" (essay)	L, I, 72, 82	1827
Oct.–Nov.	"Life and Writings of Werner" (essay)	L, I, 90, 108	1828
	1828		
Feb.–March	"Goethe's 'Helena'" (essay)	L, I, 152[13]	1828
May–June	"Goethe" (essay)	L, I, 151–152	1828
June–Aug.	"Life of Heyne" (essay)	L, I, 163	1828
Aug.–Oct.	"Burns" (essay)	L, I, 163 TNB, 129	1828
Nov.	"German Playwrights" (essay)	L, I, 178	1829
	1829		
Jan.–Feb.	"Novalis" (essay)	L, I, 178, 190 TNB, 135, 140	1829
Feb.–March	"Voltaire" (essay)	L, I, 178, 190 TNB, 135–136	1829
Summer	"Signs of the Times" (essay)	L, I, 203 TNB, 140	1829
Aug.–Sept.	"Jean Paul Friedrich Richter Again" (essay)	L, I, 203 CG, 158	1830
Fall	"My Own Four Walls" (poem)	LL, II, 355–356 & n.[14]	Posthumous

[12] The dates of composition for this item is inferred not from publication, as is the case with other inferential dates, but from its presence in "Wotton Reinfred," which was written at this time.

[13] This dating is in part inferential. Carlyle's reference comes after publication, which was in April 1828. Cf. Froude, II, 37.

[14] There is some uncertainty about which of two years is the correct one for this poem, 1829 or 1830. Alexander Carlyle is certain that, whichever of the two years is correct, the poem was written in the autumn. See source cited.

Time of Year	Work	Source	Publication
Dec.	"Schiller" (review of correspondence)	CG, 172, 195, 212–213[15]	1831
Dec.	Beginning of "History of German Literature"	L, I, 206 CG, 161–163	Posthumous[16] & 1831

1830

Jan.	"The Sigh" (poem)	Yale MS	Posthumous
By Feb.	"Richter & Mme. de Staël" (translation)	Inferential	1830
March–May	"History of German Literature"	CG, 165, 170–172, 187 L, I, 220–221, 224	Posthumous & 1831
April	"On History" (essay)	TNB, 154	1830
Aug.	Stopping of "History of German Literature"	CG, 207–210 L, I, 225	Posthumous
By Aug.	"Four Fables" (fables)	L, I, 227[17]	1830
Sept.	"The Wandering Spirits" (poem)	Yale MS	Posthumous
	"The Beetle" (poem)	Froude, II, 88	1831
Sept.–Nov.	"Teufelsdreck" (first draft of *Sartor*)	L, I, 235–239 CG, 234	1833–1834
Oct.	"Luther's Hymn" (translation)	L, I, 235	1831
By Nov.	Preface to "Nimmo"	L, I, 239	1831
Dec.	"Nouveau Christi- anisme" (translation)	L, I, 243	Lost

1831

? Jan.	"Absent" (poem)	LL, II, 356 & n.	Posthumous
Jan.	"Taylor's Historic Survey"	L, I, 242–243 245, 257 TNB, 182	1831
By Feb.	"The Kissing of the Stars" (poem)	Inferential	1831

[15] The dating is largely inferential. Shine, *Carlyle's Early Reading*, p. 205, argues persuasively for composition in December. The article was not published until March 1831.

[16] Portions of this work were detached from the manuscript, slightly revised, and published separately in 1831. But the greater part of the work was not published until Shine's edition in 1951.

[17] The reference here is not to having written the fables, but to having sent them, along with other material, to *Fraser's*. The context suggests that they had been written some time before, but it is difficult to say when. In the same package Carlyle sent "On History" and "Cruthers and Jonson."

Time of Year	Work	Source	Publication
Feb.	"The Nibelungen Lied" (essay)[18]	L, I, 261, 265	1831
March	"Early German Literature" (essay)[19]	Froude, II, 114	1831
March–Aug.	*Sartor Resartus* (the expansion and completion of "Teufelsdreck")	L, I, 257, 261–262, 268, 271, 289–290, 299–300, 307–308 CG, 285 TNB, 191	1833–1834
Nov.–Dec.	"Characteristics" (essay)	L, I, 370, 373, 378 Napier, 118	1831

1832

Time of Year	Work	Source	Publication
Jan.–March	"Biography" and "Johnson" (essays)[20]	L, I, 388 L, II, 21 TNB, 255	1832
Feb.	"Goethe's Portrait" (essay)	L, II, 26	1832
By March	"Schiller, Goethe & Mme. de Staël" (essay)	Inferential[21]	1832
April	"Death of Goethe" (essay)	L, II, 39 TNB, 265	1832
May	"Corn-Law Rhymes" (essay)	L, II, 39 TNB, 267 Napier, 125	1832
May–July	"Goethe's Works" (essay)	L, II, 39 Froude, II, 238–240	1832

[18] The essay was a reworking of material from the "History of German Literature" of the previous year, involving chiefly rearrangement of passages.

[19] This essay involved very little revision of material from the "History of German Literature." The essay is also known by the titles "German Literature of the Fourteenth and Fifteenth Centuries" and "Reinecke Fuchs."

[20] The two were originally part of the same essay, with "Biography" presumably written first. After completion Carlyle decided to separate them and publish them individually.

[21] The subject matter of this essay makes it possible that it was actually undertaken earlier in connection with the Schiller correspondence and with the Richter and De Staël translation. The inferential date, of course, is from publication.

Appendix 339

Time of Year	Work	Source	Publication
July	"Das Mährchen" (revision) & "Novelle" (translation)[22]	L, II, 44, 52	1832
Aug.–Oct.	"Diderot" (essay)	L, II, 52 L Mill, 17	1833
Nov.	"Drumwhirn Bridge" (poem)	Dyer, 72–73	1834

1833

Jan.–March	"Cagliostro" (essay)	L, II, 88, 94–95 L Mill, 37	1833
By May	"On History Again" (essay)[23]	Inferential	1833
May–Sept.	Preparation of *Sartor* for serial publication	L, II, 103–108	1833–1834
Sept.	"Crichope Linn" (poem)	Froude, II, 366	Posthumous
By Dec.	"Today," "Adieu," & "Fortuna" (poems)	Inferential[24]	1840

[22] The commentary was added to "Das Mährchen," while "Novelle" was translated for the first time.

[23] This essay is also known as "Quae Cogitavit." Wilson, *Carlyle to "The French Revolution,"* p. 308, believes that is was written in the previous year in connection with the essay on Diderot. Cf. Shine, *Carlyle's Early Reading,* p. 307.

[24] The inference here stems from the dating in the *Miscellanies,* which assigns all the poems included to the years 1823–1833. These three poems were added to the second edition of the *Miscellanies,* 1840. Although Carlyle himself is presumably responsible for the dating, it is probably not absolutely accurate.

A CHRONOLOGY OF COMPOSITION FOR
CARLYLE'S ARTICLES FOR THE
EDINBURGH ENCYCLOPAEDIA

The following chronology follows the same format as the previous one, except that where possible I have indicated the exact date. The asterisks preceding certain articles indicate those which Carlyle himself explicitly mentions. Note that "Source" is the source for *dating*, not for authorship, although in some cases it also confirms authorship.[1] When the source is given as "Inferential," the inference is from the date of publication of the volume of the *Encyclopaedia* itself.[2] The dates are in every case the latest date by which Carlyle could have written the article. In only a few cases (chiefly the 1820 and 1821 articles) does Carlyle himself explicitly state that he has completed a given article. Quite probably many of the articles were completed well before the date here assigned, and it is likely that Carlyle worked from the master list drawn up early in his association with Brewster and thus wrote some of the articles long before they were published in the *Encyclo-*

[1] The question of authorship has been treated elsewhere. The *Encyclopaedia* list of contributors (*Edinburgh Encyclopaedia*, I, x) credits Carlyle with sixteen of the twenty articles I list in this chronology. S. R. Crockett, in *Montaigne and Other Essays Chiefly Biographical* (London, 1897), added a seventeenth, the article "Montucla." Alexander Carlyle, in *Love Letters*, I, 268, added the eighteenth, "Pascal." I added the final two, "Persia" and "Quakers," in my "Unnoted Encyclopaedia Articles by Carlyle" *English Language Notes*, I (1963), 108–112.

[2] Carlyle's articles appeared in volumes XIV through XVII of the *Encyclopaedia*, published between 1820 and 1825. Not all of the volumes bear colophon dates, but from entries in *Blackwood's* and the *Quarterly Review* the following publication dates have been determined for the volumes with Carlyle's contributions: XIV, pt. I—May, 1820, pt. II—October, 1820; XV, pt. I—September, 1821, pt. II—July, 1822; XVI, pt. I—April, 1823, pt. II—December, 1823; XVII, pt. I—February, 1825.

paedia. In the absence of evidence to the contrary, however, the latest possible date had been adhered to. The
purpose, once again, is to give as accurate a picture as
possible of the sequence of Carlyle's encyclopaedia writing
and the period of his most intense activity on behalf of
the *Encyclopaedia.* Clearly this period is from 1819 to
mid-1821, after which time Carlyle no longer mentions any
encyclopaedia articles by name.

Time of Year	*Article*	*Source*	*Publication*
	1820		
Feb. 19	*Montesquieu	DAW, I, 180 EL, I, 276, 301	1820
By March 1	*Montagu	EL, I, 276	1820
By March 29	*Montaigne	EL, I, 281, 287, 301	1820
By March 30	*Dr. John Moore	EL, I, 286	1820
By March 30	*Sir John Moore	EL, I, 286	1820
March 30	Carlyle refers to "Necker" and "Nelson" as yet to be written	EL, I, 287	
May 19	Carlyle refers to "Persia" and "Quakers" as yet to be written	Archiv, CII, 321	
By Oct.	Montfaucon	Inferential	1820
By Oct.	Montucla	Inferential	1820
	1821		
By March 18	*Necker	EL, I, 328[1]	1821
By March 18	*Nelson[2]	EL, I, 335	1821
By Aug. 9	*Netherlands	EL, I, 359, 363–364 Scribner's, XIII, 418	

[1] Cf. also EL, I, 335, 343.
[2] Carlyle does not mention the article on Nelson at this time,
but from his reference to it in connection with "Necker" in the
previous year and his statement that he completed "Necker" now,
it seems highly probable that at this time he also completed "Nelson."
It follows immediately upon "Necker" in Vol. XV, pt. I.

Time of Year	Article	Source	Publication
By Aug. 9	*Newfoundland	EL, I, 359, 363–364 Scribner's, XIII, 418	1821

1822

Time of Year	Article	Source	Publication
By July	Norfolk	Inferential[3]	1822
By July	Northamptonshire	Inferential	1822
By July	Northumberland	Inferential	1822

1823

Time of Year	Article	Source	Publication
By April	Mungo Park	Inferential[4]	1823
By April[5]	Pascal	LL, I, 146, 286	1823
By Dec.	*Persia	Inferential	1823
By Dec.	Wm. Pitt	Inferential	1823
By Dec.	Wm. Pitt the Younger	Inferential	1823

1823–1825

Time of Year	Article	Source	Publication
? [Probably by 1823]	*Quakers	Inferential[6]	1825

[3] For these three articles published in 1822 see also the very general reference to writing articles in LL, I, 19. Shine, *Carlyle's Early Reading*, pp. 77–78, takes this as authority to set January 1822 as the terminal date for these articles, but I have abided with the publication date, since the articles are not mentioned by name.

[4] For these articles published in 1823 see LL, I, 146, another general reference to writing articles. See also Shine, *Carlyle's Early Reading*, p. 94. "Persia," of course, was mentioned by Carlyle earlier, in 1820 (Archiv, CII, 321).

[5] DAW, I, 233, states that "Pascal" was probably written by the spring of 1822 and, further, that it is likely that all of Carlyle's encyclopaedia work was completed by that time.

[6] "Quakers" may also have been intended by the casual reference in LL, I, 146. As in the case of "Persia," Carlyle's mention of it occurs in 1820 (Archiv, CII, 321).

Index

Entries under Thomas Carlyle relate to his life and career; works by Carlyle cited in the text are entered separately. Significant titles by other authors are also entered separately, followed by the author's name in parentheses. Authors of secondary material are entered for the first citation to a work and subsequently only when there is substantive comment from or about them. For literary devices in *Sartor* and in Carlyle's other writings see separate entries under such topics as style, structure, self-quotation, etc.

344 *Index*